Business
Britain

The essays in this textbook explore the development of British business since the Industrial Revolution. This long-term perspective facilitates an understanding of the development of skills, work practices, social structures and attitudes, all of which have bearing on twentieth-century business performance and organization. Although drawing upon existing literature the essays do give some pointers for the future development of business history. Taken together, they highlight the shift away from a Chandlerian interpretation of business, with its emphasis on vertical integration, towards one which explains why, in Britain, alternatives to the firm have often been preferred to formal internalization.

The book is divided into two broadly chronological sections which deal respectively with British business before and after 1900. The essays, all of which are written by experts in their chosen fields, provide interpretative syntheses of the principal debates in British business history, thus making a vast literature accessible to students. Themes include family business, organizational change, the shaping of business strategy, human capital investment, the competitive environment and the impact of government policy on business. They embrace both industrial and service sectors as well as Britain's multinationals.

Maurice W. Kirby is Reader in Economic History and **Mary B. Rose** is Senior Lecturer in Business History, both in the Department of Economics at Lancaster University.

**Comparative and International Business Series:
Modern Histories**
Edited by Geoffrey Jones and Mira Wilkins

Business enterprise in modern Britain

From the eighteenth to the twentieth century

Edited by
Maurice W. Kirby and Mary B. Rose

London and New York

First published 1994
by Routledge
11 New Fetter Lane, London EC4P 4EE

Simultaneously published in the USA and Canada
by Routledge
29 West 35th Street, New York, NY 10001

© 1994 Maurice W. Kirby and Mary B. Rose

Typeset in Times by Pat and Anne Murphy,
Highcliffe-on-Sea, Dorset
Printed and bound in Great Britain by
Biddles Ltd, Guildford and King's Lynn

British Library Cataloguing in Publication Data
A catalogue reference for this book is available from the
British Library

Library of Congress Cataloging in Publication Data
Business enterprise in modern Britain: from the eighteenth to
   the twentieth century/edited by Maurice W. Kirby and
   Mary B. Rose.
   p.   cm. – (Comparative and international business.
Modern histories)
   ISBN 0–415–07574–2
   ISBN 0–415–11559–0 (pbk.)
   1. Business enterprises – Great Britain – History.
   2. Great Britain – Commerce – History.   I. Kirby, M.W.
   II. Rose, Mary B.   III. Series: Comparative and
   international business. Modern histories series.
   HF3504.B87   1994   94-4462
   338.7'0941–dc20   CIP

Contents

Tables

Contributors

Martin Chick is a Lecturer in the Department of Economic and Social History, University of Edinburgh. He has written widely on nationalization, privatization and government–industry relations, and he is currently writing a book on the economic planning of the Attlee governments.

Michael Collins is currently Professor of Economic History at the Centre for Business History, University of Leeds. The focus of his research has been the historical development of modern British commercial banking and the history of central banking. His recent publications include *Banks and Industrial Lending in Britain, 1700–1939* (Macmillan, 1991), *Have the Banks Failed British Industry?* (IEA, 1992) (with Forrest Capie) and *Central Banking in History* (Elgar, 1992). He is now working (jointly, with Forrest Capie) on an ESRC-financed investigation into 'commercial banks and industrial finance in England and Wales, 1850–1914' (R000 23 2220).

Pat Hudson is Professor of Economic History in the Department of Economic and Social History, University of Liverpool. Her research and published work has mainly concerned British industrialization, pre-factory industry, industrial finance, regional and local history and the history of women's work and the family economy. Her publications include *The Genesis of Industrial Capital: a Study of the West Riding Wool Textile Industry, c. 1750–1850* (Cambridge University Press, 1986), *Regions and Industries: a Perspective on the Industrial Revolution in Britain* (Cambridge University Press, 1989) and *The Industrial Revolution* (Edward Arnold, 1992).

Geoffrey Jones is Professor of Business History in the Economics Department of the University of Reading. He is the author or editor of fifteen books mainly on the history of international business, including *The State and the Emergence of the British Oil Industry* (1981); *Banking and Empire in Iran* (1986) (ed.); *Banks as Multinationals* (1990); *The Rise of Multinationals in Continental Europe* (1993) (ed. with Harm Schroter); and *British Multinational Banking 1830–1990* (1993). He is co-editor of the journal *Business History*.

S.R.H. Jones is currently Associate Professor of Economics at the University of Auckland, New Zealand. He has published widely on the structure of markets and industry in British economic history. He has also written on the development of industry in New Zealand and is currently researching the growth of big business in that country.

Maurice W. Kirby is Reader in Economic History in the Department of Economics at Lancaster University. He has published widely on themes in British economic, industrial and business history. His latest book, a business history of the Stockton and Darlington Railway Company, has been published by Cambridge University Press as *The Origins of Railway Enterprise* (1993). Dr Kirby is a Fellow of the Royal Historical Society.

Helen Mercer was formerly Lecturer in Economic History at the University of Leeds. Her research interests have focused on the evolution of competition policy and regulation in Britain, British trade associations, and the relationship between the 1945–51 Labour governments and the private sector. She has published on government–industry relations in Britain, industrial organization and industrial policy. Her book on the history of British competition policy is to be published by Cambridge University Press in late 1994. She is currently working part-time as a lecturer and researcher.

Mary B. Rose is a Senior Lecturer in Business History in the Department of Economics at Lancaster University. Her main research interests lie in the field of business and textile history, on which she has published a number of articles and authored, edited and co-edited four books. The most recent of these are *Entrepreneurship, Networks and Modern Business* (1993) (co-edited with Jonathan Brown) and *Family Capitalism* (1993) (co-edited with Geoffrey Jones). Dr Rose is President of the Association of Business Historians for 1993–4.

Oliver M. Westall is Senior Lecturer in Economic History in the Management School at Lancaster University. His recent book *The*

Provincial Insurance Company 1903–1938: Family Markets and Competitive Growth (Manchester University Press, 1992) has provided the basis for a series of other publications which have related the history of insurance to wider themes in British business history such as the operation of cartels, business culture, goverment regulation and marketing.

Michael Winstanley is Senior Lecturer in History at Lancaster University. His publications include *The Shopkeeper's World, 1830–1914* (Manchester University Press, 1983) and, with his students, *A Traditional Grocer: T.D. Smiths of Lancaster, 1858–1981* (Centre for North West Regional Studies, Lancaster University, 1991). He has also published extensively on various aspects of northwest history and is currently writing a book on British history, *c.* 1865–1939.

Acknowledgements

The idea for an edited textbook in business history originated during a chat over a cup of coffee with Professor Balasubramanyam (Lancaster University, Economics Department) in 1989. The present volume evolved from that chat and the editors are most grateful for Baloo's encouragement and general interest throughout the project.

Wary of the well-known criticisms of edited textbooks, the editors felt that it was essential, for the coherence of the volume, that contributors should have the chance to discuss all chapters. A conference was therefore organized on 14 and 15 May 1993, in the Management School, Lancaster University. This intensive two days proved invaluable in shaping the final drafts of the chapters. The editors are grateful to the Nuffield Foundation for funding the event, to Baloo for chairing one of the sessions and to Professor Etsuo Abe (Meiji University) who attended the conference and who made a valuable contribution to discussions.

We should also like to thank our contributors, for without them there would have been no book. Throughout all stages of its production their co-operation and good humour served to make the jobs of the editors extremely easy. We were especially grateful for their general enthusiasm, for the highly stimulating discussions at the conference and for adhering so closely to our fairly tight deadlines.

Finally we should like to thank our partners, Barbara Kirby and Tony Breakell, for their support and encouragement.

Maurice W. Kirby
Mary B. Rose

1   Introduction

Maurice W. Kirby and Mary B. Rose

Business history is important for the insights it gives into the evolution and working of the modern economy. Synonymous with the study of change, a historical approach adds the dynamic dimension, lacking from much economic analysis. At the same time, economics is an essential and invaluable tool for the business historian. It provides, for example, a framework within which to study the competitive process and, in transaction cost theory, insights into the notion of the firm as an alternative to the market. Theories of comparative advantage and the product cycle, on the other hand, represent important starting points for the study of international industrial specialization. Yet understanding of business strategy, organizational structures, the competitive environment and shifts in international competitive advantage are all vastly enriched by a historical dimension.

The long historical perspective presented in this book, embracing the Industrial Revolution and the later nineteenth and twentieth centuries, is important. It facilitates an understanding of the development of skills, work practices, social structures and attitudes, all of which have bearing on twentieth-century business performance and organization. The notion that past economic and social developments may shape, promote and indeed retard business performance lies at the heart of much recent historiography. It has been shown, for example, that the financial and commercial networks, which had emerged by the mid-eighteenth century, were crucial to modern industrial development in some regions of Britain during the Industrial Revolution (Hudson 1989; Pollard 1981: 3–41). Equally, reservoirs of pre-industrial skill helped to determine the location of modern industry in the eighteenth century. They also shaped work practice and attitudes to education, in both staple and craft industries, well into the twentieth century. Chandler and Lazonick, on the other hand, have placed the nineteenth-century organizational legacy at the heart of their analysis of twentieth-century industrial decline (Chandler 1990: 235–94; Lazonick 1991: 25–7). Whatever the limitations of their interpretations there is a broad consensus that in the peculiarly British case a full understanding of twentieth-century business trends should be rooted in their historical context. As Michael Porter would remind us, the competitive advantage of national business structures is dynamic – it changes over time and its roots may be nurtured or starved by the legacy of the past (Porter 1990).

THE DEVELOPMENT OF BRITISH BUSINESS

1780–1850

The eighteenth-century British economy was predominantly agricultural. Until the 1820s agriculture, which employed over one-third of the occupied population, dwarfed the industrial sector (including manufacturing, mining and construction) as an employer of labour. Indeed, in comparison with individual industries, agriculture remained Britain's largest sector until the late nineteenth century (Crouzet 1982: 147). Similarly, as Table 1.1 shows, agriculture was the most significant source of national wealth in 1801, whilst according to Crafts productivity gains in the agricultural sector were superior to those to be found in industry. Thus, whereas between 1801 and 1831 agricultural productivity growth has been estimated to be 0.9 per cent a year, in manufacturing the rate of growth for the same period has been calculated at a mere 0.3 per cent (Crafts 1985: 115).

Controversy has long surrounded the British Industrial Revolution, and especially the productivity and growth performance of the industrial sector (Deane and Cole 1967; Harley 1982: 67–89; Crafts 1985;

Table 1.1 Industrial distribution of national income in Great Britain, 1801–1907 (%)

	1801	*1831*	*1851*	*1871*	*1907*
Agriculture	33	23	20	14	6
Industry, mining, construction	23	34	34	38	40
Trade and transport	17	17	19	22	28
Domestic and personal	6	6	5	5	3
Housing	5	7	8	8	6
Income from abroad	—	1	2	4	5
Public, professional and other	16	12	11	9	14

Source: Crouzet 1982: 67, Table 17

Crafts, *et al.* 1989; Hoppit 1990: 173−93; Berg and Hudson 1992: 24−50; Jackson 1992: 1−23). The fragility of statistical evidence means that a satisfactory resolution of the speed and implications of change in the manufacturing and mining sectors remains elusive. It has proved even more difficult to produce meaningful estimates of the growth and performance of the service sector. This has led to its relative neglect in general studies of the Industrial Revolution.

The gradualist interpretation of the British Industrial Revolution points to a relatively modest growth of national output between 1780 and 1830. In that period national product was estimated to have risen by 1.32 per cent per annum between 1780 and 1801 and by 1.97 per cent a year between 1801 and 1831 (Crafts 1985: 45). Against this canvas of slow growth, investment and productivity growth in manufacturing have also been shown to be modest (Feinstein 1978: 28−96). Only in the export-oriented cotton industry was a productivity gain of 2.6 per cent per annum, between 1780 and 1860, impressive. Crafts suggested, however, that the considerable extent of the traditional sector minimized the cotton industry's impact on the macroeconomy (Crafts 1985: 87).

This is not the place to enter into the minutiae of debate surrounding the Industrial Revolution. It is sufficient to note that in the last twenty years gradualist interpretations have proved more influential than those advanced by Rostow and Deane and Cole, who pointed to a more rapid industrial revolution (Rostow 1960: 31−5; Deane and Cole 1967). Concentration has been focused on the national economy, upon a relatively narrow range of sectors within it, and upon the productivity gains to be derived from mechanization and the factory system. This emphasis was clearly dictated by the patchiness of data. Yet it means that the operation of the microeconomy and the behaviour of businesses within and between localized business communities has been obscured. Moreover, as Berg and Hudson have argued, the factory system and manufacturing were only part of the Industrial Revolution and they acknowledge, in consequence, the symbiotic relationship between the factory and non-factory sectors (Berg and Hudson 1992: 27).

The success of the powered factory was crucially dependent on the traditional sectors of the economy and upon commercial and financial innovation. Thus in cotton textiles steam-powered spinning mills often also employed networks of handloom weavers quite late in the nineteenth century. In the Birmingham metal trades, on the other hand, the factory sector was supported by a significant community of artisans (Lyons 1985: 419−25; Berg 1993: 17−39). In addition, the

British cotton industry was overwhelmingly export oriented. By 1830 cotton textiles accounted for 51 per cent of British exports (Farnie 1979: 9). It is inconceivable that such expansion could have been achieved and sustained without innovations in the commercial sector (Chapman 1992: 81–192). Similarly, the development of British merchant banking from 1830 made a vital contribution to the ability of British manufacturers to penetrate distant markets (Chapman 1984).

The British Industrial Revolution was the heyday of the small firm, where ownership and control were normally united within a single family. Yet one of the most striking features of British business between 1780 and 1830 was diversity in scale of investment and employment. Small firms, with modest financial requirements and sometimes tiny workforces, whether associated with factories or artisan workships, characterized much eighteenth-century British manufacturing. However, technological indivisibilities in both iron making and brewing meant that even in the eighteenth century there were examples of extremely large manufacturing businesses. In these industries there were firms where levels of investment were considerable and workforces vast (Pollard 1965: 63–95). Where outwork was used, on the other hand, networks could embrace several thousand workers and be pivoted on substantial merchant capitalists. It was in agriculture, mining, commerce, transport and insurance, however, that, prior to 1850, Britain's largest scale enterprises were to be found.

Given the prominence of agriculture, it is not surprising that in the eighteenth century some of the vast landed estates were among Britain's largest business enterprises (Pollard 1965: 37–41). In addition, mines often overhauled manufacturing firms significantly in terms of scale. It was in the tertiary sector, however, which includes commerce, financial institutions and transport, that the real giants of British business emerged before 1850. As in manufacturing, commercial activity was generally organized on the basis of small, family owned partnerships. The chartered trading companies such as the East India Company and the Hudson's Bay Company, however, were vast enterprises in the eighteenth century. The product of mercantilist government policies, these trading companies enjoyed national monopolies over trade with particular regions (Braudel 1984: 427–47). In undertaking commercial activities on an international scale they were engaged in finance, overseas manufacturing and shipowning (Chaudhuri 1981). The trading companies therefore engaged in unusually large capital investments. Similarly, insurance companies, such as Royal Exchange and the Phoenix, can also be described as large-scale firms, whilst the turnpike trusts and canal companies of the eighteenth century encompassed enormous investments and vast workforces in their construction phases.

The wide range in the scale of British business was matched, before the 1850s, by variety in the legal status of firms. Between 1720 and 1825, all but the chartered companies and those gaining parliamentary assent were denied the benefits of incorporation as a result of the Bubble Act (DuBois 1971: 3). Yet it is difficult to argue that this legislation seriously inhibited business development in Britain during the Industrial Revolution. It is true that the partnership predominated in much commercial activity, in private banking and in manufacturing. But this was at least as much because of its flexibility as because the joint-stock company had been outlawed (Mathias 1979: 103–4). Moreover, wherever substantial sums of finance were required the legal profession was adept at devising schemes which, whilst within the letter of the law, were well outside its spirit. (Discussions of these issues can be found in Chapters 3, 5 and 6.)

Diversity in the scale and legal status of firms should not, however, obscure similarities in strategy and organization in business before 1850. This was an era when personal contact within and between communities was critical to business success irrespective of the scale of firm. In terms of finance, partners and information, the boundaries of the eighteenth-century and early nineteenth-century British family firm extended to embrace the local community. Nineteenth-century family firm strategy was therefore moulded within localities. In business communities shared values reduced transaction costs and meant that, despite a proliferation of small firms, collusion was not inconceivable. (These issues are explored in Chapters 3, 4 and 8.) The importance of community and personal contact was not, however, confined to family firms between 1780 and 1830. The courts of the chartered trading companies and the insurance companies (with the exception of the Phoenix) were filled by members of the City of London's commercial and financial communities. Many individuals served as directors in an array of different chartered companies and met regularly in London's numerous Coffee Houses. This significantly enhanced the flow of information between companies, and generated intelligence which could be critical to the success of a share flotation.

Even in the case of transport undertakings, which were among the most capital-hungry ventures, the power of community in generating finance and management should not be forgotten. It is well known that most finance for canals and railways was drawn from interested parties within localities. Yet in the case of the Stockton and Darlington Railway the influence of community was taken a step further. In this instance the shared values and trust of the nationwide Quaker business community generated much of the finance and managerial requirements of a joint-stock company (Kirby 1993: 26–53; Prior and Kirby 1993).

There are also striking similarities in the organization of business activity during Britain's Industrial Revolution. For the most part management was avoided rather than embraced and activities were more usually organized on the basis of external networks rather than being internalized within firms. Even in the chartered trading companies, sometimes likened to modern multinationals and certainly possessing impressive procedures to facilitate information flows, the extent of managerial hierarchies was limited. Critically, there was no middle tier of management and few professional managers. In insurance, on the other hand, expansion into provincial markets was facilitated not by an expansion of companies' internal activities but by the use of locally based agents.

The importance of outwork, subcontracting and external contracts is perhaps best known in manufacturing and mining, but they were also found in canal and railway companies before 1850. In manufacturing, for example, outwork and handworkshops persisted well into the nineteenth century. This has led to the conclusion that too much emphasis has been laid on the impact of the centralized factory in the Industrial Revolution (Berg and Hudson 1992: 24–50). What is striking, however, is the importance of external contracts and subcontracting in the strategies of factory and indeed mine owners. In these sectors, the externalization of activity reduced the burdens of management by a diverse range of activities (Pollard 1965: 23–63; Church 1986: 416–22; Berg 1993: 17–39).

1850–1914

In a brief but penetrating survey of British entrepreneurship in the period to 1914 Professor Payne commented that by the mid-nineteenth century 'British industrial organisation, characterised by the family firm' had become 'partly ossified at a relatively immature level of development' (Payne 1988: 43). Analysis of the perpetuation of family influence and control into the later nineteenth century and beyond has been a notable concern of much recent literature on British business history. This interest has been validated in part by a long-standing debate on the origins of Britain's relative decline as an industrial nation in which failings in entrepreneurship and the organization of business have been identified as critical and precipitating factors. In statistical terms the onset of decline has been interpreted in two main ways, first in relation to British growth rates of gross domestic product (GDP), industrial production and overall productivity, and second in comparisons between these indicators of economic performance and the experience of other national economies, notably Germany and the United States. In relation to trends in domestic growth rates various dates after 1870 have been identified as marking the onset of economic and industrial retardation, but with an overall consensus that the earliest years of the twentieth century were a period of unusually low growth, fully reflected in a range of industrial production indices (see Table 1.2). It is a point well taken, however, that in a relatively mature economy subject to secular economic change – as resources were switched from the industrial sector to services and elsewhere – a slowing down in the rate of industrial production or productivity was entirely compatible with rising levels of national income 'boosted by vigorously rising returns from services or foreign investments' (Pollard 1989: 17). It is salutary to remember that on the eve of the First World War Britain's visible trade deficit was generously offset by income from internationally traded services and returns from interest and dividends, the latter the product of the City of London's role as an exporter of capital. In this respect, the record of British business history from the eighteenth century points to the evolution of a dual economy in which provincial manufacturing industry was complemented by financial institutions with an increasingly metropolitan focus, the two sectors enjoying a mutually dependent relationship. As indicated already, foreign sales of British manufactures were facilitated at an early stage by merchant banks at the same time as the penetration of British exports, in increasing the volume of international commerce, redounded to the advantage of City of London financial institutions. In the light of these factors, pessimistic views of Britain's economic performance before 1914 must rest upon unfavourable comparison of growth rates at the international level (Table 1.3) reinforced by assessments of economic performance at the sectoral level. Since there can be no doubting the vigour and flexibility of the financial services sector, broadly defined, it is inevitable that manufacturing industry has provided the focus of critical attention.

In the context of British business history, relative economic retardation has been explained by a continuing failure to gain access to scale economies, especially in the period after 1880 when German, and particularly American, enterprise was adopting large-scale corporate

Table 1.2 Annual growth rates (%) of industrial/manufacturing production, UK, 1856–1913

	Hilgerdt manufacturing production	Lewis manufacturing and mining	Feinstein industrial production	Lomax industrial production	Aldroft/Richardson industrial production including building[a]
By decades					
1860–70		2.6	2.4		2.9
1870–80	1.2[b]	2.1	2.3	2.1	2.3
1880–90	2.6	2.7	2.4	1.9	1.6
1890–1900	1.5	2.1	2.4	2.6	2.8
1900–10	1.0	1.2	0.8	0.9	
1900–13	2.1	2.1	1.7	1.6	1.6
By cycles					
1855–65		2.6	3.2		
1865–74		2.9	2.5		
1874–83	1.7	2.4	2.1		
1883–90	1.7	1.8	1.9		
1890–1901	1.3	1.9	2.2		
1901–7	1.4	2.0	0.0		
1907–13	3.1	2.6	3.6		

Source: Pollard 1989: 9, Table 1.8

Notes: [a] Single years, beginning and end of decades.
[b] Start is average of 1870–1.

Table 1.3 Average annual growth rates (%) of industrial production and productivity, 1860–1913

	Industrial production	Industrial productivity
UK	2.1	0.6
Germany	4.7	1.5
United States	4.1	2.6

Source: Pollard 1989: 12, Table 1.13

organization in key exporting sectors. This was the route to international competitive advantage at a time when Britain's decentralized capital structures were firmly entrenched. That small-scale proprietary capitalism persisted in British manufacturing into the later nineteenth century is at first sight surprising in view of the companies legislation of the 1840s and 1850s which legalized the joint-stock enterprise protected by limited liability in England and Wales. The route to corporate status was therefore opened to family business. At the same time, these middle decades of the nineteenth century witnessed the foundation of impressively large corporate firms in the railway sector. Companies such as the London and North Western and North Eastern Railways adopted strategies of internalization facilitated by the recruitment of professional salaried managers differentiated by specialist function. Given the high public profile of railway enterprise in the Victorian economy the advanced managerial structures of the leading firms could reasonably be expected to have had a 'demonstration effect' on other industrial sectors.

The slow spread of corporate organization in manufacturing industry before 1914 can be explained readily by reference to a combination of supply and demand factors. In the former case the emergence of the private company endowed with limited liability permitted family firms and partnerships to combine the new legal form with control of ordinary share capital. This was a notable development from the 1880s onwards and it was of critical importance in sustaining family capitalism. As for the railway companies, all the evidence suggests that their managerial innovations were industry specific with very limited cross-fertilization to the manufacturing sector. Railway managerial hierarchies provided ample opportunity for professional advancement: leading executives were remunerated generously and enjoyed considerable social prestige. Even if private firms had sought to recruit such individuals they could not have matched the conditions of service customary in the railway sector.

Demand-side influences reinforced these patterns. Although the later nineteenth century witnessed the emergence of embryonic mass markets for small-scale items of common consumption, these were far from ubiquitous. They were also far narrower in extent than their counterparts in the United States. Moreover, the *generality* of markets for British firms, both at home and abroad, remained sufficiently fragmented to preclude access to dynamic economies of scale. In all of these respects it is significant that the retail banking sector came closest to replicating the leading railway companies in their adoption of corporate business structures in the latter half of the nineteenth century. The companies legislation was critical to this development but its permissive nature is confirmed by considerations of scale specific to the delivery of financial services. The latter included the maintenance of confidence and reduction of risk, both of which highlighted the importance of scale economies.

This is not to suggest that the industrial structure of the later nineteenth century was static. As noted already, a principal facet of retardation in Britain was the onset of foreign industrial competition emanating principally from Germany and the United States. It should also be noted that the twenty-three-year period after 1873 was subject to a sustained price deflation which made its own contribution to the erosion of profit margins. In these circumstances it is hardly surprising that the final decades of the nineteenth century should witness overt attempts at collusion in a number of industrial sectors, from coalmining to textiles. As defensive reactions to heightened competitive pressures late nineteenth-century cartels proved to be notoriously unstable, the result of atomistic business structures. In terms of the analytical structure adopted in Chapter 8 the logical response to this situation was to move from collusion to integration via the process of amalgamation. It is well known that this trend was exemplified in the textile finishing trades which witnessed a merger boom in the later 1890s. Judged by share capital and numbers employed, the resulting firms stood out as large-scale corporate enterprises in the manufacturing sector. But in adopting decentralized managerial structures they betrayed their origins as federations of proprietary capitalists intent upon gaining market power whilst preserving the prerogatives of family management. The adoption of the corporate form in the guise of the holding company was not confined to textiles. By 1914 it had spread to other industrial sectors such as metal manufacturing and foodstuffs. Thus, in combination with private limited firms, holding companies formed a substantial institutional brake on the structural evolution of British business.

BRITISH BUSINESS AFTER 1914: THE CHANDLER THESIS AND CRITIQUE

In recent years, primarily as a result of the pathbreaking work of Alfred D. Chandler Jr, much attention has been directed towards explaining the international emergence of American-style corporate enterprise in manufacturing industry. Even before 1900, the US economy had begun to experience corporate change as professional managerial hierarchies made their appearance in a range of industrial sectors. With respect to Britain debate has had three principal facets: discussion of changing levels of industrial concentration, organizational failings in business, and analysis of the relationship between industrial structure and macroeconomic performance. Yet if the analysis of organizational structure and capabilities has received a disproportionate degree of attention, it is but one aspect of business history. The performance of modern economies and the responses of firms within them can only be understood against the background of national and often local factor endowments. Equally, a historical understanding of cultural, institutional, governmental and educational influences on economic activity is critical to the appreciation of international differences in business behaviour.

The growth of modern industrial economies in the twentieth century is inseparable from the development of big business (Supple 1992: xi). This means that publication of first Chandler's *Strategy and Structure* (1962), then *The Visible Hand* in 1977, followed by *Scale and Scope* in 1990 was especially timely and made a lasting impression on business history on both sides of the Atlantic (Chandler 1962, 1977, 1990). Where once there had been isolated firm-specific case studies, there now existed a structure and compelling analysis of the development of the business corporation. In *The Visible Hand* the modernization and increased efficiency of the American economy after 1880 was viewed as synonymous with the rise of big business. In this process Chandler argued that small family firms were replaced by large corporate enterprises administered by salaried managers. As a result, the modern business enterprise replaced the market as a mechanism for coordinating economic activity, and managerial corporations became America's most powerful economic institutions (Chandler 1977: 1).

The rise of big business in the United States in the late nineteenth century was stimulated by a combination of market opportunity and technological change and involved a three-pronged investment by firms in production, marketing and management. The development of railways, and later telecommunications, unified the vast and growing

US domestic market. With the organizational models provided by rail-road companies in mind, manufacturing firms in both consumer and producer goods sectors responded by pursuing growth strategies involving high levels of investment in new technologies. Yet if the returns on such investments were to be maximized and the full benefits of economies of scale reaped, it was essential to reduce average costs by securing the further economies of speed, or rapid throughput. This was achieved in two ways. To ensure that products reached the widest possible market there was a tendency to internalize activities rather than to rely on market transactions. Thus firms complemented their initial investment in manufacturing with investments in marketing. The range and complexity of activities involved in these growth strategies and the level of investment required was, Chandler argued, beyond both the competence and resources of family proprietors and led to the growing separation of ownership from control. This encour-aged a third prong of investment – in professional managerial hier-archies. Increasingly, business corporations employed three tiers of salaried administrators, divided into functional departments, to facilitate communication and coordination and to ensure that there was no conflict between day-to-day decisions and long-term strategy (Chandler 1977: 207–344; 377–454). Internal growth, however, was but one facet of the emergence of corporate enterprise in the United States. Partly in response to the anti-trust laws of the 1890s, and partly to intensify the use of marketing and management investments, there followed merger waves which significantly increased concentra-tion levels in industry (Chandler 1977: 345–79).

Before the First World War some American corporations extended their commercial activities still further by investing overseas and by diversifying their product range. It was a move which, to be success-ful, involved further adjustment in organizational capabilities. Centralized administration was appropriate to the single product firm with only domestic factories, but not for the multiproduct, multi-national company. The response, in for example DuPont by the 1920s, was the decentralized multidivisional firm which gave access to economies of both scale and scope. Functions such as research and development and sales were located in the different product divisions, leaving the top layer of management free to determine overall corporate strategy. On the other hand, internal efficiency was ensured by competition between the constituent product divisions. In this process managerial replaced personal capitalism as the power of individual families was overhauled by that of managers. In Chandler's view the knowledge and professionalism of the increasingly highly educated career administrator meant that merit and not connections were the basis of commercial success (Chandler 1977: 455–483).

The rise of big business in America coincided, during the inter-war period, with the emergence of the United States as the world's largest industrial power and with a widening productivity gap with Europe. This led, inevitably, to the belief that there was a strong correlation between the organizational structure of business and macroeconomic performance. Faith in the superiority of American business structures has meant that, despite providing a detailed and masterful comparative analysis of American, British and German business in *Scale and Scope*, Chandler's starting and finishing point is the United States. As a result, the American-style business corporation is the benchmark against which he, and much recent historiography, have judged the structure and behaviour of firms in other countries.

It was in Britain where Chandler found the most striking contrasts with the United States before 1945. If the three-pronged investment in production, marketing and management explained the competitive success of American firms, the relatively poor performance of British business in the twentieth century, especially in the technologically sophisticated industries of the Second Industrial Revolution, could be ascribed to the nineteenth-century legacy of personal or family capitalism. Chandler explained the slower development of sophisticated managerial hierarchies and the exclusion of all but a few salaried managers from strategic decision-making in terms of the distinctive attitude of British entrepreneurs to their firms. Personal capitalism, he argued, constrained the growth of businesses whilst the owners of the relatively few large-scale family firms showed

> a distrust or dislike of losing personal control over enterprises they had either controlled or inherited. Throughout the late nineteenth century British entrepreneurs continued to view their businesses in personal rather than organisational terms, as family estates to be nurtured and passed on to heirs.
>
> (Chandler 1990: 286)

Few business historians would deny the importance of Chandler's approach in conceptualizing and systematizing the study of corporate enterprise. By combining a model of firm growth with scrupulous attention to historical detail, Chandler's work greatly enhances understanding of the way businesses grow. Yet, in applying to Europe, and especially to Britain, what could be described as an ethnocentric model based on the United States, he has met with criticism (Church 1990: 703–10; Hannah 1991: 297–309; Supple 1991: 500–14; Schmitz

1993). Controversy especially surrounds Chandler's condemnation of personal capitalism and the idea that, irrespective of circumstances, the American-style multidivisional corporation is superior to other more loosely structured organizations. It was the damaging combination of financial policies with the obsessive preservation of familial control which, according to Chandler, restricted the development of corporate enterprise in Britain.

In a perceptive analysis of the dynamics of shifting competitive advantage Lazonick has qualified, but at the same time endorsed, Chandler's interpretation. He argues that proprietary capitalism in localized industrial regions, where economies were external rather than internal to the firm, served Britain well until the late nineteenth century. By the 1890s international competitive advantage had shifted towards capital-intensive, technologically sophisticated production, for which Britain's vertically specialized family firms were ill-equipped (Lazonick 1991: 25–7, 45–9). In Lazonick's view this organizational inheritance, embracing large tracts of British industry, played a decisive role in the erosion of national competitive strength both at home and abroad in the twentieth century. Rooted firmly in Chandlerian perspectives, Lazonick's work is an original contribution to the historiography of British economic decline. His approach is grounded in the belief that the peculiarly atomistic market structures bequeathed by the nineteenth century provided a formidable *institutional* barrier to progressive economic change after 1900. In this setting, the emergence of Chandler's 'visible hand' of hierarchical managerial bureaucracies was long delayed by the British commitment to the 'invisible hand' of market competition as the arbiter of resource allocation.

The growth-inhibiting effects of entrenched institutions have certainly attracted the attention of scholars intent upon identifying the historic causes of Britain's economic malaise. This is particularly the case in Mancur Olson's classic study of economic growth and decline in mature industrial economies (Olson 1982). It is one thing, however, to highlight the phenomenon of 'institutional sclerosis' as part of a generalized hypothesis; it is quite another to advance a coherent analysis rooted in detailed appraisals of economic performance. The latter was attempted in an earlier volume co-edited by Lazonick and comprising case studies of the cotton textile, iron and steel, shipbuilding and motor vehicle industries, all of which demonstrated that British businessmen performed as well as could be expected given the obstacles to enhanced competitiveness imposed by existing institutions (Elbaum and Lazonick 1986). It could, of course, be argued from a

Schumpeterian perspective that entrepreneurial failure was present to the extent that businessmen accepted inherited constraints as given and reacted passively, rather than innovatively, in confronting them. But in endorsing this view Elbaum and Lazonick point out that failure in the Schumpeterian sense cannot be ascribed to the cultural conservatism that lies at the heart of the entrepreneurial failure thesis: 'If twentieth century British society was pervaded by conservative mores, it was in this respect no worse off than Japan or continental European countries that were pre-capitalist, tradition-bound societies when Britain was the workshop of the world' (Elbaum and Lazonick 1986: 2). Rather, Britain's decline as an industrial power was underpinned by established institutional constraints that reinforced conservatism and preempted both individualistic and collective efforts to remove them or to mitigate their growth-inhibiting effects.

An institutional approach to the assessment of national economic performance, emphasizing the historic roots of later success or failure, is especially attractive in the British context in view of the country's status as the pioneer industrial country. With an unbroken record of political and social stability, and possessing a commercial infrastructure of exceptional longevity, the notion of institutional rigidities inimical to progressive economic change fits with the idea of penalties imposed in consequence of early industrialization. That said, a number of business historians have expressed substantial reservations about Lazonick's approach and conclusions. At the most general level, the worldwide resilience of family enterprise suggests that the damaging effects of family business have been exaggerated. Even in the late 1930s almost half of America's largest manufacturing and mining companies were family controlled, whilst large- and small-scale family firms continue to be found throughout the contemporary industrial world (Church 1990: 705; Church 1993; Jones and Rose 1993). In the British context, Coleman's reservations concerning Lazonick's generalizations about business performance may be noted (Coleman 1987). For Coleman it is the very fact of uneven business performance both within and across a wide range of British industries which casts doubt on the all-pervasiveness of binding institutional rigidities. The same point is also underlined by the similar behavioural characteristics of British family and non-family firms operating within the national economy. Such considerations derive extra validity from studies of family firms in their European context. In this respect, there is an emerging consensus among business historians that Britain's proprietary capitalists, at least until 1939, were part of a European-wide structure of family enterprise subject to a variety of environmental influences in addition to their ownership structure (Jones and Rose 1993). Thus, to isolate the latter as the critical determinant of business performance is at best myopic and at worse a naive over-simplification of events.

For both Chandler and Lazonick proprietary capitalism and competitive markets were the decisive factors in delaying Britain's transition to managerial capitalism as the key determinant of international competitive advantage, at least until the 1970s. There is an alternative perspective on institutional rigidities, however, which is well reflected in the work of Olson (Olson 1982). In his view, high rates of economic growth are dependent upon the absence of narrow interest groups, or 'distributional coalitions', which stand in the way of the free movement of factors of production. Such coalitions – collusive selling organizations, trade unions and other rent-seeking bodies – have featured in all capitalist industrial societies, but their damaging effects have had particularly baleful consequences for the British economy, especially in the period since 1945. According to Olson, the superior economic growth records of West Germany, Japan, Italy and France since the Second World War can be explained substantially by the legacies of totalitarian governments, and the impact of military defeat and occupation, all of which resulted in an institutional rejuvenation denied to Britain. This is not to suggest that 'unsuccessful wars and violent revolutions' are necessary for rapid economic growth. For Olson, sclerotic institutions are susceptible to reform in response to democratic political pressures in open societies. Indeed, the Thatcherite experiment of the 1980s was underwritten by this perspective in so far as Conservative governments, for good or ill, legislated against a number of sectoral interest groups and institutions on the presumption that economic welfare is positively correlated with competitive markets.

Olson's approach to institutional rigidities thus differs profoundly from those of Chandler and Lazonick. Far from internally competitive markets being an institutional rigidity in themselves, they are the potential solvent of such rigidities, if only the rent-seeking coalitions producing market imperfections can be removed. Statistical testing of Olson's thesis has produced equivocal results (Choi 1983; Pryor 1983), but recent work by Broadberry and Crafts, focusing on the proliferation of trade associations in British industry after the First World War, has lent some support to his views (Broadberry and Crafts 1992). Moreover, for business historians the emergence of explicit collusion is all the more significant in view of the contemporary movement towards the formation of holding companies, mainly in the manufacturing sector. As indicated already, this development was foreshadowed before 1914, but their proliferation in the inter-war period served, arguably, as a powerful complement to trade associations as a source of institutional sclerosis across the divide of the Second World War. It is an indication of the research agenda confronting business historians that the number of informed business histories of British holding companies is insufficient to sustain credible generalizations as to their productivity retarding or enhancing effects. Holding companies, moreover, are an international phenomenon, being well represented in Western European and Japanese business structures. In these other national settings such companies have not been equated with managerial weakness: the evaluation of British holding company performance, therefore, should ideally embrace a comparative approach.

Competitive advantage is ever shifting and Lazonick has shown that changing conditions may render a particular organizational form redundant (Lazonick 1991: 1–25). Yet business is shaped by the legal, cultural, institutional and market environment or allocative differences. Rather than just explaining why business organization may deviate internationally from some predetermined norm it is vital to explore what factors make business strategy in a specific country or group of countries distinctive. International competitive advantage is not determined solely, or even mainly, by the managerial structure of business. Thus, if family capitalism can no longer be seen as an inevitable drag on business development, neither can it be sustained that there is necessarily a positive correlation between the American-style multidivisional firm and superior macroeconomic performance. Economists and management specialists have shown that, whilst there is some relationship between the organization and profitability of firms, it should not be assumed that the M-form was a universal panacea to economic ills (Steer and Cable 1978: 13–30; Hill and Pickering 1986: 26–50). Nor is it clear that the spread of multidivisional corporations inevitably has a favourable influence on the productivity performance of firms or on the overall competitive performance of economies (Broadberry and Crafts 1992: 531–58; Jones 1993: 7–8). It is not to be expected that a single organizational form will be the most appropriate response to all external circumstances. The experience of Britain's successful international investment groups, for example, highlights the power of networks of subsidiaries as an alternative to tighter organizational forms (Chapman 1985: 230–51). Equally, in Britain after 1945, the multidivisional form of enterprise was emerging within an often unfavourable institutional and cultural environment, which included financial short-termism and a neglect of human capital. The results for business performance were mixed whilst the major transition from personal to corporate capitalism accompanied Britain's spectacular postwar macroeconomic decline (Jones 1993: 18–20).

In terms of the consummation of the corporate economy the decades of the 1960s and 1970s may be viewed as crucial in so far as they witnessed a merger boom, complemented by the adoption of multidivisional structures on the part of a majority of Britain's leading firms. However, statistical indicators for the postwar period show clearly that these years of corporate transition coincided with a substantial retardation of growth compared with Western European experience. This is well illustrated in the manufacturing productivity figures set out in Table 1.4 and those for output set out in Table 1.5. Table 1.6 provides a further perspective on British industrial performance, indicating the substantial reduction in Britain's share of world trade in manufactures coinciding with the corporate transition (see p. 19). Equally revealing is the relatively poor performance of the US economy since the early 1960s. America's early lead in corporate capitalism notwithstanding, these years have witnessed failings in US export performance and mounting import penetration. This has been the result of vigorous competition from established manufacturing nations and newly industrialized countries possessing a wide spectrum of business structures, but generally falling far short of the high degree of corporate control characteristic of the American industrial economy (Porter 1990: 508–35). By the early 1980s the competitive decline of American industry had proceeded far enough to provoke a lively, if inconclusive, internal debate on the need for a state-sponsored industrial policy informed by Japanese practice (Thompson 1989: 11–85).

Table 1.4 Output per person-hour in manufacturing, 1951–1988: comparisons with the UK in selected years

	UK	United States	France	Germany
1951	100	270	71	68
1964	100	268	90	117
1973	100	234	101	133
1979	100	243	129	163
1988	100	224	122	138

Source: Van Ark 1990

Table 1.5 Comparative performance indicators, 1960–1988: average annual rate of growth

	Output					
	Whole economy			*Manufacturing*		
	1960–73	*1973–9*	*1979–88*	*1960–73*	*1973–9*	*1979–88*
UK	3.1	1.4	2.1	2.8	−0.7	0.8
United States	3.9	2.6	2.5	5.3	2.9	2.8
Japan	9.6	3.6	4.1	12.5	2.0	3.9
Germany	4.4	2.3	1.7	5.1	1.1	0.8
France	5.4	2.8	1.9	6.1	1.6	0.3
Italy	5.3	2.6	2.3	6.6	2.6	1.5
Canada	5.4	4.2	3.0	6.1	2.5	2.5
Average	5.5	2.8	2.7	6.3	2.1	2.4

Source: OECD, *Economic Survey: United Kingdom*, 1989

Table 1.6 Shares of world trade in manufactures, 1937–1990 (%)

	1937	*1950*	*1960*	*1970*	*1979*	*1990*
France	5.8	9.9	9.6	8.7	10.5	9.7
Germany	21.8	7.3	19.3	19.8	20.9	20.2
Japan	6.9	3.4	6.9	11.7	13.7	15.9
UK	20.9	25.5	16.5	10.8	9.1	8.6
United States	19.2	27.3	21.6	18.6	16.0	16.0

Source: Brown and Sheriff 1979; Maizels 1963; Central Statistical Office, *Monthly Review of External Trade Statistics*, London, 1991

ESSAYS AND THEMES

The essays in this book analyse the development of British business in the two hundred years since the Industrial Revolution. The book does not, however, provide a Chandlerian analysis (or even a counter-Chandlerian study) of the rise of the modern business corporation in Britain. Coverage of the evolution of British business is not comprehensive, but is wide ranging. The book comprises a number of interpretative surveys which explore the conditions, both internal and external to firms, which influenced strategic decision-making. Four of the chapters deal explicitly with aspects of organizational change. They survey the debates surrounding the rise of the factory system and the evolution of business strategy in family firms, with two more being devoted to the development of the business corporation before and after 1860. Further chapters analyse the evolution of market structures and investment on the part of British business in human capital. In recognition of the bifurcated structure of the British economy in terms of manufacturing and services two chapters are included on the development of retailing and banking. The remaining chapters highlight three of the most distinctive aspects of British business development in the twentieth century, namely the growth of multinational enterprise, state intervention in the private sector, and the rise and decline of public enterprise.

In balancing the competing theories concerning the rise of the factory system Steve Jones (Chapter 2) illustrates the range and diversity of business organization in British manufacturing in the early stages of industrialization. In many sectors the factory system was perfectly consistent with, and indeed promoted, more decentralized forms of production. Such diversity was not, however, confined to the organization of work in manufacturing. Even in the eighteenth century, business organization encompassed the full spectrum of large- and small-scale firms. As Kirby shows in Chapter 5, even though British firms were characteristically small during the Industrial Revolution, large-scale firms were to be found in many sectors of the British economy before 1860. Nevertheless, managerial structures, whilst often highly efficient, were rarely complex in the Chandlerian sense. The subcontracting of responsibility proved to be the more normal response to managerial pressure than the formal internalization of activity. Similarly, the transition to the corporate economy in Britain from the late nineteenth century did not mirror that in America. In this respect Kirby demonstrates in Chapter 6 that the rise in concentration in British business before 1960 was more closely associated with loose networks of subsidiaries than with the extensive development of internal hierarchies. Kirby also focuses on the process of corporate convergence which reached a climax in the merger-intensive decade of the 1960s. This brought in its wake the widespread adoption of multidivisional structures in the American mould, but with disappointing results. Supply and demand conditions specific to the UK were responsible for this to the extent that the 1970s witnessed growing disillusion with the corporate economy. As Kirby notes, it was this experience which provoked a renewed interest in disaggregated capitalist structures after 1980.

It has already been shown that informal networks were of fundamental importance to the formulation of business strategy in Britain's family firms. Hudson's analysis of business finance (Chapter 4) high-lights the role of localized networks of credit in the finance of business of all categories during the Industrial Revolution. It was a trend which was to continue with the development of joint-stock banking in the second and third quarters of the nineteenth century. During this period community-based banks had sufficient access to intelligence con-cerning the creditworthiness and assets of customers to ensure that finance was readily available to industrial and commercial users. The influence of community on the formulation of family firm strategies provides the central theme of Chapter 3 in which Rose illustrates that the influence of localization on business strategy in the nineteenth century went far deeper than Lazonick's external economies (Lazonick 1991: 151). Community-based networks pushed back the boundaries of the firm, so that community and business became inseparable. Thus, in Britain's localized business communities, regular contact between businessmen through a range of social and cultural as well as economic institutions facilitated information flows. The resultant net-works of trust, where transaction costs were low, reduced the incent-ive to internalize activity. Community value systems, on the other hand, influenced the strategies for survival pursued by individual families and gave shape to diversification policies.

The evolution of family firm strategy and its relationship to com-munity is extended by Winstanley in his study of retailing (Chapter 9) where a myriad of shopkeepers, often holding prominent positions within their local community, were found in Britain until the 1960s. Like Kirby and Steve Jones, Winstanley highlights the diversity in the organization of British business in the twentieth century, as well as the interrelationship between income change, consumption patterns and organizational change in retailing. The latter factors, reflecting demand-side influences, are developed further in Westall's contribu-tion (Chapter 8). Although concerned primarily with the nineteenth century, Westall underlines the limitations of supply-side explanations of Britain's relative economic decline, as set out in the Elbaum and Lazonick thesis (Elbaum and Lazonick 1986). In focusing on the three strategic options for businessmen – 'competition, collusion, or inte-gration' – he demonstrates how specific market environments, and their evolution over time, moulded business conduct in a sequence of rational responses. The fact remains that in contrast to the United States demand-side forces played a crucial role in retarding the intro-duction of mass production technology and large-scale corporate enterprise in British business. As noted already, the emergence of a mass market for small-scale items of consumption was a notable development for some British firms before 1914, but elsewhere, substantial product differentiation in home and overseas markets helped to divide and sectionalize production to the detriment of unit costs and access to scale economies.

By the 1970s Britain had come to possess a US-style corporate economy: substantial industrial concentration was complemented by professional managerial hierarchies and multidivisional structures. Chapter 6 demonstrates that these developments were foreshadowed by inter-war trends, but it was an exceptionally powerful combination of supply and demand factors which precipitated rapid corporate convergence after 1960. One important influence, identified by Mercer in Chapter 11, was the role of government in encouraging the pursuit of scale economies in the business sector. Mergers were central to this process, especially in the 1960s and 1970s when Labour and Conservative governments were concerned to accelerate national economic growth, the latter by measures of indicative planning and the former by strategic intervention in manufacturing industry. Whilst Conservative administrations placed more emphasis on the competitive process as a means of industrial restructuring, the overall thrust of policy was to favour large-scale concentrations of capital, especially when the focus of attention moved beyond domestic manufacturing to embrace the financial services sector and multinational enterprise.

The ultimate incarnation of a state-directed visible hand is public ownership in the form of the nationalized industries. The motives for nationalization are reviewed by Chick in Chapter 12. For the public utilities he demonstrates that the regulatory function in relation to natural monopoly was a critical factor in motivating public ownership, although efficiency considerations via the achievement of scale economies also loomed large. In focusing on pricing, productivity and agency problems, Chick provides important insights into the mounting disillusion with public enterprise which was to reach its apotheosis in the Conservative government's privatization programme of the 1980s. In this respect there is a close parallel with the increasing scepticism, observable in the 1980s, concerning the efficiency-enhancing potential of mergers for private sector firms. As noted above, enthusiasm for disaggregated capitalist structures was a notable feature of the 1980s. Thus governmental measures to stimulate the formation of small firms may be viewed as a complement to privatization. Certainly, the belief was widespread that small firms had a valuable role to play in stimulating structural diversity. A revitalized small-firm sector was also viewed as an offset to the risk averseness of large-scale firms, a perspective well reflected in the contemporary political rhetoric of the 'enterprise culture'.

As Mercer notes, the 1980s and 1990s have witnessed substantial government support and encouragement for inward multinational investment in both manufacturing and the financial services sector. In the former, Japanese firms have been especially welcome on the grounds both of their technological precosity and of their innovative labour policies. In this context, however, it is salutary to remember that British firms have themselves undertaken substantial foreign direct investment (FDI). Indeed, as a proportion of GDP, British FDI is currently the highest among OECD countries. In surveying the performance of British multinationals in Chapter 7, Geoffrey Jones raises an issue of critical importance for business historians, namely the mismatch between Britain's evident success in multinational corporate management and the relative growth failure of the national economy, notably in the three decades after 1950. In this setting, Jones deploys Michael Porter's analysis of the sources of competitive advantage as a possible means of reconciling such disparate trends. In other words, a clear distinction should be made between Britain's falling share of world exports of manufactures (see above, p. 19) and the relative buoyancy of the total world sales of leading British firms. In the light of disadvantageous demand and factor conditions at home the latter transferred production overseas in the form of FDI, a move which safeguarded total world sales but at the expense of domestic output and employment. From the standpoint of the individual enterprise FDI can be interpreted as a rational entrepreneurial strategy, and British successes provide some insight into the quality of corporate management at the multinational level. As is pointed out in Chapter 6, however, multinational strategies were not all-pervasive: 'uninational' firms producing in, and exporting from, Britain may well have suffered from relatively incompetent managements at the same time as they were disadvantaged by domestic demand and supply constraints. An important subsidiary theme of Jones's chapter is provided by his observation that British firms were not alone in adopting a diversity of organizational forms in undertaking FDI. Viewed in a European rather than American context, there was nothing unusual about the use of free-standing companies and other loose organizational forms.

One domestic supply constraint of considerable magnitude is the subject of Chapter 13, in which Rose traces the historic roots of the British indifference to formal and vocationally relevant education for managers and shopfloor workers alike. As Rose points out, indifference to human capital formation has been deep seated and all-pervasive, with British attitudes standing in marked contrast to

European, Japanese and American experience. Although the post-1945 period has witnessed substantial expansion in educational expenditure the consequences for industrial productivity have been disappointing. This has been the result, in Rose's view, of the deficiencies in compulsory and intermediate education which have combined to restrict the benefits and potential scope of the limited shopfloor training available.

Finally, Chapter 10 by Collins on the growth of the firm in domestic banking can be viewed as a complement to Chapter 9 in that it serves as a reminder that even before the First World War there were considerable numbers of large-scale firms in the service sector (Gemmell and Wardley 1990; Wardley 1991). Indeed, as Collins notes, banks adopted corporate structures extensively before 1914 with the sector as a whole achieving an unprecedented degree of corporate control in the overall business structure. According to Collins, the reasons for this striking development lay in a combination of supply and demand factors, from the need to monitor effective remittance systems to the absolute requirement for the maintenance of public confidence. For British business historians in particular, there can be no doubting the necessity to move beyond the Chandlerian school's preoccupation with manufacturing industry. As all students of economic history are aware, an account of British economic development which fails to recognize the critical contribution of the tertiary and particularly the financial services sector would be grossly incomplete.

REFERENCES

Berg, M. (1993) 'Small producer capitalism in eighteenth century England', *Business History* 35: 17–39.

Berg, M. and Hudson, P. (1992) 'Rehabilitating the industrial revolution', *Economic History Review* 45: 24–50.

Braudel, F. (1984) *Civilization and Capitalism: 15th to 18th century*, vol. 2: *The Wheels of Commerce*, London: Collins, 427–47.

Broadberry, S.N. and Crafts, N.F.R. (1992) 'Britain's productivity gap in the 1930s: some neglected factors', *Journal of Economic History* 52: 531–58.

Brown, C.J. and Sheriff, T.D. (1979) 'De-industrialisation: a background paper', in F.T. Blackaby (ed.) *De-Industrialisation*, London: Heinemann.

Chandler, A.D. Jr (1962) *Strategy and Structure: Chapters in the History of American Industrial Enterprise*, Cambridge, MA: MIT Press.

—— (1977) *The Visible Hand: The Managerial Revolution in American Business*, Cambridge, MA: Belknap Press.

—— (1990) *Scale and Scope: The Dynamics of Industrial Capitalism*, Cambridge, MA: Harvard University Press.

Chapman, S.D. (1984) *The Rise of Merchant Banking*, London: George Allen & Unwin.

—— (1985) 'British based investment groups before 1914', *Economic History Review* 38: 230–51.

—— (1992) *Merchant Enterprise in Britain*, Cambridge: Cambridge University Press.

Chaudhuri, K.N. (1981) 'The English East India Company, 1660–1760', in L. Blusse and F. Gaastra (eds) *Companies and Trade*, Leiden: Leiden University Press, 29–46.

Choi, K. (1983) 'A statistical test of Olson's model', in D.C. Mueller (ed.) *The Political Economy of Growth*, New Haven, C: Yale University Press, 57–78.

Church, R. (1986) *The History of the British Coal Industry*, vol. 3: *1830–1913*, Oxford: Clarendon Press.

—— (1990) 'The limitations of the personal capitalism paradigm', *Business History Review* 64: 703–10.

—— (1993) 'The family firm in industrial capitalism: international perspectives on hypotheses and history', *Business History* 35: 17–43.

Coleman, D.C. (1987) 'Failings and achievements: some British businesses, 1910–80', *Business History* 29: 1–17.

Crafts, N.F.R. (1985) *British Economic Growth during the Industrial Revolution*, Oxford: Clarendon Press.

Crouzet, F. (1982) *The Victorian Economy*, London: Methuen.

Deane, P. and Cole, W.A. (1967) *British Economic Growth, 1688–1959: Trends and Structure*, Cambridge: Cambridge University Press.

DuBois, A.B. (1971) *The English Business Company after the Bubble Act, 1720–1800*, New York: Octagon.

Elbaum, B. and Lazonick, W. (eds) (1986) *The Decline of the British Economy*, Oxford: Clarendon Press.

Farnie, D.A. (1979) *The English Cotton Industry and the World Market, 1815–1896*, Oxford: Clarendon Press.

Feinstein, C. (1978) 'Capital formation in Great Britain', in P. Mathias and M.M. Postan (eds) *The Cambridge Economic History of Europe*, vol. VII, Part 1, Cambridge: Cambridge University Press.

Gemmell, N. and Wardley, P. (1990) 'The contribution of services to British economic growth, 1856–1913', *Explorations in Economic History* 27: 299–321.

Gourvish, T.R. (1987) 'British business and the transition to a corporate economy: entrepreneurship and management', *Business History* 29: 18–45.

Hannah, L. (1980) 'Visible and invisible hands in Great Britain', in A.D. Chandler and H. Daems (eds) *Managerial Hierarchies: Comparative Perspectives on the Rise of Modern Industrial Enterprise*, Cambridge, MA: Methuen, 41–76.

—— (1991) 'Scale and scope: towards a European visible hand?', *Business History* 33: 297–309.

Harley, C.K. (1982) 'British industrialization before 1841; evidence of slower growth during the industrial revolution', *Journal of Economic History* 42: 267–89.

Hill, C.W.L. and Pickering, J.F. (1986) 'Divisionalization, decentralization and performance of large UK companies', *Journal of Management Studies* 23: 26–50.

Hoppit, J. (1990) 'Counting the industrial revolution', *Economic History Review* 43: 173–93.

Hudson, P. (ed.) (1989) *Regions and Industries*, Cambridge: Cambridge University Press.

Jackson, R.V. (1992) 'Rates of industrial growth during the industrial revolution', *Economic History Review* 45: 1–23.

Jones, G. (1993) 'Big business, management and competitiveness in twentieth century Britain', University of Reading Discussion Papers in Economics, Series A, vol. V, no. 268.

Jones, G. and Rose, M.B. (1993) 'Family capitalism', *Business History* 35: 1–16.

Kirby, M.W. (1993) *The Origins of Railway Enterprise: The Stockton and Darlington Railway*, Cambridge: Cambridge University Press.

Lazonick, W. (1991) *Business Organization and the Myth of the Market Economy*, Cambridge: Cambridge University Press.

Lyons, J.S. (1985) 'Vertical integration of the British cotton industry, 1825–1850', *Journal of Economic History* 45: 419–26.

Maizels, A. (1963) *Industrial Growth and World Trade*, Cambridge: Cambridge University Press.

Mathias, P. (1979) *The Transformation of England*, London: Methuen.

Olson, M. (1982) *The Rise and Decline of Nations: Economic Growth, Stagnation and Social Rigidities*, New Haven, CT: Yale University Press.

Payne, P. (1988) *British Entrepreneurship in the Nineteenth Century*, 2nd edition, London: Macmillan.

Pollard, S. (1965) *The Genesis of Modern Management*, Harmondsworth: Pelican.

—— (1981) *Peaceful Conquest: the Industrialization of Europe 1760–1970*, Oxford: Oxford University Press.

—— (1989) *Britain's Prime and Britain's Decline: The British Economy 1870–1914*, London: Edward Arnold.

Porter, M.E. (1990) *The Competitive Advantage of Nations*, London: Macmillan.

Prior, A. and Kirby, M.W. (1993) 'The Society of Friends and the family firm, 1700–1830', *Business History* 35: 66–85.

Pryor, F.L. (1983) 'A quasi-test of Olson's hypothesis', in D.C. Mueller (ed.) *The Political Economy of Growth*, New Haven, CT: Yale University Press, 90–105.

Rostow, W.W. (1960) *Stages of Economic Growth*, Cambridge: Cambridge University Press.

Schmitz, C. (1993) *The Growth of Big Business in the United States and Western Europe*, London: Macmillan.

Steer, P. and Cable, J. (1978) 'Internal organisation and profit: an empirical analysis of large UK Cos', *Journal of Industrial Economics* 27: 13–30.

Supple, B.E. (1991) 'Scale and scope: Alfred Chandler and the dynamics of industrial capitalism', *Economic History Review* 44: 500–14.

—— (1992) 'Introduction', in Barry E. Supple (ed.) *The Rise of Big Business*, Aldershot: Elgar.

Thompson, Graham (ed.) (1989) *Industrial Policy: USA and UK Debates*, London: Routledge.

Van Ark, B. (1990) 'Comparative levels of labour productivity in postwar Europe: some evidence for manufacturing', *Oxford Bulletin of Economics and Statistics* 52: 343–74.

Wardley, P. (1991) 'The anatomy of big business: aspects of corporate development in the twentieth century', *Business History* 33: 268–96.

Part I

2 The origins of the factory system in Great Britain

Technology, transaction costs or exploitation?

S.R.H. Jones

INTRODUCTION

One of the most striking developments to have occurred during the Industrial Revolution in Great Britain was the rise of the factory system. Until the closing decades of the eighteenth century the majority of manufactured goods were produced by the domestic or putting-out system. At the heart of the domestic system was the cottage workshop where the domestic artisan, often assisted by journeymen, apprentices and family members, used simple tools to perform one or more stages of the manufacturing process. The materials processed might belong to the artisan but they were frequently supplied by a merchant capitalist who paid for work to be done on a piece rate basis. By 1871, however, the situation had radically changed for the bulk of manufactured goods was now produced in the factory. This was certainly true for textiles, by far the largest single source of employment, whilst considerable quantities of hardware, pottery and other items of consumption also came from the factory (Usher 1921: 362). The control of production had also changed, the role of the domestic artisan being taken over by the manufacturer who now supplied plant and machinery as well as the materials and directed a factory labour force that might number hundreds of workers.

Although the factory system came to dominate production in many trades during the course of the nineteenth century, substantial manufacturing activity continued to take place outside the factory. Even in the cotton industry, the archetypal factory industry, outworkers were weaving cloth on handlooms well into the second half of the nineteenth century while in woollen textiles the spinning jenny and handloom continued to be employed in homes and workshops even longer. In some trades, such as garment manufacture, outwork was never entirely superseded. This organizational structure was welcomed by most factory masters, the existence of a body of outworkers and small subcontractors providing them with the flexibility to cope with short runs or fluctuations in demand without incurring the fixed and quasi-fixed costs of factory production. Moreover, outwork and sub-contract labour possessed the advantage that it was generally cheap, especially when it included large numbers of women and children (Jones 1987: 87−8; Berg and Hudson 1992: 31).

Yet it would be wrong to view the domestic and subcontractors' workshops that existed in mid-Victorian England as little more than marginal units of production. It is quite clear that in a number of trades, particularly those catering for a growing body of middle-class consumers who typically placed a premium on quality, craftsmanship and fashion, the small workshop represented the optimal unit of pro-duction (Samuel 1977: 56−7). This was the situation in the small arms trade where the market for sporting guns remained the preserve of small makers who relied extensively on subcontract and outwork. Large military orders for cheap, standardized products, on the other hand, were filled by firms such as the Birmingham Small Arms Company which operated a large mechanized factory at Small Heath especially to meet this segment of the market (Timmins 1967: 430−1; Allen 1966: 116−19).

The relationship between factory, workshop and outworker during the process of industrialization was thus an exceedingly complex one. Where production might be located was the result of interaction between a variety of factors, including the nature of technology, the characteristics of the market, and relations between capital and organ-ized labour which, on occasions, might block technical change (Jones 1987: 85; Robertson and Alston 1992: 330−2). Nevertheless, there was a general trend towards increasing factory production for most of the nineteenth century.

What exactly constituted a factory is difficult to say. Indeed, the debate over the definitional characteristics of the factory is almost as old as the factory system itself. Most early commentators believed that the presence of power-driven machinery was an important distinguish-ing feature of the factory. Thus in 1835 Andrew Ure wrote, 'The term Factory, in technology, designates the combined operations of many orders of work people, adult and young, in tending with assiduous skill a system of productive machines continuously impelled by a central power' (Ure 1967: 13). Not all were persuaded that plants using power-driven machinery should necessarily be described as a factory. 'I am engaged in scribbling, carding and fulling,' complained Joshua Robinson, the operator of a West Riding woollen mill, 'it is no factory – neither am I a manufacturer but work the mill for country and domestic manufacturers.' Early legislators, it seems, were not in the least concerned whether mill operators owned the materials they processed or not, deeming factories and mills to be synonymous for the purposes of inspection and regulation (Jenkins 1975: 11–13). Nevertheless, they did agree that the use of powered machinery was an important feature of factory production and factory inspectors were instructed to collect details of the nature and extent of power employed.

The Factory Acts were gradually extended to cover a wide range of plants, many without machinery, and this necessarily gave rise to doubts about the usefulness of defining factories in strictly techno-logical terms. Cooke-Taylor, writing in 1891, argued that the term 'factory' should be applied to all plants

> where several workmen are gathered together for the purpose of obtaining greater and cheaper conveniences for labour than they could procure individually in their own homes for producing results by combined efforts which they could not accomplish separately; and for saving the loss of time which the carrying of an article from place to place during the several processes necessary to complete its manufacture would occasion.
>
> (Cooke-Taylor 1891: 1)

Scale and efficiency, therefore, not technology, should be the defining characteristics of the factory.

Given the variety of definitions, it is not surprising that there should be some disagreement concerning the origins of the factory system. Contemporaries, who marvelled at the complexity of machinery intro-duced by the likes of Thomas Lombe and Richard Arkwright, were inclined to regard the spread of factories as the necessary concomitant of advances in technology. Most were well aware that not all factories contained machinery and that sometimes masters adopted factory production merely in order to sweat labour. For most, however, the triumph of the factory system was inextricably linked to the introduc-tion of new technology (House of Commons Committee on the Woollen Manufacture of England 1806: 9–11; Reports from Assistant Commissioners, Handloom Weavers 1840: 434–58; Ure 1967: 12–13; Wing 1967: v–viii).

Economic historians, too, have tended to point to the technological origins of the factory system. Mantoux, writing at the beginning of the twentieth century, was quite unequivocal. 'The factory system', he states, 'was the necessary outcome of the rise of machinery' (Mantoux

1961: 246). Most have followed in the Mantoux tradition. Heaton, whose research was conducted a few years later, concludes:

> the major part of the economic advantage of the factory springs from the use of machinery capable of performing work quickly, and the use of power which can make machinery go at high speed. Until these elements of speed became possible, the factory system did not possess any great advantage over the cottage industry.
>
> (Heaton 1965: 352)

And finally David Landes, in a recent restatement of his position: 'No, what made the factory successful in Britain was not the wish but the muscle: the machines and the engines. We did not have factories until these were available, because nothing else would have overcome the advantages of dispersed manufacture' (Landes 1986: 606–7).

The view that the rise of the factory system can be explained largely in technological terms has attracted increasing criticism since the mid-1970s, especially from those who are not economic historians. For example, Stephen Marglin, writing from the perspective of the New Left, focused on the exploitative aspects of the factory system. According to Marglin, factories were introduced not because they were technologically superior, but because they enabled capitalists to control the work process more closely and thereby extract greater output from workers for a given cost. Capitalists (who Marglin suggests were irrelevant to the productive process, be it the putting-out or the factory system) were thus able to obtain an even 'larger share of the pie' (Marglin 1974: 62).

New institutional economists, while rejecting the exploitation thesis of the New Left, have also questioned the technological underpinnings of the factory system. Oliver Williamson, for example, argues that putting-out was superseded by the hierarchically organized factory because the latter economized on transactions costs. Economies were achieved as factory production enabled transportation and inventory costs to be cut, embezzlement to be reduced and manufacturers to respond more readily to changes in fashion and demand. For Williamson, therefore, the main reason why the factory system was adopted was that it was organizationally more efficient than putting-out and other earlier modes of production (Williamson 1980: 28–9).

These challenges to traditional explanations for the rise of the factory system have not remained unanswered. Landes, for example, has questioned the empirical basis of Marglin's work arguing that, while Marglin's argument is logically elegant, it explains what might have happened rather than what actually did happen (Landes 1986).

Williamson, too, has been criticized, both for using a model that ignores key variables and for the empirical deficiencies of his work (Jones 1982, 1983). More recently Rick Szostak has suggested that a fall in transport costs led to a shift in comparative advantage from putting-out to the factory system just prior to major advances in technology at the end of the eighteenth century (Szostak 1989). His argument, too, has been attacked, on both methodological and empirical grounds (Jones 1992).

That the debate has continued unresolved for almost twenty years is not entirely surprising, for there is disagreement as to what is actually meant by 'the factory system', when it is supposed to have emerged, whether the empirical evidence has been properly addressed, and what was typical and what was not. Before we examine the merits of the various arguments, therefore, it might be helpful to establish the broad outlines of factory development in the centuries leading up to and including the Industrial Revolution.

FACTORIES BEFORE THE INDUSTRIAL REVOLUTION

Factories employing scores of workers using simple hand technology can be found in England as early as the sixteenth century. The most celebrated of these, perhaps, are the woollen textile factories of Jack of Newbury and William Stumpe but there were similar establishments elsewhere (Patterson 1967: 151–2). How cost effective these early factories were is difficult to say although their ability to survive may well have been due to the unusual demand conditions of the time. Suffice it to say that they disappeared during the second half of the sixteenth century, the collapse in demand together with anti-factory legislation probably hastening their demise (Heaton 1965: 90–1).

For the next two centuries the putting-out system was increasingly adopted by those industries where processes were divisible, technology was simple and semifinished materials were not costly to transport. Rural labour surpluses encouraged this development, with a system of outriders and agents emerging that enabled capitalists to put out work to underemployed and unemployed labour throughout the countryside. Putting-out work was not only confined to the countryside, for a number of urban trades came to rely on outwork too, but it was cheap rural labour that underpinned the growth of the putting-out system. In some industries technological non-separabilities and other characteristics meant that production in the domestic workshop was simply inappropriate. Manufacturers of iron, porter, glass, paper and seasalt, for example, required plants of a certain scale if they were to realize production economies. For many goods, however, the small workshop with its simple technology constituted the least cost mode of production. Certain stages of the manufacturing process, such as fulling cloth, might require a more capital-intensive technology, but it was often possible to integrate this within the broad structure of domestic production.

Putting-out conferred substantial advantages on the merchant capitalists who organized production. Labour was usually cheap, fixed costs were low, an extensive division of labour could be practised and, in times of depression, production could be easily curtailed. Despite these advantages, however, the hand factory or *manu*factory, which utilized essentially the same technology as that employed by outworkers, began to appear in a variety of trades from the end of the seventeenth century onwards. The term 'proto-factory' has been coined by Freudenberger and Redlich to describe these technologically simple factories but, given its wider connotations within the proto-industrialization debate, it will not be adopted here (Freudenberger and Redlich 1964: 381).

Some of the earliest factories were established as a means of setting the poor to work. The view that the poor might be usefully employed by the parish gained ground during the course of the seventeenth century and by 1700 pauper factories run by the parish had come into being in London, Bristol and elsewhere (Furniss 1957: 108–10; Thirsk and Cooper 1972: 301–2). Philanthropists also set up factories in an attempt to alleviate the twin evils of poverty and unemployment (Heaton 1965: 354–5). The history of pauper factories, however, is scarcely a glowing testament to their efficiency. A study of forty-five workhouses-cum-factories undertaken in 1725 revealed that none earned sufficient to cover the costs of maintaining their inmates (Furniss 1957: 108–9). Nevertheless, paupers continued to be set to work, often performing tasks in the workhouse on materials supplied by a manufacturer and under the supervision of an agent. This was particularly common in that archetypal factory industry, pin-making, where manufacturers continued to contract with overseers of the poor (and gaols) to supply work well into the nineteenth century.

An increasing number of manufacturers also employed paupers on their own premises (Rose 1989: 5–29). One of the earliest factories in the hosiery industry, that of Samuel Fellowes of Nottingham, employed more than forty parish apprentices by the early 1720s. A few other hosiers followed suit but factories were not widely adopted by the rest of the Nottingham trade, not even in the 1760s when competition was at its fiercest (Aspin and Chapman 1964: 34). Indeed, domestic outwork continued to dominate the hosiery trade until the 1840s (Nelson 1929–30: 469).

At the same time that experiments were being carried out with pauper factories, a growing number of hand factories came into being that relied on free labour. One of the earliest was that established by Ambrose Crowley at Winlaton, near Newcastle, which was set up in 1691 to manufacture nails. Expansion soon followed with a new vertically integrated plant being erected in nearby Swalwell, and ultimately the firm possessed blast-furnaces, slitting mills and a range of large workshops producing numerous items of hardware and ships' chandlery. The Crowley enterprise was undoubtedly 'a giant in the age of pygmies'. It also represented an attempt to break new ground by introducing the factory to an industry hitherto organized on traditional domestic lines. Yet in spite of the advantages of a reduction in embezzlement, an improvement in scheduling, better quality control and the evident profitability of the Crowley empire, few manufacturers sought to emulate Ambrose Crowley. Thus most items of hardware continued to be produced in small domestic workshops for a century or more. Indeed, the Crowley iron works found it increasingly difficult to compete with the domestic nailmakers of the West Midlands, the production of nails finally ceasing at Winlaton in 1816 (Flinn 1962: 94, 184–93, 252–4).

There were nevertheless, examples of factory production in other hardware trades, especially in the production of fancy boxes and japanned ware. Amongst the first manufactories to appear was that of Charles Osborne, a tobacco box maker of Wolverhampton who set to work 'a large shop of workmen' during the 1720s. Others in the Birmingham district also gathered workers into the factory, including John Baskerville, who, by 1745, employed 300 hands in japanning, and the celebrated firm of Boulton and Fothergill. Yet in spite of contemporary interest in large factories, few manufacturers were prepared to adopt them. As Marie Rowlands points out: '[t]he large workshop with elaborate machinery and numerous employees aroused the admiration of visitors in the mid-eighteenth century precisely because it was exceptional. Only a minority of the workforce were employed in such places' (Rowlands 1975: 155–7). This continued to be the case well into the nineteenth century.

Technology and the factory

At the same time that the hand factory was beginning to make an appearance in the Midlands, a very different type of factory was coming into being in the silk trade. This took the form of a multi-storied water-powered silk throwing mill. The first English silk mill was erected in Derby by Thomas Lombe who, with his brother John, had acquired, improved and patented Italian technology. Defoe described Lombe's silk mill in some detail, evidently fascinated by machinery that incorporated '26,586 wheels and 97,746 movements, which work 73,726 yards of silk thread every time the water wheel goes round' (Chaloner 1963: 13).

Thomas Lombe's patent for silk throwing expired in 1732. Thereafter new entry occurred and over the next four decades a number of mills were built incorporating the latest technology. By 1769 there were six silk mills at work in Stockport, principally supplying Spitalfields weavers, with a further twenty in operation in nearby Macclesfield. Additional mills were to be found at Derby, Congleton, Leek and Knutsford, further mills coming into operation in the south of England towards the end of the century. The success of these early throwing mills did little, however, to persuade silk manufacturers to employ factories in the weaving section of their trade. A few weaving factories were introduced at the end of the Napoleonic Wars, mainly in order to force down wage rates, but the majority only came into being following the introduction of new technology later in the nineteenth century (Jones 1987: 71–96).

Despite the lead given by the silk industry in erecting large water-powered mills, the rise of the factory system has traditionally been associated with cotton manufacture. The first cotton spinning factories came into being during the 1740s, based on the patented machinery of Lewis Paul and John Wyatt, but they proved to be commercially unsuccessful. It was only after Arkwright patented his roller-spinning machine, or water frame, in 1769 that cotton began to overtake silk as the premier factory industry in the country. The expiration of the roller-spinning patent in 1783, followed shortly afterwards by the revocation of Arkwright's omnibus patents for preparatory processes, removed the principal barriers to entry to the factory-spinning section of the trade. By 1795 some 300 Arkwright type factories had come into existence (Chapman 1972: 30).

Substantial changes also took place in the woollen and worsted industries from around 1770 onwards. Power was applied to the preparatory processes of carding, slubbing and spinning, and to finishing with processes such as milling and shearing being mechanized. The result was a proliferation of mills to house the new technology, with old fulling mills being converted and extended and new water and steam mills being erected. There were some 243 mills in operation in the West Riding by the beginning of the nineteenth century as well as a number elsewhere (Jenkins 1975: 17). Whether all should be termed factories is a matter for debate, for some employed less than a dozen hands and performed only a limited range of processes. Nevertheless, many operated on an integrated basis, using power for processes such as scribbling and carding (and sometimes worsted spinning) and hand-powered machines to produce slubbings and weft, while some contained looms as well. The larger mills of this type often employed scores of workers and clearly merited the description 'factory' however that term might be defined.

Yet not all advances in spinning technology required a large mill with a central power source. The spinning jenny, which was first introduced in the 1760s, was a hand-powered machine small enough for workers to operate in their cottages. Improvements in the method of construction soon permitted the jenny to be enlarged, however, and by the 1770s modest factories housing the larger hand-powered jennies were to be found in both Lancashire and Somerset (Wadsworth and Mann 1965: 500−1). The larger jenny was slower to make its way in woollens than in cotton, mainly for technical reasons, although by the early nineteenth century there were a number of jenny workshops in both Yorkshire and Gloucestershire (Aspin and Chapman 1964: 56−8).

Crompton's mule, which first appeared in the 1780s, was also a hand-powered machine suitable for domestic use. As with the jenny, enlarged versions were soon to be found in the factory, the application of power to the mule in the 1790s hastening its departure from the cottage (Kennedy 1819: 129). By 1812, according to Samuel Crompton's census, there were 573 mule workshops or factories, although how many of these were reliant on mechanical power is not known (Daniels 1930: 109).

The introduction of what might be regarded as 'intermediate technology' was also linked to the spread of hand factories in other trades. The stamp and press, for example, was introduced into a number of Birmingham trades, transforming the button industry, making inroads into the pin industry, and ensuring that an increasing proportion of the needle manufacturing process was henceforth carried out in the factory. Like the early jenny, the stamp and press was small enough to be used in the cottage although the quantities of material processed, the fact that some of the machines were subject to patent, and the need for occasional adjustment by a fitter meant that there was a tendency to locate them in a large workshop or factory. In spite of these developments, outworkers and subcontractors using intermediate technology found themselves placed under increasing pressure as power-driven machinery was introduced, with those making pins, for example, being almost completely supplanted by automatic machinery by the middle of the nineteenth century.

The introduction of capital-intensive equipment that significantly lowered the costs of production did not always rob artisans of their independence. In the West Riding woollen industry, domestic clothiers gained access to the new technology by forming joint-stock mills which performed a variety of processes for shareholders, including carding, slubbing, fulling and sometimes spinning wool (Hudson 1983: 135). In nearby Sheffield, labour chose to hire capital equipment rather than become petty capitalists themselves. Thus craftsmen in the cutlery trades were able to retain their independence by renting grinding-troughs at steam powered public wheels at which they worked for themselves, factors and larger manufacturers (Pollard 1959: 54–7). Similar arrangements were arrived at by pointers and scourers in the Redditch needle industry (Jones 1980: 187), while in the Birmingham sporting gun trade a combination of subcontract and the extreme division of labour ensured the survival of artisans and small local and country gunmakers long after the application of steam power to barrel-boring and grinding (Timmins 1967: 387–93; Greener 1910: 407–10). Even in the cotton industry the practice of inside contracting meant there was a role for the semi-independent artisan, with employers attempting to reduce the costs of hiring and supervision by employing labour through mule-spinners rather than directly themselves (Lazonick 1979: 233; see also Chapter 5, p. 127).

In these and other industries, therefore, the introduction of factory machinery with a high technical optimum did not result in all processes being carried out by large-scale hierarchically organized firms. Where technology was sufficiently flexible and the characteristics of the market permitted, contracting-out was seen by merchants, manufacturers and artisans as one way of sharing the costs and risks of production. Nor was this structure necessarily lacking in vitality, for the existence of large numbers of small producers appeared to provide a competitive environment that encouraged invention and innovation, with new designs and new methods helping to ensure that the workshops of Birmingham and Sheffield were able to survive in an age of factories (Sabel and Zeitlin 1985: 146–7).

The symbiotic relationship that existed between factory, workshop and outworkers undoubtedly contributed to the growth in numbers of both power-driven and hand factories between 1780 and 1850. Precise figures are not available, for the early returns from factory inspectors tended to exclude plants without power and provide only an imperfect record of the remainder. Even so, the returns for 1835 reveal 1,245 cotton mills at work throughout the United Kingdom, more than 1,300 woollen and worsted mills, 345 flax mills and 238 silk mills (Jenkins 1973: 26–46). In addition, there were scores of hardware factories that produced pins, needles, nails, buttons, cutlery and other items, together with a limited number of factories and workshops in other branches of industry. The majority of these establishments employed advanced technology, using steam and water power in conjunction with the latest machinery to ensure that by the middle of the nineteenth century Britain had become the workshop of the world.

TRADITIONAL EXPLANATIONS FOR THE RISE OF THE FACTORY SYSTEM

The rise of the factory system was an exceedingly complex phenomenon. Factories appeared in certain trades long before others; there were differences in timing both between branches of a single trade and between the geographical areas in which that trade was found; the shift to factory production was sometimes accompanied by the introduction of new technology and sometimes not, and on occasions artisans retained independence even though working within the factory. Generally speaking, though, the movement into the factory took place in most trades after 1780 and, from the turn of the century, was associated with steam power and the growth of factory towns.

In spite of its complexity, the essential features of factory development have long been familiar to most economic historians. Certainly those who have argued for the technological origins of the factory system are well aware of the wide variety of circumstances in which factories were adopted and that, in a number of instances, technological considerations were unimportant. Why, then, have so many economic historians, including Mantoux, Heaton, Usher, Ashton, Landes, Mathias and others, chosen to place so much emphasis on the role of technology?

Before one can understand why these scholars consider technology so important, it is necessary to appreciate the nature of the dominant paradigm at the time they wrote. The dominant paradigm, it seems, was a general belief in the existence of an Industrial Revolution. Indeed, the notion of developments that resulted in fundamental – even revolutionary – changes in economy and society finds precise expression in the titles of the seminal works of both Mantoux and Ashton and, more allegorically, in Landes' *The Unbound Prometheus*.

At the same time, each of these scholars is aware that, in certain respects, change was more evolutionary than revolutionary. But, to quote Ashton, 'the phrase "Industrial Revolution" has been used by a long line of historians and has become so firmly embedded in common speech that it would be pedantic to offer a substitute' (Ashton 1962: 2).

Thus qualified, the belief in the existence of an Industrial Revolution has proved to be a powerful influence shaping the ideas of economic historians and others in the twentieth century (Coleman 1992: 1–42). But what was it that so radically transformed the nature of economy, society and environment in late eighteenth-century England? A major force for change, in the eyes of many, was the *modern* factory system. This appeared in its embryonic form in the silk industry, reached its full bloom in cotton, was adopted by the rest of the textile industry and, in the nineteenth century, spread to other manufacturing sectors.

The essential features of the modern factory system have been carefully spelt out by both Mantoux and Landes. First, there was the substitution of inanimate sources of power for the limited and irregular effort of human and animal muscles. And second, machines – as opposed to mere tools – performed tasks previously undertaken by hand. The difference between a tool and a machine is a matter for debate but, for the purposes of their argument, both Mantoux and Landes envisage machinery that was of a scale that required sizable premises and a central power source for efficient operation (Mantoux 1961: 246; Landes 1969: 2). In other words, both regard technological indivisibilities to have been a major feature of the modern factory system.

For many historians, however, the development of the modern factory system entailed rather more than just the introduction of power-driven machinery. It also entailed the transformation of an industry that was capable of growing in size until it had major ramifications for the rest of the economy. Thus even though there were more than thirty power-driven silk mills at work prior to Arkwright's experiments, cotton is regarded as the key to the Industrial Revolution. This is because the cotton industry, unlike silk, enjoyed a favourable combination of highly price-elastic demand schedules and rapidly shifting cost curves (Landes 1969: 81–3; Mathias 1983: 116–17). The result was almost exponential growth, described by one contemporary as 'absolutely unparalleled in the annals of trading nations' (Aiken 1968: 3), and by the 1820s few commentators doubted that, as a result, both economy and society in Great Britain had undergone a radical change (Berg and Hudson: 1992).

A modern factory system based on power-driven cotton mills is thus seen as having been at the heart of the first Industrial Revolution. There is less unanimity concerning the processes that lay behind the appearance of the factory system, with Ashton stressing, amongst other things, a reduction in the cost of capital, Mantoux paying particular attention to inventors and inventions, and Landes linking developments in technology with changes in the structure of demand. Indeed, the growth of demand, especially domestic demand, is seen by some as crucial to the development of the industry, with bottlenecks in supply leading to invention and innovation. Most are agreed, however, that the rapid expansion in the number of cotton factories placed substantial demands on capital goods and other industries. This induced further innovation, capital deepening and the increases in labour productivity that were so important for sustained economic growth.

Yet at the same time that power was being applied to spinning and other processes, there was also an increase in the number of hand factories that did not require power. The 1770s witnessed the spread of jenny factories, especially in Lancashire cottons, whilst towards the end of the century large loom shops began to appear in both the Yorkshire and Gloucestershire woollen industries. Given such activity, why have generations of economic historians tended to regard hand factories as unimportant, in their contribution both to the development of the modern factory system and, more generally, to the process of industrialization? The answer would seem to be that while there was indeed an increase in jenny factories, spinning capacity was relatively small compared with that of power-driven factories. Loomshops were even less significant, being dwarfed by outwork until the 1830s. Furthermore, such establishments yielded neither the cost savings nor the linkage effects attributed to the power-driven mills that prepared and spun cotton and wool. Their introduction did not, therefore, represent a radical change in the organization of production.

Few would deny that there were advantages to be gained from gathering workers together in manufactories. The centralization of production meant that the manufacturer was able to avoid the transportation and other costs of putting-out and, through closer monitoring, reduce embezzlement, improve scheduling and exercise greater quality control. Yet, as Heaton, Landes and others point out, there were disadvantages too: the need to provide both plant and equipment leading to an increase in fixed costs and a reduction in the manufacturers' ability to respond to fluctuations in demand. Nor was it easy to persuade a labour force unaccustomed to time discipline to work regularly or diligently in the manufactory, especially in the absence of machinery that imposed its own work discipline (Pollard 1968: 189; Harte 1977: 41).

But the principal disadvantage of the factory system, it is argued, is that masters were usually obliged to pay factory workers higher rates of pay than outworkers. This was the result not only of the premium that factory masters were obliged to pay labour to work in the much disliked factories, but because they were not able to tap rural and distant labour markets in which employment opportunities were limited and people were prepared to work for substantially lower wages. Putters-out faced no such constraints, being able to employ men, women, children and the otherwise unemployable on a casual basis, paying wage rates that might be below subsistence and sometimes had to be made up by the parish (Select Committee on the Silk Trade 1831–2: 195; Bischoff 1968: 185–6; Landes 1986: 606–7).

The judgement of a succession of historians, therefore, is that the gains from factory organization were generally insufficient to offset the additional costs involved. When raw materials were particularly expensive, quality a consideration, prompt delivery important, secret processes in use, or other fixed costs involved, it might pay masters to have a proportion of their goods produced in the factory (Ashton 1962: 109; Aspin and Chapman 1964: 33; Landes 1986: 603). The absence of substantial numbers of hand factories prior to the Industrial Revolution, however, is taken as *prima facie* evidence of the fact that such conditions were rarely met.

The modern factory system, like the Industrial Revolution of which it was such an essential element, is thus seen by traditional historians to have been based on new technology that ultimately overwhelmed putting-out and other earlier modes of production. This technology was not usually to be found in the hand factory or manufactory but in more technologically advanced establishments, of which the cotton factory with its power-driven machinery was the exemplar.

FACTORIES, DISCIPLINE AND THE NEW LEFT

The first major challenge to the view that the rise of the modern factory system was due to advances in technology was mounted by Stephen Marglin. In a seminal article published in 1974, Marglin argues that the adoption of factories had nothing to do with their technological superiority. Rather, it was so that the capitalist and not the worker might control the work process and quantity of output. This innovation in the organization of work enabled the capitalist to get 'a larger share of the pie'. The change in relative income shares was achieved through supervision and discipline, the closer monitoring and control of the factory system making it possible for masters to force the worker to work harder and produce for little or no extra remuneration (Marglin 1974: 62, 84).

The advantages conferred by supervision and discipline were sufficient, according to Marglin, to persuade manufacturers to adopt the factory system even though it was not more *technologically efficient* than putting-out. These advantages, he maintains, are widely recognized by a number of leading authorities, including Mantoux, Ashton and Landes, even though none are prepared to admit that supervision and discipline played more than a minor part in accounting for the success of the factory system. The reason for their agnosticism, according to Marglin, is because most have employed a model in which greater output has been achieved through technical innovation. The technologically simple factory, he says, which only obtained greater outputs through dint of greater inputs, does not fit easily within their model (Marglin 1974: 82–3).

Hand factories, as Marglin is first to admit, have a long history prior to the Industrial Revolution. Why then, if factories offered manufacturers the possibility of obtaining 'a larger share of the pie', did they not appear in significant numbers before the end of the eighteenth century? Marglin offers two related explanations. First, he suggests that the factory system was slow to arrive because of the lengthy struggle between the guilds and capitalism. Thus in the sixteenth and seventeenth centuries, the small master and journeyman took advantage of divisions between more powerful classes 'to forge temporary alliances that for a time at least were successful in stalling the advent of the factory'. Gradually, however, as the power and interests of the various classes changed, the statutory provisions that protected journeymen and small masters fell into disuse and were ultimately repealed. This opened the way for the introduction of factories (Marglin 1974: 102).

Second, Marglin argues that, even after power relationships changed, pressures to switch to the factory system did not become critical until the latter part of the eighteenth century when outworkers sought to take advantage of buoyant product markets by demanding higher real wage rates. With greater remuneration, outworkers could afford to substitute leisure for work and take time off. If the wage rates offered still seemed inadequate, they might embezzle raw materials and engage in other types of fraud. Capitalists attempted to control such activities by recourse to the law, with statutes being passed to ensure work regularity and reduce embezzlement. 'But', says Marglin, 'more direct action proved necessary. The capitalists' salvation lay in taking immediate control of the proportions of work and leisure.' Thus the very success of the putting-out system in exploiting demand at home and abroad 'contained within it the seeds of its own transformation' (Marglin 1974: 92–5).

Although the need to control the work process is seen as the primary reason for the movement into the factory, Marglin is prepared to accept that technology also became important in later years. Technology, however, was not the independent cause of the factory system as Mantoux and Landes would suggest.

> On the contrary, the particular forms that technological change took were shaped and determined by factory organization. It is not accidental that technological change atrophied within the putting-out system after Hargreaves jenny but flourished within the factory.

Why was technological change apparently biased towards the factory? Marglin suggests that it is because, on the demand side, factory owners provided a better market for patented inventions than domestic outworkers while, on the supply side, it was easier to exercise control than in a myriad of country cottages (Marglin 1974: 89–90).

Marglin, the factory system and the evidence

The Marglin thesis is carefully structured and is buttressed with numerous quotations drawn from both contemporary works and those of economic historians. What evidence is there, however, to support his principal contention, namely, that the success of the factory system 'had little or nothing to do with the technological superiority of large scale machinery'?

Mantoux and Landes, as we have seen, carefully spell out what they mean by 'factory system'. Indeed, they employ a definition which excludes a 'system' consisting of hand factories. Marglin is less specific, for after initially referring to the 'factory system' he then refers to the success of 'the factory'. The confusion is compounded by his choice of examples that include factories that neither Mantoux nor Landes would consider as part of the 'factory system'. Consequently, it is never entirely clear whether he is discussing the origin of hand factories or a factory system based on power. Such a distinction is probably unimportant to Marglin who believes that hand factories represent the first stage in a process that paved the way for the introduction of power-driven machinery.

Yet although a considerable proportion of factory spinning was initially based on the hand-powered jenny, what evidence is there to suggest that manufacturers set up jenny factories because closer supervision enabled them to extract more output from workers? For Marglin, the fact that the cottage and jenny factory spinners used the same 'basic machine' is conclusive proof that the success of the jenny factory 'could only have been for organizational reasons' (Marglin 1974: 86–7). What, one may ask, does Marglin mean by the term 'basic machine' and, more importantly, was there any significant difference between the small cottage machine (which was certainly basic) and the larger factory jenny? Certainly those in the cotton trade believed there was a difference, with riots in Lancashire in the late 1770s leading to jennies of more than twenty-four spindles either being destroyed or reduced in size by having the excess spindleage lopped off. Following the riots a proposal was put forward to tax all jennies of over twenty-four spindles. The rate of taxation was to increase as the size of jennies rose, presumably to offset economies of scale and enable those with smaller machines to compete (Wadsworth and Mann 1965: 496–502). In the woollen industry, too, attempts were made to limit the number of spindles per jenny or workshop (Aspin and Chapman 1964: 57).

Given the economies of scale that the operators of large jennies clearly enjoyed, why were they not adopted by the cottage spinner? Sometimes they were, especially in Yorkshire where small clothiers might incorporate them into their operations. Space, however, was often a limiting factor, with many persons finding it difficult to house machines that might have a 3 foot draw and be more than 12 feet in length. Finding additional space, moreover, was not always easy, especially if William Radcliffe's comments on the shortage of workshops are to be believed. Furthermore, the cost of renting, setting up and maintaining a small jenny (or mule) shop was probably beyond the resources of most workers (Podmore 1923: 38–9; Aspin and Chapman 1964: 44; Lazonick 1979: 233; Landes 1986: 606).

It is difficult, therefore, to accept Marglin's contention that the jenny factory was adopted for purely organizational reasons. Large jennies were simply more efficient than small ones, their very size ensuring that they were usually located in workshops and factories. Here they were often to be found running in tandem with power-driven carding engines and slubbing billies which, because of their size, throughput and power requirements, were also unsuitable for use in the cottage (Aspin and Chapman 1964: 50–1; Landes 1986: 604).

The reason for the adoption of handloom factories is also seen by Marglin to be due to the organizational advantages they conferred:

> Long before the powerloom became practicable, handloom weavers were brought together into workshops to weave by the same techniques that were employed in cottage industry. Clearly, handloom shops would not have persisted if it had not been profitable for the entrepreneur, and just as clearly the source of profits could not have been in a superior technology. There is no evidence that the handloom in the capitalist's factory was any different from the one in the weaver's house.
>
> (Marglin 1974: 87–8)

It is by no means clear, however, that the spread of handloom factories was due to the advantages conferred by better supervision and discipline. Technical parameters did change, for improvements in the quality of yarn due to power-spinning reduced the levels of weaving skill required, opening the way for the employment of cheap unskilled labour working in factories under skilled supervision. Even so, Landes believes that the rationale for such factories usually lay elsewhere, pointing out that both loomshops and jenny factories were often part of integrated concerns. These might include mechanized preparatory processes such as slubbing and carding as well as heat-intensive and power-driven finishing processes such as dying and fulling. Landes concludes: 'If clothiers were going to invest in factories at both ends of the production process, they wanted to be able to keep plant and equipment busy' (Landes 1986: 604). Capacity utilization, he suggests, not the gains from supervision and discipline, was the *raison d'être* for many loomshops and jenny factories.

There were, nevertheless, exceptions to this pattern of development that lend a measure of support to the Marglin thesis. In 1815, for example, a strike by Macclesfield silk weavers over a reduction in piece-rates led manufacturers to establish hand factories and employ erstwhile apprentices and others at significantly lower rates of pay. Elsewhere in the trade, a system of 'half-pay apprentices' was employed in which nine or ten young persons were gathered together under one roof and set to work under the supervision of a skilled silk weaver. Silk weaving factories were not widely adopted, however, even though power-driven throwing mills had been in existence for almost a century by this stage. Moreover, the century-long lag before weaving followed throwing into the factory suggests that the cost advantages that were supposed to flow from factory organization cannot have been glaringly obvious to those engaged in the silk industry (Jones 1987: 78–80).

Handloom factories were also introduced by Gloucestershire woollen manufacturers as a means of forcing down wage rates. A few large loomshops appeared around 1800 but they were not adopted on any scale until a succession of strikes against reductions in wage rates in the 1820s finally led, in 1828, to 'the more general establishment of the shoploom system'. Whether manufacturers would have been so quick to transfer weaving to the factory had they not been so con- cerned about the 'value of buildings and machinery rendered inactive by this strike' is a matter for conjecture (Reports from Assistant Com- missioners, Handloom Weavers 1840). Moreover, even though the Gloucestershire industry was burdened with significant fixed costs due to investment in fulling mills, shearing engines and so forth, hand- loom factories were surprisingly slow to be adopted.

Marglin is therefore correct to suggest that *some* hand factories were introduced so that capitalists might exploit their positions of power to extract more labour from workers for a given cost. What he fails to establish, however, is that the majority of jenny factories and large loomshops, upon which his argument is largely based, were adopted for those reasons. Far more compelling are arguments con- cerning the size and interrelatedness of much of the new equipment – and this brings us back to technology.

Paradoxically, although Marglin is quick to play down the role of technology, his treatment of it is surprisingly cursory. Certainly he offers no empirical evidence to support his contention that, because of the patent system, invention was biased towards producing technology more suited to the factory than putting-out. Had he examined the cotton industry in greater depth, he would have discovered that the mule, which was not initially subject to a patent, was rapidly trans- formed from the cottage to the workshop or factory because of its size and power requirements. Indeed, as Berg has observed, many advances went unpatented (Berg 1991: 187).

More generally, Marglin fails to analyse the reasons for the intro- duction of power-driven factories in silk, cottons or wool, or to assess their importance relative to hand factories. Nor does he comment on the timing of their introduction which, in the silk industry, occurred almost a century prior to the adoption of hand factories, and in the case of cotton and wool, took place round about the same time as the growth in the number of jenny factories and large loomshops. For many economic historians, the introduction of these power-driven factories is precisely what constitutes 'the rise of the factory system', and on this subject Marglin remains largely silent.

TRANSACTION COSTS AND THE FACTORY SYSTEM

Marglin's account of the origins of the factory system, although receiving a somewhat guarded response from traditional economic historians, has been welcomed more enthusiastically elsewhere. Thus Oliver Williamson, whilst not agreeing with Marglin's central thesis, welcomes the attention paid to the way in which work is organized. Economists, he argues, are too wedded to the 'production function orientation of received microtheory' and this approach makes us blind to the fact that increases in efficiency can be brought about by improvements in internal organization as well as by advances in technology. For Williamson, therefore internal organization matters, so much so that he seeks to explain many institutional developments in terms of organization rather than technology. This includes the displacement of putting-out by what Williamson refers to as the *authority relation*, another term for Marglin's hierarchically organized factory (Williamson 1980: 11, 29).

For the purposes of his analysis, Williamson is first obliged to journey inside the 'black box' of the neoclassical firm in order to unravel its internal structure. What we generally find, he tells us, is that a firm does not consist of a large single workstation transforming raw materials into finished products but a series of adjacent workstations, each of which adds value to an intermediate product before passing it on. In principle, therefore, one can envisage independent (and possibly dispersed) workstations transferring product to each other via a series of market exchanges. Alternatively, production might be undertaken on a co-operative basis, or certain processes might be subcontracted out to others, either working in the same plant or elsewhere. Williamson maintains that the reason why the hierarchically organized firm is generally used to co-ordinate product flow instead of the market or these alternative organizational modes is because it usually incurs fewer transaction costs. Hierarchy, therefore, by economizing on transaction costs, serves important efficiency purposes, a proposition that runs counter to Marglin's thesis concerning the role of the boss and the rationale for the factory. Williamson concludes that the historical progression from putting-out to the authority relation (factory) is thus best explained in terms of the superior efficiency properties of the latter (Williamson 1980: 11–12, 29).

To substantiate his argument, Williamson embarks on a 'comparative institutional assessment' in which he compares the efficiency properties of a variety of organizational modes, including putting-out and the factory. Eleven efficiency criteria are chosen against which to compare performance. These fall under three broad headings: *product flow attributes*, which include transportation expenses, inventory requirements and leakages of product from the system; *assignment attributes*, which reflect the efficiency with which the work is assigned to those with the relevant skills, the need for co-ordination and leadership, and the capacity to contract for specialist services; and *incentive attributes*, which cover matters such as work intensity, equipment utilization, local shock responsiveness, the incentive to innovate locally, and the capacity to respond to system shock. Technology and factor inputs are assumed to be identical. Having established his criteria, Williamson then uses a combination of *a priori* reasoning and a little historical evidence to assign a score of zero or one to each mode against each of the efficiency criteria (Williamson 1980: 22–4). His findings reveal that the factory was organizationally more efficient than putting-out (Table 2.1).

Williamson's conclusions have received a mixed response from economic historians. All accept that the adoption of the hand factory was, on some occasions, due to a desire on the part of manufacturers to economize on transaction costs, especially 'interface leakages'. Thus when one Huddersfield merchant was asked whether he derived an advantage from employing looms in the factory, he replied: 'We have them in factories principally to prevent embezzlement as we now manufacture [expensive] Spanish wool.' The advantages were not entirely clear cut, however, for he continued: 'but if we meet with men we can depend on for honesty, we prefer having them wove at their own houses' (House of Commons Committee on the Woollen Manufacture of England 1806: 220). Notwithstanding such evidence, however, there are those who believe that the broader methodological and empirical weaknesses of Williamson's paper undermine its validity as a general explanation for the emergence of the hand factory and, by extension, the rise of the factory system (Jones 1982, 1983).

The principal weakness of the paper, it is argued, is that Williamson's basic assumptions are flawed. Thus the assumption that all organizational modes had access to identical inputs ignores the fact that putters-out and factory masters frequently operated in quite separate labour markets. As we have already seen, the ability of putters-out to tap rural and distant labour markets effectively shifted their supply curve of labour to the right. At the same time, a reluctance

Table 2.1 Simple efficiency properties of the putting-out and factory systems

	Product flow attributes			Assignment attributes					Incentive attributes			Score
	Transportation expenses	Buffer inventories	Interface leakages	Station	Leadership	Contracting	Work intensity	Equipment utilization	Local responsiveness	Local innovation	System responsiveness	
Putting out												
Williamson score	0	0	0	1	1	0	1	1	0	1	0	5
Revised score	0	1	0	1	1	0	1	1	0	1	1	7
Factory system												
Williamson score	1	1	1	1	1	1	0	1	1	0	1	9
Revised score	1	0	0	1	1	1	0	1	1	0	0	6

to enter the factory on the part of eighteenth-century labour due to working conditions and connotations with the workhouse shifted the factory supply curve to the left. The result was that factory masters might pay at least a third more for their labour than putters-out (Bischoff 1968: 185–6). Given the labour-intensive nature of production, the organizational economies of the factory would have to have been substantial indeed for it to have offset the lower labour costs of putting-out. Williamson's failure to address this question is a serious omission.

Williamson, of course, believes that the factory was organizationally much more efficient, scoring it 9–5 against putting-out in his evaluation of efficiency properties. Unfortunately, his method of scoring leaves much to be desired, with no attempt being made to ascribe weights to the various efficient criteria used. Thus savings in terms of transportation expenses, a daily occurrence, is given the same weight as the capacity to respond to shocks which, by definition, occurred irregularly. Moreover, the various efficiency criteria employed are not strictly additive, with some measures relating to short-run costs and others to the ability to innovate and respond. Williamson is not unaware of these problems but argues that they are unimportant as his results seem to be pointing in the right direction! (Jones 1982: 124–5; Williamson 1983a: 59).

Yet even if one is prepared to go along with Williamson's method of scoring, a number of objections can be raised against the scores that he allocates. The most important set of efficiency criteria would seem to be product flow, in which the factory or authority relation is judged to be superior to putting-out under all three headings (see Table 2.1). Few would disagree that the factory system incurred fewer transportation expenses. However, the advantage that the factory held under the second heading, interface leakages, of which embezzlement was the principal component, is rather less clear cut than one might suppose. For a start, embezzlement continued to occur inside the factory, even within the archetypal pin factory! (Jones 1976: 41–2). Moreover, there is ample evidence to show that manufacturers incorporated embezzlement in their costings and adjusted the wage rate accordingly. They, like the workers, also went behind the wage contract, indulging in long pays, truck, arbitrary deductions and other deceits so that they actually paid less than the agreed rate. Embezzlement and truck etc. may therefore be seen as opposite sides of the same coin and, although an inefficient method of contracting, were part of the process by which real wage rates were established in the marketplace. Legislation was repeatedly introduced to abolish both, but there is little evidence to suggest that this was a reflection of increasing problems or the way to solve them (Jones 1982: 129–32; Styles 1983: 173–204).

Williamson's treatment of inventories also raises questions, for he concentrates on buffer inventories between workstations as opposed to the overall level of inventories. Although he is correct in suggesting that factory masters may have been better able to economize on buffer inventories, it is quite clear that they frequently accumulated large inventories of finished goods simply in order to keep their plant moving and hands together (Jones 1982: 129). Unlike putters-out who might easily discharge hands when depression struck, factory masters, faced with fixed costs and an investment in a trained labour force, were obliged to stay in production. This ran them heavily into stock and drained them of liquidity at a time when money was tight. These disabilities far outweighed any savings they might make on buffer inventories.

The other two broad efficiency categories are those of assignment and incentive attributes, and here also the hierarchically organized factory or authority relation is seen by Williamson as being more efficient than putting-out. His evaluation of assignment attributes would seem to be broadly correct. He is on less certain ground when it comes to incentive attributes, however, especially in his judgement that the factory system was more responsive to changes in market circumstances. Most commentators view the responsiveness of putting-out as one of its major attributes, unlike the factory system where masters hoarded labour simply in order to meet fluctuations in demand. The factory, therefore, was generally less responsive than putting-out, quite the reverse of what Williamson would have us believe (Jones 1982: 133; 1987: 87–8; Hudson 1983: 142).

Far from being clearly superior in terms of product flow, assignment and incentive attributes therefore, a re-evaluation of the evidence suggests that, overall, there was little difference in organizational efficiency between the hierarchically organized factory and putting-out (see Table 2.1). Moreover, even if the factory did hold a slender organizational advantage, this was usually more than offset by the cheaper labour available to putting-out. Indeed, access to cheap labour enabled the outwork system to compete long after factories had been established using more advanced technology (Landes 1969: 118–19).

Methodological and empirical deficiencies thus cast serious doubt on the validity of Williamson's conclusions. More generally Williamson, unlike Marglin and Landes, offers no explanation as to why the transition from putting-out to the factory should have suddenly speeded up during the closing decades of the eighteenth century. Indeed, his comments on the bankruptcy of technological approaches to work organization seem to indicate a certain myopia on his part in this area, so much so that it has been suggested that he is merely attempting to replace 'the determination of technological production efficiencies with the determinism of transaction cost efficiencies' (Englander 1988: 339). Traditional economic historians who, for many years, have grappled with the trade-offs that existed between cheap labour, transaction cost efficiencies and technology, would probably agree.

TRANSPORT IMPROVEMENTS, TRANSACTION COSTS AND TECHNOLOGY

A recent attempt has been made by Rick Szostak to provide the Williamson thesis with the temporal dimension that it has hitherto lacked. He suggests that, while putting-out may have been the transaction cost minimizing method of production until the middle of the eighteenth century, improvements in transport thereafter tended to be biased in favour of the hand factory which then took over as the least cost mode of production. Technology only accelerated the shift to the factory at a later date, by which time the factory system (based on hand factories) was already fairly widespread (Szostak 1989: 346–7).

Szostak uses the eleven criteria proposed by Williamson as a basis for determining the way in which transportation improvements affected the efficiency of the two systems. He regards the debate about absence of weights and the scores assigned as irrelevant for his purposes – he is only concerned with relative changes in efficiency. Szostak concludes that, 'In terms of ten of the eleven criteria, transport improvements served either to make factories look more advantageous or less disadvantageous' (Szostak 1989: 345–9). Transportation and not technology, therefore, explains why the factory system emerged in the late eighteenth century.

But were transport improvements biased in favour of the factory? Like Williamson, Szostak bases his conclusions not on a careful appraisal of historical data, but on impressionistic judgements that are arrived at through a combination of *a priori* reasoning and limited empirical evidence. Indeed, Szostak admits that, 'To "prove" that the net effect of transport improvements during this period was in favour of factories would require extensive data on the costs of putting-out and early factories, and such data does not exist (Szostak 1989: 351).

The problem with Szostak's judgements, therefore, is that they rely more upon logic than fact and reflect what may have happened given certain assumptions as opposed to what actually happened in practice. Whether one believes that Szostak's hypothetical constructs reflect reality is largely a matter of faith.

Yet even if the factory was the major beneficiary of transport improvements, it does not necessarily follow that its costs fell far enough relative to those of putting-out for it to offset the lower unit labour costs of the latter. To establish that this was the case, Szostak has first to provide some estimate of the initial cost advantages of putting-out and, second, to demonstrate that changes in relative costs due to transport improvements were sufficient to overcome those advantages. This cannot be done without explicitly considering labour costs and the way they also changed during the period under consideration. Szostak, unconvinced both by historical evidence and by a wealth of scholarship on the existence of cheap outwork labour, refuses to accept that putters-out were able to lower wage costs by exploiting the lower reservation wage of outwork labour (Szostak 1992: 396). Even so, to argue that the hand factory displaced putting-out simply because of a favourable and unquantified bias in transport improvements is not terribly persuasive.

Finally, it must be said that the weight of empirical evidence does tend to run counter to Szostak's thesis. If transport improvements did provide the hand factory with such competitive advantage after the middle of the eighteenth century, why did the putting-out system continue to expand so vigorously? Why in Yorkshire, where the number of broad and narrow cloths stamped annually *increased* by 125,000 pieces between 1791 and 1805, did factories account for only 8,000 of those pieces? (House of Commons Committee on the Woollen Manufacturers of England 1806: 11–13). Szostak, taking refuge in *a priori* reasoning, suggests that the continued coexistence of hand factories and putting-out was probably due to the fact that diffusion commonly follows an S-shaped path and it simply took time to learn about the advantages of factory organization (Szostak 1992: 397). The real answer, it seems, is because in Yorkshire, as elsewhere, the putting-out system was still able to produce a product at a competitive price, notwithstanding the improvements in transportation that had taken place.

CONCLUSION

Monocausal explanations in economic history should always be viewed with suspicion, especially where there are ambiguities in both evidence and terminology. Nevertheless, the argument that the rise of the 'modern factory system' in the latter part of the eighteenth century was largely the result of the introduction of new technology would appear to be substantially correct. This is not only a reflection of the fact that authors such as Mantoux and Landes define the 'modern factory system' in terms of new technology, but because the majority of factories that appeared from 1780 onwards incorporated new technology which, because of both size and/or power requirements, could not be easily located in the cottage.

At the same time, it must be said that there is a body of evidence that lends credence to the views of Marglin and Williamson. Some manufacturers clearly did turn to the factory to cut costs, both by extracting greater output from their workers and by economizing on transaction costs. In spite of such evidence, the arguments of Marglin and Williamson contain a number of weaknesses. The processes they outline, while they may have occurred occasionally, fail to reflect what generally occurred in late eighteenth- and early nineteenth-century England. They focus on the atypical rather than the typical and build logically sound but historically inaccurate models to justify their central theses. Landes has dubbed this type of economic reasoning 'economoneirics' or dream economics – what may have happened but in actual fact did not (Landes 1986: 591). This is not to imply that the organization of production was completely technologically determined, and Landes would doubtless not wish for such an inference to be drawn from his writings. Yet although institutional factors had a real bearing on the choice of productive mode, one cannot understand the rise of the factory system without a proper appreciation of the vital role of technology.

NOTE

I am grateful to Grant Fleming, Keith Rankin and members of a symposium on 'Business Enterprise and Industrialisation' held at the University of Lancaster, May 1993, for their helpful comments on earlier drafts of this work.

BIBLIOGRAPHY

Aiken, J. (1968) *Description of the Country from Thirty to Forty Miles Round Manchester*, Newton Abbot: David & Charles.

Allen, G.C. (1966) *The Industrial Development of Birmingham and the Black Country: 1860–1927*, London: Frank Cass.

Ashton, T.S. (1962) *The Industrial Revolution 1760–1830*, London: Oxford University Press.

Aspin, C. and Chapman, S.D. (1964) *James Hargreaves and the Spinning Jenny*, Preston: Helmshore Local History Society.

Berg, M. (1991) 'On the origin of capitalist hierarchy', in B. Gustafsson (ed.) *Power and Economic Institutions*, Aldershot: Edward Elgar.

Berg, M. and Hudson, P. (1992) 'Rehabilitating the industrial revolution', *Economic History Review* 45: 24–50.

Bischoff, J. (1968) *A Comprehensive History of the Woollen and Worsted Manufactures*, vol. 1, London: Frank Cass.

Chaloner, W.H. (1963) *People and Industries*, London: Frank Cass.

Chapman, S.D. (1972) *The Cotton Industry in the Industrial Revolution*, London: Macmillan.

Clarkson, L.A. (1971) *The Pre-industrial Economy of England, 1500–1750*, London: Batsford.

Coleman, D.C. (1992) *Myth, History and the Industrial Revolution*, London: Hambledon.

Cooke-Taylor, R.W. (1891) *The Modern Factory System*, London: Paul, Trench, Tribner.

Daniels, G.W. (1930) 'Samuel Crompton's census of the cotton industry in 1811', *Economic History* 2: 107–10.

Englander, E.J. (1988) 'Technology and Oliver Williamson's transaction cost economics', *Journal of Economic Behaviour and Organization* 10: 339–53.

Flinn, M.W. (1962) *Men of Iron*, Edinburgh: Edinburgh University Press.

Freudenberger, H. and Redlich, F. (1964) 'The industrial development of Europe: reality, symbols, images', *Kyklos* 17: 372–403.

Furniss, E.S. (1957) *The Position of the Labourer in a System of Nationalism*, New York: Kelley & Millman.

Greener, W.W. (1910) *The Gun and its Development*, London: Cassell.

Hammond, J.L. and Hammond, B. (1919) *The Skilled Labourer*, London: Longman.

Harte, N.B. (1977) 'The growth and decay of a hosiery firm in the nineteenth century', *Textile History* 8, 7–55.

Heaton, H. (1965) *The Yorkshire Woollen and Worsted Industries*, Oxford: Clarendon Press.

House of Commons Committee on the Woollen Manufacture of England, *British Parliamentary Paper*, 1806, III.

Hudson, P. (1983) 'From manor to mill: the West Riding in transition', in M. Berg, P. Hudson and M. Sonenscher (eds) *Manufacture in Town and Country before the Factory*, Cambridge: Cambridge University Press, 124–44.

—— (1992) *The Industrial Revolution*, London: Edward Arnold.

Jenkins, D.T. (1973) 'The validity of the factory returns 1833–50', *Textile History* 4: 26–46.

—— (1975) *The West Riding Wool Textile Industry, 1770–1835: a Study in Fixed Capital Formation*, Edington: Pasold.

Jones, S.R.H. (1976) 'Hall, English & Co., 1813–41: a study of entrepreneurial response in the Gloucester pin industry', *Business History* 18: 35–65.

—— (1980) 'John English & Co., Feckenham: a study of entrepreneurship in the British needle industry in the eighteenth and nineteenth centuries', Unpublished PhD thesis, London University.

—— (1982) 'The organization of work', *Journal of Economic Behaviour and Organization* 3: 117–37.

—— (1983) 'Technology and the organization of work: a reply', *Journal of Economic Behaviour and Organization* 4: 63–6.

—— (1987) 'Technology, transactions costs and the transition to factory production in the British silk industry, 1700–1870', *Journal of Economic History* 47: 71–96.

—— (1992) 'The emergence of the factory system in eighteenth century England', *Journal of Economic Behaviour and Organization* 19: 389–94.

Kennedy, J. (1819) 'Observations on the rise and progress of the cotton trade in Great Britain', *Literary and Philosophical Society of Manchester: Memoirs and Proceedings* 3(25): 115–37.

Landes, D.S. (1969) *The Unbound Prometheus: Technological Change and Industrial Development in Western Europe, 1750 to the Present*, Cambridge: Cambridge University Press.

—— (1986) 'What do bosses really do?', *Journal of Economic History* 46: 585–623.

Lazonick, W. (1979) 'Industrial relations and technical change: the case of the self-acting mule', *Cambridge Journal of Economics* 3: 231–62.

Mantoux, P. (1961) *The Industrial Revolution in the Eighteenth Century*, London: Cape.

Marglin, S. (1974) 'What do bosses do?', *Review of Radical Political Economy* 6: 60–112.

Mathias, P. (1983) *The First Industrial Nation*, London: Methuen.

Nelson, E.G. (1929–30) 'The putting-out system in the English framework-knitting industry', *Journal of Economic and Business History* 2: 467–94.

Patterson, R. (1967) 'Spinning and weaving', in C. Singer, E.J. Holmyard, A.R. Hall and T.I. Williams (eds) *A History of Technology*, London: Oxford University Press.

Podmore, F. (1923) *Robert Owen: A Biography*, London: Hutchinson.

Pollard, S. (1968) *The Genesis of Modern Management*, Harmondsworth: Penguin.

Reports from Assistant Commissioners, Handloom Weavers, British Parliamentary Papers, 1840, XXIV.

Robertson, P.L. and Alston, L.J. (1992) 'Technological choice and the organization of work in capitalist firms', *Economic History Review* 45: 330–49.

Rose, M.B. (1989) 'Social policy and business; parish apprenticeship and the early factory system', *Business History* 31: 5–29.

Rowlands, M.B. (1975) *Masters and Men in the West Midlands Metalwares Trades before the Industrial Revolution*, Manchester: Manchester University Press.

Sabel, C. and Zeitlin, J. (1985) 'Historical alternatives to mass production: politics, markets and technology in nineteenth century industrialization', *Past and Present*, 108, 133–76.

Samuel, R. (1977) 'Workshop of the world: steam power and hand technology in mid-Victorian Britain', *History Workshop* 3: 6–72.

Select Committee on the Silk Trade (1831–2) *British Parliamentary Papers*, XIX.

Styles, J. (1983) 'Embezzlement, industry and the law in England, 1500–1800', in M. Berg, P. Hudson and M. Sonenscher (eds) *Manufacture in Town and Country before the Factory*, Cambridge: Cambridge University Press, 173–205.

Szostak, R. (1989) 'The organization of work: the emergence of the factory revisited', *Journal of Economic Behaviour and Organization* 11: 343–58.

—— (1992) 'Transport improvements and the emergence of the factory', *Journal of Economic Behaviour and Organization* 19: 395–9.

Thirsk, J. and Cooper, J.P. (1972) *Seventeenth Century Economic Documents*, Oxford: Clarendon Press.

Timmins, S. (ed.) *Birmingham and the Midland Hardware District*, London: Frank Cass.

Ure, A. (1967) *The Philosophy of Manufactures*, London: Frank Cass.

Usher, A.P. (1921) *An Introduction to the Industrial History of England*, London: Harrap.

Wadsworth, A.P. and Mann, J. de L. (1965) *The Cotton Trade and Industrial Lancashire*, Manchester: Manchester University Press.

Williamson, O.E. (1980) 'The organization of work', *Journal of Economic Behaviour and Organization* 1: 5–38.

—— (1983a) 'Technology and the organization of work: a reply to Jones', *Journal of Economic Behaviour and Organization* 4: 57–62.

—— (1983b) 'Technology and the organization of work: a rejoinder', *Journal of Economic Behaviour and Organization* 4: 67–8.

Wing, C. (1967) *Evils of the Factory System Demonstrated by Parliamentary Evidence*, London: Frank Cass.

3 The family firm in British business, 1780–1914

Mary B. Rose

Whether as a source of economic growth or a harbinger of conservatism and stagnation, the family firm has long been the subject of debate among economic and business historians. Few would doubt that the rapid formation of new family firms contributed a vital dynamism during the early phases of industrialization. Yet the potentially inhibiting impact of such firms in the later stages of development has given rise to extensive comment. In the case of Britain, it has been argued that, whilst the origins of early industrial prowess may have lain in the family firm, the survival of this 'personalized capitalism', as the economy matured, contributed to economic decay. In the late nineteenth century international competitive advantage, in many sectors, moved towards large-scale, vertically integrated, hierarchically organized firms. In such an environment Britain's smaller, more specialized businesses lost market share. Similarly, it has been argued that even those that did expand, whether by merger or internal growth, grew more slowly and were less efficiently managed than their American counterparts (Florence 1953: 173; Chandler 1990: 236–94; Lazonick 1991: 48–9). Equally the lacklustre performance of the French economy in the nineteenth century has been traced to the intrinsic conservatism of family-oriented business (Landes 1951: 334–53).

Influential though the Chandlerian interpretation of the decline of British business has been, the causal relationship between family run firms and economic decay can be overdrawn. Some historians have signalled caution in the general censure of the family firm and especially to any blanket application of the third generation thesis (Barker and Lévy-Leboyer 1982: 12–13; Hannah 1982: 3; Payne 1984: 188–9). Similarly it has been shown that 'the family firm' cannot be used as a generic term which somehow embraces the strategy and structures of all firms which are managed by families rather than by administrators. It is of course possible to identify the family firm as being one where ownership and control were united in a family. Yet it is clear that the scale, scope, boundaries, organization and legal status of family firms vary historically between sectors and, even more important, internationally. Differing economic and social conditions can therefore vastly alter the performance and role of such firms. Family firms are not, for example, always small and conservative (see Broehl 1992). Thus the Japanese Zaibatsu, which were diversified vertical groupings owned exclusively by a single family or group of families, were as much family firms as the often tiny partnerships to be found in Britain during the Industrial Revolution (Morikawa 1992: xviii). Equally, the internalization of economic activity in large-scale firms cannot be seen as a universally appropriate business strategy. It is not then to be expected that, in all societies and in all markets, businesses will take on identical forms (Porter 1990: 108). The international success achieved by small-scale Italian family firms, producing textiles and knitwear for fashion-oriented markets, highlights the potential of this type of business, even in the twentieth century (Toyne *et al.* 1984: 150–1). This is not to suggest that there are not some characteristics of family firms which are problematic, but rather to warn against any general condemnation on the grounds of inevitable inefficiency and conservatism. Moreover, the relatively poor performance of some managerial enterprises means that the case in favour of the overwhelming efficiency of Chandler's modern business enterprise is by no means proven (Church 1993).

It is the purpose of this chapter to explore the role, strategies and performance of British family firms from the late eighteenth century to the eve of the First World War. It will emerge that the strategy and structure of family firms in the nineteenth and early twentieth century can only be understood against the economic, social and cultural influences of the period. This is hardly novel since it is a truism that business is shaped by national cultural characteristics. It has been demonstrated, however, that nothing so simple as a national economy existed in Britain, at least until quite late in the nineteenth century. In the eighteenth century the existence of islands of industrialization amid a sea of pre-industrial practice made for a dual economy which persisted at least until the second half of the nineteenth century. In manufacturing industry, therefore, there was a significant sectoral variation in the strategies of family firms. Equally, before the railway age and beyond, business activity in Britain was heavily localized, making the region, as opposed to the nation, the realistic basis for the study of business strategy (Pollard 1981: 25; Hudson 1989). Capital and labour markets, for example, were often heavily localized, making for significant economic interdependence at the regional level (Langton 1984: 157; Hudson 1986: 212–55; Rose 1989: 5–32). It is thus at the level of the region and most particularly at that of the community that family firm strategy in British business can be best interpreted. It will be demonstrated that the policies of family businesses were a reflection of family priorities. Yet it will become clear that subtle differences in community culture within Britain could lead to significant variations in the pattern of development of family firms, the way in which they diversified and even their longevity. In addition, it will be shown that the early development of regionally specialized, community-oriented business had long-term consequences for family firm strategy in the late nineteenth and early twentieth century.

The chapter will be divided into four sections. The first provides a chronological overview of the position of the family firm in British economic development from the eighteenth to the twentieth centuries. The second will explore the relationship between family firm strategy and British economic performance, whilst a third will show the ways in which community culture can be used to explain these distinctive policies. In a fourth section the long-term consequences of the pattern of family firm development in Britian will be indicated and conclusions will be drawn.

LEGAL, ECONOMIC AND SOCIAL ENVIRONMENT AND THE FAMILY FIRM

During the eighteenth century and for much of the nineteenth, family partnerships proliferated in Britain in most branches of manufacturing, commerce and finance. Best known in the staple industries, they were also the norm in brewing, shipbuilding, glassmaking, chemicals and provincial banking. Similarly, the retail trade remained the citadel of the family firm, even in the twentieth century. In the City of London, too, ownership and control was united in both the commercial houses and the merchant banks (Chapman 1984, 1992; Lisle-William 1984a: 241–71, 1984b: 333–62; Daunton 1988: 269–86, 1989: 154–77). Even in railways, the ultimate corporate enterprise, there is evidence that families could exert financial and managerial influence. The Stockton and Darlington Railway, for example, has been described as a family firm in which an extended network of Quaker industrialists and financiers owned and controlled the firm from the 1820s until 1860 (Kirby 1993: 105–26).

The popularity of family-oriented enterprise in eighteenth- and nineteenth-century Britain was a product of a complex array of legal, economic and cultural forces. With the spectre of bankruptcy ever present, a combination of the common law partnership and unlimited liability meant that many businessmen preferred to be associated with their family connections than with outsiders. This was less a reflection of conservatism than a strategy to ameliorate the worst effects of uncertainty. Once established, it will be shown that a peculiary British type of familial capitalism persisted and evolved through the nineteenth century and into the twentieth.

The legal environment encountered by eighteenth-century British businessmen was distinctive, with both the joint stock company and limited liability outlawed and the partnership the favoured business form. Yet the impact of the Bubble Act of 1720 in shaping business organization should not be exaggerated, nor should the ingenuity of the legal profession, in skirting round it, be underestimated. Incorporation was quite simply unnecessary for the majority of enterprises. Where, on the other hand, substantial sums of finance were required, as in mining or insurance, lawyers were adept at using the law of trust to avoid the constraints which this legislation placed upon the transferability of shares (DuBois 1971: 3). In making the benefits of incorporation dependent upon parliamentary assent, the government had intended to favour the partnership whilst guarding against the speculative excesses, which had reached a peak in the South Sea Bubble of 1720 (DuBois 1971: 1, 38–9). Yet it failed to foresee the mobility of shares through large partnerships, joint associations or unincorporated joint stock companies (DuBois 1971: 39; Mathias 1979: 103–4). Even though incorporation brought with it the added benefit of limited liability (DuBois 1971: 94–104) many of those embarking on capital-hungry enterprises preferred to avoid the costs and time involved in a parliamentary application. For the majority of late eighteenth-century businessmen, however, the limited financial requirements of their firms rendered such legal gymnastics unnecessary. For manufacturers, merchants and retailers the common law partnership, which united ownership with control, was the obvious business form, and one they were in no hurry to abandon when the Bubble Act was finally repealed in 1825 (Jeffreys 1977: 6; Cottrell 1979: 42; Payne 1988: 14). Only in provincial banking was there any shift towards the joint-stock company. The wave of failures in the private banking sector had undoubtedly exacerbated the 1825 crisis, and persuaded the government in 1826 of the need to rescind the Bank of England's monopoly over non-metropolitan, joint-stock, banking. Even so, it was not until 1838 that joint stock banks exceeded private banks in importance (Pressnell 1956: 1, 507).

The partnership therefore predominated in a large part of British economic activity for much of the nineteenth century and proved exceptionally adaptable to the needs of business in this period. Thus where additional resources were needed, whether financial, technical or managerial, they could be accommodated merely by extending the partnership. In addition, since the liability of partners was unlimited, this form of business organization brought with it its own managerial regulation. This in turn made it increasingly likely that business partners would be drawn from the family circle.

Unlimited liability, far from being a source of complaint, was for much of the nineteenth century believed to be essential if business prudence was to be ensured. Suspicion of limited liability can be found in the eighteenth century where the founders of the unincorporated Phoenix Insurance Company argued that incorporation was a handicap to good business practice because 'the holders of shares in such corporations stand sheltered from any responsibilities beyond the extent of their chartered capital' (quoted by DuBois 1971: 96). Amongst the majority of members of partnerships suspicion, indeed abhorrence, of limited liability persisted for much of the nineteenth century. In the 1830s, for example, Kirkman Finlay believed that:

> the greatest danger [from limited liability] would arise and great losses be occasioned by relieving parties, who, in consequence of taking no management of the business and having no control over its arrangements were not made liable for the debts either participated in the profits or were entitled to do so.
>
> *(Report on the Law of Partnership* 1837: 48)

Nearly twenty years later, Henry Ashworth was even more vehement in his condemnation of the introduction of any limitations to liability, claiming they would mean that:

> failure and success would be shielded from reproach; the law would become the refuge of the trading skulk, and as a mask over the degradation and moral guilt of having recklessly gambled with the interests of trades, and then the stain which now attaches to bankruptcy would cease to exist. . . . The position of our mercantile character is a treasured object, and demands the best security we can obtain for the upholding of it. On that account we cannot hesitate to prefer the security of a man who without reservation offers to stake his whole property and the treasured estimate of his

own respectability upon the result . . . as against the pretentions of another who requires to be fenced in by conditions.

(quoted by Hunt 1936: 11)

Similarly one critic described the Limited Liability Bill of 1856 as 'An Act for the better enabling Adventurers to interfere with and ruin established traders, without risk to themselves' (quoted by Jeffreys 1977: 28).

Unlimited liability, therefore, generally found favour with the British business community before the introduction of full limited liability in 1862. Each member of a partnership was personally liable for all debts 'to his last shilling and acre'. As a result creditors of a troubled firm could call on both the stock of the partnership and members' personal estates in order to recover monies owing to them (Cottrell 1979: 39–40). Such a responsibility meant that businessmen were especially careful in their choice of associates, unlimited liability and the family firm becoming synonymous. In a world where malpractice or an imprudent debt policy could bring personal ruin, it was logical to turn to trusted members of one's family and circle of connections in any quest for new partners, whether active or sleeping. This is not to say that unlimited liability was the only reason for the importance of family firms in the British Industrial Revolution. The predominance of familial capitalism in France, where sleeping members of *en commandite* partnerships enjoyed limited liability, indicates that other considerations were also important (Cottrell 1979: 50). Nevertheless, in Britain the link between ownership and full liability for debts reinforced a natural tendency towards the family firm in the uncertain world of the late eighteenth and early nineteenth century. In such a world 'the whole thrust of partnership was active participation [and] its essence was the personal nature of the relationship [where] no stranger could be substituted' (Davidoff and Hall 1987: 201).

Individual businessmen thus faced a deeply uncertain world where bankruptcy rates were high (Hoppit 1987: 48–9) and where the unlimited liability of partnerships meant that imprudent management could lead to personal ruin. It was a period, moreover, where imperfect and often slow communications over poor roads, or by sea, vastly increased the hazards of business by impeding information flows and increasing the danger of loss or damage to goods. Equally, the much applauded bill of exchange, which oiled the wheels of commerce in the eighteenth century (Crouzet 1972: 44; Mathias 1979: 88–115) was open to abuse and was thus itself a source of business uncertainty (Hoppit 1987: 64–78). In addition, the expanding number of country banks, based as they were on private partnership and unregulated in their debt and note issuing policies, were themselves a source of instability (Pressnell 1956: 507).

The hazardous economic environment goes a long way towards explaining the predominance of family firms in the British Industrial Revolution. The owners of mainly small-scale firms were keen to reduce the risks of business activity. In such a world the family, widely defined to include the extended kinship group of cousins, in-laws and connections, especially from within religious groupings, represented more than just a reservoir of skill, labour and finance. It was a network of trust, the use of which reduced the transaction costs and the dangers of business activity. Thus whilst the family represented an internal market of skilled and managerial labour and a source of funds for establishment and expansion, family connections could also be reliable sources of market information (Casson 1982: 302–7; Pollak 1985: 582–93; Casson 1991: 169–70). Such involvement of family and connections could be especially helpful in transactions between provincial industrial centres and London or in overseas trade. In such long distance dealings, either the planting of a partner in the metropolis or abroad, or the reliance upon a middleman who was also connected with the family, was not uncommon amongst manufacturers and merchants (Wadsworth and Mann 1931: 263). In country banking, too, intricate and often nationwide webs of intermarriage, especially among Quakers, created a network of trust, which spanned commercial, financial and industrial interests. Such family groupings could also, as in the case of links between Richardson Overend and Company, the London Bill brokers and the Gurneys of Norwich, create a foothold for provincial bankers in the London money market (Pressnell 1956: 114–15). Familial enterprise, therefore, by ensuring a degree of trust within firms, represented a business strategy designed to combat external uncertainty. Equally, reliance upon a business network which, whilst external to the firm, was internal to the family reduced transaction costs without the need for any formal integration of activity.

Once established, the family firm tradition proved remarkably resilient, influencing business organization well into the twentieth century. Changes in the competitive environment and in legislation during the second half of the nineteenth century were met less by a radical transformation in the form which firms took as by a shift, sometimes fairly subtle, in family firm strategy. Thus, in contrast to experience in the United States, where from the 1880s onwards ownership and control became increasingly divorced, in Britain personal capitalism persisted well into the twentieth century. That this should be so is hardly surprising given Britain's relatively protracted industrialization. The coming of limited liability in 1856 and 1862, for example, theoretically freed firms from their financial roots. Yet since the British family firm tradition had matured over eighty years, this change did not herald any radical alteration in business organization, the umbilical chord between ownership and control remaining largely intact. The spread of limited liability was slow until the 1880s, only making any significant progress in the staple industries, though without any marked impact upon control (Payne 1967: 520). Thus in commenting on the industrial organization of 1886–7 Clapham, for example, concluded that family firms were the norm:

> in nearly all the wool firms, outside Oldham, nearly all the cotton firms and the same in linen, silk, jute, lace and hosiery. Most of the smaller and some of the largest engineering firms and nearly all the cutlery and pottery firms were still private. Brewing was a family affair. So with certain outstanding exceptions, were the Birmingham trades and the great, perhaps the major part of the shipbuilding industry. In housebuilding and the associated trades there were very few limited companies; few in the clothing trades, few in the food trades . . . add the many scores of thousands of retailing businesses, unlimited almost to a shop.
>
> (quoted by Payne 1988: 17)

It was therefore not until the 1880s that there was any significant decline in the use of the partnership. Even then a rise in the proportion of limited companies should not be equated with substantial changes in control in British business (Payne 1984: 171–3). On the eve of the First World War four-fifths of registered joint stock companies were private. These were predominantly one-time partnerships, availing themselves of limited liability (Cottrell 1979: 163; Hannah 1983: 23–4). At the same time, although the number of public companies grew threefold, even in these the degree of family control remained striking. Where either new technology or market growth meant that the financial needs of firms exceeded family resources, or where families wished to reduce proportionately their financial commitment to their firm, it was not unusual to go public. Yet by ensuring that equity, with its attendant voting rights, remained in the family, whilst any external finance was raised through the sale of debentures, familial control was maintained. In brewing, for example, when Truman Hanbury and Company went public in the 1880s, the families owned 67 per cent of the company's share capital and all the equity (Cottrell 1979: 169).

The internal preoccupations of family firms were but part of the explanation for the increase in public companies in this period. External considerations, especially in the form of foreign competition during the 1890s and into the inter-war period, encouraged a wave of mergers in Britain's staple industries. These amalgamations resulted not in sophisticated managerial hierarchies, but in loose horizontal federations of family firms, united in a holding company, a mere financial device. Lacking in direction, with the independence of the constituent companies largely intact, these firms were once thought to have damaged the performance of British business during the inter-war period (Payne 1967). Doubt has been cast, however, on the managerial diseconomies habitually associated with the holding company form. As a result, rather than a blanket condemnation, there is a growing recognition that loose networks of subsidiaries represented an alternative to the multidivisional form rather than an inferior organizational form (Hannah 1983: 86–7; Church 1993; the holding company is discussed at greater length in Chapters 5 and 6).

FAMILY FIRM AND ECONOMIC PERFORMANCE

The heyday of the British family firm was during the Industrial Revolution, when 'the power of heredity and the vitality of the family as an economic group [was quite remarkable]' (Payne 1984: 171; Heaton 1972: 88–9). It is clear that in the eighteenth and early nineteenth centuries family firms, far from being incompatible with economic growth, were the principal agents of change and dynamism (Habakkuk 1955: 155). It would be all to easy to conclude, as was once assumed, that it was the heroic entrepreneurship of the founders of these pioneering families which stimulated the beginnings of structural change in the British economy. Yet for every successful innovator there was a string of failures, with bankruptcy rates rising sharply during the Industrial Revolution. Economic opportunity may have stimulated business enterprise, but it created a minefield for the inexperienced or the unwary. In the eighteenth century, the annual rate of growth in the number of bankruptcies was 1.15 per cent, whilst national income grew by 0.87 per cent a year (Hoppit 1987: 48–9). The strong correlation between rising economic activity, especially when financial barriers to entry were low, and business failure is confirmed at the level of the region. Thus London, with its rapidly expanding commercial base, exhibited the highest bankruptcy rates throughout the eighteenth century. Equally, within the textile trades, the growing regions of Lancashire and Yorkshire exhibited a higher rate of business failure than the West of England and East Anglia (Hoppit 1987: 63, 75). So it would seem that it was the rapid entry and exit of many small firms in commerce and manufacturing, rather than the outstanding success of a few, that proved an important source of change in the eighteenth-century British economy. It was not that failure outweighed success, but that a turnover of firms was both a symptom and a cause of expansion. It would be wrong, however, to suggest that no firms displayed longevity or that lasting enterprises played an insignificant role in the prosperity of particular communities. At the micro level some firms, even those founded in the eighteenth century, displayed remarkable resilience and created demand for a range of ancillary services, and hence new firms, within particular areas.

As the nineteenth century progressed the rate of growth of economic activity slowed down. The so-called Great Depression of 1870–96 is no longer seen as a watershed for the economy as a whole, with a deceleration discernible from as early as the 1850s (Floud 1981: 6). It is clear, however, that, by the last three decades of the nineteenth century, the industrialization of Germany and the United States irreversibly altered the competitive environment of the international economy. As a result of this rising tide of foreign competition, Britain's share of the world's manufacturing output declined from nearly 20 per cent in 1860 to 14 per cent on the eve of the First World War (Capie 1983: 5). For an economy heavily reliant upon exports it was the even sharper decline in the share of world trade in manufactures that was potentially more damaging, even if at least part of the decline was the result of the entry of more players to the game. Whilst still the world's pre-eminent industrial trading nation, therefore, Britain's share had fallen from 41.4 per cent in 1880 to 29.9 per cent in 1913. (Saul 1967: 12).

The relative decline of Britain's share of world trade in manufactures is of less importance than the suspicion that it was not merely a reflection of the international spread of industrialization. Instead it has been seen as a result of diminished competitive advantage in world markets by businessmen who, for whatever reason, were slow to innovate. Interpretations range from outright condemnation of British entrepreneurs for their tardy adoption of new technology, modern corporate enterprise and adventurous marketing techniques at the one extreme (Aldcroft 1964: 113–14), to their relative exoneration on the grounds of economic rationality on the other (Sandberg 1969:

25–43). Yet in their search for an explanation of the relative decline of the British economy, historians have most often looked to the family firm. No longer a source of dynamism, the family firm has been said

> to have sinned against economic efficiency, and hence against growth, by limiting expansion – failing both to extend into new markets when finance was available from internal funds and to seek outside funds when these were required for expansion. . . . Recruiting was undertaken from within the family, except for faithful retainers who assisted the firm against the revolutionary working force.
>
> (Kindleberger 1964: 115)

Whether as a source of conservatism, of inefficiency or as an institutional rigidity, the mature family firm in the changing economic environment of the late nineteenth century has therefore most frequently been identified as a negative influence.

The debate has focused on a number of interrelated issues. In the first place, it has been argued that by the late nineteenth century the once dynamic family firms of the Industrial Revolution had become moribund (Landes 1965: 563–4). The Buddenbrook syndrome has thus been seen by some as a cause of Britain's economic ills. Alternatively it has been argued that Britain's family firm tradition both slowed down the emergence of corporate enterprise and meant that many of the large-scale firms that did emerge were the result of defensive mergers. Equally it has been argued that with the survival of the resultant holding company structure where structure constrained strategy, rationalization and organizational change was inhibited (Payne 1984: 196–7; Chandler 1986: 51–2).

The detrimental impact of the holding company on British business performance may have been exaggerated. Although American style governance structures were slow to develop in Britain, it is by no means proven that this necessarily retarded the performance of all British firms (Jones 1993). Nor is it proven that outside the United States there is a strong correlation between the multidivisional form and business performance. The holding company may be different from the U-form or M-form of organization, but this does not necessarily make it inferior, even when used to prolong family control. The experience of Britain's highly successful international investment groups, for example, indicates the power of networks of subsidiaries (Chapman 1985: 230–51). In Japan, on the other hand, the vertical holding company emerged as an alternative, highly flexible organizational mode, rather than an inferior one. It was, indeed, a family firm strategy in which family control was perfectly consistent with growth in scale and scope (Morikawa 1992).

The association between a family firm legacy and the lack-lustre performance of British business thus has a long pedigree. It was Chandler, however, who provided the most wide-ranging condemnation of personalized capitalism. He is convinced that the persistence of family control in British business led to loss of competitive advantage in world markets in the twentieth century. The family firm, he has suggested, rarely pursued dynamic growth strategies, since the desire to placate family shareholders with high dividend payments inhibited profit retention. He also pointed to management deficiencies, since the suspicion of outsiders meant that even where firms did grow, as in the food and drink sector, sophisticated managerial structures were slow to appear (Chandler 1990). Building on the Chandler thesis, it has been forcibly argued that, whilst the family firm may have been the basis of Britain's competitive prowess in the nineteenth century, this proprietary capitalism contributed to long-term economic decline in the twentieth (Lazonick 1991: 48–9). Yet the case that there was a strong correlation between the persistence of personal capitalism in Britain and the decline of competitive advantage remains to be proven (see Church (1993) for an excellent critique of Chandler's view of the family firm).

Irrespective of whether Chandler is correct to be so dismissive of family capitalism in Britain, it is apparent that, for the most part, the strategies pursued by British firms were markedly different from those in the United States in the same period. Whereas in Britain, business remained in the hands of families, in the vertically integrated corporations of the United States the control of founding families diminished as firms grew. Precisely why what amounts to family firm strategy should diverge can only be understood by looking beyond conventional economic considerations.

The strategy of any family firm can only be interpreted in the context of the priorities and aspirations of the family. It is equally clear that such personal considerations remain opaque, except in their appropriate cultural context. This is not to say that economic influences are unimportant in family firm decision making, but rather that such personalized business strategy was informed and moulded by prevailing attitudes and value systems. Differing national cultural characteristics have been widely used to explain divergent business strategies. In the United States, for example, it has been suggested that familial capitalism was less resilient and owners more innovative than in Britain, because of differences in attitudes to and within the family.

Thus Cochran has observed:

> High mobility, both geographic and social, also weakened family
> ties; men expected to leave home early, and in many cases the farm
> of their early childhood memories was soon sold. The same was
> true of family business firms. Few sons felt the obligation, common
> in continental Europe, to perpetuate the farm or firm as a family
> enterprise. Money, or 'economic rationality' rather than land and
> family ties, was the common measuring rod of the society.
>
> (Cochran 1971: 12)

In America, therefore, where partible inheritance rather than primo-
geniture was the norm, there was seemingly less of a tendency to
'found a family' by diversifying into landholding (Farber 1972:
77–8). By implication, American business became more dynamic and
responsive to change than their British counterparts. Similarly, it was
peculiarly British cultural influences that manifested themselves as an
anti-industrial spirit which, according to Wiener, accounted for
Britain's economic decline (Wiener 1981: 5–6).

For Wiener industry lacked social cache, in a country where
prestige, power and privilege came with landownership and gentility.
By the late nineteenth century, he argued, the sons and grandsons of
founding entrepreneurs chose a public school education for offspring
and preferred landed leisure to the trials of business. The implication
is that it was British cultural values which gave family firms their distinctiveness. These meant that families in long-established industrial
firms in the late nineteenth century pursued social rather than business
objectives, to the detriment of British economic performance. This
would seem to be a classic example of family firm strategy, being
moulded by familial objectives, which ultimately conflicted with
business health. Yet a compelling narrative masks a superficiality and
selectivity in the use of evidence which has left him open to criticism
(see especially essays in Collins and Robbins (1990) for a wide ranging
critique).

From the perspective of the performance of the family firm in the
late nineteenth century, with its support of widespread gentrification
and implied endorsement of the Buddenbrooks syndrome of third
generation decline, the Wiener thesis is deeply flawed. This is less
because well-known examples of dynamic long-lived family firms can
provide a counterpoise to those which faltered (Barker and Lévy-
Leboyer 1982: 10–20), as because of the low survival rate of family
firms. It has been demonstrated that, in part as a result of the difficulties of arranging generational succession, very few firms survived

for more than one generation, let alone three (Saul 1967: 195–7; Payne 1984: 184; Rose 1993: 140). If there was a relationship between macroeconomic decline and the mature family firm, it was not that the majority of firms were old and conservative. Instead there was a slowing in the rate of formation of new firms. This was especially so in the regions and communities dependent upon the staple industries, where barriers to entry began to rise and some markets to stagnate during the second half of the nineteenth century. Here there was a proportionate rise in the importance of hereditary firms (Jeffreys 1977: 92; Howe 1984: 9–10), whilst in communities which did not diversify into more rapidly growing sectors the dynamism which comes from new business formation was lost.

Considerable doubt has been cast upon the extent and even the supposed damaging impact of gentrification amongst industrial families. At the level of the individual firm, it is perfectly true that some families became gentrified, purchasing land, country houses, sending their sons to public schools and engaging in politics. Yet it is extremely difficult to sustain the argument as *the* principal cause of the loss of dynamism in nineteenth-century family firms. The comparatively small scale of most businesses, and the modesty of most industrial fortunes, even in the late nineteenth century, meant that gentrification of a degree sufficient to be damaging to a firm's performance was a luxury denied to many families. Whilst some regional variation in landownership can be detected, a modest villa in the leafy suburbs of industrial towns was likely to be the full extent of conspicuous expenditure on property by the majority of late nineteenth-century industrialists (Farnie 1982: 54–5; Howe 1984: 310; Trainor 1989: 193; Koditschek 1990: 47). For Wiener to be correct in his contention that the social aspirations of her industrialists accounted for the downturn in Britain's economic fortunes, it would also be necessary to show that the rate of gentrification increased markedly after 1870. Yet this was not so. If anything the opportunity to move from the 'wrong' to the 'right' side of the social divide was greatest in the late eighteenth and early nineteenth centuries, when business was at its most dynamic, rather than in the late nineteenth century (Coleman 1973: 97).

It should not be concluded that there were no problems in older family businesses. Intergenerational disputes and inward-looking business cultures stemming from a suspicion of outsiders could seriously damage the vitality of older firms (Boswell 1973: 128; Rose 1993: 135–40). Nor should the inference be drawn that cultural influences and attitudes played an insignificant role in creating distinctive

British family firms. Rather, it would seem that the cultural influences which shaped family firm strategies in Britain were far more complex than Wiener implied. The idea that nineteenth-century businessmen merely fell prey to a set of nationally determined social priorities is to deny the importance of locally shaped values and attitudes, which were themselves the product of economic change. There is ample evidence that there emerged distinctive elites in the industrial regions, whose status derived from their local standing and power. In Lancashire, for example, the cotton masters were a 'cohesive self sustained industrial elite' (Howe 1984: 314). London's banking community, on the other hand, shared the values, habits and standing of Britain's aristocracy (Cassis 1985: 210–29). To understand why the owners of some older family firms were apparently conservative and why they formed defensive mergers rather than responding positively to the pressures of foreign competition, it is therefore necessary to look more closely at the formulation of family firm strategy. More particularly it is important to explore the extent to which the policies of individual firms were shaped by the economic and cultural influences, not of the nation, but rather of the local business community.

FAMILY FIRM STRATEGY AND COMMUNITY

The nineteenth-century British economy was characterized by a high level of regional specialization, whilst anything like a national economy cannot be identified until the railway age. Even then, the business community, rather than Britain as a whole, remained the canvas for the owner of the typical family firm. Business communities derived their distinctiveness both from their economic base and from the complex array of traditions, attitudes, skills and values which together made up their culture. Historical differences in the development of communities, even within the same region or in similar sectors, could lead to contrasts in values and attitudes and in the measures adopted to ensure familial security (Berg *et al.* 1983). Family firms did not therefore act in isolation. The existence of locally based networks of trust, which reflected far more than flows of finance, ensured that the strategy and structure of family firms was closely bound up with the culture and institutions of the surrounding community. Equally, since business communities were composed of the owners of family firms, depending upon the relative importance of a business group, the culture of the firms helped to mould that of the surrounding society.

Within individual business communities there existed informal networks of mutual trust and interest, which were the product of economic and social interdependence. Shared values and attitudes were reinforced by an impressive array of institutions as well as more informal arrangements. This meant that transaction costs were usually comparatively low. Whether the principal function of an institution was economic, religious or educational, it fulfilled similar functions. In the first place, as a reflection of the common interests of a community, institutions like Chambers of Commerce, literary and philosophical societies, churches and chapels helped to reinforce the culture of a community. Membership of such institutions could also give a sense 'of belonging' and a common set of values. Of even more importance, however, was the sense in which these bodies represented meeting places within which judgements could be made and information flow. Thus the Manchester Royal Exchange has been described as 'a power house of Manchester and Lancashire [which acted] as the nerve centre of the most nervous form of life in the kingdom of commerce', which strengthened personal links within the business community. Attendance was strictly limited to members, who saw it as a 'coffee house, a news room and a trading floor [where] Manchester's merchants [could meet with] country manufacturers' (Farnie 1979: 97–8). The Exchange therefore acted as a centralized source of business information where regular daily contact with both suppliers and competitors was inevitable.

When the role of religious groups is evaluated, Christian beliefs undoubtedly influenced business ethics and attitudes towards paternalist community development (Child 1964: 393–415; Campbell 1988: 27). In nineteenth-century business communities, however, especially before 1850, churches and chapels represented some of the most powerful social institutions. Irrespective of denomination, they were meeting places in which there was a common set of values and endogamous behaviour, which tied together extended families. Membership of a church or chapel could also provide the respectability crucial to business success (Davidoff and Hall 1987: 100, 208–9). Intermarriage between commercial and industrial families from within a sect ensured a common outlook. This was not all, however, because such alliances augmented the supply of partners and finance to each participating family, thus facilitating the growth of individual firms (Howe 1984: 78). Amongst Quakers, where the religious network and common values spanned communities, intermarriage and the exchange of business information through the Meetings, a nationwide and cross-sectoral community existed (Prior and Kirby 1993).

In general terms the institutional development of different business communities may be similar, with all inevitably having their own channels of information. It was the peculiar juxtaposition, however, of economic characteristics and cultural considerations which made individual business communities and hence the family firm strategies pursued in them distinctive. This tendency is especially noticeable when the value systems of such industrial, commercial and financial centres as Leeds, Manchester, the West Midlands and the City of London are compared. In Leeds, for example, the mercantile elite was generally Tory in politics and Anglican in religion (Wilson 1971: 172). Similarly, in Birmingham and the Black Country there was a tendency for the elites in the business community to take on the values of the landed aristocracy and gentry (Trainor 1989: 181). This tendency, however, was most marked in the City of London where the merchant banking community emerged as a kind of aristocracy and occupied a poll position in both British banking and British society (Cassis 1985: 212). Bankers generally, and most especially London's bankers, enjoyed an aristocratic way of life. At the same time there existed a network of familial connections which spanned banking, commerce and the aristocracy. Whereas in the Jewish and Quaker minorities this network of connections was densest, intermarriage with the landed aristocracy was most common by the families such as the Barings which constituted the 'banking aristocracy' (Cassis 1985: 218–19). In Manchester, by contrast to the other communities, wealthy merchant–manufacturers became factory owners and emerged as a self-contained elite, with their own distinctive set of values. A 'charmed circle' of Unitarian commercial–industrial families was dominant there until at least 1850. Intermarriage between such families as the Philips, Potters and Gregs created 'a web of family connection [which] was the source of Manchester Unitarians' great strength' (Gatrell 1982: 25). Manchester's Unitarian chapels were more than just religious meeting houses; they were social institutions which brought together the town's wealthiest families (Seed 1986: 25–46). The same group has been shown to have dominated the Manchester Literary and Philosophical Society, whose meetings, by providing further opportunities for contact cemented the coherence of the elite (Seed 1982: 4). This combination of commercial and industrial wealth meant that this group enjoyed considerable power and status within Manchester in the first half of the nineteenth century. As a result they helped to mould a set of values that were distinct from those of the British establishment. Thus Manchester emerged as the only English city that can look London in the face, not merely as a regional capital, but as a rival version of how men should live in a community. . . . Manchester is the last and greatest of the Hanseatic towns – a civilisation created by traders without assistance from monarchs or territorial aristocracy.

(Taylor 1976: 307–8)

Far more research is needed to establish precisely why there should be such variations in the outlook of nineteenth-century business communities. Nevertheless, differences in the values and attitudes of various groups can be explained by the interaction of historical, economic and social influences. If for example the behaviour of Leeds and Manchester merchants in the eighteenth and early nineteenth century are compared it is possible to gain some insight into the differences in their community culture. Whereas in Manchester it was from the mercantile elite of merchant manufacturers that many of Lancashire's leading industrialists were drawn, Leeds merchants showed little inclination to diversify into manufacturing industry (Chapman 1970: 235–66; Wilson 1971: 136).

The differing attitudes of the two commercial elites may have stemmed initially from historical variations in the development of textiles in the two regions. In the West Riding, in the eighteenth century, rather than the outwork networks which fanned out from Manchester, domestic manufacturing was undertaken by a large number of independent clothiers, who sold their goods via the wealthy merchants. In his search for familial security the successful merchant was therefore unlikely to move into manufacturing, preferring consols or land as a source of extra security and good trouble-free income (Wilson 1971: 136). As this trend proceeded during the eighteenth century the boundaries between the landed and commercial communities became blurred as established mercantile families, such as the Milners, Ibbetsons and Dennisons, 'made a fortune in [Leeds] and then transferred their riches and talents to the country' (Wilson 1971: 221). As a result the value system of the landed groups became grafted onto the Leeds commercial elite. They formed, as a result, a socially distinct group set apart from the industrialists and small traders who tended to be Unitarian and Whig. It is clear that the values of the Leeds business elite were moulded by the landed groups in a way which is not to be detected in Manchester. There and indeed in Lancashire as a whole the trend towards gentrification was less noticeable, with remarkably few amongst the elite cotton families owning substantial estates (Howe 1984: 268–9).

In explaining why value systems in commercial and industrial communities diverged, it is of course necessary to look beyond differences in patterns of industrial development. Variations in the level of wealth generated was also significant and is especially important in explaining the shaping of attitudes in London's City community. It has been shown that the wealth generated by financial and commercial activities was well in excess of that created in industrial communities (Rubinstein 1981). Thus whilst, as elsewhere, land was often seen as a strategy which would bolster family security, the ability to buy large estates was far greater than in other sectors. Aesthetics, too, were not an insignificant influence on gentrification. The sheer ugliness of the industrial landscape of the Black Country and Birmingham encouraged businessmen to adopt a landed life style though not it seems to the detriment of their businesses (Trainor 1989: 179).

Irrespective of the motivation behind differences in landholding patterns in business communities or the effect on value systems, property in the first instance was seen as one aspect of family strategy designed to increase both security and comfort. In the nineteenth century family and firm remained inseparable, so that the reduction of uncertainty, combined with the maintenance of regular income, remained the prime objectives of all businessmen. It was critical to strike a sustainable balance between the interest of the family and those of the firm. As a consequence it was vital that the family received adequate protection from failure and that the firm enjoyed a fair chance of success (Nenadic 1990: 1; Daunton 1988: 270–81). For the majority of owners of family firms, then, their 'primary business' came to represent just one aspect of an increasingly diversified array of activities. The balance in complementary activities varied between communities and with the life cycle of firms, but generally comprised a judicious mix of active and rentier activities.

It has already been demonstrated that the initial purchase of land by eighteenth-century Leeds merchants represented a form of familial diversification. By the second quarter of the nineteenth century, the Leeds business elite saw land as part of a portfolio of investments which could be purchased to guarantee retirement income, whilst also providing security for mortgage loans (Morris 1990: 322). In the City business community, on the other hand, landownership enhanced business reputation. In addition, by offering an alternative route to the less able brethren of a family, it allowed commercial firms and merchant banks to maintain a familial meritocracy (Chapman 1984: 176, 64). Amongst the Manchester elite, whilst the trend towards gentrification was much less pronounced, the purchase of property allowed businessmen to spread risk, especially in times of particular uncertainty. Thus, during and after the Napoleonic Wars, Samuel Greg merchant and cotton millowner developed a diversified investment portfolio. It embraced rural, urban and overseas property, government stocks and shares in public utilities, and meant that quite apart from income from the cotton industry his family enjoyed an annual non-industrial income which annually averaged £4,900 between 1822 and 1832 (Rose 1977: 50; 1986: 45). In some instances, diversification even took the family out of one sphere of activity into another. Thus Westall has observed that in 1903 the prime objective of the founder of Provincial Insurance was to create a vehicle that would transmit wealth made in the cotton industry to later generations of the family (Westall 1992: 1–22). Similarly it is possible to interpret the emergence of investment groups in the late nineteenth century as part of a family firm strategy by London's general merchants to maintain familial power and wealth, despite growing specialization in the commercial world. These groups, which raised finance for a wide array of overseas enterprises, were dependent upon 'the loyalty and capital of family connections and friends' within the City and in their foreign spheres of influence (Chapman 1992: 231–2). Nor was such diversification of activity confined to larger firms: amongst the Birmingham artisan business community an array of interests was more normal than a singularity of purpose (Berg 1993: 17–39).

In seeking to protect the security of the family through diversification, collective activity by a group of families was not unusual. In the first place, the combination of wealth and social cohesion provided the opportunity for a collective response to the potential erosion of their family security. Pearson has identified such co-ordinated behaviour by members of mercantile communities in Leeds, Manchester and Norwich. It was in Manchester in the 1820s, however, that he identified the most notable example of collective action. Then a group of cotton lords successfully moved into insurance, first in an attempt to combat the risks of mill fires but also to widen their investment portfolios. The Manchester Fire and Life Assurance Company was thus a 'club of cotton lords, the directors of which were woven into a "Byzantine network of intermarriage and business partnerships"' (Pearson 1991: 379–414). Collective strategies by groups of families bound by community interest can also be identified in both banking and commerce. Thus the foundation of Barclays Bank in 1896 represented the amalgamation of twenty private banks, the partners of which were all linked by strong family ties (Cassis 1985: 218).

Community-based family firm networks are thus critical to the understanding of the distinctiveness of British family firm strategy. So far attention has been directed towards the evolution of familial and business strategy within elites. The business culture and policies of smaller family firms were also intimately related to their communities. The proliferation of small firms, during the Industrial Revolution and the increasing levels of specialization thereafter, has been likened to atomistic competition. Certainly the high turnover of firms during this period would give credence to this view. Recent work, however, has shown that firms in business communities where a reservoir of skilled artisans existed were able to pursue highly successful niche market policies. In such an environment, competitive advantage was dependent upon flexibility deriving from a skilled artisan workforce working in an interlocking web of workshops within business communities. In these circumstances of mainly 'proprietary capitalism', networks of expertise, which were external to the firm but nonetheless internal to the community, reinforced specialization. There was therefore simply no incentive to internalize activities through formal integration. Community ties of common outlook, shared attitudes and craft culture were just as effective.

In nineteenth-century Britain, what amounted to a 'just in time' system dependent upon a cross-community network of trust and accumulated skill has been identified in the Birmingham metal trades and the Sheffield cutlery trades (Berg 1993: 25–6). Such a trend was not confined to the West Midlands, however, and meant that even quite late in the nineteenth century in some industries community-based craft production coexisted with factories. In Lancashire, for example, new estimates suggest that in 1851 there were over 50,000 handloom weavers with as many as 10,000 remaining in the country in 1871 (Timmins 1993: 110). In the production of finer and fancier cloths, where demand was most volatile, factory spinners who employed outworkers in their community were able to counteract technological deficiencies in power weaving, whilst enjoying the flexibility of community-based subcontracting (Lyons 1985). Horrockses of Preston, for example, combined handloom weaving with factory spinning and some power weaving until 1853 (Timmins 1993: 142). In Lancashire such community-based networks were not confined to handloom weaving. By the 1830s an impressive array of specialist ancillary services had also developed, meaning that economies were to a large degree external to the firm (Farnie 1990: 150). Far more research is needed to establish the full extent of intra-community independence and its implications for business strategy in family firms.

Nevertheless it seems safe to conclude that family firms in many business communities engaged 'in an informal "between firm" strategy of internalisation which corresponds in some respects to the formal "within firm" strategy of internalisation seen among large Chandlerian firms' (Nenadic 1990: 6).

CONCLUSION

The family firm in Britain emerged as the personal response of businessmen to the uncertain legal and economic environment of the eighteenth century. Similarly the subsequent nineteenth-century strategies developed by the owners of family firms also reflected the desire of owners to guarantee the safety, income and future prosperity of their offspring. In order to achieve these aims combined with a desire for social betterment, family firms have been presumed to have pursued business stability at the expense of dynamic growth strategies. Yet this chapter has revealed that, whilst nothing so simple as national cultural values can be identified in nineteenth-century Britain, it was families rather than firms which diversified.

The explanation of why British families diversified the overall range of their interests rather than merely increasing the scale and scope of their firms in the way of their American contemporaries is complex. Indeed far more research is needed if conclusive interpretation is to be put forward. Yet a few tentative observations can be made. The different compositions of markets and contributions of technology have long been identified as sources of differing business strategies in the two countries; equally, differing legal structures and attitudes towards collusion have also been highlighted as important. In addition in America land was too plentiful to be valued either as a store of wealth or a source of prestige.

Yet the opportunities for familial diversification were also different. In Britain, the relative advanced economic canvas for industrial development in the eighteenth century bred increasing specialization and market segmentation. This meant that economies were external rather than internal to firms. Thus quite apart from constraints, which have been seen as financial, technological, managerial and social, to the growth of firms, families had little to gain from internalization of activities. Their American counterparts, in other words, had larger gaps to fill if their businesses were to be successful. By way of amplification of this point it is instructive to find that in the 1820s and 1830s the Boston mercantile elite pursued collective familial strategies of diversification in the face of a need to protect wealth and position.

These were very similar in character to those found in Britain. Yet since Northern Massachusetts was relatively innocent of economic development, they embraced manufacturing and machine making, as well as banking, insurance and public utilities (Dalzell 1987).

By the late nineteenth century a combination of economic, demographic, social and technological pressures began to alter British business and British business communities. Railways, by making longer distance commuting possible, began to reduce the cohesion of localized business communities. The institutions remained, yet regular social interaction and the sharing of common value systems began to break down in the late nineteenth century and into the Edwardian era. Similarly a combination of foreign competition and technological change altered both the competitive environment and the threshold of entry in British business, whilst smaller family size after 1870 altered the character of both family and firm. In this environment it became increasingly common to substitute the formal co-operation of the trade association for the informal information flows of the business community. Nevertheless in cotton, and doubtless in other sectors also, the cohesion of industry-wide associations of manufacturers was inhibited by the continued distinctiveness of interests and outlook of individual business communities (Turner 1962: 376; McIvor 1988: 2–3).

BIBLIOGRAPHY

Aldcroft, D.H. (1964) 'The entrepreneur and the British economy, 1870–1914', *Economic History Review* 17: 113–34.

Barker, T.C. and Lévy-Leboyer, M. (1982) 'An inquiry into the Buddenbrooks effect in Europe', in L. Hannah (ed.) From Family Firm to Professional Management, Budapest: Akademiai Kiado.

Berg, M. (1993) 'Small producer capitalism in eighteenth century England', *Business History* 35: 17–39.

Berg, M., Hudson, P. and Sonenscher, M. (eds) (1983) *Manufacturing in Town and Country*, Cambridge: Cambridge University Press.

Boswell, J. (1973) *The Rise and Decline of Small Firms*, London: Allen & Unwin.

Broehl, W.G. (1992) *Cargill. Trading the World's Grain*, Hanover, NH: New England University Press.

Campbell, R. (1988) 'A critique of the Christian businessman and his paternalism', in D.J. Jeremy (ed.) *Business and Religion in Britain*, Aldershot: Edward Elgar.

Capie, F. (1983) 'Tariff protection and economic performance in international trade', in J. Black and L.A. Winters (eds) *Policy and Performance in International Trade*, London: Allen & Unwin.

Cassis, Y. (1985) 'Bankers in English society in the late nineteenth century', *Economic History Review* 38: 210–29.

Casson, M.C. (1982) *The Entrepreneur*, London: Mark Robertson.

—— (1991) *The Economics of Business Culture: Game Theory, Transaction Costs and Economic Performance*, Oxford: Oxford University Press.

Chandler, A.D. (1986) 'Managers, families and financiers', in K. Kobayashi and H. Morikawa (eds) *The Development of Managerial Enterprise*, Tokyo: Tokyo University Press.

—— (1990) *Scale and Scope: The Dynamics of Industrial Capitalism*, Cambridge, MA: Harvard University Press.

Chapman, S.D. (1970) 'Fixed capital formation in the British cotton industry, 1770–1815', *Economic History Review* 23: 235–66.

—— (1984) *The Rise of Merchant Banking*, London: Allen & Unwin.

—— (1985) 'British based investment groups before 1914', *Economic History Review* 38: 230–51.

—— (1992) *Merchant Enterprise in Britain: From Industrial Revolution to World War I*, Cambridge: Cambridge University Press.

Child, J. (1964) 'Quaker employers and industrial relations', *Sociological Review* 12: 293–315.

Church, R. (1993) 'The family firm in industrial capitalism: international perspectives on hypotheses and history', *Business History* 35.

Cochran, T. (1971) *Frontiers of Change: Early Industrialism in America*, New York: Oxford University Press.

Coleman, D.C. (1973) 'Gentlemen and players', *Economic History Review* 26: 92–116.

Collins, B. and Robbins, K. (1990) *British Culture and Economic Decline*, London: Weidenfeld & Nicholson.

Cottrell, P.L. (1979) *Industrial Finance, 1830–1914: The Finance and Organization of English Manufacturing Industry*, London: Methuen.

Crouzet (1972) *Capital Formation in the Industrial Revolution*, London: Methuen.

Dalzell, R. (1987) *Enterprising Elite: The Boston Associates and the World They Made*, Cambridge, MA: Harvard University Press.

Daunton, M. (1988) 'Inheritance and succession in the City of London in the nineteenth century', *Business History* 30: 269–86.

—— (1989) 'Family and firm in the City of London in the nineteenth century: the case of F.G. Dalgety', *Historical Research* 62: 154–77.

Davidoff, L. and Hall, C. (1987) *Family Fortunes: Men and Women of the English Middle Class, 1780–1850*, London: Hutchinson.

DuBois, A.B. (1971) *The English Business Company after the Bubble Act, 1720–1800*, New York: Octagon.

Farber, B. (1972) *Guardians of Virtue: Salem Families in 1800*, New York: Basic Books.

Farnie, D.A. (1979) 'An index of commercial activity: the membership of the Manchester Royal Exchange, 1809–1948' *Business History* 21: 97–106.

—— (1982) 'The structure of the British cotton industry, 1846–1914', in A. Okochi and S.-I. Yonekawa (eds) *The Textile Industry and its Business Climate*, Tokyo: Tokyo University Press.

—— (1990) 'The textile machine-making industry and the world market, 1870–1960', *Business History* 32: 150–70.

Florence, P.S. (1953) *The Logic of British and American Industry*, London: Routledge & Kegan Paul.

Floud, R.C. (1981) 'Britain 1860–1914', in R.C. Floud and D. McCloskey (eds) *The Economic History of Britain since 1700* Cambridge: Cambridge University Press.

Gatrell, V.A.C. (1982) 'Incorporation and the pursuit of liberal hegemony in Manchester, 1790–1839', in D. Frazer (ed.) *Municipal Reform and the Industrial City*, Leicester: Leicester University Press.

Habakkuk, H.J. (1955) 'The historical experience of the basic conditions of economic progress', in L.H. Dupriez (ed.) *Economic Progress*, Louvain: Louvain University Press.

Hannah, L. (ed.) (1982) *From Family Firm to Professional Management*, Budapest, Akademiai Kiado.

—— (1983) *The Rise of the Corporate Economy*, London: Methuen.

Heaton, H. (1972) 'Financing the Industrial Revolution', in F. Crouzet (ed.) *Capital Formation in the Industrial Revolution*, London: Methuen.

Hoppit, J. (1987) *Risk and Failure in English Business, 1700–1800*, Cambridge: Cambridge University Press.

Howe, A. (1984) *The Cotton Masters, 1830–1860*, Oxford: Clarendon Press.

Hudson, P. (1986) *The Genesis of Industrial Capital: A Study of the West Riding Wool Textile Industry, c. 1750–1850*, Cambridge: Cambridge University Press.

—— (ed.) (1989) *Regions and Industries*, Cambridge: Cambridge University Press.

Hunt, B.C. (1936) *The Development of the Business Corporation in Britain, 1800–1867*, Cambridge, MA: Harvard University Press.

Jeffreys, J.B. (1977) *Trends in Business Organization in Great Britain since 1856*, New York: Arno Press.

Jones, G. (1993) 'Big business, management and competitiveness in twentieth century Britain', University of Reading Discussion Papers in Economics, Series A, vol. V, no. 268.

Jowitt, J.A. and McIvor, A.J. (eds) (1988) *Employers and Labour in the English Textile Industries, 1850–1939*, London: Sage.

Kindleberger, C.P. (1964) *Economic Growth in France and Britain, 1851–1950*, Cambridge: MA: Harvard University Press.

Kirby, M.W. (1993) 'Quakerism, entrepreneurship and the family firm in North East England, 1780–1860', in J. Brown and M.B. Rose (eds) *Entrepreneurship Networks and Modern Business*, Manchester: Manchester University Press.

Koditschek, T. (1990) *Class Formation and Urban Industrial Society: Bradford, 1750–1850*, Cambridge: Cambridge University Press.

Landes, D.S. (1951) 'French business and businessmen in social and cultural analysis', in E.M. Earle (ed.) *Modern France*, Princeton, NJ: Princeton University Press.

—— (1965) 'Technological change and development in Western Europe, 1750–1914', in M. Postan and H.J. Habakkuk (eds) *Cambridge Economic History of Europe*, Cambridge: Cambridge University Press, vol. 6, 563–4.

Langton, J. (1984) 'The industrial revolution and the regional geography of England', *Transactions of the Institute of British Geographers* 9: 145–67.

Lazonick, W. (1986) 'The cotton industry', in B. Elbaum and W. Lazonick (eds) *The Decline of the British Economy*, Cambridge: Cambridge University Press.

—— (1991) *Business Organization and the Myth of the Market Economy*, Cambridge: Cambridge University Press.

Lisle-Williams, M. (1984a) 'Beyond the market: the survival of family capitalism in the English merchant banks', *British Journal of Sociology* 35: 241–71.

—— (1984b) 'Merchant banking dynasties in the English class structure: ownership, solidarity and kinship in the City of London', *British Journal of Sociology*, 35: 333–62.

Lyons, J.S. (1985) 'Vertical integration of the British cotton industry, 1825–1850: a revision', *Journal of Economic History* 45: 419–26.

Mathias, P. (1979) *The Transformation of England*, London: Methuen.

McIvor, A.J. (1988) 'Introduction', in J.A. Jowitt and A.J. McIvor (eds) *Employers and Labour in the English Textile Industries, 1850–1939*, London: Sage.

Morikawa, H. (1992) *Zaibatsu. The Rise and Fall of Family Enterprise Groups in Japan*, Tokyo: Tokyo University Press.

Morris, R.J. (1990) *Class, Sect and Party: The Making of the British Middle Class: Leeds, 1820–50*, Manchester: Manchester University Press.

Nenadic, S. (1990) 'The family and the small firm in late nineteenth century Britain', in *Strategy and Structure in Small and Medium Size Enterprise*, A4 session, Tenth International Congress, Leuven.

Payne, P. (1967) 'The emergence of the large scale company in Great Britain', *Economic History Review* 20: 519–42.

—— (1984) 'Family business in Britain: an historical and analytical survey', in A. Okochi and S. Yasuoka (eds) *Family Business in the Era of Industrial Growth*, Tokyo: Tokyo University Press.

—— (1988) *British Entrepreneurship in the Nineteenth Century*, 2nd edn, London: Macmillan.

Pearson, R. (1991) 'Collective diversification; Manchester cotton merchants and the insurance business in the early nineteenth century', *Business History Review* 65: 379–414.

Pollak, R.A. (1985) 'A transaction cost approach to families and households', *Journal of Economic Literature* 23: 581–608.

Pollard, S. (1981) *Peaceful Conquest: the Industrialization of Europe 1760–1970*, Oxford: Oxford University Press.

Porter, M.E. (1990) *The Competitive Advantage of Nations*, London: Macmillan.

Pressnell, L.S. (1956) *Country Banking in the Industrial Revolution*, Oxford: Oxford University Press.

Prior, A. and Kirby, M.W. (1993) 'The Society of Friends and the family firm, 1700–1830', *Business History* 35.

Report on the Law of Partnership (1837) Parliamentary Paper 1837 (530) XLIV.

Rose, M.B. (1977) 'The role of the family in providing capital and managerial talent in Samuel Greg and Company, 1784–1840', *Business History* 19: 37–54.

—— (1979) 'Diversification of investment by the Greg family, 1800–1914', *Business History* 21: 79–96.

—— (1986) *The Gregs of Quarry Bank Mill: the Rise and Decline of a Family Firm, 1750–1914*, Cambridge: Cambridge University Press.

—— (1989) 'Social policy and business: parish apprenticeship and the early factory system, 1750–1834', *Business History* 31: 5–32.

—— (1993) 'Beyond Buddenbrooks: the family firm and the management of succession in nineteenth century Britain', in J. Brown and M.B. Rose (eds) *Entrepreneurship, Networks and Modern Business*, Manchester: Manchester University Press.

Rubinstein, W. (1981) *Men of Property*, London: Croom Helm.

Sandberg, L. (1969) 'American rings and English mules: the role of economic rationality', *Quarterly Journal of Economics* 73: 25–43.

Saul, S.B. (1967) 'The market and the development of the mechanical engineering industries in Britain, 1860–1914', *Economic History Review* 20: 101–19.

Seed, J. (1982) 'Unitarianism, political economy and the anatomies of liberal culture in Manchester', *Social History* 7: 1–25.

—— (1986) 'Theologies of power: unitarianism and social relations of religious discourse', in R.J. Morris (ed.) *Class, Power and Social Structure in British Nineteenth Century Towns*, London: Leicester University Press.

Taylor, A.J.P. (1976) *Essays in English History*, London: Penguin.

Timmins, G. (1993) *The Last Shift: the Decline of Handloom Weaving in Nineteenth Century Lancashire*, Manchester: Manchester University Press.

Toyne, B., Arpan, T.S., Ricks, D.A., Shimp, T.A. and Barnett, A. (eds) (1984) *The Global Textile Industry*, London: Allen & Unwin.

Trainor, R. (1989) 'The gentrification of Victorian and Edwardian industrialists', in A. Beier, D. Cannadine and L. Rosenheim (eds), *The First Modern Society*, Cambridge: Cambridge University Press.

Turner, H. (1962) *Trade Union Growth*, Toronto: Toronto University Press.

Wadsworth, A.P. and Mann, J. de L. (1931) *The Cotton Trade and Industrial Lancashire, 1600–1780*, Manchester: Manchester University Press.

Westall, O.M. (1992) *The Provincial Insurance Company, 1903–38: Family, Markets and Competitive Growth*, Manchester: Manchester University Press.

Wiener, M.J. (1981) *English Culture and the Decline of the Industrial Spirit, 1850–1980*, Cambridge: Cambridge University Press.

Wilson, R.G. (1971) *Gentlemen Merchants: the Merchant Community in Leeds*, 1700–1830, Manchester: Manchester University Press.

4   Financing firms, 1700–1850

Pat Hudson

Forty years ago a significant increase in capital formation was regarded as a hallmark of industrialization (Lewis 1955: 201–303; Rostow 1956: 25–48) and the subject of how industrial and commercial firms were financed was of central importance. In recent years this question has become less fashionable because it appears less urgent. New estimates of national income and of the pace and nature of capital formation have suggested that growth and change in the eighteenth and early nineteenth centuries was very slow and significant transformation and capital deepening was confined to a small advanced sector of the economy (Crafts 1985: 9–47). Capital requirements were generally modest and the slow expansion of most manufacturing and mercantile activities was easily accommodated by the ubiquitous credit network and through the gradual growth of a variety of largely informal conduits which eased the flow of plentiful funds between and within sectors of the economy (Mathias 1989: 69–85).

There are several reasons why these easy assumptions should be questioned and why commercial and industrial finance during these decades should continue to be addressed. First, slow-moving national capital figures tell us little about the processes of capital utilization and accumulation experienced by individual firms in different sectors and regions of the country. Despite generally easy conditions of capital supply relative to overall demand, the fragmented nature of the capital market, different capital requirements of major sectors, different trade and credit arrangements, and regional variations in capital availability meant that many firms faced difficulties in gaining both the long-term capital and the credit which they needed to survive. These problems contributed to the high failure rates characteristic of enterprise in the period and influenced the pace of development and the nature of larger-scale undertakings in several sectors. We thus need to know more about them.

Second, the largest potential savers and investors in the economy, landowners and financiers, generally invested their money outside of domestic industrial or commercial ventures in government bonds and stocks, imperial expansion, estate improvement or conspicuous consumption. The majority of manufacturers and traders had little access to big money and were forced to rely upon local and family connections, on credit stretched to cover long-term needs and on delays and truck in wage payments (Crouzet 1972: 162–222; Shapiro 1967: 118–19, 141–2, 219–20). New work in these areas can help us to reassess earlier conclusions about the easy financial circumstances of firms during the Industrial Revolution.

Finally, there remains debate and disagreement about the nature of capital requirements and capital sources even with respect to the most straightforward and central questions. Where did businesses find the funds to embark on commercial manufacturing or trading? How easy was it to get capital to expand the scale of operations or to invest in new plant and equipment? How important were different forms of business organization in facilitating or constraining capital expansion? What role did financial intermediaries and the banking and credit infrastructure play? How vital were landowners in underpinning non-agricultural enterprise? What were the financial connections between inland and overseas merchanting and other forms of business? How significant was reinvestment? And how do our answers to all of these questions change between regions, over time and through cycles of shifting commercial and investment opportunity?

This chapter will address these issues. It starts with an overview of the structure of business enterprise, paying attention to organizational forms, sectoral and regional differences, variations in the structure of capital assets and the implication of these for the nature of capital demand and supply. The four remaining sections consider financial links between agriculture, landownership and commercial enterprise; relationships between mercantile and other business activity in the financing of firms; the impact of banks on business finance; and the role of ploughed-back profits. The final section draws the evidence together and analyses shifts in the nature and sources of capital accumulation over time, regionally and in relation to the origins and life cycles of firms and individuals.

THE STRUCTURE OF BUSINESS ENTERPRISE

After the speculative crisis of 1720 formal joint stock organizations were forbidden (until 1825) and incorporation and limited liability became dependent upon the expensive process of gaining parliamentary consent. Firms requiring a large financial base, for example in mining, insurance, grain and cloth milling or overseas trade, could form unincorporated joint stock businesses by using the law of trust or could apply to Parliament for incorporation. Similarly for investment in utilities such as canals, turnpikes and docks, equitable trusts gave legal powers of compulsory purchase as well as limited liability and incorporation. These arrangements are analysed in some detail in Chapter 5 of this volume. In overseas trade it was common to create joint stock associations for each voyage and/or to break down the ownership of ships into transferable fractions of a sixty-fourth or less. Other devices which effectively circumvented legal obstacles to finance included the Cornish 'cost-book' system whereby tin mines could operate as companies with transferable shares. Institutional arrangements were thus, in practice, flexible but, for most manufacturers, merchants and retailers, private (unlimited liability) partnerships (of six persons or fewer) remained the most popular form of business arrangement throughout our period. Partnerships had the advantage of uniting ownership with control (sleeping partners were not allowed by law) which was important in an age which regarded unlimited liability favourably as a spur to prudent management.

Private partnerships dominated across the board from City merchant houses and banks to firms in all manufacturing branches including textiles, brewing, shipbuilding and metal wares. They ranged from heavily capitalized businesses and large employers to small-scale artisanal and workshop concerns with little capital and limited labour. Partnerships were usually family or extended family concerns with partners having close links through birth, marriage, community or religious affiliation. Mutual trust between partners and knowledge of each other's business affairs and assets was important in the face of unlimited liability (Hudson 1986: 269). High failure rates, coupled with high risk, uncertainty and continuous change in the business environment (Hoppit 1987: 42–55, 122–39), encouraged the predominance of family concerns (as is discussed in Chapter 3 of this volume).

This had several implications for the financing of enterprise. First, following the dominant patterns of family and kinship settlement, bolstered by overlapping communal and religious affiliations and loyalties, the ownership and finance of most firms tended to be local or regional, depending on localized capital supply conditions, local knowledge and influence and the development of local financial networks and institutions. Second, families were frequently the main source of capital extension raised through personal bonds and loans or by taking on additional partners from within the family. The origins and fortunes of the family and its connections shaped the fortunes of the firm through marriage settlements for example. But, at the same time, familial goals such as ensuring the respectability, stability or continuity of the family and providing for several offspring could affect withdrawals of capital from the business, the fragmentation of operations, and the spreading of investment outside the firm (Hudson 1986: 245–55; Rose 1986: 64–7; Davidoff and Hall 1987: 215–22).

The size of firms and their capital composition as well as the institutional structure of business were important influences upon financial demands and sources. Overseas merchants were regarded as the most prosperous group in the business community. Their number appears to have expanded only slowly from around 10,000 in 1690 to reach 15,000 or so in the early nineteenth century despite a sixfold increase in external trade. Overseas merchants required between £1,500 and £10,000 to establish in business in the eighteenth century (Chapman 1992: 26–9). But they needed to be able to call upon much more than this to cover the lengthening periods of realization incurred in dealings with distant markets. Some trades involved outlays over two years or more and one year was normal (Hudson 1986: 155–81; Chapman 1992: 27–8). Thus overseas merchants required much short- and medium-term 'accommodation', especially in periods of trading uncertainty such as during the Napoleonic Wars when new markets were being pursued and risks were high (Hudson 1986: 160–7). Lengthy credit extension coupled with high risk and uncertainty of markets resulted in overseas merchants being very prominent in eighteenth-century bankruptcy figures (Hoppit 1987: 96–102).

The late eighteenth and early nineteenth centuries also saw the increasing extension of manufacturers into merchanting as well as more investment by overseas merchants back into production to increase their control over markets and commodity supplies respectively in difficult times. Although some of the larger manufacturers continued to trade directly with overseas clients, after the Napoleonic Wars and especially after the crisis of 1825 more of Britain's external trade came to be conducted through a limited number of accepting houses in Liverpool and London.

The internal trade comprised a vast spectrum of concerns from large wholesalers involved in both domestic and foreign ventures, through a variety of middlemen to lowly retailers and shopkeepers. Their numbers may have increased around fourfold in the eighteenth century alone and the nineteenth century brought further opportunities for marked expansion in the number of wholesalers and retailers especially in servicing the growth of industry and towns (Westerfield 1915; Alexander 1970). Middlemen had various functions. Some, such as the Manchester merchants, ran warehouses and others attended fairs or markets to which manufacturers came to sell their wares for cash or short bills. Others were more heavily involved in seeking out and developing a client relationship with particular producers from whom they took the bulk of production. Sometimes this also involved direct investment in production, a role which became more common especially with industrial goods by the end of the eighteenth century (Westerfield 1915: 218–320; Hoppit 1987: 5–6). Merchant manufacturers also grew in number by their direct involvement in putting-out raw materials to domestic producers, co-ordinating and financing both production and sale. The degree of involvement of merchants and middlemen in production depended on the form of production and the nature of the market.

Domestic industry was the most prevalent form of manufacturing organization in the eighteenth century and it was slow to be displaced thereafter. It was most common in rural or semi-rural areas where households also had access to land and were simultaneously involved in agricultural activities. In some regions, for example in South Lancashire, the West Country and the worsted area of Yorkshire, merchants were pivotal agents in co-ordinating complex and geographically widespread divisions of labour between and within households. Merchants often owned the raw materials and sometimes also tools and equipment as well as directly involving themselves in various finishing processes (generally running urban workshops for this purpose) and in marketing. In other areas, for example in the Midlands, amongst Sheffield cutlers and scythemakers and in the Yorkshire woollen belt, domestic industry was predominantly the province of semi-independent artisan households and small producers who owned their own tools and raw materials and sold their products to merchants either at urban warehouses or at local, often specialized, market halls (Hey 1972: 18–30; Rowlands 1975: 39–53; Hudson 1986: 25–41; Berg 1993). Urban and rural workshop industries also flourished during industrialization. These required more overhead finance but, using mainly hand skills and labour-intensive methods, their fixed capital needs remained modest. Financial demands grew if and when workshop masters sought out markets on their own account as occurred to some extent in Yorkshire, Birmingham, Sheffield and elsewhere in the eighteenth and early nineteenth centuries (Hudson 1986: 160–7; Berg 1993: 24).

Finally, in the late eighteenth and early nineteenth centuries water- and later steam-powered factories were becoming more prominent especially in the textile sector. These required much more fixed capital (sunk in plant and equipment) and necessitated a new and longer gestation view of investment which was slow to develop (Hudson 1977: 11; cf. Fleischman and Tyson 1993: 508–19). The expansion of the iron industry and of coalmining also brought fixed capital demands to new levels (Feinstein and Pollard 1988: 35–104). For the cotton industry of the early nineteenth century it appears that fixed capital may commonly have accounted for more than 50 per cent of investment needs (Richardson 1989: 488–502; cf. Pollard 1964: 303–5; Lee 1972: 164–7; Gatrell 1977: 103). In the more typical wool textile sector ratios of 20–40 per cent were more common (Jenkins 1975: 175–90; Hudson 1986: 51). Thus fixed capital was in some sectors becoming a major factor by the 1820s and 1830s but circulating capital (for holding stocks, extending credit to purchasers and for paying wages) remained the most important requirement for the vast majority of concerns and especially for those outside the technologically advanced and steam-powered manufacturing sector (Weatherill 1982: 243–58). Even in the more capital-intensive sector it was common to rent rather than buy premises, to purchase second-hand machinery and to pay for expensive equipment by instalments (Jenkins 1975: 196–205; Gatrell 1977: 103). Furthermore, most firms even in the cotton textile sector remained small. In 1841 a typical cotton factory had fixed capital of £15,000 and employed 200 workers (Gatrell 1977: 127) whilst an average mill in the wool textile sector was much smaller – under £4,000 fixed capital as late as 1835 (Jenkins 1975: 154–6). Thus capital demands, though growing, remained generally modest in most sectors of manufacturing because of a variety of capital economizing devices such as renting and because of the diversity of small firms in specialized niches of production where economies of scale were insignificant. But as Heaton argued some years ago, capital needs were 'frequently large enough to harass and perplex those who needed funds' (Heaton 1937: 4). This was particularly the case when the web of credit, within which business concerns operated, tightened to their disadvantage: when they were forced, in the competitive search for markets, to extend more credit to their purchasers than they in turn were granted by suppliers. Liquidity problems and fluctuations varied between sectors depending upon the nature of markets and the credit practices which had evolved in particular trades (Weatherill 1982; Hudson 1986: 107–207; Hoppit 1987: 56–103). But when the credit matrix tightened, internal resources were necessarily diverted from employment in the longer term renewal or expansion of productive or trading capacity. Thus, in understanding industrial finance in these years, the historians' distinction between fixed and circulating capital needs and sources is not always a helpful one. Any change which eased a firm's credit position released resources which could be used to extend premises and equipment.

As technology became more advanced and capital hungry in some sectors and as improvements in communications, merchanting and distribution increased the turnover time of capital and shifted some of the costs of stockholding from producers to merchants, brokers and middlemen, the composition of manufacturing capital within firms changed. This was a process sometimes aided by vertical disintegration and horizontal specialization, notably in textiles in the second quarter of the nineteenth century, which speeded the turnover time in production. But cyclical changes also occurred: if markets were temporarily overstocked, manufacturers stockpiled or were forced to offload goods on their own account rather than dealing through merchants or middlemen. This involved the employment of increased working capital.

Finally, the Industrial Revolution was marked by sectoral concentration within industrial regions and the specialization of port cities in particular trades. These involved external economies of agglomeration with respect to the provision of trade credit and loan capital. Industrial regions developed their own institutions and practices to serve the needs of their area (Westerfield 1915: 273–323; Buchanan 1986: 80–93; Hudson 1989: 182–234). The Cloth Halls where clothiers sold their wares under regulated conditions and the role of the woolstapler in extending lengthy credit to manufacturers were two specialized developments which underpinned the financial position of West Yorkshire woollen manufacturers, for example. Private and, later, joint stock banks grew from the dominant sectors of the regions which they served and developed policies appropriate to the needs of their partners, shareholders and clients whether they were mainly factory entrepreneurs, overseas merchants, wholesalers or workshop masters (Collins and Hudson 1979: 69–79). Networks of trading, business and social contact within regions developed the forms of trust and knowledge upon which the informal market in bonds, loans and bill discount was based. And the pivotal role of attorneys in linking lender to borrower operated within a dense regional network of contacts formed through county court business or local estate agency (Anderson 1969: 223–55; Miles 1981: 127–46).

In all, the institutional structure, the functions, the typical size and capital composition of firms before the mid-nineteenth century all favoured local, regional and personal financial links. But inter-regional and international financial flows were also important in financing firms as we shall see.

FINANCE FROM THE LAND

It was natural for commercial and industrial concerns to look to local landed wealth as a potential source of finance and in some regions and sectors landlords themselves were active in initiating and expanding extractive, transport and manufacturing developments, particularly on their own estates. But not every region of agriculture generated a significant surplus or had a resident landowning group concerned with extra agricultural estate development (Evans 1989: 206–19; Short 1989: 172–4; Walton 1989: 57–63). Rural areas with the greatest potential surplus of funds in the form of high profits and farm rents were often those most removed geographically from industrial concentrations. Although the network of country banks was expanding in the second half of the eighteenth century and these institutions were capable, via the London clearing banks, of effecting a transfer of funds from areas of agricultural surplus to areas of industrial need, it is likely that their impact with respect to this was slight until well into the nineteenth century. The development of specialist bill brokers during the Napoleonic Wars did facilitate the transfer of short-term funds interregionally via the discount market. But the liquidity needs of both arable and industrial/commercial sectors peaked at the same time – in the summer months and just before harvest – leaving only limited surpluses to be shifted at the times of industry's greatest needs. Furthermore, the capital flow created by the growth of the insurance business may have been a major factor in ensuring a reverse drift of capital from industry and trade to the land. Premiums from the rising insurance companies were most often invested in the secure arena of the mortgage market for farmers and landowners (although an unquantified amount did find its way into private commercial concerns) (Dickson 1960: 244, 260–4; Collins 1988a: 30–1).

Many landowners invested in transport, notably in local canal developments, river improvements and turnpikes. In many canal companies landed finance represented about a third of shareholdings between 1760 and 1815 (Ward 1974), whilst in cities like Liverpool and Birmingham landowners put considerable capital into urban housing concerns. Some landlords were closely involved in coal and mineral mining on their estates, the northeast coalfield and Cornish tin mining being important examples. Direct enterprise and investment appears to have been more common in the early stages of exploration and exploitation of mines in particular. This was certainly the case in the Black Country in the late eighteenth century (Raybould 1984: 59–86). And in the brewing industry it appears that landed finance played a major role both at the initiation and during the later expansion of concerns (Mathias 1952: 249–57). There are also examples of landowners becoming involved in textile businesses by building and leasing mills. The Lowther family established a linen factory in Westmorland as early as the 1740s, initially for the benefit of the poor (Beckett 1977: 56–65) and Lord Dartmouth owned and leased out nineteen mills in the Leeds/Huddersfield area in the early nineteenth century. Dartmouth was just one of several landowners in the West Riding who made a contribution to the provision of fixed capital for local industry although only 6 per cent of Yorkshire's wool textile mills were owned by landowners in 1835. Some landowners, like Sir James Graham at Kirkstall and Thomas Thornhill in Calverely, invested in the wool textile industry by encouraging domestic clothiers to settle on their estates by providing cottages and agricultural plots as well as building mills (Hudson 1986: 85–104).

Much landed investment in manufacturing and mining firms appears to have been of a rentier type. The leasing of mineral rights, mines, farm plots and other industrial premises by landowners was seen as an aspect of estate improvement. Extensions and improvements to installations or premises were accompanied by rising rents and in some cases rents can clearly be seen to be creaming off the profits of industrial concerns and depriving them of funds for reinvestment (Hudson 1986: 86–93). Thus it may be as O'Brien suggests that 'High prices had to be paid to those who had charge of English agriculture and its investable surplus in order to persuade them to lend serious and positive support to industrialization' (O'Brien 1985: 785).

Many landowners were opposed to industrial development and took steps to prevent it, particularly where it spoiled the view from their windows. Some regarded canals with suspicion because they feared that an easier flow of grain would glut markets and depress prices and rents, and landowners often sold off their industrial and commercial assets to finance farm improvement. Sir Christopher Sykes sold his interests in stock and shipping in order to develop the Yorkshire Wolds at the end of the eighteenth century (Jones 1967: 26, 32–3). The intersectoral terms of trade favoured such shifts of investment as did the high costs of enclosure. And estates often carried a heavy burden of mortgage debt, supposedly raised from professional and commercial sources, which must be added to the substantial dowries brought to the land by the heiress daughters of merchants. It is likely that in the decades of heavy eighteenth-century enclosure British agriculture was taking as much capital as it was giving to the rest of the economy, while in the Napoleonic War period when food prices spiralled, 'the net flow of resources was probably towards the land' (Landes 1969: 77). Wartime uncertainty further encouraged defensive diversification of assets away from industry to the land or to government stocks as a way of spreading risks in these years (Rose 1986: 25–6).

It is the informal and formal capital market at local level which appears to have been most important in linking agriculture with the finance of firms. Small agriculture holdings or just access to common-lands on the part of domestic workers subsidized manufacturing households and reduced the cost of putting-out employers, enabling them to pay industrial wages below subsistence level. Thus capital from land and industry was intimately linked in the functioning of rural domestic and workshop concerns. Ownership of a farm or small-holding could also facilitate borrowing and hence the ability to survive and to expand. At a time when such a large proportion of national wealth was in agricultural assets, it is not surprising that land was the major security upon which loans could be raised and upon which financial status, respectability and creditworthiness rested. So important was the mortgage of land to raise industrial capital in the West Riding that the Registry of Deeds was established in 1725 to document ownership transfers and thus to promote the finance of industry. Raising finance on the security of land was also of crucial importance in Lancashire, the West Midlands and other areas. The sale and mortgage of farms and fields appears from the evidence of title deeds and business papers in Yorkshire and elsewhere to have been a major channel for the transfer of capital into industry, but as most of the mortgagees were merchants, manufacturers and, later, banks one can see that land mortgage and sale was acting more as a means for the transfer of wealth within the commercial and industrial classes than as a way of shifting capital from agriculture to industry. The same was true of the activities of attorneys in connecting lenders to borrowers: they organized some loans to commercial firms from widows and spinsters of landed families and from landowners but merchants appear to have been a much more important source of loan finance for both trade and industry (Miles 1981: 127–46; Hudson 1986: 211–18).

Capital flowed in both directions between agriculture and industrial and commercial firms via national taxation, local rates, investment by landowners in government stock as well as via the formal and informal capital markets. It is impossible to quantify all these flows but it appears that income from farming and the security of landed assets for raising loans was vital to the initiation and success of small-scale rural industries in particular. Very few larger commercial and industrial firms appear to have benefited greatly in net terms from landed wealth outside of canal and railway companies.

MERCHANT CAPITAL

The extent to which profits gained from trade were invested in wider business and commercial undertakings has long been debated. Merchants invested in landed estates but it is likely that this did not represent a significant leakage of capital from trading and manufacturing enterprise (Chapman 1992: 36). Many merchants in the trans-Atlantic trade were also heavily involved in West Indian sugar plantations (often by default through the extension of credit to planters) and there is no doubt that mercantile profits found their way into government bonds and stock. But much mercantile wealth appears to have been invested productively in industrial and commercial firms (Price 1989: 267–284; Chapman 1992: 37–8, 58–62, 118–20, 122–4).

From the perspective of a firm requiring funds merchants presented several possibilities; equity investment, direct loans, a partnership or the extension of credit. The majority of investors in early joint stock companies appear to have been merchants, especially City merchants. In the Bank of England, the East India Company and in South Sea shares Dutch merchants and investors were more important than British before the later eighteenth century. In the growing trades of insurance broking and underwriting, shareholders were again predominantly merchants. In 1780 over 60 per cent of directorships in the Sun, Royal Exchange and London Assurance Companies were merchants. Only the Phoenix was dominated by manufacturers (Dickson 1967: 302; Chapman 1992: 36). Merchants also commonly invested in industrial partnerships and shareholdings especially where capital requirements for setting up centralized and mechanized industry were beyond the means of workshop and artisan concerns. They were thus less commonly involved in the Yorkshire woollen mill industry than in the worsted sector (Wilson 1971: 230–6; Hudson 1986: 261). Manchester merchants and Yorkshire woolstaplers involved themselves in textile mills and London merchants underpinned the calico printing industry both in London and during its transfer to the northwest. In Glasgow in the eighteenth century, tobacco merchants appear to have been the prime movers in the growth of an industrial economy, investing in textile factories, tanneries, iron works, soap works and sugar refining. More than half of Glasgow merchants in the American trades had at least one partnership in manufacturing or extractive industry (Devine 1975: 34–5, 46–7). The South Wales and Derbyshire iron industries were largely generated and financed by mercantile capital as there was little indigenous industry or capital from land or manufacturing in these areas (Evans 1989: 208–10; Chapman 1992: 39). Merchant investment was also important in canal and later in railway investment. The bulk of canal capital was raised from merchants, much attracted by the need to ensure steady supplies of the goods in which they dealt (Ward 1974). Other transport investment was in equity. In the railway mania of the 1840s speculation in rail shares was responsible for bringing several merchanting firms to grief and preventing them from honouring their long-dated bills (Chapman 1992: 103).

The emergence of merchant manufacturers in the industrial regions of the Industrial Revolution was a general trend. Manufacturers extended into merchanting and merchants extended their financial and entrepreneurial interests backwards into manufacturing. Some of the biggest concerns such as the Drinkwaters, Dales, Gregs, Fosters, Salts and Gotts in textiles built up integrated concerns with capital merged in combinations of transport, banking, mining and estate development as well as the importing of raw materials, factory building and exporting. But as industrial regions established themselves and as marketing and credit conditions changed, economies of specialization tended to reassert themselves. After the difficult years of the Napoleonic Wars and especially after the commercial crisis of 1825–6, a new breed of specialist rose to take the place of older forms of overseas merchant enterprise which were dying out through failures and retirements. Accepting houses rose to dominate the overseas commercial activities of the major ports of London and Liverpool by the 1830s and 1840s. Much of their business involved endorsing bills of exchange signed by their clients. They specialized in the finance of particular branches of trade and were less involved in direct investment in industry than their forebears. Most of the merchants of major industrial centres such as Manchester, Birmingham, Sheffield came to depend on accepting houses for the bulk of export finance. The accepting houses advanced up to two-thirds of the invoice to their clients for three to four months for sales in North America and for twelve months on sales to the Far East. This economized on the working capital of manufacturing firms and manufacturing generally became less involved with direct foreign trading by the second quarter of the nineteenth century (Hudson 1986: 170−81; Chapman 1992: 51−78).

Some merchant−manufacturers did continue direct trading after the 1820s in order to offload their stocks and to keep heavy fixed capital working during depressions. They had to trade further afield in South America and the Orient as American and European merchants were increasing their hold over the trade of British manufactures in more established overseas markets. This placed severe liquidity difficulties on firms and caused bankruptcies. Robert Gardner of Manchester became bankrupt in the 1847 crisis with debts of £100,000 but his assets were worth nearly £350,000, mostly in goods shipped to Brazil and the United States. Many manufacturers (in less spectacular style) came to grief because of such overextension of credit in overseas trade in the first half of the nineteenth century. As a self-made man (starting up in 1810) Gardner had neither the wider family resources nor sufficient creditworthiness to see him through the crises. The Bank of England suggested that he was a

> wild speculative man, dogmatical in all his opinions and views, and not easily guided . . . he is always borrowing money and he conceives the only use of a banker is to lend money.
>
> (quoted by Chapman 1992: 102)

Credit which merchants and middlemen created for each other and for manufacturers was vital in keeping firms afloat. Wholesalers were important in the credit supply to manufacturers and to inland and export merchants. Six to eight months credit was common in the inland trade and twelve to eighteen months for overseas ventures (Price 1989: 273−4). The extension of credit on raw material purchases before the 1820s and 1830s was usually substantial and in some sectors was sufficient to cover the full period of manufacture and sale of goods. Inland merchants buying from manufacturers bought on short credit or for cash so that the net book credit position for manufacturers not involved in direct trade themselves was often positive before the Napoleonic War period (Hudson 1986: 182−207; Price 1989: 274). There were important exceptions to this pattern, however, which testify to the complexity of eighteenth-century credit arrangements between manufacturers and their clients. In the pottery sector, for example, the producers themselves extended the bulk of the credit upon which the extensive distribution network depended (Weatherill 1982: 252).

Thus merchant capital was very important in the finance of firms in all sectors from mining to textile manufacture, transport and insurance. Direct investment was common in most sectors although after the 1820s merchanting was becoming more specialized in overseas trade. By the 1830s and 1840s specialized acceptance houses began to dominate external trade but commonly advanced on invoices to manufacturers and inland middlemen for considerable periods as we have seen. Thus, as earlier, merchant capital remained particularly important in creating the conditions for manufacturing expansion by the provision of credit in the trade in raw materials and finished goods. By the 1830s and 1840s, however, open or book credit was generally contracting from six to twelve months in many trades down to three to four months and the provision of working capital for all types of firms was becoming increasingly dependent upon accommodation provided by the banking sector.

BANKS AND INDUSTRIAL FINANCE

Banks have always been regarded as playing an important role in the financing of industrial and commercial ventures (Pressnell 1956: 322–43, 356–65). Historians have concentrated on their function in providing credit and short-term working capital but more recent research has emphasized that banks were also important in the provision of longer term finance which could be used to extend fixed capital in industry and trade (Collins and Hudson 1979: 67–79; Hudson 1986: 218–34). Most bank credit extended to industry came via their role in discounting bills of exchange, but rediscounting further extended the length of credit which a bank's clients might receive and in addition most bank customers were allowed overdraft and short-term loan facilities. In the trade oscillations of the late eighteenth and early nineteenth centuries, short-term loans frequently became longer term by default and banks often became rather unwilling long-term investors in commerce and industry to prevent their clients from going to the wall.

The private banks which proliferated from the second half of the eighteenth century were founded by firms already well established in the major branches of commerce and manufacture in each locality. They commonly extended overdraft and loan facilities to their own partners as well as to a wider circle of trusted family and business contacts. Bank accounts were at first rarely separated from the accounts of firms as a whole; thus the opportunity arose for the strategic transfer of funds between banking and other business activity. The Bros Swaine and Company of Halifax, bankers from 1779, were simultaneously engaged in worsted manufacture and trade, owning three large mills by the early nineteenth century. At the time of their bankruptcy petition in 1807, only 1.7 per cent of their total assets were held in London as a cash reserve; a large proportion of the remaining £523,000 (excluding mills and estates worth £90,000) was employed in the locality, half in drafts of the textile firm W.S. and J. Crossley (Hudson 1986: 220). Private banks generally agreed overdraft limits and the deposit of collateral with their clients when an account was opened. In 1809 Rawsons Rhodes and Briggs listed securities valued between £1,000 and £15,000 on eleven debtor accounts covering unspecified overdrafts. Five years later, seven of the eleven accounts still owed amounts between £1,711 and £3,403; about a third of these debtors were local firms involved, like Rawsons, in wool textile manufacture. Hartley and Company, cotton warp manufacturers, owed the bank £2,400 in 1819 on security of the cotton mill and contents; James Hartley was a partner in the bank. The same firm was heavily tied up with loans to woollen mills which suffered in the crisis of 1815. Sums of several thousand pounds had for example been extended to James Moore and Sons of Brockwell. Their bankruptcy resulted in the bank having rights to the mill, estates and goods in Halifax, New York and London and in shipment to the value of £14,700 which took two years to redeem. Similarly Wentworth, Chaloner and Rishworth, the Wakefield bank which collapsed in 1825, owned (largely by default) much commercial and industrial property including four textile mills. They had extended considerable sums to industrial concerns; four alone owed £183,700 in 1825 and two of these belonged to the banking firm itself (Hudson 1986: 221).

More conservative and stable private banks of West Yorkshire yield similar, if not such extreme, evidence of longer term involvement in other businesses. Beckett and Company of Leeds, Leatham Tew and Company of Wakefield and Benjamin Wilson and Son of Mirfield and Dewsbury all lent up to and over agreed overdraft limits to a variety of trading and manufacturing concerns. Loans remained outstanding for several years, most secured by a variety of personal bonds, life policies, mortgages and deed deposits. In 1832 Wilson's documented the overdraft limits on 216 accounts which varied from £50 to £5,000. Leatham and Company had over a hundred overdrafts on their books in 1837 totalling £153,758 (Hudson 1986: 223). Beckett's generally advanced money to merchants and manufacturers . . . to manufacturing firms who keep their accounts with us and consequently they are often for a long time owing us money. . . .

(Report from the Committee on Renewing the Bank of England Charter, 1831–2 (722) VI, QQ 1238–1436)

Beckett was 'not in the habit of refusing advances' to anyone in Leeds who came to him. Sometimes the loan was for a fixed period but most were on current account with the repayment period left open (Hudson 1986: 222). The practice of private banks in other industrial and commercial regions appears to have been similar to that of Yorkshire although much research remains to be done, particularly on London (Pressnell 1956: 322–43; Collins 1991: 30).

Loans and assessment of the creditworthiness of clients reflected the business involvement of proprietors of private banks and their local knowledge. Similar policies were followed by the expanding numbers of joint-stock banks in the industrial regions but these were generally able to mobilize greater funds. As was the case with private banks, lending depended on the extent of resources from proprietors' capital, deposits and notes, and lines of credit with the rest of the money market and it was always influenced by the competing demands for liquidity and profit. In the highly competitive atmosphere of banking expansion in the 1830s and 1840s, banks appear to have been tempted into heavy lending. In many cases the value of loans and overdrafts by banks was greater than the banks' assets held in bills of exchange. The deeds of settlement of most banks emphasized their willingness to lend either upon open account or upon real and personal security, bills of exchange, promissory notes, letters of credit, or the deposit of deeds or mortgages, goods, wares, merchandise, bills of lading, delivery orders, life assurance policies and various bonds and shares (Collins and Hudson 1979: 73).

It was common to allow unsecured overdrafts, particularly for seasonal credit needs of up to 10 per cent of the turnover on accounts. Loans and extended overdrafts were granted to retailers, wholesalers, merchants and industrialists. In West Yorkshire manufacturers and merchants relied heavily on banks. Average debts to banks of a group of Yorkshire bankrupts in the period 1839–47 ranged from over £80,000 in the case of cloth and yarn merchants to £49,000 in the case of worsted spinners and to just over £1,000 on average for small-scale clothiers (Hudson 1986: 233). The majority of loans in Yorkshire appear to have been secured by mortgages upon urban and industrial real estate whereas loans to merchants on the security of merchandise or claims to ships were common in Liverpool. The Liverpool Union Bank held mortgages on the *Reliance* and the *Briton* against a loan of £5,000 to William Sharp, merchant and shipowner, and in 1844 held mortgages on five vessels valued at £10,000 to Cannon Miller and Company, merchants (Collins and Hudson 1979: 77).

Much short-term credit was given to clients via the banks' business in discounting bills of exchange. Often bill discounts for customers were renewed when the bills matured and sometimes this was done explicitly to finance loans over a longer period. The bulk of bank discount was straightforward, however, the banks being pivotal in oiling the wheels of commerce and facilitating the flow of funds between provincial and London money markets by the discount of foreign bills of exchange in particular. Slave traders' ships from Liverpool, for example, generally returned from the West Indies with bills which were presented in London to a small number of West India houses who took final responsibility. Foreign bills from Europe and elsewhere commonly went to London for payment. In this manner funds were drawn north from the capital to the industrial regions where they underpinned the expansion of trade and productive capacity (Anderson 1977: 59–61, 77; Black 1989: 377; Hudson 1992: 198–9). The ability of provincial banks to provide credit via discounting always depended upon their links with the rest of the money market and particularly with London and the buoyancy of these links was increasingly affected by the Bank of England's discounting policy (Pressnell 1956: 75–125, 401–40; Collins 1988a; 1988b: 25–9; Black 1989: 377–81; Neal 1993).

To gain bank finance it was important to have a trusted and respectable position in local trade, to have some form of collateral security and or to be a partner or shareholder as well as a customer of a banking concern. Firms who could gain access to this source of credit and loans had more opportunity to prosper. They could soak up the available credit in periods of expansion although overextension was always a danger, particularly at the downturn of trade cycles. In depressions creditors, including banks, could be forced to contract their credit or call in loans resulting in waves of bankruptcies. Banks generally regarded this action as a last resort, however: it was in their interests to keep clients afloat if at all possible to avoid heavy losses and many firms may have been assisted through commercial crises by contracyclical investment on the part of their bank (Collins 1988b). Firms, particularly manufacturing concerns, who were left out of this network of banking and business finance, whilst perhaps avoiding the worst excesses of speculation in trading, faced major problems particularly in the 1830s and 1840s when open credit practices were changing in favour of shorter credits and when it became more essential than in the past to have access to banking credit.

PLOUGHED BACK PROFITS

'Industrial capital has been its own chief progenitor' wrote Ashton in 1948 (Ashton 1948: 97) and all accounts of the finance of manufacturing and other businesses during industrialization place stress on the role of ploughed back profits in the process of accumulation. Usually this has been related to the peculiarly thrifty and ascetic nature of entrepreneurs. But the mechanism of profit accumulation and reinvestment and how this changed over time in relation to changing entry thresholds and to the life cycles of firms and businessmen has seldom been addressed. Where these have been studied it appears that although ploughback was important it was rarely the dominant source of capital investment particularly during periods of major expansion of capacity which called for a sudden injection of larger amounts of finance. It was also more important in the early years of a firm when retention of profits was a matter of how little to draw rather than how much to leave in: a firm had to build up a name for itself in trade and develop a reputation for stability before it could call upon any extensive credit or capital from external sources. The Broadbent brothers started in the woollen industry in 1825 with £4,500 which their father gave them and a further £6,000 which he loaned at interest. Until 1832 interest payments were delayed and the brothers themselves made no withdrawals. Fosters of Black Dyke Mills Queensbury made few withdrawals over £1,000 (above interest and rent charges) in the 1840s, following the building of the mill, but in the 1850s withdrawals rapidly increased, reaching a peak of over £130,000 in 1859–60 (Hudson 1986: 245–53).

Once a firm and its partners became firmly established commercially and financially it was no longer imprudent to make larger withdrawals. Sometimes these withdrawals were related to marriage or retirement in the business family which could alter the net worth of concerns quite radically (Rose 1986: 44–6; Davidoff and Hall 1987: 198–228). Often, as firms and families prospered, conspicuous consumption was a reason for greater withdrawals. A fine house, an art collection and a well stocked wine cellar were badges of status for business families demonstrating their prosperity and creditworthiness as well as wealth (Hudson 1986: 251). The transfer of wealth from business enterprise to community development, philanthropic and civic endeavour was also common. Analysis of investment by Manchester cotton merchants in insurance in the 1820s suggests that it cannot be explained by short-term financial or commercial considerations but as

> part of a broader attempt to create a system of interlocking services by an urban oligarchy seeking both to improve the economic infrastructure of their region and to consolidate the economic and political power of their group.
>
> (Pearson 1991: 380)

By the 1830s and 1840s the search for alternative and more stable investment opportunities may have been increasingly important in tempting profits away from reinvestment in industry and commerce. Foreign and domestic railways shares and overseas government stocks appeared commonly in the portfolios of the more substantial Yorkshire manufacturers in particular (Hudson 1986: 251–2, 267–88).

Established concerns could also draw more readily on external sources of capital and credit from banks and suppliers and did not have to rely as heavily as newcomers on internal sources. Ploughback did remain important, however. In periods of contraction of external credit in the downturn of trade cycles, firms were often thrown back on their own devices and the maintenance of profitability for reinvestment became vital. Much depended on an entrepreneur's ability to juggle with costs, prices and the credit matrix. Study of the Yorkshire wool textile manufacturing industry in the second quarter of the nineteenth century has shown a high degree of association between profits, export performance and raw wool prices. At the same time wages, the most important single cost of production and by far the most flexible, appear to have been squeezed, during the crises of the 1830s and 1840s, by the use of truck, long delays and payment in kind. In the Lancashire cotton industry, in Yorkshire and elsewhere workers were often paid in coal, vegetables or substandard cloth which had to be mended before it was sold. Abuses of the truck system were widespread (Report from the Select Committee on the Payment of Wages 1842 (471) IX; Shapiro 1967: 118–19, 141–2, 219–20; Hudson 1986: 235–55).

CONCLUSION

The British economy of the eighteenth and early nineteenth centuries was not short of capital but manufacturing and commerce was expanding most rapidly away (socially and geographically) from the main concentrations of landed, rentier and mercantile wealth, in the industrial and exporting regions of the provinces. Family based partnerships were the prevalent form of business enterprise and few had direct access to metropolitan or landed finance. They had to rely heavily on internal resources and upon the formal and informal networks which arose in the industrial regions to meet the peculiar and specific capital and credit needs of the dominant patterns of local industry and trade. The bill system had reached a high level of sophistication in Lancashire by the later eighteenth century as had the activities of attorneys in arranging longer term transfers of funds (Ashton 1954; Anderson 1969). The land mortgage market in West Yorkshire and the leasing and investment policies of some West Riding landowners furnish other examples of the regional response to specific regional needs. Where firms could take advantage of well developed local capital markets and benefit from a favourable credit matrix and a ready capital supply, commercial opportunity expanded for both large- and small-scale concerns. The success of Liverpool slave traders, for example, was predicated upon their ability to organize voyages into shares, accept long credits from wholesalers, utilize the regional and intraregional bill discount arrangements to the full, and insist on immediate remittances for slave sales (Price 1991: 293–339).

Generalizing on the basis of the small number of empirical studies of regions and sectors is difficult as there appear to have been a great variety of localized and sector-specific credit arrangements, financial institutions and practices. With this warning in view there are some points which can be suggested about the financial experiences of different sorts of concerns in different periods.

In the eighteenth century, initial capital in the generally small-scale firms came from family and personal connections aided by the subsidies created by landholding and farming and by a credit environment in most sectors which could be entered relatively easily provided one maintained a sober, respectable and creditworthy status in the locality. Bank and mercantile connections helped in securing the extended financial requirements required by larger concerns. On the whole this structure encouraged the extension of industry and trading on the part of small firms with low capitalization.

The economic circumstances of the last three decades of the eighteenth century and into the nineteenth century placed new demands on firms in their search for finances. The gradual concentration of fixed capital, particularly in the textile sector, and a more integrated structure of external credit provision introduced greater vulnerability to fluctuations and crises (Hoppit 1986: 55–8). And credit became stretched in the competitive search for markets in the difficult years of the Napoleonic Wars, further adding to the financial problems of firms. Many concerns came to grief in these years because of overextension of credit and liquidity problems. Some historians argue that wartime borrowing by the State also crowded-out (or was at the expense of) civilian investment. Interest rates rose and there were signs of a failure in the capital market (Williamson 1984; Black and Gilmore 1990; cf. Heim and Mirowski 1987). But a significant proportion of public funds came from abroad or from increasing the money supply. And nearly 60 per cent of the additional finance raised to prosecute the War between 1793 and 1814 came from regressive taxation, not borrowing: it was at the expense of consumers and not diverted from potential private investors. Government finance during the Napoleonic Wars is thus unlikely to have been the *prime* cause of rising interest rates or a slowing in the pace of economic growth. Furthermore, the marketing and resale of government bonds during and after the Wars encouraged the development and improved efficiency of institutional arrangements throughout the money market (O'Brien 1989: 347–50).

The pattern of financing firms which emerged after the Wars and in the second quarter of the nineteenth century was different. Regional and inter-regional capital markets were served by a more sophisticated array of institutions. Industrial regions had further developed their specialized patterns of manufacture and trading and their vital links with metropolitan capital. The easy and long open credits, which had kept entry thresholds low in many sectors and had underpinned the survival of a multitude of small firms in manufacturing in particular, declined. Banks multiplied to provide a highly competitive and hence ready source of credit and loans bolstered by their agency networks and links with the London money market, the Bank of England and its regional branches. Acceptance houses rose to dominate and financially underpin external trade and its finance. The opportunities were there in financial terms for the extension and growing capitalization of firms but the structure was unstable: liable to credit-driven speculative crises, periodic overstocking of markets and waves of bankruptcies which weeded out sound as well as unsound concerns. Many firms had a distinct cohort experience of these charges; some for example found it easy to start out in boom conditions only to be faced by extinction in the next crisis. Much depended upon the timing of fluctuations relative to points of stress in the life cycle of firms and business families. The only enduring key to stability and longer term survival was to be able to fall back upon internal and familial resources in crises, to foster close links with banks, to avoid the temptation of easy profits through speculations and to maintain a respectable status with one's peers in the local business community.

BIBLIOGRAPHY

Alexander, D. (1970) *Retailing in the Industrial Revolution*, London: Athlone.

Anderson, B.L. (1969) 'The attorney and the early capital market in Lancashire', in J.R. Harris (ed.) *Liverpool and Merseyside. Essays in the Economic and Social History of the Port and its Hinterland*, London: Frank Cass; reprinted in Crouzet, F. (1972) *Capital Formation in the Industrial Revolution*, London: Macmillan.

—— (1977) 'The Lancashire bill system and its Liverpool practitioners: the case of a slave merchant', in W.H. Chaloner (ed.) *Trade and Transport: Essays in Honour of T.S. Willan*, Manchester: Manchester University Press, 59–97.

Ashton, T.S. (1948) *The Industrial Revolution, 1760–1830*, Oxford: Oxford University Press.

—— (1954) 'The bill of exchange and private banks in Lancashire, 1790–1830', in T.S. Ashton and R.S. Sayers (eds) *Papers in English Monetary History*, Oxford: Oxford University Press.

Beckett, J.V. (1977) 'The eighteenth-century origins of the factory system: a case study from the 1740s', *Business History* 19: 55–67.

Berg, M. (1993) 'Smaller producer capitalism in eighteenth century England', *Business History* 35: 17–39.

Black, I. (1989) 'Geography, political economy and the circulation of finance capital in early industrial England', *Journal of Historical Geography* 15(4): 366–84.

Black, R.A. and Gilmore, C.G. (1990) 'Crowding out during Britain's industrial revolution', *Journal of Economic History* 47: 109–31.

Buchanan, B.J. (1986) 'Aspects of capital formation: some insights from north Somerset, 1750–1830', *Southern History* 8: 73–93.

Chapman, S. (1992) *Merchant Enterprise in Britain from the Industrial Revolution to World War I*, Cambridge: Cambridge University Press.

Collins, M. (1988a) *Money and Banking in the UK: a History*, London: Croom Helm.

—— (1988b) 'English banks and business cycles, 1848–80', in P. Cottrell and D.E. Moggridge (eds) *Money and Power: Essays in Honour of L.S. Pressnell*, Basingstoke: Macmillan.

—— (1991) *Banks and Industrial Finance in Britain 1800–1939*, London: Macmillan.

Collins, M. and Hudson, P. (1979) 'Provincial bank lending; Yorkshire and Merseyside, 1826–60', *Bulletin of Economic Research* 31: 69–79.

Crafts, N.F.R. (1985) *British Economic Growth during the Industrial Revolution*, Oxford: Oxford University Press.

Crouzet, F. (1972) *Capital Formation in the Industrial Revolution*, London: Macmillan.

—— (1985) *The First Industrialists*, Cambridge: Cambridge University Press.

Davidoff, L. and Hall, C. (1987) *Family Fortunes: Men and Women of the English Middle Class, 1780–1850*, London: Hutchinson.

Devine, T.M. (1975) *The Tobacco Lords. A Study of the Tobacco Merchants of Glasgow and their Trading Activities c.1740–90*, Edinburgh: John Donald.

Dickson, P.G.M. (1960) *The Sun Fire Insurance Office, 1710–1960*, London: Oxford University Press.

—— (1967) *The Financial Revolution*, London: Macmillan.

Evans, N. (1989) 'Two paths to economic development: Wales and the north East of England', in P. Hudson (ed.) *Regions and Industries: a Perspective on the Industrial Revolution in Britain*, Cambridge: Cambridge University Press, 201–27.

Feinstein, C.H. (1978) 'Capital formation in Great Britain', in P. Mathias and M.M. Postan (eds) *Cambridge Economic History of Europe*, vol. VII, Part 1, *The Industrial Economies: Capital, Labour and Enterprise*, Cambridge: Cambridge University Press.

Feinstein, C.H. and Pollard, S. (eds) (1988) *Studies in Capital Formation in the United Kingdom 1750–1920*, Oxford: Clarendon Press.

Fleischman, R.K. and Tyson, T.N. (1993) 'Cost accounting during the industrial revolution: the present state of historical knowledge', *Economic History Review* 56: 503–17.

Gatrell, V.A.C. (1977) 'Labour, power and the size of firms in Lancashire cotton in the second quarter of the nineteenth century', *Economic History Review* 30(1): 95–139.

Heaton, H. (1937) 'Financing the industrial revolution', *Bulletin of the Business History Society* II: 1; reprinted in Crouzet, F. (1972) *Capital Formation in the Industrial Revolution*, London: Macmillan, 84–93.

Heim, C.E. and Mirowski, P. (1987) 'Interest rates and crowding out during Britain's industrial revolution', *Journal of Economic History*, 47: 117–39.

Hey, D. (1972) *The Rural Metalworkers of the Sheffield Region*, Leicester: Leicester University Press.

Honeyman, K. (1982) *Origins of Enterprise*, Manchester: Manchester University Press.

Hoppit, J. (1986) 'Financial crises in eighteenth century England', *Economic History Review* 39: 39–58.

—— (1987) *Risk and Failure in English Business*, Cambridge: Cambridge University Press.

Hudson, P. (1977) 'Some aspects of accounting development in the West Riding textile industry', *Accounting History* 2: 4–22.

—— (1986) *The Genesis of Industrial Capital*, Cambridge: Cambridge University Press.

—— (1989) *Regions and Industries: a Perspective on the Industrial Revolution in Britain*, Cambridge: Cambridge University Press.

—— (1992) *The Industrial Revolution*, London: Edward Arnold.

Jenkins, D.T. (1975) *The West Riding Wool Textile Industry 1770–1835. A Study in Fixed Capital Formation*, Edington: Pasold.

Jones, E.L. (ed.) (1967) *Agriculture and Economic Growth in England*, London: Macmillan.

Landes, D.S. (1969) *The Unbound Prometheus: Technological Change and*

Industrial Development in West Europe from 1750 to the Present, Cambridge: Cambridge University Press.

Lee, C.H. (1972) *A Cotton Enterprise, 1795–1840: a History of M'Connel and Kennedy, Fine Spinners*, Manchester: Manchester University Press.

Lewis, W.A. (1955) *The Theory of Economic Growth*, London: Allen & Unwin.

Mathias, P. (1952) 'Agriculture and the brewing and distilling industries in the eighteenth century', *Economic History Review* 5: 249–57.

—— (1989) 'Financing the industrial revolution', in P. Mathias and J.A. Davis (eds) *The First Industrial Revolution*, Oxford: Blackwell, 69–85.

Miles, M. (1981) 'The money market and the early industrial revolution: the evidence from West Riding attorneys, 1750–1800', *Business History* 23: 127–46.

Neal, L. (1994) 'The finance of business during the industrial revolution', in R. Floud and D.N. McKloskey (eds) *The Economic History of Great Britain since 1700*, 2nd edn, vol. 1, Cambridge: Cambridge University Press.

O'Brien, P.K. (1985) 'Agriculture and the home market for English industry', *English Historical Review* 344: 733–800.

—— (1989) 'The impact of the Revolutionary and Napoleonic Wars, 1793–1815 on the long run growth of the British economy', *Review of the Fernand Braudel Centre* 12: 335–95.

Pearson, R. (1991) 'Collective diversification: Manchester merchants and the cotton business in the early nineteenth century', *Business History Review* 65: 379–414.

Pollard, S. (1964) 'Fixed capital in the industrial revolution in Britain', *Journal of Economic History* 24: 299–314.

Pressnell, L.S. (1956) *Country Banking in the Industrial Revolution*, Oxford: Oxford University Press.

Price, J.M. (1989) 'What did merchants do? Reflections on British overseas trade, 1660–1790', *Journal of Economic History* 49: 267–84.

—— (1991) 'Credit in the slave trade and plantation economies', in B. Solow (ed.) *Slavery and the Rise of the Atlantic Slave System*, Cambridge: Cambridge University Press, 293–339.

Raybould, T. (1984) 'Aristocratic landowners and the industrial revolution; the Black country experience', *Midland History* 9: 59–86.

Richardson, P. (1989) 'The structure of capital during the industrial revolution', *Economic History Review* 42: 484–584.

Rimmer, W.G. (1960) *Marshalls of Leeds, Flax Spinners, 1788–1886*, Cambridge: Cambridge University Press.

Rose, M.B. (1986) *The Gregs of Quarry Bank Mill: the Rise and Decline of a Family Firm, 1750–1914*, Cambridge: Cambridge University Press.

Rostow, W.W. (1956) 'The take-off into self sustained growth', *Economic Journal* 66: 32–51.

Rowlands, M.B. (1975) *Masters and Men in the Midlands Metalware Trades before the Industrial Revolution*, Manchester: Manchester University Press.

Shapiro, S. (1967) *Capital and the Cotton Industry in the Industrial Revolution*, Ithaca, NY: Cornell University Press.

Short, B. (1989) 'The deindustrialisation process: a case study of the Weald, 1600–1800', in P. Hudson (ed.) *Regions and Industries: a Perspective on the Industrial Revolution in Britain*, Cambridge: Cambridge University Press, 156–74.

Sigsworth, E.M. (1958) *Black Dyke Mills: a History with Introductory Chapters on the Development of the Worsted Industry in the Nineteenth Century*, Liverpool: Liverpool University Press.

Walton, J. (1989) 'Proto-industrialisation and the first industrial revolution: the case of Lancashire', in P. Hudson (ed.) *Regions and Industries: a Perspective on the Industrial Revolution in Britain*, Cambridge: Cambridge University Press, 41–68.

Ward, J.T. (1974) *The Finance of Canal Building in Eighteenth Century England*, Oxford: Oxford University Press.

Ward, J.T. and Wilson, R.G. (1971) *Land and Industry: the Landed Estate and the Industrial Revolution*, Newton Abbot: David & Charles.

Weatherill, L. (1982) 'Capital and credit in the pottery industry before 1770', *Business History* 24: 243–58.

Westerfield, R.B. (1915) 'Middlemen in English business particularly before 1760', *Transactions of the Connecticut Academy of Arts and Sciences* 19: 111–445.

Williamson, J.G. (1984) 'Why was British economic growth so slow in the industrial revolution', *Journal of Economic History* 44: 687–712.

Wilson, R.G. (1971) *Gentleman Merchants: the Merchant Community in Leeds 1700–1830*, Manchester: Manchester University Press.

5 Big business before 1900

Maurice W. Kirby

INTRODUCTION

The notion of 'big business' conjures up images of Chandlerian corporate structures with their associated managerial hierarchies and vertically integrated production and distribution, more in keeping with the twentieth century than the eighteenth. However, the justification for a chapter with this heading for the period up to 1860 rests on the fact that even in the eighteenth century there existed business organizations which aspired to the status of large-scale enterprise, demarcated from other contemporary concerns by the size of their labour forces and capitalization and the extended nature of their commercial operations. This is not simply a matter of highlighting the activities of those firms which were unusually large by contemporary standards in industries such as ironmaking and coalmining. It is more a question of focusing attention on business and commercial endeavours which, even by the standards of later generations of firms, were notable for the sheer scale and scope, not to mention the complexity, of their organizational structures and trading relationships. This was 'big business' in its eighteenth-century context, as reflected in 'the great monied companies'. By 1720 several such organizations existed, with the Bank of England, the East India Company and the South Sea Company at the apex, and the Hudson's Bay and Royal African Companies occupying lesser positions in the hierarchy. Indeed, in that year the ranks of big business were swelled by the foundation of the London Assurance and the Royal Exchange Assurance as large-scale corporations embodying substantial concentrations of capital (Supple 1970: 68). Some of the early corporate enterprises were also distinctive in possessing relatively integrated structures in the sense that the outer boundaries of the firm were quite distinct and continued to be so throughout their independent existence. Elsewhere, however, one notable response to emergent problems of managerial co-ordination as the firm grew in size was to subcontract out certain activities to independent agents, thereby curtailing the extent of direct supervisory functions. The practice became widespread in the mining industry, broadly defined, during the course of the eighteenth century, but it also existed in textiles, ironmaking and insurance. Perhaps the best known examples of subcontracting were to be found in the emergent transport sector, notably in the case of canal companies. Eighteenth-century canals were both built and operated on the subcontract principle and their experience in this respect was to cast a shadow forwards into the nineteenth century. It is well known that the greater part of Britain's railway network, from its inception in the 1820s, was constructed by subcontractors operating on behalf of the sponsoring railway companies. There was one fundamental difference, however, between canal and railway companies with respect to managerial procedures. Whereas the former carried subcontracting into their operational phase, the railway companies, especially from the 1840s onwards, chose to internalize the great majority of managerial functions. In doing so they were obliged to establish sophisticated organizational procedures at the behest of a newly emergent class of professional salaried managers, differentiated by specialist function. In their contemporary setting the major trunk line companies which began to emerge after 1840 were truly giant enterprises, as indicated by the volume of their commercial transactions, the size of their workforces and their capital market valuations.

In concentrating attention on large-scale enterprise it should be emphasized that the chapter is concerned with untypical business structures. The title of a well known work by Professor J.D. Chambers, commenting on Britain's industrial achievements in the mid-nineteenth century, is indicative of the small-scale nature of the generality of firms (Chambers 1961). In the textile trades the factory system was well established by this time, but taking British industry as a whole Chambers was fully justified in choosing *The Workshop of the World* as his title, denoting the focus on the small unit of production and management. In the nineteenth century, the railway sector may have given birth to corporate management in its 'modern' form but all the evidence indicates that, until the 1920s at least, the corporate revolution encapsulated in the recruitment of professional salaried management was largely confined to this sector. In the following section the chapter comments on the nature and extent of large-scale enterprise in agriculture, manufacturing and mining. The second section examines the characteristics of the monied companies, paying particular attention to the Royal Exchange Assurance and the East India Company as exemplars of the type. The third section discusses subcontracting as a reaction to the problem of size, whilst the final section examines the emergence of professional management in the early railway sector and comments on its limited impact elsewhere in the nineteenth century.

LARGE-SCALE ENTERPRISE IN AGRICULTURE, MANUFACTURING AND MINING

In the early eighteenth century the largest manufacturing units, as indicated by capital and labour employed, were controlled by public authorities in the form of royal arsenals and naval dockyards. According to Defoe, writing in the early 1720s, the royal arsenal at Chatham possessed buildings which were 'the largest in dimension, and the most in number, that are anywhere to be seen in the world', whilst the associated docking facilities were 'all like the whole, monstrously great and extensive, and . . . not easily describ'd' (Defoe, cited in Ashton 1972: 113). In relation to other contemporary productive enterprises the defining feature of governmental establishments was that they did not have to demonstrate commercial success in a competitive environment. In this respect their nearest eighteenth-century equivalents were agricultural or landed estates, organizations which rarely competed against each other, whether for markets or for factors of production. Moreover, the point has been made that estate economies were 'as much a function of social status and social aspirations as of economic calculation' (Pollard 1968: 39). Political undertones were also present to the extent that controlling landlords had ready access to levers of power which could wholly offset the effects, for good or ill, of market forces. But despite the fact that 'the mainspring of the capitalist economy was missing' (Pollard 1968: 39), estate agents and stewards as managerial functionaries came closest in the eighteenth and early nineteenth centuries to developing codes of managerial practice enjoying wide currency. As Pollard has pointed out, whereas industrial managers in general in the period to 1830 had no access to anything approaching management textbooks, estate agents in need of guidance on such issues as keeping accounts and paying taxes and rates could consult a range of published guidebooks. It is also impossible not to be impressed by the extent to which the landed estate could give rise, on its own account, to large-scale industrial enterprise, especially in the coalmining regions of northern England and Scotland. Indeed, where landowners chose to exploit mineral deposits on their estates directly, rather than lease them out, it was not unusual for estate agents to act as mine managers, thus ensuring that the early organization and administration of substantial parts of the coal industry was based upon techniques devised originally for landed estates (Pollard 1968: 41–2). Good examples of this were to be found in the Duke of Bridgewater's Worsley estates, the Fitzwilliam estates in Yorkshire and the Whitehaven collieries of the Lowther estates. Perhaps the best known example of landowner involvement in coalmining is provided by the experience of several gentry families in northeast England. In 1726 the Montagu family of Wortley, the Liddells of Ravensworth and George Bowes of Gibside agreed 'to join some of their collieries and to enter into a friendship and partnership for the purchase or taking other collieries, and for winning and working of coals thereout, and to exchange benefits and kindnesses with each other, upon a lasting foundation' (Tomlinson 1967: 9). This family grouping, henceforth known as the Grand Allies, functioned as a partnership, bringing together capital for the purpose of joint-stock mining. By 1750 the Allies controlled, either as owners or lessors, sixteen of the twenty-seven seasale collieries south of the Tyne. Dominating the London coastal trade in coal, the Allies were also renowned for their policy of output regulation, buttressed by the acquisition of further wayleaves (rights of way) and leases 'for the sole purpose of denying them to competitors' (Flinn 1984: 41).

The growth of the coalmining industry was also stimulated by substantial investments on the part of ironmaking companies, especially in South Wales, Shropshire and Derbyshire, areas where vertically integrated concerns began to emerge during the course of the eighteenth century. Excellent examples are provided by the Coalbrookdale and Butterley iron companies in England and the Carron Ironworks combine in Scotland. The latter, founded in 1759–60, was originally capitalized at £12,000. In 1773 this was raised to £150,000, far higher than the £96,000 capital valuation of the Coalbrookdale company in 1798 (Campbell 1961). All three companies were large employers of labour, the Carron company employing 2,000 workers in 1792, Coalbrookdale more than 1,000 in 1800, and the Butterley company approximately 1,500 in 1825.

It has been said that businessmen needed to possess 'large horizons' in the iron industry (Mathias 1983: 113). Nowhere was this more true than in South Wales, where a favourable combination of raw materials, cheap leases and good transport facilities encouraged the development of 'giant concerns which for a time put the rest of the country in the shade' (Pollard 1968: 96). This was exemplified in the case of the Cyfarthfa, Dowlais, Penydaren and Plymouth Ironworks, all of them in the neighbourhood of Merthyr Tydfil. Dowlais, the largest iron making concern in the country, employed 5,000 workers by 1830 (inclusive of mining labour), a figure matched only by the Cyfarthfa works.

In focusing attention on large-scale enterprise it should be emphasized that, for the eighteenth century at least, 'The merchant, the putter out – and the farmer – remained the pivotal figures of most branches of production. . .; and as a corollary to this the domestic system, the cottage workshop or the small urban workshop remained the typical unit of employment for most workers' (Mathias 1983: 148). It is, of course, a truism that large-scale production is dependent upon large-scale markets serviced by efficient transport systems and cost-effective marketing networks (Supple 1977: 427). Although the latter half of the century witnessed substantial improvements in transport facilities which, in extending the market, provided an impetus towards increased scale, the fact remains that the relevant facilities were geographically uneven and populations sufficiently scattered to sustain the economic advantages of the small-scale entrepreneur. Where large-scale enterprise developed it can be safely assumed that special factors were at work, embracing economic, geographical and technological influences. Thus, access to economies of scale might be conferred by marketing opportunities in response to unusually large urban concentrations. In the eighteenth century it is significant that only London breweries were able to deploy large-scale operations at a time when transport costs for beer were prohibitive over anything more than short distances. Moreover, the dominant position of the northeast coal industry and the activities of the Grand Allies themselves were wholly dependent upon a localized system of waggonways giving excellent access to the Tyne and Wear shipping staiths for coastal shipment to the metropolitan market. Even there, however, the risks entailed by heavy investment in fixed facilities, compounded by the sheer uncertainty of mining operations, combined to encourage organization in restraint of trade. As for the technological influences encouraging large-scale enterprise these were most evident in their eighteenth-century context in the iron industry where relatively heavy fixed investments were dictated by indivisibilities in plant size and a minimum-efficient scale of production.

In terms of structural organization large-scale enterprise in mining and manufacturing embraced the full range of proprietary arrangements, from state ownership in the case of dockyards and arsenals to the joint stock form in coalmining. But large-scale enterprise in the eighteenth century was entirely consistent with single proprietorships in the guise of family firms or, in the case of mineral exploitation, aristocratic houses. In fact, the most common form of organization was the common law partnership which in unincorporated form rendered the Bubble Act of 1720 a dead letter. Designed to prevent the flotation of unauthorized joint stock companies, this legislation was effectively circumvented by the legal device of the trust operating within the framework of the law of equity. Unincorporated partnerships were thereby able to operate in a joint-stock mode with their continuity of existence secured, the right to have their property held on behalf of trustees, and the authority to issue transferable shares (Supple 1970: 54−61; DuBois 1971).

An excellent example of a large-scale partnership is provided by the Cyfarthfa Ironworks in which the capital was divided between William Crawshay senior (£100,000) and Benjamin Hall (£60,000). Interest on capital was calculated on an annual basis with the net surplus being divided between the partners in the proportions 5:3. A significant attraction of this kind of organization was that it enabled entrepreneurs to diversify their own investments and to tap passive sources of capital. Leading partners were thus able to take the predominant entrepreneurial and managerial roles. Nevertheless, the need for continuous management, and especially technical expertise, could encourage the recruitment of professional managers, as in the London brewery trade and in some branches of the iron industry. Indeed, it was not unusual in large-scale mining and ironmaking concerns for dynasties of managers to emerge well before 1800, and whilst by 1830 there was still 'hardly a managerial profession as such', the time had long passed in British industry where 'ambitious men could without qualms make a managerial career, with a partnership at the end of it, their target' (Pollard 1968: 186, 188).

CORPORATE ENTERPRISE: THE MONIED COMPANIES

Legalized joint-stock businesses endowed with corporate personality owed their existence to the grant of royal charters. Such concerns date back to the sixteenth century and in the period to 1700 they played a significant role in overseas trade, and also in mining and smelting. It was in the later seventeenth century that there was a marked upsurge in the rate of incorporation (Braudel 1982: 448−52). The Hudson's Bay Company was founded in 1670 and the Royal African Company in 1672. Most spectacular of all, however, were the establishment in 1694 of the Bank of England and in 1698 of the new East India

Company. The former, capitalized at £1.2 million, undertook to lend the equivalent sum to the State in return for exclusive banking privileges, whilst the East India Company was awarded special privileges in the trade with India in return for a loan of £1,662,000. It has been said that these monied companies brought into being 'business' in the modern conception of the term (Laslett 1971: 166). It is ironic, therefore, that it was one of their number – the South Sea Company, floated in 1711 – whose gross speculative excesses led to the Bubble Act of 1720 which was designed specifically to inhibit incorporation by requiring the promoters of joint stock companies to engage in the costly process of parliamentary authorization.

A significant feature of the large-scale incorporations after 1690 was their close link with the finances of government focusing on the growth of the national debt. The South Sea Company itself, capitalized at more than £9 million, was used to fund the government's floating debt and it was this aspect of their activities which produced the contemporary charge that the new monied companies were 'the pretended servants, but in many respects the real masters of every administration' (Bolingbroke, cited in Supple 1970: 4). In retrospect this was an unfair judgement in so far as it overestimated the companies' ownership of the national debt and also because it neglected their valid economic rationale and functions. However, as Professor Supple has commented,

> the judgement stripped of its political overtones, had grasped an important truth: the economic needs of private enterprise and the financial needs of government *had* produced a set of newly powerful institutions. At one extreme large-scale corporate organisations could not be disassociated from the new and interlocking patterns of finance and commerce which helped shape, even if yet they did not dominate, the economic life of the country. And the Stock Exchange, rooted in the necessities of corporate and public finance, now served as a link (not always a welcome one) between the vicissitudes of the capital market and the course of business in general.
> (Supple 1970: 4)

The context for this comment is provided by Supple's business history of the Royal Exchange Assurance (REA) founded by Royal Charter in the year of the Bubble Act as 'the pioneer marine insurance company'. As in the case of its immediate predecessors the new company, together with its sister corporation the London Assurance, were inaugurated in the context of government borrowing needs. Its corporate privileges were validated by a promise to pay £300,000 into the

Exchequer, but it too had vital economic functions to perform in relation to the expansion of foreign trade. In view of the fact that the founding of the REA 'marks an important stage not only in the development of insurance but in that of the business corporation and of the capital markets in Britain' (Supple 1970: 5) it is worthwhile examining the company's structure and organization.

In the first instance, there is the very fact of the corporate form, arguably unnecessary in view of the readily available and relatively simple process of establishing partnerships or syndicates. In marine insurance private underwriting was well established before 1700 in the context of a well developed market demand. But partnerships could prove unwieldy or unstable, and there was always the danger that their capital resources could prove inadequate. Corporations, however, had a well defined legal personality, reinforced by perpetual succession, and although this fact was of less relevance to the world of insurance than to overseas trading companies, they could also own substantial fixed assets as well as statutory and exclusive trading rights. In terms of its managerial structure the REA conformed closely with established practice in other monied companies. Thus management and policy making was the responsibility of the Court of Directors, twenty-four in number, and subject to re-election every three years. Voting rights and electoral eligibility were determined by the ownership of stock with an upper limit of four votes for each proprietor. Supple's account of the history of the REA in the eighteenth century provides ample evidence of the managerial role fulfilled by the directorate. Professional managers were noted for their absence until the nineteenth century, and as late as 1838 the REA employed 'less than fifty officials, clerks and messengers' (Supple 1970: 70), despite the expansion of its business to include life and fire insurance. The Court therefore consisted of 'working Directors' whose responsibilities extended even to the acceptance or rejection of 'routine proposals' for insurance via their membership of a substructure of Court Committees. The rationale for this active directorial role lay in the company's position within the eighteenth-century mercantile economy. As Supple points out,

> Deploying a very large capital, with its financial and commercial influence closely affecting a wide variety of other sorts of business, and even its purely underwriting work involving it directly and continuously in the business of overseas trade, the Corporation could only be effectively managed with an awareness of the larger setting within which its underwriting and its investments played their part.
> (Supple 1970: 45)

That 'larger setting' is exemplified in the relationship between the Court of Directors and the economic and social life of the City of London. Thus, during the course of the eighteenth century significant numbers of directors were directly involved in overseas trade, reflecting the REA's original commitment to marine insurance. The Levant trade was well represented, as was the West India trade. Some directors were even listed as 'Captains' in the service either of the East India Company or of Trinity House. An equally significant but smaller group of directors was also distinguished by its links with other monied companies in the City. Twelve REA directors were at some time members of the court of the Bank of England and six were on the board of the East India Company. The Royal African and Russia Companies were also well represented. Moreover, at least fifteen REA directors served as members of Parliament before 1800 and this, together with the fact that at least twenty directors were directly descended from Hugenot immigrants, can be taken as substantial evidence of the REA's enmeshment in London's cosmopolitan political and business life (Supple 1970: 76). Given the close relations between these groups it is unsurprising that commercial ties were reinforced by marital and kinship links, both of which gave rise to a strong dynastic element in the directorate. As Supple comments, 'It was almost as if a hereditary place was made available for particular families; and the explanation can only be that the relevant family firm stood in some special business relationship with the Royal Exchange Assurance' (Supple 1970: 79). In this respect the experience of the REA is entirely representative of other family based networks in British business life, from Jews to Quakers, where kinship links were of critical importance in sustaining commercial trust and confidence. It is this very fact of an interlocking mercantile elite – well represented also in the London Assurance Company and the Sun Fire Office – which provides the strongest possible contrast with the Phoenix Assurance Company, founded in the 1780s and destined to become Britain's leading insurer of industrial properties. In the period to 1870 the managing board of the Phoenix contained far more manufacturers and fewer directors with City connections, whether direct or indirect, than its contemporaries. Indeed, during the first twenty-five years of its existence the company was dominated by sugar refiners. The individuals involved may have disposed of impressive wealth holdings by the standards of industrialists in other trades, but they hardly ranked with the 'gilded capitalists' at the REA, the Sun and London Assurance. According to the company's most recent historian the large sugar houses of the 1780s and 1790s were on a par with 'extensive cotton mills and capacious iron works' in terms of capital values. But in comparison with 'cosmopolitan financiers or company nabobs' they were 'no more than men of middling weight seeking safe passage' (Trebilcock 1985: 36).

Despite significant differences in the composition of their managing boards, the REA and the Phoenix company shared one common feature in their structure and organization. Both companies made use of the agency system as a means of extending their activities beyond London. In embarking on the business of fire insurance, for example, the REA recruited 'shop-keepers, well-to-do artisans, merchants and professional men' as agents in a range of provincial centres (Supple 1970: 90). In 1758 these included Dublin, Liverpool, Newcastle, Bury St Edmunds, Manchester and Plymouth, by which time agents had also been authorized to undertake a limited amount of life business. Whilst the spread of an agency network was gradual for the REA before 1800, in the case of the Phoenix company two factors prompted a more rapid expansion, first the desire to capitalize on the limited non-metropolitan business of other companies, and second, a determination to take the decisive lead in industrial fire insurance. The latter factor in itself dictated the spread of activities to the industrial north. By 1821 the company possessed eighteen agencies in Yorkshire and thirteen in Lancashire with the two regions occupying first and second positions in a rank order of counties according to agency numbers (Trebilcock 1985: 81–90). For the REA the adoption of the agency system reflected the overwhelming dominance of London in its corporate affairs, whilst for the Phoenix it facilitated a relatively rapid and cost-effective means of commercial expansion. In both cases, however, its effect was to produce a dualistic corporate structure, combining tightly knit directorates with indistinct outer boundaries to the firm. In this respect there is a clear parallel with the practice of subcontracting which was emerging in contemporary industrial concerns and the transport sector (see below).

The earlier reference to nabobs is a direct reminder of the immense fortunes accumulated during the eighteenth century by a number of the overseas servants of the East India Company, notable as the largest by far of the early chartered trading corporations. Condemned by contemporary observers as the cause of a drain of England's national currency in response to the export of precious metals to the Orient, and by economic historians for its monopolistic trading practices, the company has received more favourable attention from business historians. K.N. Chaudhuri's work in particular (Chaudhuri 1978; 1981) has pointed to 'a complex world of entrepreneurship under conditions of business uncertainty in which sophisticated methods of economic forecasting were not uncommon' (Arkin 1981: 91), whilst other business historians have gone as far as to portray it as an 'analogue' to modern multidivisional and multinational corporations (Anderson *et al.* 1983; Carlos and Nicholas 1988). These recent analyses are complementary in that they focus attention on the East India Company's hierarchical management system whereby the London-based Court of Committees framed the commercial policy to be executed by the President and supporting Council in each of the Company's major trading areas. The third and subordinate tier of the organization was provided by outlying trading stations and local manufacturing establishments. For Chaudhuri this structure was an essential means of reducing uncertainty in an unpredictable and occasionally hostile trading environment. Indeed, it was the fact of uncertainty which encouraged the company to construct the 'semi-autonomous strongholds' in India which were to transform it during the course of the eighteenth century into a quasi-military organization with public administration rather than commerce as the company's *raison d'être*. Whilst Chaudhuri's analysis is based upon the concept of an input–output flow, with the London Court's control of shipping as the key operational variable, Carlos and Nicholas use modern transaction cost theory to validate their multinational perspective. Transaction costs arise whenever goods and services are traded in the market. There are costs, for example, in gaining commercial information and in negotiating and enforcing contracts, and the more extended the market in geographical terms the greater will be the resulting transaction costs (Coase 1937). In order to economize on these costs firms can adopt a strategy of internalization, that is, the supersession of market functions by hierarchical managerial co-ordination (Williamson 1981). It was precisely this strategy, according to Carlos and Nicholas, that the East India Company adopted by developing a subcommittee system staffed by salaried managers. It was thus the emergence of a recognizable managerial hierarchy which, in facilitating higher volumes and frequencies of transactions, propelled the growth of the company. The multinational analogy is carried further by Carlos and Nicholas in their reference to the East India Company's investment in overseas manufacturing facilities. Whilst the relevant factories fulfilled military and diplomatic functions, in economic terms they were an example of vertical integration designed to reduce transaction costs. As Carlos and Nicholas point out,

The factory acted as both a symbolic and physical bond, representing the [East India Company's] long-term commitment to a new
market as well as providing a building for holding inventories of
trade goods to supply the foreign market and to fulfil the yearly
shipments to Europe.

(Carlos and Nicholas 1988: 411)

Whilst transaction cost theory provides some revealing insights into
the structure and organization of the East India Company it is
arguable that Carlos and Nicholas have adopted an unduly narrow
interpretation of the company's activities. Wilkins, for example, has
suggested that the early chartered companies, rather than being
analogues to present-day multinational firms, were in reality anomalies, distinct from not only other contemporary enterprises but also
their twentieth-century counterparts (Wilkins 1986a: 488; 1986b: 82).
Modern multinational firms are integrated by means of the 'rapid
transmission of information between and among the associated companies in a grouping'. The resulting 'economies of speed' were denied
to chartered companies with the shipping factor in particular bristling
with uncertainties on account of a multitude of maritime hazards and
the vagaries of trade wind cycles. Moreover, in the case of the East
India Company it is equally valid to argue that its international
activities were propelled not so much by transaction cost considerations but by the search for monopoly rents, a view which receives
some credence from the political environment in which it operated. It
is salutary to remember that the later seventeenth and early eighteenth
centuries were a period of national rivalries focusing on England,
France and Holland. Translated into economic terms this was the
classic era of mercantilism, a view of the world which saw international trade as a zero-sum game and the amassing of bullion as a
critical factor in determining national power. It is instructive to note
that Thomas Mun, a leading contemporary advocate of mercantile
beliefs, was himself a director of the East India Company (Dunning *et
al.* 1986: 28). In conformity with Mun's beliefs, the company may
have had a monopoly of British trade, but the existence of the Dutch
East India Company and periodic interventions by French traders
suggests that internalization of the firm's activities was a reflection
not so much of transaction costs but of mercantilist-inspired colonial
rivalries (Braudel 1982: 444–7). In this setting the naval and military
activities of the East India Company are readily understandable as a
means of reducing commercial uncertainty induced by national power
political rivalries.

In claiming that the East India Company operated as a multidivisional organization Anderson, McCormack and Tollison have highlighted the difficulties of monitoring the behaviour of overseas managers as the most significant institutional impediment to the commercial success of the chartered companies. Whilst 'The Court of Directors made strategic decisions for the firm, including the establishment of long-term goals, administrative organisation, and capital allocation', responsibility for localized trading operations and investment lay with the individual division, or 'presidencies' (Anderson *et al*. 1983: 228). As noted already, however, the East India Company was denied access to economies of speed, a profound handicap for a multidivisional concern in that it prevented effective control of managerial behaviour. In view of the existence of asymmetrical information and uncertainty what was there to prevent the company's overseas employees from acting in their own self-interest as private traders to the detriment of overall profitability? One solution to this difficulty, adopted by the Hudson's Bay Company, was to pay its local managers high salaries, supplemented by generous gratuities and salary revisions. Thus, by increasing the opportunity cost of opportunistic behaviour the company felt justified in barring all private trade by its managers after 1672 (Carlos and Nicholas 1990: 862–3). Financial incentives, moreover, were buttressed by oaths of fidelity to the company, the requirement to put up bonds as tokens of good faith, and the rigorous searching of ships, baggage and letters. In the case of the East India Company an opposite strategy was adopted in that relatively low managerial salaries were complemented by the freedom to engage in private trade. Additional shipping space and trading capital were allocated to the company's Indian factories according to relative rates of return. Thus, as the volume of official trade expanded, so too did the opportunities for private transactions. Successful employees were rewarded with extra shipping space at the expense of laggards (Anderson *et al*. 1983: 228–9). This is not to suggest that these strategies were sufficient to eliminate all monitoring difficulties: the evidence available at present suggests that the Hudson's Bay Company achieved a greater degree of success, not least as a result of the creation of a company 'social structure' which rested on strong moral imperatives. But even in the case of the East India Company it would appear that monitoring and control problems were contained at least until the later 1750s from which time the company's commercial operations became increasingly subordinate to political functions based upon the levying of extortionate taxation.

What is striking about the experience of the chartered trading companies is that confronted by complex decisions over production, distribution and prices they devised hierarchical managerial structures which were far in advance of other contemporary business organizations. Anomalies they may have been, but in one notable respect they cast a long shadow forwards into the later nineteenth and twentieth centuries in laying the foundations for London's status as an international commodity market, a development exemplified in the tea auctions administered by the East India Company from the 1720s onwards (Chaudhuri 1978). This does not mean that firms possessing less ambitious structures and which did not adopt a strategy of internalization were lacking in entrepreneurial leadership and quality. As the following section indicates, internalization was not a universally valid imperative in the eighteenth and early nineteenth centuries. Almost by definition, the chartered trading companies, operating in a truly global environment, could set no organizational precedents for firms with a narrower market compass and a lower volume of market transactions.

SUBCONTRACTING AS AN ALTERNATIVE TO LARGE-SCALE DIRECT MANAGEMENT

If the East India Company was an early and distinctive example of the internalization of managerial functions the practice of subcontracting was its antithesis. During the eighteenth century a wide range of firms in different sectors of the economy resolved emerging managerial constraints on the scale and scope of their operations by subcontracting all or part of their functions. Subcontracting had precedents in the early modern economy and it could be justified even when the extent of a firm's operations was not a problem. Whatever its context, the rationale of subcontracting lay in the reduction of direct supervisory functions and also in the sharing of risks, capital and technical knowledge with the subcontractor. Where the latter was in receipt of a fixed price per unit the originating firm was relieved of a complicating element in its cost structure. Most importantly, in the early phases of industrialization, when work incentives for managers and workers alike could be uncertain, 'the great advantage of this system . . . was that it supplied a "self-acting stimulus", which dispensed with the necessity of incessant supervision of the managing foreman by the employer' (Taylor 1960: 216). The disadvantages of subcontracting lay in the maximizing of short-run returns, as when subcontracting in mines and quarries led to physical damage which preempted effective programmes of mineral exploitation. The coalmining industry provides one of the best examples of subcontracting in the eighteenth century. Pits were invariably sunk on behalf of the mine owner by subcontractors. In the operational phase, moreover, it was not unusual for miners to take on contracts to work as equals, although by the 1790s the butty system, whereby subcontracting miners employed labour on their own account, was widespread. Elsewhere, the 'delegation–subcontract method' was popular, as in the early coke blast furnace industry, and the textile and engineering industries. The Carron Iron Company, for example, 'sprouted subsidiaries which acted like subcontractors', a practice which was followed by the Coalbrookdale iron combine, the Furness ironmasters and the Midland glass industry (Pollard 1968: 54–5). In the manufacturing sector perhaps the best known example of subcontracting, replicating in some respects the butty system in mining, was to be found in cotton spinning. As Pollard explains,

> Here, the method was not . . . to let the mill as a whole to a substantial group of skilled workers nor yet to an entrepreneur but to put skilled spinners in charge of extensive machinery on the understanding that they paid and recruited their own child assistants, the 'scavengers' to clean the machines, and the 'piecers'.
>
> (Pollard 1968: 57)

Child employees were initially directly related to or known to the spinners, and it was not unusual for early factory masters to pay wages to family units. That the practice continued well into the nineteenth century is confirmed by the Factory Commission returns of 1833–4 covering approximately one-third of the total employment in British mills. Of 20,000 child workers investigated, approximately half were employed by other operatives, the remainder being direct employees of the firm. The survival of subcontracting into the factory era is *prima facie* evidence of the unwillingness or inability of factory masters to maintain labour discipline in their mills. As such, it was an acceptable interim solution to the problem of combining access to scale economies with only partial internalization of the managerial function.

The industry *par excellence* of subcontracting, notable for having retained the practice to this day, is civil engineering. In the eighteenth-century context it was exemplified in the case of canals, the great majority of which were built by subcontract labour. Most canal companies were corporate concerns with their identity confirmed by parliamentary statute. As joint-stock enterprises their outer boundaries were unusually indistinct in that, not only were they built by subcontractors, they also operated on the basis of independent carriers utilizing the toll-road principle, the carriers being, in effect, subcontractors. In the nineteenth century the transport sector in the guise of railways was to give birth to a new era of large-scale corporate management in British business, marked by substantial internalization of market functions facilitated by the recruitment of professional salaried managers. These developments, which were inaugurated in the 1840s, are the subject of the next section and in order to illustrate their significance the nature of railway enterprise at its inception in the 1820s and 1830s can be highlighted, in so far as it straddled the organizational divide between reliance on the market as the arbiter of resource allocation and internalization as the ultimate transaction-cost-reducing strategy.

The joint-stock pioneer of the public steam railway was the Stockton and Darlington Railway Company founded by Act of Parliament in 1821. In conformity with canal practice it was constructed on a subcontract basis, but in marked contrast with subsequent trunk line railway companies it persisted with subcontracting throughout its independent operational phase (Kirby 1993). The practice became less important in the company's administration after 1850, but at its peak in the mid-1830s subcontracts ranged from the comparatively trivial, such as the winding and maintenance of clocks, to the upkeep of the permanent way, locomotives and rolling stock, and haulage by locomotives and permanent engines. The extent of subcontracting was reflected in the company's managerial structure. Until the end of its independent existence in 1863 the Stockton and Darlington Company employed few individuals who could be described as salaried professional managers. Beyond the offices of company engineer, surveyor and secretary, the managerial hierarchy was virtually non-existent. Significantly, when the company appointed a civil engineer to its staff in 1842 his remit was to oversee the work of the permanent way subcontractors. That said, the few salaried officials employed were assisted in their task by members of the directorate, the more active of whom performed direct managerial functions in addition to determining the company's broader competitive strategy.

The Stockton and Darlington Railway Company occupies an unusual position in British business history. It was innovative and profitable and helped to propel regional economic growth in the maturing phase of Britain's industrialization. Yet in its managerial procedures it was antidiluvian, looking back to precedents set in the canal era of the eighteenth century. The question remains why the company persisted with subcontracting in the face of sustained expansion both in route mileage and traffic flows. One obvious reason is that it was cost effective. The directorate clearly thought so, as evidenced by the regular statements in the annual reports to shareholders drawing attention to reduced contract prices. It is one thing, however, to reduce the cost of a contract and quite another to secure a satisfactory standard of service. As indicated already, a potential weakness of sub-contracting as a response to the problem of size was that the elimina-tion of 'direct supervisory functions' rendered the originating company open to the maximizing of short-run returns on the part of the contractor. The records of the Stockton and Darlington Company indicate that lapses in subcontractors' standards did occur, but they were a rare occurrence and quickly rectified to the satisfaction of the directorate (Kirby 1993:109). Despite the expansion of its business the volume and range of commercial transactions handled by the com-pany was highly focused. The route network was geographically compact along the line of the Tees and upper Wear valleys and traffic flows were concentrated overwhelmingly on an interrelated group of minerals – coal, ironstone and limestone – supplied in quantity to a quite narrow range of heavy industrial customers. It was thus the limited compass of the company's activities which facilitated close internal surveillance of subcontractors' standards, thereby reducing the impetus towards internalization.

THE MANAGERIAL REVOLUTION OF THE NINETEENTH CENTURY: THE TRUNK LINE RAILWAY COMPANIES

In a number of industrializing countries in the nineteenth century rail-way networks bore the impress of centralized planning, the product in part of governmental interest in a form of transport with important strategic implications. In Britain, however, railway development was, from the outset, infused with the spirit of competitive private enter-prise. The inevitable result in a small island with localized transport requirements was the proliferation of small undertakings. Indeed, by the end of 1844, of the 104 railway companies then in existence, only eleven, accounting for more than half the total route mileage laid down, possessed lines in excess of fifty miles in length. As the system developed, the management of through traffic necessitated co-operation between companies and this was facilitated at a relatively early stage by the establishment of the London-based Railway Clearing House in 1842. Initially restricted to nine companies, by the end of the decade it embraced most of the larger undertakings then in existence. It is a point well taken that although the organization 'aimed at removing one of the penalties of dispersed control of rail-way operations [it] probably tended in practice to demonstrate some of the advantages which amalgamation would bring, and it is arguable that its very existence hastened the process for which it had been designed as an alternative' (Dyos and Aldcroft 1974: 38). In this context the movement towards large-scale combination which gathered momentum after 1844 becomes readily understandable as a rational response to the practical difficulties of railway operations.

In many ways the most impressive amalgamation scheme of the later 1840s was the formation in 1846 of the London and North Western Railway (LNWR) following the merger of the trunk line London and Birmingham and Grand Junction Railways. Five years later, the new concern was capitalized at more than £29 million, employed a workforce in excess of 12,000, and operated more than 800 miles of track. By contemporary and later standards the LNWR was a giant enterprise, bearing in mind that as late as 1905 only three manufacturing firms were capitalized in excess of £10 million. A concern as large as this was dependent for its success upon an effective managerial structure and in this respect the LNWR was one of a number of large-scale railway companies which recruited military men with administrative experience to senior managerial positions. Indeed the company's first and most influential general manager was Captain Mark Huish, the former chief executive of the Grand Junction Railway and one-time serving officer in the East India Company's Bengal Native Infantry. In a detailed study of the managerial structure of the LNWR Dr Gourvish has provided a graphic reminder of the organizational problems imposed by the sheer size of the amalgamated undertaking (Gourvish 1972). On a geographically extensive rail network carrying a variety of goods, including large numbers of passengers, the traffic management requirements were intricate to a degree. Methods had to be devised to keep track of rolling stock and to avoid jams and the accumulation of idle stock along the network. Such a large commercial operation, moreover, entailed more than rudimentary accounting procedures. With revenues collected on a daily basis from numerous ticket offices, as well as freight and passenger conductors, the system gave rise to large cash flows, the efficient handling of which was an art in itself. This aspect of the company's operations was matched in complexity by the interregional movement of traffic with all the difficulties that this entailed for the fixing of agreed rates for goods travelling across more than one railway system. Complicating matters even further was a company financial structure characterized by high fixed costs and mounting capital expenditures as the volume of traffic expanded. In the light of all these factors an undertaking the size of the LNWR required precise information about maintenance and operating costs, and this entailed some degree of sophistication in the collection of statistics, the recording of data and the transmission of information to company managers.

The managerial strategy adopted by the LNWR to cope with extensive commercial operations was to opt for a geographically divided structure but with strongly centralized overall control. Three divisions were created, Northern, North Eastern and Southern, each possessing its own secretary, superintendent, locomotive superintendent and goods manager. All of these senior company officials were responsible to Captain Huish as general manager. Huish in turn possessed his own managerial staff directly responsible to the London-based board of directors. As Gourvish reveals, Huish made effective use of this structure to implement new administrative and managerial procedures. His innovations included accounting methods which made appropriate allowances for depreciation and plant valuation, and extensive collection of operating statistics, thereby facilitating the continuous revision of long-run costs and an element of forward planning. The board of directors, meeting monthly, was presented with detailed information on costs, augmented where necessary by working papers from Huish and his senior managers, some of which in Huish's case represented path-breaking contributions to the theory and practice of railway management. Thus, the hallmarks of Huish's managerial regime were threefold: first the recruitment of professional salaried managers, differentiated by specialist function; second the collection and interpretation of operating statistics; and third the internalization of market functions in order to reduce transaction costs. The strategy of internalization was exemplified by the early policy of the LNWR in expanding to the point of self-sufficiency its own locomotive and rolling stock building capacity. The motives for this were the desire to monitor construction techniques and costs closely, to create a locomotive fleet attuned to the company's specific requirements, and to ensure security of supply at those times in the business cycle when private locomotive building establishments enjoyed full order books (Kirby 1988).

The management of the LNWR thus provides major points of contrast to the Stockton and Darlington Company. Subcontracting would never have been an appropriate strategy for the larger company: its route mileage was sixteen times as great and its daily managerial arrangements far more complex in view of a much higher volume of transactions and the concentration on a varied merchandise and passenger traffic. As the co-ordinator of activities at the centre and responsible for the LNWR's strategic direction, Huish 'approximates to the modern chief executive to an extent remarkable for a founder member of a new profession, a man merely on the threshold of a nascent science' (Gourvish 1972: 262). In Gourvish's considered judgement, therefore, it was the early trunk line railway companies, and the LNWR in particular, which 'made the first concerted attempt to solve the overriding problems of large-scale business, and developed important and possibly novel forms of business management' (Gourvish 1972: 265).

In a comparative setting the management of railway companies is of particular significance for business historians in that it is the railroad sector which pioneered the visible hand of professional managerial hierarchies in the United States after 1850, a movement which had enormous repercussions for managerial practice in American manufacturing industry before it was transmitted overseas during the course of the twentieth century (Chandler 1977: chs 3–6). However, there was no such 'Chandlerian effect' emanating from Britain's railway companies before 1914, despite the fact that the railway sector in general enjoyed a high profile in Victorian society, the product of sustained governmental interest in its operations, and reflected in persistent journalistic concern with the pricing policies of the larger companies. As Chapter 3 reveals, there were many factors which led to the longevity of family or personal capitalism in British business on the side both of demand and of supply. The fact remains that until the outbreak of the First World War railway management techniques were sector specific in Britain, in marked contrast to American experience. It is a telling point that in the Victorian and Edwardian periods very few firms in the manufacturing sector could match the high salaries paid to senior railway managers. Neither could they offer the kind of social prestige and rewards emanating from service on government commissions and committees of enquiry. Dr Gourvish's sample study of railway company chief executives reveals that in the late nineteenth century only 10 per cent of the total were connected with other industries as directors and even then there was a marked bias in favour of electricity supply and insurance companies (Gourvish 1973). Although such men were more likely to take an active than a passive view of their directoral responsibilities it seems unlikely that the small numbers involved could have had any real impact on managerial practice in non-rail sectors.

The fact that railway companies failed to precipitate a corporate revolution in British industry is superficially surprising in view of the changes to company law in England and Wales between 1844 and 1856. During this period the joint stock form and limited liability received general parliamentary sanction, thus permitting firms in the manufacturing sector to adopt corporate status at minimal expense. However, it is well known that although 'The way was open for the emergence of the corporate economy . . . few trod the path' (Payne 1988: 17). In the service sector banking was a notable exception (see Chapter 10) but elsewhere in manufacturing industry in general, the response was muted. The reasons are not far to seek. In the first instance, there was the phenomenon of the private company, legally unrecognized until the Companies Act of 1907. In the period from 1880 to 1914, 132,000 firms adopted limited liability with a majority combining the legal form with the control of ordinary share capital by partners and their families. Private registration thus preserved pre-existing managerial structures (Gourvish 1987: 24). Second, although the development of the stock market encouraged some firms in pursuit of scale economies in marketing and production to combine together for a public flotation, the overall numbers were small, even when augmented by the activities of company promoters in advertising the attractions of monopoly profits (Hannah 1983: 20). Third, where large-scale, even giant corporate enterprises were founded in the manufacturing sector, the effect of their distinctive organizational form was to place a significant institutional barrier in the way of American style corporate development. This was especially noticeable in the merger boom between 1898 and 1900 when as many as 650 firms with a combined value of £42 million were involved in 198 mergers. Prominent in this movement towards greater industrial concentration were the textile finishing trades. The Bradford Dyers' Association, for example, formed in 1898, combined twenty-one firms, the Calico Printers Association in 1899, forty-five firms, and the Bleachers Association in 1900, fifty-two firms. Although these were corporate enterprises of exceptionally large scale, they were in reality holding companies, or family firm federations. This is well illustrated in the case of the Calico Printers' Association, a firm which controlled over 80 per cent of the calico-printing industry with an original capital of £9,200,000 but which possessed a board of directors numbering eighty-four, eight of whom were managing directors (Payne 1967: 528). The main impetus for the formation of such federations was provided not by the desire to gain access to scale economies, but by the perceived necessity to achieve effective market regulation in the face of falling prices and profit margins, and where structural fragmenta-tion precluded the formation of effective trade associations. Thus, in relation to the themes pursued in Chapter 8 holding companies embraced both collusion and integration and as such they represented a fundamentally conservative response to heightened competitive pressures in the late Victorian economy. The holding company form does, indeed, provide critical insights into the delayed adoption of American style managerial hierarchies in British manufacturing industry. The perpetuation of family influence and control is an obvious factor and this was complemented by disinterest in vertical integration as a means of achieving high-throughput scale economies. Inter-country differences in the legal framework for business are also of relevance. In this respect, the American Sherman Anti-Trust Act of 1890, in outlawing cartels and in rendering the legal position of holding companies uncertain, imparted a powerful impetus towards the creation of 'large functionally departmentalised managerial enterprises' (Chandler 1976: 48). In Britain, however, the absence of such legislation permitted holding companies to thrive as evidenced by their proliferation beyond the textile trades to include metal manufacturing, armaments, chemicals and foodstuffs.

CONCLUSION

In focusing on big business in the period to 1900 this chapter has been concerned with islands of giantism within a generally disintegrated business structure. In the case of the chartered trading corporations of the seventeenth and eighteenth centuries and the trunk line railway companies it is apparent that their advanced managerial structures were effectually intelligent and pragmatic responses to their specific trading environments. It is possible to admire their innovatory capacities, their coherent responses to problems of large-scale management and their evident and successful results. But in their managerial procedures they set no precedents beyond their own spheres. In respect of the railway companies the Victorians themselves regarded them in an entirely different light to other business sectors, restricting their commercial freedom by legislation and establishing the Railway and Canal Commission as a judicial surveillance body. In 1912 the President of the Board of Trade in the then Liberal government even conceded the case for railway nationalization, thus confirming the railway companies' status as nascent public utilities. So too with the chartered companies, their organizational form and the geographical scope of their activities can be understood fully only in the context of contemporary international political rivalries rooted in mercantilist perceptions of national power. It is also clear that growth in firm size need not be accompanied by increased sophistication in managerial structures. The development of the agency system in insurance was one indication of this and it bore close resemblance to the practice of sub-contracting which penetrated even into the early railway era. At the very end of the period the proliferation of holding companies confirms the point that in the British context the adoption of corporate status could be precipitated by factors other than the desire to enhance business performance through the achievement of scale economies.

REFERENCES

Anderson, G.M., McCormack, R.E. and Tollison, R.D. (1983) 'The economic organisation of the English East India Company', *Journal of Economic Behaviour and Organisation* 4: 222–38.
Arkin, M. (1981) 'Entrepreneurship and the English East India Company', *Business History* 23: 91–5.
Ashton, T.S. (1972) *An Economic History of England: the 18th Century*, London: Methuen.
Braudel, F. (1982) *Civilization and Capitalism 15th–18th Century*, vol. II, *The Wheels of Commerce*, London: Collins.
Campbell, R.H. (1961) *Carron Company*, Edinburgh and London: Oliver and Boyd.
Carlos, A.M. and Nicholas, S. (1988) ' "Giants of an earlier capitalism": the chartered trading companies as modern multinationals', *Business History Review* 62: 398–419.
—— and —— (1990) 'Agency problems in early chartered companies: the case of the Hudson's Bay Company', *Journal of Economic History* 50: 853–75.
Chambers, J.D. (1961) *The Workshop of the World*, London: Oxford University Press.
Chandler, A.D. (1976) 'The development of modern management structure in the US and UK', in L. Hannah (ed.) *Management Strategy and Business Development: An Historical and Comparative Study*, London: Macmillan, 23–51.
—— (1977) *The Visible Hand: The Managerial Revolution in American Business*, Cambridge, MA: Belknap Press.
Chaudhuri, K.N. (1978) *The Trading World of Asia and the English East India Company 1660–1760*, Cambridge: Cambridge University Press.
—— (1981) 'The English East India Company in the 17th and 18th centuries: a pre-modern multinational organisation', in L. Blusse and F. Gaastra (eds) *Companies and Trade*, Leiden: Leiden University Press, 24–46.
Coase, R.H. (1937) 'The nature of the firm', *Economica, New Series* 4: 386–405; reprinted in Supple, B.E. (ed.) (1992) *The Rise of Big Business*, Aldershot, Elgar, 111–30.
DuBois, A.B. (1971) *The English Business Company after the Bubble Act, 1720–1800*, New York: Octagon.
Dunning, J.H., Cantwell, J.H. and Corley, T.A.B. (1986) 'The theory of international production: some historical antecedents', in P. Hertner and G. Jones (eds) *Multinationals: Theory and History*, Aldershot: Gower, 19–41.

Dyos, H.J. and Aldcroft, D.H. (1974) *British Transport: An Economic Survey from the Seventeenth Century to the Twentieth*, Harmondsworth: Pelican.

Flinn, M.W. (1984) *The History of the British Coal Industry*, vol. 2, *1700–1830: The Industrial Revolution*, Oxford: Clarendon Press.

Gourvish, T.R. (1972) *Mark Huish and the London and North Western Railway*, Leicester: Leicester University Press.

—— (1973) 'A British business elite: the chief executive managers of the railway industry, 1850–1922', *Business History Review* 47: 289–316.

—— (1987) 'British business and the transition to a corporate economy', *Business History* 29: 18–45.

Hannah, L. (1983) *The Rise of the Corporate Economy*, London: Methuen.

Kirby, M.W. (1988) 'Product proliferation in the British locomotive building industry: an engineer's paradise?', *Business History* 30: 287–305.

—— (1993) *The Origins of Railway Enterprise: the Stockton and Darlington Railway, 1821–1863*, Cambridge: Cambridge University Press.

Laslett, P. (1971) *The World We Have Lost*, London: Methuen.

Mathias, P. (1983) *The First Industrial Nation: An Economic History of Britain, 1700–1914*, 2nd edn, London: Routledge.

Payne, P. (1967) 'The emergence of the large-scale company in Great Britain, 1870–1914', *Economic History Review* 20: 519–42.

—— (1988) *British Entrepreneurship in the Nineteenth Century*, 2nd edn, London: Macmillan.

Pollard, S. (1968) *The Genesis of Modern Management: A Study of the Industrial Revolution in Great Britain*, Harmondsworth: Penguin.

Supple, B. (1970) *The Royal Exchange Assurance: A History of British Insurance 1720–1970*, Cambridge: Cambridge University Press.

—— (1977) 'The nature of enterprise', in E.E. Rich and C.H. Wilson (eds) *The Cambridge Economic History of Europe*, vol. V, *The Economic Organisation of Early Modern Europe*, Cambridge: Cambridge University Press, 394–461.

Taylor, A.J. (1960) 'The subcontract system in the British coal industry', in L.S. Pressnell (ed.) *Studies in the Industrial Revolution: Essays Presented to T.S. Ashton*, London: Athlone Press.

Tomlinson, W.W. (1967) *The North Eastern Railway: its Rise and Development*, Newton Abbot: David and Charles (first published 1915).

Trebilcock, C. (1985) *Phoenix Assurance and the Development of British Insurance*, vol. 1, *1782–1870*, Cambridge: Cambridge University Press.

Wilkins, M. (1986a) 'The history of European multinationals: a new look', *Journal of European Economic History* 15: 483–6.

—— (1986b) 'Defining a firm: history and theory', in P. Hertner and G. Jones (eds) *Multinationals: Theory and History*, Aldershot: Gower, 80–95.

Williamson, O.E. (1981) 'The modern corporation: origins, evolution, attributes', *Journal of Economic Literature* 19: 1537–68.

Part II

6 The corporate economy in Britain
Its rise and achievements since 1900

Maurice W. Kirby

INTRODUCTION

There can be little doubt that the most impressive developments in
British industry since 1900 have been the growth in industrial concentration and the emergence of the business corporation as the predominant organizational form in a range of sectors. In 1930 the share
of the largest 100 companies in manufacturing net output stood at 26
per cent. By 1948 the figure had fallen back to 22 per cent, but thereafter it rose persistently with a notable surge in the 1960s. Thus, in
1970, the 40 per cent share of Britain's largest manufacturing firms
was 5 per cent higher than their American counterparts (Hannah and
Kay 1977; Hart and Clarke 1980). Perhaps the clearest indication of
the extent to which the Victorian legacy of personal capitalism had
been eroded is provided by Derek Channon's 1970 survey of the
managerial organization of the 100 largest industrial enterprises in
Britain. Of these, no less than seventy-two had adopted a multidivisional structure, characterized by semi-autonomous production
and marketing divisions administered by a general or corporate office
(Channon 1973: 73). As the ultimate embodiment of the professional
managerial hierarchies identified by Professor Chandler as the mainspring of international competitive advantage there is a *prima facie*
case for the view that the widespread adoption of multidivisional
structures was a highly desirable development if only because
managerial enterprises 'have been the engines of economic growth and
social transformation in industrial nations for the past 100 years'
(Chandler 1990a: 132). It is an apparent paradox, therefore, that the
consummation of Britain's corporate economy was accompanied by
increasing concern over British industry's competitive decline, well
reflected in the 1970s debate on 'deindustrialization' and mounting
enthusiasm after 1979 for the return of a Victorian-style 'enterprise

culture' invigorated by small owner-managed firms (Blackaby 1978; Morris and Stout 1985).

The coincidence of the maturation of the corporate economy in Britain with relatively low economic growth and declining industrial competitiveness has been interpreted in two main ways. First, in conformity with the 'declinist' tradition in British economic history, it has been suggested that 'Major shortcomings in company organisation and management have been at the centre of Britain's unsatisfactory performance since 1945' (Alford 1988: 66). This is not to pre-judge the possible causes of these shortcomings, but rather to explain Britain's macroeconomic competitiveness by reference to the quality of microeconomic performance. Second, as indicated in Chapter 7, the very fact of Britain's successful role as a multinational investor, especially after 1960, fits uncomfortably with allegations of poor managerial performance in the corporate sector. In this setting, the coincidence of a sharply falling share of world exports of manufactures with the relative stability of the total world sales of Britain's leading firms can be readily explained. Within the framework of Michael Porter's analysis (Porter 1990: 499–501), the corporate sector, confronted by sluggish growth in the domestic market, transferred production overseas to richer markets with more favourable demand and factor conditions. This was an entirely rational entrepreneurial response, facilitated by improvements both in managerial standards and corporate practice. Thus, Britain's relative economic decline cannot be ascribed to managerial deficiencies, especially in the context of demonstrable public policy failures both in economic management and in the provision of education and training for industry. Judging between these opposing standpoints raises acute problems of historical interpretation. It is undeniably true that some British firms in both their corporate structures and multinational strategies have been of world class standard as evidenced by their successful penetration of highly competitive markets in Europe and North America after 1960. As such, they should not be tarred with the brush of relatively low rates of economic growth and declining trade shares of the British national economy. That said it is important to note that multinational strategies were far from ubiquitous in the corporate sector, and some firms were more multinational than others. In other words, there were many firms whose productive base lay either wholly or substantially within the British economy. Competitive failings on their part, therefore, would certainly be reflected in declining national competitiveness, all the more so if they were reinforced by vagaries of public policy and institutional barriers to progressive change. It is this perspective of inferior 'uninational' production which informs this chapter. In the following section the phenomenon of British industry's 'corporate lag' behind the United States is examined briefly as a prelude to consideration of the factors which led to corporate convergence in the period to 1939. In the latter context specific attention will be devoted to interpretations of the onset of convergence – its timing and defining characteristics. The third section considers the consummation of the corporate economy after 1945, noting continuities in causal factors and circumstances specific to the period. It will be argued that Britain's relative economic and industrial decline was entirely compatible with the triumph of the corporate economy in the light of inherited deficiencies in business performance and their interaction with contemporary failings in managerial standards. The concluding section offers insights into the growing disillusion with large-scale enterprise in the 1970s as a precursor to the trend towards decentralization and structural diversity observable in the 1980s.

CORPORATE LAG AND CORPORATE CONVERGENCE, 1914–1939

On the eve of the First World War the single-unit family owned firm was the norm in British industry. Where large-scale firms existed outside the railway sector they invariably took the form either of integrated 'entrepreneurial' companies (i.e. manager-manned, but owner-controlled), or holding companies encompassing decentralized federations of family or entrepreneurial firms. In Professor Chandler's words, 'At the top, owners managed and managers owned' (Chandler 1976: 40). In the very few instances where recognizable administrative hierarchies existed in the manufacturing sector, their smaller size and restricted functions relative to their American counterparts 'helped to perpetuate a commitment to personal ways of management' (Chandler 1990b: 242) which effectively precluded both managerial innovation and access to the economies of scale and scope which even before 1914 were beginning to determine international competitive advantage in a range of product markets (Elbaum and Lazonick 1986).

The pre-1914 dominance of 'personal' or 'family' capitalism in Britain's industrial structure has been explained by reference to a number of interrelated factors which derive their validity from explicit comparisons with the United States. The British domestic market, for example, was relatively slow growing and disintegrated, whilst real incomes were lower and income distribution more highly skewed. For many firms, moreover, export markets, both in composition and geographical extent, were highly fragmented, thus compounding the limitations of the home market as a source of scale economies. The incentives, therefore, to create integrated firms with managerial hierarchies were far less compelling than in the continental United States, all the more so because of the existence in Britain of a sophisticated and entrenched network of marketing middlemen, operating both nationally and internationally, which placed a substantial institutional brake on integration (Chandler 1980: 402). A further institutional restraint on corporate development in Britain was provided by the legal framework for business. As Chapter 5 has noted, the Sherman Anti-Trust Act of 1890 played a critical role in moulding corporate structures in the United States, whereas in Britain lack of competition in the form of the holding company 'extended the life of many family and entrepreneurial enterprises' (Chandler 1976: 48). It also underpinned a 'live-and-let-live' business environment where the determination to avoid price competition was complemented by disinterest in the possibilities for growth and expansion of the firm (Chandler 1990b: 294).

If the pre-1914 decades provide confirmation of Professor Payne's judgement that the structure of British industry in the nineteenth century remained 'ossified at an immature level of development' (Payne 1988: 43), there is a well founded case for the view that the inter-war decades witnessed a decisive structural shift, marking the rise of the modern corporate economy. This development redounded to the competitive advantage of British industry via the process of integration and the achievement of scale economies and it may even have helped to boost the growth of the economy as a whole, in so far as improved business efficiency was translated into enhanced total factor productivity. The case for regarding the interwar period as demarcating a major discontinuity in Britain's business structure in general and the manufacturing sector in particular has been advanced most forcefully by Leslie Hannah (Hannah 1983: 90–122). Statistical trends certainly lend powerful support to his case. Taking the share of the largest 100 firms in manufacturing net output, this share stood at approximately 16 per cent in 1910, 18 per cent in 1920, with a surge forward to 26 per cent by 1930. Thereafter, there was a falling off in the level of concentration so that the 1930 percentage was not reached again until the mid-1950s. What is especially striking about the increasing concentration of British industry in the 1920s is that it was correlated closely with merger activity, with peak years in 1920 and 1929. With an average of 188 firm disappearances a year by merger taking the decade as a whole, this represented three times the average number for the forty years to 1920. When it is borne in mind that the merger peaks of 1920 and 1929 were not surpassed again until after 1959, Hannah is undoubtedly correct in his assertion that the 1920s were the first merger-intensive decade in British business. Although internal growth in response to the acquisition of new plant and capacity made a powerful contribution to the growth of firm size in the vehicles, textiles and clothing and footwear sectors, Table 6.1 shows that growth through mergers was especially prominent in foodstuffs, chemicals, metal manufacture, shipbuilding, electrical engineering and building materials. In terms of the direction of corporate growth, therefore, increased concentration in response to mergers affected both old and new industrial sectors. It also encompassed substantial real increases in market value and significantly larger firms as measured by employment levels. In 1919, for example, the largest manufacturing enterprise, J. and P. Coats, was valued at £45 million with Lever Brothers in second place valued at £24.3 million. By 1930, however, five firms exceeded Coats's valuation – in order of size, Unilever, Imperial Tobacco, ICI, Courtaulds and Distillers – and in the case of Unilever and Imperial Tobacco their market valuations exceeded £130 million. As for employment levels, the largest manufacturing employer in 1905 was Fine Cotton Spinners and Doublers with 30,000 workers. By 1930, at least ten British firms employed in excess of 30,000, with ICI and Unilever in the lead with workforces of approximately 50,000. In view of the fact that the very largest firms *in situ* by 1930 tended thereafter to maintain their positions in the hierarchy of the top fifty firms by capital valuation, the case for regarding the 1920s as of critical importance in determining the future structure of British business appears all the more compelling.

Hannah's argument that 'The foundations of the modern corporate economy of large-scale firms had been laid' in the inter-war period is buttressed by qualitative evidence of managerial innovation in response to increased firm size. The diffusion of the telephone, for example, greatly facilitated managerial control and co-ordination, as did the introduction of office machinery such as the Hollerith 'which could process accounting data with great speed, and which were recognised to have caused important developments in the collection and diffusion of information, notably in large companies' (Hannah 1974: 257). Equally significant as a response to company growth was the rise of the functional managerial specialist, with a particular focus on new methods of accounting. In this respect the spread of cost accounting as an established technique of managerial control was complemented

Table 6.1 Concentration in industry groups, 1919–1930

Industry	1919 population (%)	1930 population (%)	Counterfactual 'merged population' (%)	Proportion of the increase due to mergers (%)
Shares of the largest five firms				
Food	39.0	74.0	67.7	82
Drink	25.7	40.6	33.9	55
Tobacco	94.5	99.7	97.7	62
Chemicals	61.3	86.3	84.0	91
Metal manufacture	28.7	45.9	42.7	81
Non-electrical engineering	46.3	56.2	53.7	75
Electrical engineering	43.8	51.9	56.8	160[a]
Shipbuilding	64.6	89.7	84.9	81
Vehicles	34.1	66.5	41.2	22
Metal goods not elsewhere specified	68.0	87.1	80.8	67
Textiles	47.4	64.0	51.3	23
Clothing and footwear	33.1	58.0	40.1	28
Building materials	59.5	83.0	81.4	93
Paper and publishing	40.8	73.8	64.6	72
Miscellaneous manufacturing[b]	49.2	84.8	70.5	60
Share of the largest 100 firms				
All manufacturing	56.4	77.4	72.5	77

Source: Hannah 1983: 98

Notes: [a] A merger contribution above 100 per cent implies that, but for merger activity, concentration would have declined in this industry.
[b] Includes industry groups conventionally listed separately as 'leather, leather goods and fur' and 'timber and furniture' in addition to the conventional 'miscellaneous manufacturing' category.

by innovations in internal audit and forecasting procedures. An indication of the extent of their dissemination is provided by the rapid rise in the proportion of accountants employed in industry: in 1913 most accountants had been in private practice whereas by 1939 more than half were in direct business employment (Hannah 1974: 259). Accountants even began to aspire to leading managerial roles in business. This was exemplified in the case of F.R.M. de Paula, formerly Professor of Accounting at the London School of Economics, who was appointed Controller of Finance at the Dunlop Rubber Company in 1929 and presided thereafter over a sequence of highly effective financial innovations. An even more spectacular example of upward managerial mobility was provided by Francis D'Arcy Cooper, recruited to Lever Brothers from an accounting partnership in 1923. After succeeding Lord Leverhulme as company chairman in 1925, he was subsequently appointed chairman of the newly merged Unilever company after its formation in 1929 (Hannah 1974: 259).

The reference to Unilever is a reminder that some British inter-war firms overcame potential diseconomies of scale by establishing relatively advanced corporate structures. The product of a merger between Lever Brothers and the Dutch Margarine Unie, Unilever's initial aim of co-ordinating the purchase of raw materials was soon followed by the development of a multidivisional structure 'with a corporate office of general and staff executives, with product divisions for its domestic (British) markets, and with geographical divisions for its markets overseas' (Chandler 1990b: 385). As the largest multinational merger of the inter-war period Unilever had, as its purely British counterpart, Imperial Chemical Industries (ICI), at the time of its formation in 1926 the largest merger in British manufacturing industry in terms of capitalization and 'the first merger in Britain to consolidate major sectors of a basic industry in the American manner' (Chandler 1990b: 358). By the 1930s ICI had introduced an American-style divisional structure with a functionally specialized head office as the principal agency of managerial and financial co-ordination. Investing heavily in research and specialist personnel, the new corporation's product divisions were responsible for some impressive innovations and their successful commercial exploitation during the course of the 1930s (Reader 1970).

Whilst it is important to note that Unilever, and ICI in particular, were the only British companies with structures approximating to 'the paradigm of the multidivisional corporation', there were other firms which were adopting a strategy of decentralization as a means of containing scale diseconomies. Hannah cites the case of three such companies – Spillers in flour milling which adopted a regional divisional structure in 1926, Dunlop which combined functional control of tyre manufacturing with decentralization for rubber goods, footwear, garments and sports goods, and Turner and Newall, the leading manufacturer of asbestos products, which created separate divisions for mining, textile manufacture, asbestos, cement and magnesia insulation in 1931. Elsewhere, however, strategies of decentralization were notable for their absence. It was, in fact, the holding company which was the most common form of control for subsidiaries. This was notably the case in such firms as Associated Electrical Industries, Tube Investments, Imperial Tobacco, Guest Keen and Nettlefold, Tootal Broadhurst Lee, Hawker Siddeley, and Electrical and Musical Industries (Hannah 1983: 87). Whilst Hannah concedes that their loose federal structures prevented these and other firms from gaining access to the full range of managerial and technical economies, he is nevertheless of the opinion that even the holding company form could give 'access to the benefit of pooled overheads, risk spreading, the interchange of commercial and industrial methods, collusive pricing policies, and some degree of coordination of new investment'. To that extent, such company structures need not be a brake on the achievement of managerial economies of scale (Hannah 1983: 87).

In generalizing about the motives for merger activity in British business in the half century to 1939 Chandler has stated explicitly that their goal was to restrain competition in order 'to maintain family control' (Chandler 1980: 404, 406). Whilst there are substantial elements of truth in this, especially for the period to 1914, it is an unduly myopic interpretation of inter-war developments. One factor of considerable importance in the 1920s was the emergence of the 'rationalization' movement in British industry. 'Rationalization' was to become a vogue word in the 1920s in the context of the market collapse of Britain's staple export industries and the increasing perception that large-scale business organization, in promoting scale economies, was also of relevance to newer, relatively capital-intensive sectors, such as motor vehicles and electrical products. Although castigated by *The Economist* as a 'cloak for confused ideas and sometimes . . . a badge of respectability for processes of doubtful value' (*Economist* 1929), rationalization came to be synonymous with the contemporary merger movement as a panacea for the loss of competitive efficiency endemic in the existence of surplus productive capacity. If horizontal integration was a direct means of overcoming the slowness of market forces in securing the elimination of marginal concerns in structurally fragmented industries, vertical integration could be viewed as essential for the achievement of large-scale economies in industries such as cotton textiles and, more especially, iron and steel. Rationalization owed its popularity in part, therefore, to increasing dissatisfaction with the invisible hand of market mechanisms as the critical determinant of resource allocation. It was even viewed by government and its leading business advocates as a structuralist solution to the mounting problem of unemployment. Whilst it was conceded that amalgamations would have the immediate effect of increasing unemployment, in the longer term, as industrial efficiency improved in response to scale economies, lost export markets would be regained and rationalized industries would begin to recruit more workers (Kirby 1987: 131–2).

The belief that rationalization would lead to industrial and commercial rejuvenation was grounded clearly in contemporary perceptions of the virtues of German and American business organization. This is confirmed by the flood of literature pointing to foreign competitive strengths based upon large-scale organization. Official publications were no exception to this trend, as evidenced by the reports of the Balfour Committee on Trade and Industry, and the Samuel and Lewis reports on the coal industry (HM Government 1926a, b, 1929), all of which extolled the virtues of 'scientific' marketing and management as the paramount sources of commercial success in German and American business. Hannah has taken the issue of foreign emulation further by pointing to 'the direct intrusion' into the British business scene of industrialists or firms with American and German origins (Hannah 1983: 38). Excellent examples are provided by Sir Hugo Hirst of GEC, the Renolds of the Renold and Coventry Chain Company and, for his role in founding ICI, Sir Alfred Mond (later Lord Melchett). Mond claimed to have inaugurated the rationalization movement in Britain, and it is significant that his enthusiasm for a large-scale merger in the British chemical industry was prompted by the desire to emulate the competitive power of the recently formed German combine, I.G. Farben. At the level of the firm it was American companies which spurred on the rationalization movement by acquiring and then merging British firms in sectors such as electrical products and vehicles. The General Electric Company, for example, was responsible for the merger of four electrical manufacturers to form Associated Electrical Industries, whilst General Motors, in taking over Vauxhall Motors, complemented Ford's presence as a large-scale producer in the British domestic market. As Hannah has concluded, these foreign incursions served as highly visible reminders to British businessmen to reform their managerial and organizational practices in order to safeguard their independence at a time when competitive pressures were severe and American capital internationally mobile (Hannah 1983: 38–9).

Reference to the rationalization movement and foreign influence by no means exhausts the range of factors encouraging increased firm size. ICI's investment in research has already been cited as a critical ingredient in the firm's commercial success. Indeed, ICI's research budget quadrupled between 1926 and 1930, and in so far as this expansion paved the way for product innovations it offered substantial confirmation of the contemporary belief that effective research and development (R&D) programmes could be implemented only by firms employing more than 1,000 workers. A further impetus towards expanded firm size was provided by the presence of scale economies in finance. Whilst it is true that family owned enterprises such as Pilkingtons and Morris Motors (until its public flotation in 1935) grew in the customary manner via the plough-back of profits, many other firms had recourse to the stock market as a means of financing a larger scale of operations. The new issues market boomed in the merger-intensive decade of the 1920s, and whereas in 1907 Britain had possessed only 569 publicly-quoted companies with a market valuation of £500 million, the respective figures for 1939 were 1712 and £2.5 billion. Several factors account for stock market interest in company finance: first the impact of the rationalization movement in underlining the enhanced commercial prospects of large-scale firms; second the opportunities that company flotations provided for speculative gains; and third the attractions of financing new mass production technology, as at Ford's Dagenham plant, opened in 1931. That said, the growth-promoting role of the stock market should not be overestimated. Most firms in the inter-war period financed new capital projects internally and, more to the point, there were some industries which were effectively precluded from using the stock market to achieve rationalization. This was certainly true in the iron and steel and cotton textile industries owing to entrenched vested interests and depressed market conditions. It was by no means coincidental, therefore, that the limited corporate growth achieved in these sectors was the product mainly of pressure from creditor banks such as Barclays and Lloyds and the Bank of England via its rationalizing subsidiary, the Bankers' Industrial Development Company (Tolliday 1987; Bamberg 1988).

Finally, the impact of market demand in precipitating the growth of the firm should be considered. In the pre-1914 period mass markets had made only limited headway in Britain. In the case of motor vehicles, for example, the restricted demand for what was still regarded as a luxury product was catered for by a plethora of small-scale, mainly family firms, employing labour-intensive production methods. This was at a time when the American automobile industry had already made the breakthrough to the mass production assembly line epitomized by Ford's 'Model T'. Not only was the American market broader, it was also deeper as a result of higher real income levels. Thus, mass markets where they existed in Britain were confined to small-scale items of common consumption in the form of low-priced branded and packaged products (Chandler 1990b: 262–8). In the inter-war period, however, a combination of rising real incomes and supply-side innovations created the conditions for the expansion of a range of so-called 'new' industries so that by the end of the period an emergent mass market was in evidence in such sectors as motor vehicles, electrical products and artificial fibres. This was especially so for the 1930s, a decade traditionally associated with long-term unemployment and social distress, but which also experienced a private sector housebuilding boom of unprecedented proportions and strongly rising real incomes for the majority of the working population. Direct evidence of the buoyancy of consumer demand is provided by the phenomenal expansion in the number of radio licences, from 2,269,644 in 1927 to 8,968,388 in 1939, together with the boom in motor vehicle output from 238,805 in 1929 to 507,000 in 1937 (Richardson 1967). Expansion of this magnitude could only be facilitated by the introduction of mass production technology and the development of complementary marketing and distribution networks (Chandler 1990b: 345).

In surveying the evolution of Britain's business structure between the wars Hannah has concluded, optimistically, that

Many of the features that distinguish the modern corporate economy from the Victorian economy of small family firms were . . . firmly established in Britain by the early 1930s. Over large sectors of manufacturing industry the position of large integrated firms had been strengthened by vigorous internal growth and by the unprecedented merger waves of the dozen years following the First World War. These firms were also diversifying their product ranges through the acquisition of businesses in related fields, and some of them had laid the basis for continued growth by investment in new technologies and well-equipped research laboratories. The possibilities of expansion through vertical integration at home and abroad, and through overseas manufacturing subsidiaries, were also being more fully explored than they had been in earlier decades. Typically the large corporations were quoted companies and their shareholdings were widely dispersed beyond the entrepreneurial families to which most of them owed their Victorian origins. Some of them, like ICI, had begun to solve the problems of maintaining efficiency through management decentralization, and this enabled them to sustain the rapid pace of expansion, which the reduction of financial constraints on firm size and the diversification of their activities had made possible.

(Hannah 1983: 123–4)

Whilst conceding the 'gradual' and 'evolutionary' nature of structural change in the economy in view of the Victorian legacy of personal capitalism, Hannah is nevertheless concerned to present the inter-war years in general, and the 1920s in particular, as marking a major discontinuity with previous experience, a period when 'corporate lag' was being reduced and the foundations of the modern corporate economy were being laid. This is a legitimate interpretation of events as far as it goes, validated by the statistical trends and qualitative evidence noted above. But it is possible to adopt a different perspective on 'the rise of the corporate economy' by emphasizing its faltering progress as a result of significant barriers to structural change, both historic and contemporary. Far from the inter-war period laying down conditions for rapid industrial progress on the basis of increasing access to scale economies, it resulted in a business structure riddled with imperfections, the consequence of a widespread retreat from competition manifesting itself in the form of cartelization. This alternative view is well reflected in the work of Chandler, but it has recently been augmented by the gloomy pronouncements of the new school of 'institutional pessimism' led by Elbaum and Lazonick, Olson and Broadberry and Crafts (Elbaum and Lazonick 1986; Olson 1982; Broadberry and Crafts 1990, 1992). For Chandler it is the very fact of evolutionary change, taking the entire period from the later nineteenth century to 1939, which underpins his case for the enduring survival of personal or family capitalism in British business. This is well illustrated in the case of those firms which had responded successfully to the development of urban mass markets before 1914. As Chandler points out,

As late as the 1930s the great majority of the leading firms making packaged, branded goods continued to be run by one or two families. The Cadburys, Frys, Rowntrees, Colmans, Reckitts, Ranks, Lyles, Barratts, Beechams, Sangers, Courtaulds, Albrights, and Wilsons, and the families who owned Crosse and Blackwell, Peek Frean, Huntley and Palmers, Gilbeys Gin, Cerebos, Liebig, Bovril, Carreras, Yardley, Pinchin Johnson and Goodlass, Wall, and Borax Consolidated continued to manage their firms into the third and even fourth generations.

(Chandler 1980: 402)

Growth by merger and acquisition, moreover, was also consistent with the perpetuation of family influence and control. Although the merger wave of the 1920s gave birth to such corporate giants as ICI and Unilever, the pre-war practice of constructing federations of autonomous family enterprises in the form of holding companies was the norm. As noted already, Hannah has suggested that the holding company need not be a constraint on the achievement of scale economies, but as he has also concluded,

It may reasonably be suspected . . . that a looser form of holding company structure with few managerial advantages, was common in Britain. Companies like AEI, Hawker Siddeley, Liebigs, Cadbury–Fry, Stewarts and Lloyds, Tube Investments and Reckitt and Colman appear to have been little more than loose confederations of subsidiaries, and it may reasonably be doubted whether such a structure can have achieved many of the potential economies of large scale. Suspicion is inevitably aroused that they were a form of cartel – albeit a strong and permanent control – which could achieve many of the private benefits of monopoly power whilst forgoing the social benefits which strategic and organisational innovation were likely to bring.

(Hannah 1976: 199)

In the absence of a cross-section of academically credible business histories of holding companies, it is not possible to confirm or deny Hannah's suspicions concerning their productivity-retarding effects. Clearly, more research is needed in the area. If an interim judgement is to be offered it must lie on the pessimistic side, especially in the context of the recent analysis of Britain's productivity achievements in the 1930s carried out by Broadberry and Crafts (1990, 1992). Writing at the end of a decade which had witnessed a 50 per cent increase in manufacturing productivity leading to substantial convergence towards the German level – the product of the 'cold bath' of Thatcherism – these authors suggest that the intense recession of 1929–32 might reasonably be expected to have exerted a similar effect in boosting labour productivity. However, as Broadberry and Crafts note, the policy stance of government in the 1930s was to shield firms from competitive pressures through protectionist legislation, the encouragement of cartels and collusion, and the devaluation of sterling. In marked contrast to the 1980s, therefore, the economic policy environment of the 1930s 'could be expected to militate against productivity improvement by raising barriers to entry, by reducing the rate of exit of the inefficient and by encouraging restrictive practices' (Broadberry and Crafts 1992: 535). The significance of this conclusion for the assessment of business performance is that it moves the focus of attention away from the Chandlerian emphasis on corporate structure to 'the competitive environment as a key determinant of conduct'. The link between the two approaches is provided by the holding company in its cartel guise, but there is considerable evidence in favour of the Broadberry and Crafts perspective.

Recent analysis of government macroeconomic policy in the 1930s has concluded that a principal aim was to stimulate a mild price inflation in order to lower real wages and boost profits (Peden 1985: 92–4; Booth 1987). Protectionism and encouragement of collusion were critical ingredients in this policy in the belief that rising profits, in stimulating business confidence, could underwrite industrial modernization along the lines indicated by the rationalization movement. In reality, however, the retreat from competition placed substantial barriers in the way of modernization. This was exemplified in the case of the iron and steel industry, a sector which government wished to see rationalized on the basis of a well-founded plan for regional amalgamations devised in 1930 by American consulting engineers. But following the introduction of a general tariff in 1932 the iron and steel manufacturers were able to circumvent governmental pressures for reorganization. It is true that the industry as a whole reluctantly came to accept the need for a national co-ordinating body – the British Iron and Steel Federation founded in 1934 – but lack of consensus ensured that the restructuring powers of this body were severely limited. As the industry's most recent historian has concluded, 'the final scheme was not one of reorganisation but solely of price maintenance' and until 1939 'the state sponsored a cartel over which it had little control' (Tolliday 1984: 69, 74). The dominant element in the iron and steel industry, the heavy steelmakers, were determined to adopt a defensive posture behind a tariff wall buttressed by the suppression of internal competition. In the face of their intransigence a predominantly Conservative national government was obliged to accept the industry's view that rationalization could only be secured by 'natural market forces'. Radical state-sponsored programmes were therefore ruled out by the government's desire to avoid direct involvement in industrial affairs for fear of falling into a policy morass which would lead very quickly to the undermining of private managerial prerogatives (Kirby 1987: 134). Similarly, in the case of the coal industry the National Government remained committed to the compulsory merger of colliery companies throughout the 1930s as an efficiency-enhancing measure. Decisive action to bring it about, however, was ruled out in favour of an increasingly restrictive statutory cartel system which was perceived as a device to maximize employment levels in the country's most depressed industrial regions (Kirby 1977; Supple 1987).

Broadberry and Craft's work can be related to much broader themes of interest to business historians. It certainly conforms to Mancur Olson's well-known thesis of institutional sclerosis. This places 'distributional coalitions' at the centre of growth-retarding influences and indicates that faster economic growth is dependent upon 'freer trade and fewer impediments to the free movement of factors of production' (Olson 1982: 141). In this light the 1930s can be viewed as a period when economic recession strengthened political pressures and restrictive coalitions which would operate to retard modernization of the economy as a whole and the business structure in particular. In the business world the rise of such coalitions can be gauged by the increase in the number of trade associations – from 500 in 1919 to approximately 2,500 in 1943, by which time approximately 60 per cent of British manufacturing output may have been subject to restrictive agreements (Gribbin 1978). Institutional sclerosis at the inter-firm level was compounded by Britain's distinctive structure of labour relations which produced its own variant of the rent-seeking coalition. This applied both to old and new industries. In the motor vehicle industry, for example, rather than emulate American practice, British manufacturers rejected high throughput, capital-intensive technology with payment by day rates. Fearing labour resistance to advanced process innovations they opted for relatively labour-intensive methods. Profits were maintained at acceptable levels only by offsetting low productivity on the shopfloor by the payment of low wages. By the end of the inter-war period the piece-work system with low throughput was the norm in the industry, permitting the trade unions to exercise deleterious control over the pace of work (Lewchuk 1987). The cotton textile industry was also subject to labour rigidities which, in combination with its structural fragmentation, retarded productivity advance. Lazonick's commentary on the malevolent effects of the nineteenth-century inheritance of entrenched labour organizations is well known

(Lazonick 1983: 1986). Labour-intensive, low-throughput techniques were underwritten by wage lists which determined the relationship between work effort and pay. The end result was that, when employers sought to increase capital intensity in the later 1920s and 1930s in a bid to restore their competitive advantage, they were largely frustrated by defensive but powerful unions, presiding over entrenched wage lists.

The Broadberry–Crafts analysis of productivity movements provides valuable insights into Britain's business performance. In some respects it is complementary to the Chandlerian approach, but in others it serves to qualify the assumption, writ large in the work of Elbaum and Lazonick, that corporate strategy and structure were the key variables in explaining business conduct (Kirby 1992). That said, an emphasis on the competitive environment, however valid, should not be allowed to detract from the importance of other critical factors which have been advanced by business historians in explanation of Britain's productivity lag behind the United States. It is possible, for example, to point to some further failings in business performance which were first highlighted in the debate on British entrepreneurial standards inaugurated by Aldcroft and Landes (Aldcroft 1964; Landes 1972). Their analyses concentrated on the staple industries in the later nineteenth century, a period which they regarded as critical in marking the onset of Britain's relative industrial decline. In this setting they highlighted two factors in business performance which are of direct relevance to the inter-war period, first the issue of marketing standards, and second investment in human capital formation. In the former case emphasis was placed on crude and amateur sales techniques, especially in overseas markets where heavy reliance on the traditional merchanting system created a barrier in communication between manufacturer and customer. Moreover, the fragmented structure of British industry precluded the establishment of the direct selling and overseas distributive organizations which were such an important factor in aiding the expansion of German and American manufactured exports after 1880. Whilst the evidence available at present is by no means extensive it would appear that these weaknesses lingered on well into the present century even in such technologically advanced sectors as rayon and aero engines (Coleman 1969: chs 11, 13; Richardson 1961: 371). A striking illustration of British marketing deficiencies is provided by motor vehicles, the 'new' industry *par excellence*. In 1937, for example, 'the six leading British producers, making roughly 350,000 private cars, turned out more than forty different engine types and an even greater number of chassis and body models, which was considerably more than the number offered by the three leading producers in the United States, making perhaps 3,500,000 cars' (Kahn 1946: 112–13). As for human capital formation, the pre-1914 decades are noted for British industry's indifference to formal technical and managerial education on the German and American models, compounded by the education system's reluctance to engage in vocational training beyond legal and medical studies (Locke 1984). Although Sidney Pollard has sought recently to redeem Britain's reputation in this respect (Pollard 1989: 194–213) the overall impression remains of a society which accorded low social prestige and priority in economic terms to applied science and technology (Chandler 1990b: 292–4). As in the case of marketing, evidence suggests that these attitudes persisted well into the present century. There are isolated examples of progress after 1920, as in the case of ICI which established a Central Staff Department in 1927 and Pilkington's which inaugurated a training programme in 1933, but as Gourvish observes 'these rather limited responses were far from typical . . . and even large companies retained a cosy amateurishness' entirely consistent with 'the "club" atmosphere of most boardrooms' (Gourvish 1987: 34).

The fact remains that by the end of the inter-war period, after two decades of turbulent economic conditions, only two British firms had introduced managerial structures which bore comparison with the best practice in the United States. It is true that economic crisis had produced managerial innovation in British business but there are numerous instances of tentative responses falling far short of funda-mental change. Gourvish's recent study of British business, based upon a number of single-firm case studies, has pointed to 'a continua-tion of the unitary or departmental form, a preference for internally-recruited directors, and the retention of owners in entrepreneurial positions' (Gourvish 1987: 33). Above all, the period had witnessed a merger wave which gave the appearance of substantially increased industrial concentration. In reality, it had given birth to enforceable cartels in the form of holding companies. In this setting, Professor Chandler's conclusion that in comparison with their German and American competitors such firms enjoyed 'every source of market power . . . except the ability to compete' is apposite (Chandler 1990b: 391).

THE CONSUMMATION OF THE CORPORATE ECONOMY AFTER 1945

Reference was made at the beginning of this chapter to Channon's study of the rapid diffusion of multidivisional managerial structures in Britain's largest companies during the 1950s and 1960s, leading to the consummation of the corporate economy. Taking British business as a whole there was far more evidence of 'Harvard Business School-approved' diversification strategies than at earlier periods. By 1970 managerial hierarchies had advanced significantly at the expense of owner-managers whilst research and development expenditures were running at unprecedented levels in peacetime. The general business environment, moreover, was radically changed from that of the inter-war period. In terms of market demand, buoyant levels of domestic consumption were complemented by expanding markets overseas, the product of American financial underwriting of a revitalized international economy and successive rounds of negotiated tariff reductions. The associated diminution of protectionist influences as a barrier to structural change was buttressed by the changed policy stance of government to the suppression of internal competition. In this respect there is a clear link between the wartime coalition government's official statement on *Employment Policy after the War* (HM Government 1944) and the establishment of the Monopolies and Restrictive Practices Commission in 1948 and the Restrictive Practices Court in 1956. In referring to the possibility that the achievement of fuller employment in peacetime via measures of aggregate demand management might be frustrated by the pricing policies of collusive selling organizations the *Employment Policy* white paper had clearly in mind the inter-war legacy of cartels and producers' associations (Kirby 1987). In fact, the great bulk of restrictive agreements extant in British industry were outlawed by the 1956 legislation. Thus, in relation to the themes identified in this chapter, the postwar years marked a discontinuity in Britain's business structure at least as significant as that of the 1920s' merger boom. In Chandlerian terms this period witnessed the elimination of corporate lag behind the United States, and in accordance with Olson's perspective on economic growth it appeared to provide far less fertile ground for the restrictive activities of rent-seeking coalitions.

In statistical terms increases in concentration among large-scale firms were not as impressive as in the 1920s, but as Table 6.2 reveals, taking the period between 1957 and 1969, concentration in manufacturing industry was substantial. The table also shows that mergers

Table 6.2 Concentration in industry groups, 1957–1969

Industry	1957 population (%)	1969 population (%)	Counterfactual 'merged' population (%)	Proportion of the increase due to mergers (%)
Shares of the largest five firms				
Food	41.3	52.7	49.9	75
Drink	32.7	69.5	68.9	98
Tobacco	96.5	100.0	100.0	100
Chemicals	71.0	73.7	74.5	130[a]
Metal manufacture[b]	45.7	59.5	63.9	132[a]
Non-electrical engineering	29.8	25.3	33.7	[c]
Electrical engineering	47.2	68.0	59.1	57
Shipbuilding	62.1	74.2	70.9	73
Vehicles	50.4	71.0	76.2	125[a]
Textiles	44.2	65.1	71.0	128[a]
Clothing and footwear	63.8	78.4	71.1	50
Building materials	53.1	51.1	53.1	[c]
Paper and publishing	47.5	63.2	65.1	112[a]
Share of the largest 100 firms				
All manufacturing[d]	60.1	74.9	75.3	103

Source: Hannah 1983: 144

Notes: [a] A merger contribution above 100 per cent implies that, but for merger activity, concentration would have declined in this industry.
[b] Excluding the nationalized British Steel Corporation and its constituents.
[c] Concentration declined.
[d] Including the four industry groups – leather, timber, metal goods not elsewhere specified and miscellaneous – not separately listed in the table.

were once again of critical importance in increasing concentration. Indeed, as the counterfactual 'merger' population indicates, the overall level of concentration would have declined in the absence of mergers, in some cases markedly (Hannah 1983: 145). A further continuity with the inter-war period was that the major industrial groups *in situ* in 1939 provided 'the core of corporate growth' in the 1950s and 1960s. Such growth was also dominated by existing corporations, thus confirming Hannah's observation that the structural changes of the 1920s were of long-term significance.

In accounting for this second surge of concentration propelled mainly by mergers, it is possible to identify a constellation of causal factors, some specific to the postwar period, but others repetitious of interwar circumstances. In the latter category, for example, rising demand at home and abroad facilitated access to scale economies in terms of both production and finance and marketing. Established advertising techniques, augmented by commercial television, reinforced these trends, as did a growing appreciation of the importance of scale economies in industrial research (Hannah 1983: 146–7). Among factors specific to the post-1950 period the revival of competitive forces alluded to above appears critical. In this respect, international treaty obligations and domestic legislation were complemented by the influx of foreign direct investment from the United States in intensifying competition. The net result of these trends 'was a widespread desire to reduce such competitive pressures within the British market', manifesting itself in the form of 'compensating mergers' (Hannah 1983: 148–9). Whilst mergers may be viewed as defeating the ends of a pro-competition policy, government itself was directly responsible for their encouragement. This was especially the case in the defence-related industries where the state as a monopsonist was in a powerful position to promote mergers in pursuit of more efficient procurement policies, notably in the aircraft industry. In the later 1960s, moreover, the then Labour government adopted policies of direct intervention in the industrial sector in the hope of boosting competitive performance. In the present context, the establishment of the Industrial Reorganisation Corporation 'to promote or assist the reorganisation or development of any industry' in pursuit of scale economies was significant. In its brief existence as a merger broker the corporation presided over the formation of significantly larger firms in a range of industries, from motor vehicles and computers to ball bearings and scientific instruments (Hague and Wilkinson 1983). Within industry itself a combination of technological change, focusing on computer applications, and increased professionalism in management is notable. The British Institute of Management was founded in 1947 and the inauguration of business schools in the 1960s was followed by an upsurge in 'management education' in the universities and polytechnics generally after the mid-1970s. Finally, the rise of the takeover bid should be noted. As Hannah has commented, 'Directors of firms which had slept on their assets in the 1930s and 1940s found that in the new postwar full employment conditions, takeover bidders could acquire their shares and make substantial profits by selling off assets at their higher current prices (or sometimes by operating them more efficiently themselves)' (Hannah 1983: 149). Legislation also had a role to play in creating 'a more fluid market in corporate control', in so far as the 1948 Companies Act forced the disclosure of financial information which could then be used as the basis of a takeover bid. Indeed, in the ten years after 1957 38 per cent of firms quoted on the London Stock Exchange were acquired by other quoted companies.

It has been suggested that takeover bids 'represented the development of skills in the arts of corporate finance'. As firms grew in size they acquired the status of 'mini capital markets' and this fact, together with other financial advantages in merger activity, encouraged takeover bids as 'a form of corporate conspicuous consumption' (Alford 1988: 63). This critical note has been well reflected in the recent debate on the quality of 'corporate governance', or control, in British business which has focused on the frequency of takeover bids. In an international setting takeover activity in the UK from the 1960s onwards has been notable for its unusually high level and also for its hostile nature leading to dramatic substitutions of executive personnel. Although a market-based theory of corporate control would suggest that this was a desirable outcome – in the sense that inferior managers were being replaced by the more talented – concern has been expressed that hostile takeovers may be an inappropriate means of enhancing corporate governance (Jenkinson and Mayer 1992: 3). The funding of takeover bids is a costly process, involving substantial payments to specialist advisers and financial institutions. They are clearly a significant distraction from normal managerial functions, and to compound matters, may not even target deficient managerial performance (Franks and Mayer 1992). Most significant of all, there can be no presumption that they will lead to improved corporate performance, a judgement which receives some confirmation from empirical studies of post-merger results in the UK (see below). All of this is in marked contrast to experience in Continental Europe and Japan. In the case of Germany, for example, where takeover activity of any description has been relatively low, it has been argued that the monitoring of corporate governance has proceeded effectively without reference to a market for corporate control (Schneider-Lenné 1992). In marked contrast to the UK, firm shareholdings have been highly concentrated in the hands of small numbers of other firms, banks and founding families, a structure reinforced by cross-shareholdings between firms. This 'insider' system of concentrated shareholdings – replicated in large measure in Japan (Franks and Mayer 1992: 4–7) – may well have encouraged higher managerial standards, whereas the UK norm of portfolio diversification, in reducing risks to investors, may have removed important incentives for the monitoring of corporate control. Further research is necessary to validate these presumptions, but the suspicion remains that German firms in particular have gained important advantages from the closer monitoring of corporate governance facilitated by concentrated shareholdings and a far greater degree of continuity in managerial control.

In view of the more favourable demand and supply conditions during the quarter-century after 1950 it is intriguing to find that in a twentieth-century context the three decades after 1950 were a period of unusually rapid relative economic and industrial decline for Britain, as evidenced by growth rates of output and productivity and the country's share of world manufactured exports (Crafts 1991). In so far as this comparative growth failure was the product of competitive weakness in the domestic economy there is an apparent inconsistency with contemporary demand and supply conditions. It is, of course, possible that the elimination of corporate lag, combined with legislative assaults on Olsonian coalitions, did result in enhanced business performance, but that there were countervailing factors elsewhere in the economy which limited their positive growth impact. This possibility is, indeed, well provided for in the most recent 'declinist' literature pointing to the baleful effects of government economic policies on the business sector, whether in the form of bloated and inefficient public services (Bacon and Eltis 1978) or Treasury concerns with macroeconomic symbols, in particular the value of sterling and the balance of payments (Pollard 1982; Newton and Porter 1988). This is not the place to evaluate these hypotheses, and in any event there is substantial evidence to indicate that the supply-side rejuvenation of British business after 1950 was more apparent than real. In examining British competition policy from the 1940s to the passing of the Restrictive Practices Act of 1956 Helen Mercer has shown how ineffectual it was despite a sequence of damning reports on the adverse consequences for industrial efficiency of restrictive practices prepared by the Monopolies and Restrictive Practices Commission. Responsible officials and ministers quite simply succumbed to 'regulatory capture' by vested interests, and 'unwillingness to antagonise industry permeated to Cabinet level' (Mercer 1991: 93). Mercer's conclusion that the failure of the Commission was the product of 'rigidities' within the British political and economic system' is entirely consistent with Olson's thesis of institutional sclerosis. Similarly, it is all too easy to assume that the 1956 Act did provoke a supply-side revolution in British business, as evidenced by the widespread surrender of restrictive agreements in the later 1950s and 1960s. Quite apart from the subsequent upsurge in 'information agreements' which served to break the spirit, if not the letter, of the Act (Allen 1966), there is the possibility that this legislation was in some degree responsible for the upsurge in merger activity after 1957 as a defensive response to the loss of cartel arrangements (Gribbin 1978; Cowling 1982; Walshe 1991). As noted above, the American Sherman Anti-Trust Act had been followed in the 1890s by a merger boom, but whereas this unleashed favourable Chandlerian effects on America's business structure (Chandler 1977) there is substantial evidence that its British counterpart of the 1960s produced disappointing results in terms both of productivity gains and profit maximization 'at least through the early 1970s' (Crafts 1988: xi). There were, of course, successes, represented at one end of the spectrum by the early history of Lord Weinstock's GEC in gaining access to a range of static and dynamic efficiency benefits (Coleman 1987: 1–17). There were, however, equally spectacular failures, notably British Leyland which, despite the receipt of major public subventions, experienced progressive market collapse almost from its inception in 1967. UK mergers undoubtedly contributed towards large-firm dominance of markets and higher managerial salaries, but as studies by industrial economists have shown, the overall performance of merged firms in the period 1954–72 was consistent with reduced profits and productivity (Singh 1971; Utton 1974; Meeks 1977; Firth 1979; Kumar 1984). Efficiency gains, moreover, tended to be modest with even GEC achieving productivity improvements only in the 15–25 per cent range (Cowling *et al.* 1980). One study of the merger movement, in adopting a long-term perspective, took the view that efficiency losses from mergers could be ascribed to 'managerial chaos' arising from inherited unitary-form managerial structures. Such chaos could therefore be expected to disappear following the adoption of improved M-form structures (Cowling 1982). It is significant, therefore, that in those cases where multidivisional structures were introduced (often on the basis of advice from North American management consultants) the results in terms of enhanced productivity performance were disappointing. In 1970 the 72 per cent of the top hundred British companies to adopt the Chandlerian M-form structure was far ahead of the 40 per cent in Germany (Channon 1973; Dyas and Thanheiser 1976). Yet by that date German labour productivity in manufacturing exceeded the UK level by 30 per cent, having been 30 per cent below it in 1950 (Van Ark 1990). Econometric testing has shown that multidivisional structures did have a positive effect on industrial productivity but with increases confined to the range between 15 and 20 per cent (Steer and Cable 1978). What seems incontrovertible is that British firms proceeding towards 'multidivisionalization' failed to adopt the full range of managerial practices which had come to be the norm in US enterprise. Critical deficiencies were the lack of uniform and effective accounting procedures both within and between divisions, weaknesses in marketing and technical innovation and, in the case of the numerous holding companies adopting M-form structures, a tendency to insert a cosmetic layer of management falling far short of fundamental reform (Pagnamenta and Overy 1984; Clark and Tann 1986; Alford 1988: 64; Payne 1990: 35). The net result was that British multidivisional firms were less profitable than their US counterparts operating in comparable product markets. In this light, therefore, it is a gross assumption that the early and widespread adoption of advanced American-style corporate structures, in imitation of ICI and Unilever, would have produced a more dynamic British economy in the context of global competition (Kirby 1992).

Before concluding this chapter consideration should be given to two further factors which had an adverse impact on business performance, the first relating to the industrial relations environment and the second to the interface between government and industry. In so far as Britain's postwar labour difficulties can be related directly to the absence of effective managerial hierarchies they were the product of historical continuities reaching back to the nineteenth-century inheritance of personal capitalism. Mention has already been made of Lewchuk's work on shopfloor organization in the motor vehicle industry before 1939, stressing the industry's commitment to low-throughput production and piece-work. After 1950, rapid market expansion placed a new premium on automation and standardization, but the transition to direct managerial control of the shopfloor was difficult and protracted. British managers, lacking training and experience in the organization of large plants, were confronted by worker resistance to capital intensity. The strike-proneness of the motor vehicle industry is readily explained in this context, but productivity studies have shown that the problem was widespread, embracing such sectors as shipbuilding, brewing, tobacco, tyres, metal boxes and typewriters (Pratten and Atkinson 1976; Prais 1981). It should also be noted that worker resistance to new technology and patterns of work was compounded by the poor training and low levels of skills prevalent among shopfloor personnel (Daly *et al.* 1985). The evidence suggests that this 'industrial relations sclerosis' only began to weaken during the 1980s when a combination of large-scale unemployment and legislative assaults on trade union privileges encouraged greater managerial control over work processes (Broadberry and Crafts 1990).

In terms of government–industry relations beyond the nationalized sector, their interface was closest in the matter of military-defence procurement with particular reference to the aerospace industry, broadly defined. Within this setting the mutually dependent relationship between the aircraft manufacturers and the state is of long standing, reaching at least as far back as the First World War. The aircraft industry has long been reliant on state funding and orders, and successive governments have underwritten the industry, first as a supposedly cost-effective way of sustaining imperial cohesion and a balance of power in Europe, and latterly as a means of preserving a world political and military role semi-independent of the United States (Edgerton 1991). After 1945 the manufacturers of aircraft and aero-engines were joined in the defence procurement process by firms in the electrical engineering and electronics sector, a reflection both of weapons proliferation and technological embellishment (Kaldor 1982). Institutional rivalries between the military services were critical, and in encouraging non-price competition on the part of defence contractors they underwrote short production runs, a trend compounded by the growth of international collaboration as different countries insisted on 'maintaining broad national capabilities rather than . . . on a true division of labour' (Kaldor *et al.* 1986). It is true that in the later 1950s and 1960s the aircraft industry was rationalized by mergers in the expectation of gaining access to the kind of scale economies available to the large American producers. Indeed by 1965 the new Hawker Siddeley group (Hawker Siddeley Aviation) had emerged as Britain's second largest manufacturing employer with 123,000 workers. At the same date the recently formed British Aircraft Corporation employed 37,000 workers, but was itself owned jointly by the much larger engineering firms of Vickers, English Electric and Bristol Aeroplane. In 1966 British Siddeley Engines was absorbed by Rolls Royce, resulting in total firm employment of 88,000 workers. Collectively, these firms were responsible for some outstanding technological successes, but they failed to be translated into the kind of international commercial success achieved by their American counterparts enjoying virtually exclusive access to a substantially larger domestic market (Hayward 1989). The influential Elstub report, published in 1969 (Elstub 1969), in analysing the 3:1 productivity gap between the British and American industries, concluded that the greater efficiency of the latter was the product not so much of the greater capital intensity of US production, but of differences in the scale of production. In Britain, comparatively short production runs meant fewer units over which to amortize the fixed costs of new aircraft and the 'learning curve' was correspondingly shorter. At the same time, the US industry benefited from an organizational structure where the large prime contractors could take advantage of scale economies via the production of sub-assemblies by specialist suppliers. A smaller scale of production also meant that the British industry experienced periodic productivity declines as the workforce contemplated the more frequent prospect of unemployment.

A further critical consequence of the development of a British-style 'military–industrial complex' was a distinctive pattern of R&D expenditures. In 1955 total R&D expenditure in the UK amounted to £187 million, the highest figure for any country in Western Europe, yet 63 per cent of the total was spent on military projects with less than one-third funded by private industry. More to the point, nearly two-thirds of private industry research was related directly to defence contracts (Channon 1973: 231; Freeman 1978: 66). Thereafter, there was some reduction in defence-related R&D in the light of numerous project failures and a trend after 1960 to purchase American equipment. However, from the early 1970s the proportion of total R&D spent on defence projects began to rise with the result that by 1983 the UK was spending proportionately more on military R&D and less on civil R&D than any of her main industrial competitors. The point to be made in this context is that some of Britain's leading manufacturing firms were operating for much of the postwar period in a noncommercial environment conducive to risk averseness and low financial returns. This stands in marked contrast to the two most dynamic OECD economies, West Germany and Japan. Devoid of large military commitments and investing heavily in commercially oriented R&D in machinery, vehicles and electronics, these countries achieved substantial export successes at the expense of British and also American industry (Freeman 1978). In the British case, moreover, the high prestige accorded to military–industrial endeavours drained off the most talented scientists and engineers who, from the standpoint of Britain's international competitive advantage, would have been better employed in commercially oriented manufacturing industry (Peck 1968). As Chapter 13 reveals, with only limited access to highly qualified personnel, British industry could ill afford this human 'crowding out'.

CONCLUSION

In surveying the rise of the corporate economy in Britain a superficial approach grounded in Chandlerian perspectives might assume that British business had everything to gain in moving from personal to corporate capitalism. If the small-scale family firm stood at one end of the structural spectrum, then the opposite end was occupied by the multidivisional corporation representing the ultimate paradigm of corporate excellence and efficiently functioning managerial hierarchies. It is salutary to note, therefore, that contrary to some recent interpretations Chandler himself did not advocate the wholesale adoption of M-form structures. They were particularly inappropriate for the manufacturers of semi-finished products dependent on a small number of large industrial consumers. This certainly applies to the iron and steel industry, not least in the United States itself where the steelmakers after 1900 opted for large functional departments rather than the M-form precisely because their marketing processes were comparatively simple (Hannah 1976: 197). In Britain the United Steel Company 'established centralised control over its subsidiaries in the 1920s, with strong functional departments handling administration, purchasing and sales'. A centralized programme of works rationalization was introduced together with budgetary control, leaving local boards of management with 'power only over production and works management'. As Hannah observes: 'Multidivisional organisation was neither created nor required'. In textiles the Lancashire Cotton Corporation, formed in 1929 as the vehicle for a multifirm merger among coarse yarn manufacturers, encountered severe managerial problems as the result of the attempt to introduce a divisional structure. Following the resignation of the managing director responsible 'a centralised, functionally departmentalised management structure was adopted . . . , a structure which was almost certainly more appropriate to an undiversified company selling a standardised semi-finished product like cotton yarn to a limited range of industrial consumers' (Hannah 1976: 197). This case validates Chandler's own perception that unitary, or U-form, structures are the appropriate organizational mode for single product firms. Hannah has also questioned the assumption, well reflected in the work of Elbaum and Lazonick, that the visible hand of managerial hierarchies is always superior to the market in allocating resources. In the textile depression of the 1970s it was the medium-size vertically integrated firms which performed best, while Courtaulds, as a relative corporate giant, suffered due to a market strategy which rendered it especially vulnerable to import competition (Blackburn 1982; Toyne *et al.* 1984: 151–3). Even a firm such as ICI could not escape the adverse financial consequences of an inappropriate investment decision for the manufacture of nitrogenous fertilizers at Billingham in the early 1930s. Although the same firm engaged in effective R&D programmes before the Second World War it was slow to appreciate the importance of plastics, partly as a result of vested interests located within existing divisions (Reader 1975).

That the market could impose severe penalties on managerial hierarchies receives some confirmation from the fact that 'the two countries with the most concentrated structures and largest corporations since World War II, Britain and the United States, are also those with the least impressive economic performance' (Hannah 1980: 71). As a recent authoritative survey has concluded, the promulgation of a universally valid model of big business based on American manufacturing industrial experience is misplaced.

> because the attempt to generalize it to other societies smacks of an ethnocentricity that neglects a host of vital, nation-specific determinants of productivity and competitive success. Differences in corporate structures and managerial hierarchies are undoubtedly relevant to the discussion of national economic performance. But so are resource and factor endowments, cultural institutions, educational experiences, social structures and attitudes etc. Indeed, in the last resort, big business is at least as much a product as a cause of economic and social activity.
>
> (Supple 1992: xxv)

In the United States the onset of 'corporate self-doubt' after 1970 in the wake of faltering export performance and mounting import penetration unleashed a new interest in 'flexible specialization' with diversified product strategies, especially in the light of contemporary West German, Japanese and Italian experience in resisting the trend towards 'deindustrialization' observable both in Britain and the

United States. Thus, at the very time when Chandler was proclaiming the virtues of the visible hand and managerial hierarchies, an alternative literature was in preparation based on the presumption that corporate industrial society was moving towards 'multi-structured dualism' with 'core' and 'peripheral' firms coexisting (Kaufman 1982; Piore and Sabel 1984; Sabel and Zeitlin 1985). This trend, foreshadowed in the structural changes consequent upon de-industrialization and shifts in international competitive advantage in the 1970s, gave every sign of coming to fruition in the 1980s. Notable developments in this decade were the rationalization of activities by large multinational firms, the information technology revolution giving rise to externalization of functions and the birth of new small firms in the burgeoning service sector, and the creation of 'niche' markets and products by small-scale manufacturers. In the specifically British context the period witnessed a change of public policy in favour of 'disaggregated' capitalist structures. There was a renewed emphasis on competition policy and this went hand in hand with the reduction of the monopoly powers of public corporations as a prelude to privatization. In manufacturing considerable attention was devoted to encouraging the formation of small firms in the belief that they had a role to play in stimulating structural diversity and in offsetting the aversion to risk of large-scale firms. This was all in accord with an attempted reversion to a Victorian-style 'enterprise culture' stimulated by market forces. However, the ambiguous nature of the government's policy stance was encapsulated in the hopes expressed in the mid-1980s that an upsurge in small-firm formation in the service sector could fill the structural void created by deindustrialization in manufacturing (Kirby 1991: 258–9). If there are shades here of the movement towards a 'post-industrial society', light years removed from Victorian capitalism, business trends in the 1980s were consistent with the emergence of a new kind of corporate economy, still dominated by large-scale firms but subject to internationalization and decentralization, the product of the globalization of business in combination with the information technology revolution (Supple 1992: xviii).

REFERENCES

Aldcroft, D.H. (1964) 'The entrepreneur and the British economy, 1870–1914', *Economic History Review* 17: 113–34.
Alford, B.W.E. (1988) *British Economic Performance 1945–1975*, London: Macmillan.

Allen, G.C. (1966) *The Structure of Industry in Britain*, 2nd edn, London: Longmans.

Bacon, R. and Eltis, W. (1978) *Britain's Economic Problem: Too Few Producers*, 2nd edn, London: Macmillan.

Bamberg, J.H. (1988) 'The rationalisation of the British cotton industry in the interwar years', *Textile History* 19: 83–102.

Blackaby, F. (ed.) (1978) *De-industrialisation*, London: Heinemann.

Blackburn, J.A. (1982) 'The vanishing UK cotton industry', *National Westminster Bank Quarterly Review* November: 42–52.

Booth, A. (1987) 'Britain in the 1930s: a managed economy?' *Economic History Review* 40: 499–522.

Broadberry, S.N. and Crafts, N.F.R. (1990) 'The implications of British macroeconomic policy in the 1930s for long run growth performance', *Rivista di Storia Economica* 7: 1–19.

—— and —— (1992) 'Britain's productivity gap in the 1930s: some neglected factors', *Journal of Economic History* 52: 531–58.

Chandler, A.D. (1976) 'The development of modern management structure in the US and UK', in L. Hannah (ed.) *Management Strategy and Business Development: An Historical and Comparative Study*, London: Macmillan, 23–51.

—— (1977) *The Visible Hand: The Managerial Revolution in American Business*, Cambridge, MA: Belknap Press.

—— (1980) 'The growth of the transnational industrial firm in the United States and the United Kingdom: a comparative analysis', *Economic History Review* 33: 396–410.

—— (1990a) 'The enduring logic of industrial success', *Harvard Business Review* 68: 130–40.

—— (1990b) *Scale and Scope: The Dynamics of Industrial Capitalism*, Cambridge, MA: Belknap Press.

Channon, D.F. (1973) *The Strategy and Structure of British Enterprise*, London: Macmillan.

Clark, P. and Tann, J. (1986) 'Cultures and corporations: the M-form in the USA and Britain', Paper presented to the International Academy of Business.

Coleman, D.C. (1969) *Courtaulds: An Economic and Social History*, vol. 2, Oxford: Oxford University Press.

—— (1987) 'Failings and achievements: some British businesses, 1919–80', *Business History* 29: 1–17.

Cowling, K. (1982) *Monopoly Capitalism*, London: Macmillan.

Cowling, K., Stoneman, P., Cubbin, J., Hale, R., Domberger, S. and Dutton, P. (1980) *Mergers and Economic Performance*, Cambridge: Cambridge University Press.

Crafts, N.F.R. (1988) 'The assessment: British economic growth over the long run', *Oxford Review of Economics and Policy* 4: i–xxi.

—— (1991) 'Economic growth', in N.F.R. Crafts and N. Woodward (eds) *The British Economy since 1945*, Oxford: Oxford University Press, 261–90.

Daly, A., Hitchens, D.M. and Wagner, K. (1985) 'Productivity, machinery and skills in a sample of British and German manufacturing plants', *National Institute Economic Review* 111: 48–61.

Dyas, G.P. and Thanheiser, H.T. (1976) *The Emerging European Enterprise*, London: Macmillan.

Edgerton, D. (1991) *England and the Aeroplane: An Essay on a Militant and Technological Nation*, London: Macmillan.

Elbaum, B. and Lazonick, W. (eds) (1986) *The Decline of the British Economy*, Oxford: Clarendon Press.

Elstub, St J. (1969) *Productivity of the National Aircraft Effort*, London: Macmillan.

Firth, M. (1979) 'The profitability of takeovers and mergers', *Economic Journal* 89: 316–28.

Freeman, C.F. (1978) 'Technical innovation and British trade performance', in F. Blackaby (ed.) *De-industrialisation*, London: Heinemann, 56–77.

Franks, J. and Mayer, C. (1992) 'Hostile takeovers and the correction of managerial failure', London Business School Discussion Paper.

Gourvish, T.R. (1987) 'British business and the transition to a corporate economy', *Business History* 29: 18–45.

Gribbin, J.D. (1978) 'The postwar revival of competition as industrial policy', Government Economic Service Working Paper 19.

Hague, D. and Wilkinson, G. (1983) *The IRC – An Experiment in Industrial Intervention*, London: Allen & Unwin.

Hannah, L. (1974) 'Managerial innovation and the rise of the large scale company in interwar Britain', *Economic History Review* 27: 252–70.

—— (1976) 'Strategy and structure in the manufacturing sector', in L. Hannah (ed.) *Management Strategy and Business Development: An Historical and Comparative Study*, London: Macmillan, 184–202.

—— (1980) 'Visible and invisible hands in Great Britain', in A.D. Chandler and H. Daems (eds) *Managerial Hierarchies: Comparative Perspectives on the Rise of the Modern Industrial Enterprise*, Cambridge, MA: Harvard University Press, 41–76.

—— (1983) *The Rise of the Corporate Economy*, 2nd edn, London: Methuen.

Hannah, L. and Kay, J.A. (1977) *Concentration in Modern Industry: Theory, Measurement and the UK Experience*, London: Macmillan.

Hart, P.E. and Clarke, R. (1980) *Concentration in British Industry, 1935–75*, Cambridge: Cambridge University Press.

Hayward, K. (1989) *The British Aircraft Industry*, Manchester: Manchester University Press.

HM Government (1926a) *Report of the Royal (Samuel) Commission on the Coal Industry*, vol. 1, Cmd 2600.

HM Government (1926b) *Report of the Departmental (Lewis) Committee on Co-operative Selling in the Coal Industry*.

HM Government (1929) Committee on Industry and Trade, *Final (Balfour) Report*, Cmd 3282.

HM Government (1944) *Employment Policy after the War*, Cmd 6527.

Jenkinson, T. and Mayer, C. (1992) 'The assessment: corporate governance and corporate control', *Oxford Review of Economic Policy* 8: 1–10.

Kahn, A.E. (1946) *Great Britain and the World Economy*, New York: Columbia University Press.

Kaldor, M. (1982) *The Baroque Arsenal*, London: Andre Deutsch.

Kaldor, M., Sharp, M. and Walker, W. (1986) 'Industrial competitiveness and Britain's defence', *Lloyds Bank Review* October: 31–49.

Kaufman, R.L. (1982) 'Economic dualism: a critical review', *American Sociological Review* 47: 727–39.

Kirby, M.W. (1977) *The British Coalmining Industry, 1870–1946: A Political and Economic History*, London: Macmillan.

—— (1987) 'Industrial policy', in S. Glynn and A. Booth (eds) *The Road to Full Employment*, London: Allen & Unwin, 125–39.

—— (1991) 'Supply-side management', in N.F.R. Crafts and N. Woodward (eds) *The British Economy since 1945*, Oxford: Clarendon Press, 236–60.

—— (1992) 'Institutional rigidities and economic decline: reflections on the British experience', *Economic History Review* 45: 637–60.

Kumar, M.S. (1984) *Growth, Acquisition and Investment*, Cambridge: Cambridge University Press.

Landes, D.S. (1972) *The Unbound Prometheus: Technological Change and Industrial Development from 1750 to the Present*, Cambridge: Cambridge University Press.

Lazonick, W. (1983) 'Industrial organisation and technological change: the decline of the British cotton industry', *Business History Review* 107: 230–6.

—— (1986) 'The cotton industry', in B. Elbaum and W. Lazonick (eds) *The Decline of the British Economy*, Oxford: Clarendon Press, 18–50.

Lewchuk, W. (1987) *American Technology and the British Vehicle Industry*, Cambridge: Cambridge University Press.

Locke, R.R. (1984) *The End of the Practical Man: Entrepreneurship and Higher Education in Germany, France and Great Britain*, Greenwich, CT: JAI Press.

Meeks, G. (1977) *Disappointing Marriage: A Study of the Gains from Merger*, Cambridge: Cambridge University Press.

Mercer, H. (1991) 'The Monopolies and Restrictive Practices Commission, 1949–56: a study of regulatory failure', in G. Jones and M.W. Kirby (eds) *Competitiveness and the State: Government and Business in Twentieth Century Britain*, Manchester: Manchester University Press, 78–99.

Morris, D.J. and Stout, D.K. (1985) 'Industrial policy', in D.J. Morris (ed.) *The Economic System in the UK*, 3rd edn, Oxford: Oxford University Press, 851–94.

Newton, S. and Porter, D. (1988) *Modernization Frustrated: the Politics of Industrial Decline in Britain since 1900*, London: Unwin Hyman.

Olson, M. (1982) *The Rise and Decline of Nations: Economic Growth, Stagflation and Social Rigidities*, New Haven, CT: Yale University Press.

Pagnamenta, P. and Overy, R. (1984) *All Our Working Lives*, London: British Broadcasting Corporation.

Payne, P. (1988) *British Entrepreneurship in the Nineteenth Century*, London: Macmillan.

—— (1990) 'Entrepreneurship and British economic decline', in B. Collins and K. Robbins (eds) *British Culture and Economic Decline*, London: Weidenfeld & Nicholson, 25–58.

Peck, M.J. (1968) 'Science and technology', in R.E. Caves and associates (eds) *Britain's Economic Prospects*, London: George Allen & Unwin, 448–84.

Peden, G.C. (1985) *British Economic and Social Policy: From Lloyd George to Margaret Thatcher*, Oxford: Philip Allan.

Piore, M.J. and Sabel, C.F. (1984) *The Second Industrial Divide: Possibilities for Prosperity*, New York: Basic Books.

Pollard, S. (1982) *The Wasting of the British Economy: British Economic Policy, 1945 to the Present*, London: Croom Helm.

—— (1989) *Britain's Prime and Britain's Decline: The British Economy, 1870–1914*, London: Edward Arnold.

Porter, M. (1990) *The Competitive Advantage of Nations*, London: Macmillan.

Prais, S.J. (1981) *Productivity and Industrial Structure*, Cambridge: Cambridge University Press.

Pratten, C.F. and Atkinson, A.G. (1976) 'The use of manpower in British manufacturing industry', *Department of Employment Gazette* 84: 571–6.

Reader, W.J. (1970) *Imperial Chemical Industries: A History*, vol. 1, *The Forerunners 1870–1926*, London: Oxford University Press.

—— (1975) *Imperial Chemical Industries: A History*, vol. 2, Oxford: Oxford University Press.

Richardson, H.W. (1961) 'The new industries between the wars', *Oxford Economic Papers* 13: 360–84.

—— (1967) *Economic Recovery in Britain 1932–1939*, London: Weidenfeld & Nicholson.

Sabel, C. and Zeitlin, J. (1985) 'Historical alternatives to mass production: politics, markets and technology in nineteenth century industrialisation', *Past and Present* 108: 133–76.

Schneider-Lenné, E.R. (1992) 'Corporate control in Germany', *Oxford Review of Economic Policy* 8: 11–23.

Singh, A. (1971) *Takeovers*, Cambridge: Cambridge University Press.

Steer, P. and Cable, J.R. (1978) 'Internal organisation and profit: an empirical analysis of large UK companies', *Journal of Industrial Economics* 27: 13–30.

Supple, Barry (1987) *The History of the British Coal Industry*, vol. 4, *1913–1946: The Political Economy of Decline*, Oxford: Clarendon.

—— (ed.) (1992) *The Rise of Big Business*, Aldershot: Edward Elgar.

Tolliday, S. (1984) 'Tariffs and steel, 1916–1934', in J. Turner (ed.) *Businessmen and Politics: Studies of Business Activity in British Politics*, London: Heinemann, 50–75.

—— (1987) *Business, Banking and Politics: The Case of British Steel, 1918–1939*, Cambridge, MA: Harvard University Press.

Toyne, B., Arpan, T.S., Ricks, D.A., Shimp, T.A. and Barnett, A. (eds) (1984) *The Global Textile Industry*, London: Allen & Unwin.

Utton, M.A. (1974) 'On measuring the effects of industrial mergers', *Scottish Journal of Political Economy* 21: 95–121.

Van Ark, B. (1990) 'Comparative levels of labour productivity in postwar Europe: some evidence for manufacturing', *Oxford Bulletin of Economics and Statistics* 52: 343–74.

Walshe, J.G. (1991) 'Industrial organisation and competition policy', in N.F.R. Crafts and N. Woodward (eds) *The British Economy since 1945*, Oxford: Clarendon Press, 335–80.

7 British multinationals and British business since 1850

Geoffrey Jones

BRITISH MULTINATIONALS IN INTERNATIONAL PERSPECTIVE

The high propensity of British enterprises to undertake foreign direct investment (FDI) outside the United Kingdom has been a striking feature of British business history. In the nineteenth century, when FDI first became significant in the world economy, British firms were uniquely prominent. During the twentieth century, when world FDI both grew rapidly and changed its shape in fundamental ways, British business remained exceptionally active in multinational investment.

Table 7.1 indicates the long-term relative importance of the UK as a home economy for FDI. It gives the best available estimates of FDI stock levels at various benchmark dates, but it has to be acknowledged immediately that these figures must be treated with caution. Because no reliable FDI statistics exist before the 1960s, estimates for earlier years have to be calculated from total foreign investment figures, which are themselves disputed in the case of pre-1914 Britain (Platt 1986; Feinstein 1990). These estimates also depend, as will be discussed in the following section, on contestable assumptions as to what constitutes FDI as opposed to portfolio investment. The post-1960 FDI statistics are very much more reliable, though the effects of exchange rate movements have to be borne firmly in mind.

The United Kingdom emerges from these statistics as the largest holder of FDI in the world before the Second World War. Subsequently, the British lost first place to the United States, but they remained the second largest multinational investor until the present day. Nor was the significance of British-owned multinational investment limited to absolute size. Throughout the twentieth century FDI has been a relatively more important part of British business activity than for any comparable country. This can be illustrated by relating

Table 7.1 Percentage share of estimated stock of accumulated foreign direct investment held by the UK, the United States, Germany and Japan, 1914, 1938, 1960, 1970,[a] 1980 and 1990 (%)

	1914	1938	1960	1970	1980	1990
UK	45	40	16	14	15	15
United States	18	28	49	48	40	26
Germany	10	1	1	4	8	9
Japan	0	3	1	3	7	12
Total world (US$ billion[b])	14	26	67	172	517	1644

Sources: Dunning 1993: 17, 117; Stopford and Dunning 1983; United Nations 1992

Notes: [a] 1971.
[b] Current US dollars.

FDI to domestic output, but the frailty of pre-1960 data renders statistical calculations for the first part of this century speculative. The speculations of Houston and Dunning are, however, startling. They estimate that the ratio of UK FDI to UK national income was 'above 57 per cent' in 1913, before falling to around 33 per cent in 1938. The US ratio was 9 per cent in 1914 and 1929 (Houston and Dunning 1976: 12).

Table 7.2 demonstrates the importance of British FDI to the British economy for two benchmark years, 1967 and 1990, when reliable statistical data are available. It can be seen that in 1967 the size of UK FDI compared with the British gross domestic product was much larger than for the United States and other large Western European countries, and was only surpassed by the Netherlands, two of whose largest multinational corporations – Shell and Unilever – were Anglo-Dutch. Twenty-three years later the relative importance of FDI to the British economy was higher, and remained of a different magnitude from that of the United States and the large Western European economies. A similar point emerges if FDI flow data are used rather than stock figures. A calculation of British FDI flows as a percentage of gross domestic fixed capital formation reveals an average of 5 per cent for 1960–2 and 7.6 per cent for 1978–80. The comparative averages for the United States are 3 and 4.7 per cent; for Germany 1 and 2.5 per cent; for France 2.2 and 1.9 per cent; and for Japan 0.5 and 0.8 per cent. In the entire 1960–80 period, only the Netherlands approached the UK level (Stopford and Dunning 1983: 11).

The size of British multinational investment raises important questions about British business performance since the nineteenth

Table 7.2 Stock of outward foreign direct investment of the UK and other countries compared with gross domestic product, 1967 and 1990

	1967		1990	
	Stock ($billion)	% GDP	Stock ($billion)	% GDP
UK	15.8	14.5	244.8	25.1
Germany	3.0	1.6	155.1	10.4
France	6.0	7.0	114.8	9.6
Italy	2.1	2.8	60.0	5.5
Netherlands	11.0	33.1	99.2	35.5
Switzerland	2.5	10.0	64.9	28.8
United States	56.6	7.1	426.5	7.9
Japan	1.5	0.9	201.4	6.8
Total[a]	112.3	4.0	1644.2	8.0

Sources: Dunning 1993: 17; United Nations 1992

Note: [a]Total world outward FDI calculated against world gross domestic product.

century. At the most basic level, it confronts a literature oriented towards explaining the relative competitive failure of British business with a story of apparent international vitality and success. Few economic histories of twentieth-century Britain refer to the extensive multinational investments of its enterprises. The subject is also not mentioned in Michael Porter's analysis of the 'slide of Britain'. How is the proposition that 'Britain has been losing competitive advantage in industry since well before the second world war' (Porter 1990: 482) to be reconciled with the vigour of its companies overseas? The evidence from British multinational enterprise poses questions for prevailing interpretations of British business history. It would not be possible to sustain international business activity on such a scale without a level of competence in management and organization. How can Chandlerian and other critiques of British organizational capability be reconciled with the evidence of British multinational activity?

This chapter surveys the growth of British multinational enterprise over the last hundred years. Within this context, it addresses two main issues. Why has British multinational investment been so high? And how has this high level been sustained, especially after 1945, despite the relative decline of the British economy and the perceived weaknesses of its management? A complete answer to these matters would need to consider also Britain's position as a leading host economy for foreign multinationals. It has attracted a disproportionate share of US FDI in Europe throughout the twentieth century, and in the last decade has attracted a disproportionate share of Japanese FDI in Europe (Dunning 1985, 1986; Jones 1988; Bostock and Jones 1994). The UK currently accounts for 10 per cent of the world stock of inward FDI, considerably more than France and Germany (4 per cent and 5 per cent respectively), and very considerably more than Japan (2 per cent). Foreign companies accounted for almost 20 per cent of gross value added in the British manufacturing sector in 1990. It is beyond the remit of this chapter to discuss this extensive inward investment into the UK, which has in any case received more attention than British outward investment (Young *et al*. 1988), but its implications for the interpretation of British-owned multinational investment will need to be considered.

BRITISH MULTINATIONALS BEFORE 1914

The size and corporate forms of British foreign direct investment

Few subjects in modern British business history have undergone such a substantial reinterpretation as the pre-1914 history of British multinational enterprise. Although Britain has always been recognized as the world's leading capital exporter before the First World War, most of this foreign investment was regarded as portfolio in nature, involving no significant element of managerial control. In his pioneering study of the origins of British-based multinational manufacturing enterprises, Stopford estimated that only 10 per cent of British overseas investment was FDI in 1914. British multinational manufacturing was regarded as retarded compared with that of the United States: British firms were 'ostrich-like . . . viewing the world at a distance' (Stopford 1974: 182). This view has persisted in the work of many economic historians, such as W.P. Kennedy, who regarded British foreign investment as overwhelmingly portfolio and risk averse before 1914 – and sought to explain this by alleged biases in British capital markets (Kennedy 1987: 110–63). There are strong echoes of this tradition in *Scale and Scope*, where Chandler argues that the British lack of organizational capability deriving from their 'personal capitalism' meant that British enterprises 'moved overseas more hesitantly and less successfully than those of many of their foreign competitors' (Chandler 1990: 294, 337, 372).

However, a very different interpretation has developed alongside this 'pessimistic' one. A critical problem faced by those seeking to estimate the size of British FDI before 1914 is the diversity of institutional forms used by British-owned business abroad. From its origins in the nineteenth century, American and German FDI primarily took the form of a company with pre-existing domestic business establishing a subsidiary in a foreign country, over which it exercised management control. This became the 'classic' form of multinational enterprise which dominated international business activity in the world from the First World War until at least the 1970s. British manufacturing companies made investments of this nature from the 1860s, and in greater numbers than the 'ostrich' thesis would suggest. Nicholas has identified over 200 of such British manufacturing multinationals before 1914 (Nicholas 1991: 135). It is almost certain that there were more of such British-owned multinationals than American ones before the First World War. However, the British also undertook a considerable amount of foreign investment using different corporate forms than the 'classic' multinational enterprise, although still involving sufficient managerial control to justify regarding it as FDI. This point was made by Houston and Dunning (1976: 36), Wilkins (1977: 13–14), and Svedberg (1978), and it was incorporated by Dunning into the estimates of world FDI in 1914 given in Table 7.1 above. Dunning believed that over one-third of total UK foreign investment abroad in 1914 fell into the category of direct rather than portfolio.

According to Wilkins, the predominant form of British FDI before 1914 was the 'free-standing' company. These firms, of which there were thousands, were registered in Britain 'to conduct business overseas, most of which, unlike the American model, did *not* grow out of the domestic operations of existing enterprises that had headquarters in Britain' (Wilkins 1988b: 261). They usually specialized in a single country, where they might own a railway, electricity company, a plantation or a cattle ranch. Stopford (1974: 161–3) considered such enterprises to be a special category of foreign investment distinct from both portfolio and FDI, but the combination of ownership and control from Britain does make them appear far more as a form of FDI. These free-standing firms, which were found extensively in the United States, formed only part of an extensive galaxy of British overseas business activities, which included trading companies, managing agencies and other corporate forms active throughout the world.

The free-standing and other types of firm were nominally independent from one another, but often linked in various ways, somewhat like Japanese-style 'enterprise groups'. Wilkins has identified ten different types of 'clusters' of free-standing firms organized around various interest groups and producers of services, such as firms of solicitors, accountants and mining engineers. Chapman has explored a similar theme in his identification of thirty British 'investment groups', consisting of networks of British companies associated through cross-shareholdings or interlinking directorships. These were particularly prominent in India, China and the Far East: the diversified activities of Jardine, Matheson were one example. Beyond Asia, British investment groups were active in South Africa, Russia and Latin America, where trading companies such as Anthony Gibbs & Son and Balfour, Williamson diversified before 1914 from international commerce to shipping, mining and agricultural activities (Chapman 1992: 231–61).

It should be added that this diversity of corporate forms undertaking FDI before 1914 was not uniquely British but rather a feature of most European capital-exporting and imperial nations. Much of the FDI of France, Belgium and the Netherlands also utilized free-standing and other types of business enterprise quite different from the 'classic' multinational. As in many other matters, the British experience is best considered in its European context rather than in comparison with the United States.

Sectoral distribution

The diversity of British FDI before 1914 was not limited to its corporate form. British-owned enterprises were active abroad in an exceptionally wide-range of economic sectors. By the middle of the nineteenth century, British firms were already extensively involved in multinational service sector investment, especially in trading companies, financial services and public utilities. The activities of British 'overseas banks' are one example. These banks, promoted and largely owned in the UK, where they had their corporate headquarters, were designed to undertake banking overseas rather than in Britain. The first banks, founded in the 1830s, went to the British colonies in Australia, the West Indies and Canada. Subsequently they went to Asia and Latin America also. By 1913 just over thirty British overseas banks operated almost 1,400 branches outside the UK, principally in Asia, Latin America and Australasia (Jones 1993a: 414). British insurance companies were also very active in FDI. In 1913 forty-two British insurance companies were involved in fire and marine insurance in the United States alone (Wilkins 1989: 531).

British companies, usually of the free-standing type, invested extensively in foreign public utilities. By 1913 the British had £340 million of FDI in Latin American railways (Stone 1977: 699). British-owned and managed railway companies were dominant in Argentina, Uruguay, Peru and Columbia, and occupied a strong position in Brazil, Chile, Venezuela and elsewhere. British-owned and managed gas and electricity companies, tramways and other utilities were also spread all over Latin America (Rippy 1959). Beyond Latin America, British-owned utilities were present in many parts of the world, even including Continental Europe. An early and spectacular instance was the Imperial Continental Gas Association, formed in 1824 to introduce gas lighting from Britain to the rest of Europe. By 1850 it owned and operated sixteen gas utilities spread over the German states, France, Belgium, the Netherlands and Austria. Fifty years later it operated gas utilities in ten major European towns outside the UK – of which Berlin was the largest operation – and in twenty-nine smaller towns, and had a total workforce of almost 8,000 (Hill 1950). British-owned shipping companies, such as the Ellerman Lines and the P & O Steam Navigation Company, provided another example of British service sector multinational investment before 1914.

British FDI in the primary sector also occurred early in the nineteenth century, and became extensive from the 1870s. Thirty-five British companies were active in non-ferrous metal mining outside Britain in 1875 with a total of £11.4 million invested; by 1913 there were 957 companies with £240 million invested (Harvey and Press 1990: 102). In the 1870s British firms were most active in copper and silver extraction, with around one-third of the investment in Continental Europe and another third in the United States, but by 1913 gold accounted for around 60 per cent of total British FDI in metals, with South Africa as the main focus of attention. An early example of British FDI in gold mining was the St John d'el Rey Mining Company, organized in 1830 to exploit Brazilian goldfields. By 1913 this freestanding company operated the deepest mine in the world, and employed over 2,500 workers in Brazil (Eakin 1989: 49).

British FDI in metals before 1914 usually took the free-standing form, although larger and more diversified enterprises also developed, such as the Rio Tinto Company, founded in 1873 to exploit copper mines in Spain. It began life with a large capital and captured for a time a leading part in world markets for sulphur and copper. It had also diversified into North Africa and the United States by 1914 (Harvey 1981).

Before 1914 the foundations had also been laid for Britain's large multinational investment in the world oil industry. Both the Shell Group and BP originated in this period. The 'Shell' Transport and Trading Company's origins lay in the Far East trading interests of the Samuel family, London merchants. During the 1880s the Samuels began selling Russian oil to the Far East, and a major coup was achieved in 1892 when they secured permission for their oil tankers to pass through the Suez Canal, which greatly reduced the cost of Russian oil in Asia and permitted it to compete with American oil. Fears that Russian supplies might be reduced led to a search for oil-fields nearer the Far Eastern markets, and in 1898 a major oilfield was discovered in the Dutch colony of Borneo, a year after the 'Shell' Transport and Trading Company was founded. However, in the early 1900s a loss of entrepreneurial drive and a series of misjudgements weakened Shell's position, and in 1907 the British were obliged to accept a minority position in a merger with the Royal Dutch Petroleum Company. The Dutch held 60 per cent and the British 40 per cent of the shareholding of the new group. By 1914 the Shell Group had extensive production and marketing FDI in Asia, Russia, Latin America and the United States (Jones 1981: 19–23, 77). In addition to Shell, British free-standing type oil companies were to be found in Russia, Southeast Asia, Mexico and – most importantly – Iran. In Iran, a small British oil company with a concession from the Shah's government discovered a huge oilfield in 1908. When the firm's lack of downstream facilities and capital threatened its independent existence, the British government was persuaded to take a majority shareholding in the company in 1914 (Ferrier 1982: 158–201). Within twenty years Anglo-Iranian – or BP as it later became known – had become one of the world's largest oil companies.

There was also extensive British FDI in agriculture and raw materials before 1914. In India and Ceylon, British companies introduced the cultivation of tea from the 1840s and hundreds of British-owned tea plantation companies were in operation by 1900, usually controlled and partially owned by the large British agency houses active in the region. In the United States, the British invested heavily in cattle raising and meat processing (Wilkins 1989: 299–307). A few British manufacturing companies also undertook backward integration to secure supplies of raw materials. Lever Brothers began in the 1900s to establish plantations in order to guarantee supplies of vegetable oil, first in the Pacific and then – on a huge scale – in the Belgian Congo (Fieldhouse 1978: 448–55).

British FDI in manufacturing was smaller than in the service and primary sectors, but nonetheless extensive. The staple industries which dominated the domestic economy saw little outward FDI, as they generally preferred exporting. Lancashire cotton textile firms did invest abroad before 1914, but the largest multinational investment came from the specialized cotton thread and rayon sectors. In the former product, J & P Coats opened an American factory in 1869, and by the mid-1890s the firm was already manufacturing in the

United States, Canada, Russia, Austria and Spain (Wilkins 1989: 363). In rayon, Courtaulds, having acquired the British patents to the chemical processes in 1904 and the American rights five years later, established an American factory in 1911, which dominated the US market for the next twenty years (Coleman 1969: II, 104–54).

Multinational investment occurred frequently in the 'new' industries of the late nineteenth century. In consumer products, Lever Brothers after 1890 established soap factories in the United States, Canada, Australia, South Africa, Japan and several European countries (Wilson 1954, I: 98–110, 188–210). By 1914 British firms manufactured abroad a range of branded food products, from dog food and toffee in the United States, to marmalade in Germany. The Gramophone Company had six musical record factories outside Britain by 1914, in Germany, Russia, Spain, France, Austria–Hungary and India (Jones 1985: 85–6). Dunlop established tyre factories in France and Germany in 1892, in the United States in 1893 (sold five years later) and in Japan in 1909 (Jones 1986a: 24–8). By 1914 Vickers owned and controlled dockyards and arsenals in Spain, Italy, Austria–Hungary, Russia, Turkey, France, Japan and Canada, often in the form of joint ventures with other British companies or local interests (Davenport-Hines 1986a: 46–7). The overall impression of British multinational manufacturing investment before 1914 was that it was spread over a wide range of product groups (Nicholas 1991).

Determinants

What caused the rapid growth of British FDI from the mid-nineteenth century? Why were the British the most prolific foreign investors in the world? The British experience formed part of a worldwide trend. A number of important environmental influences in the world economy caused world FDI to grow quickly from a very low base in 1850. Both access to markets and the control of international business activities were facilitated by improvements in transportation, notably the spread of railways and, from the 1870s, the use of steamships. Managerial control was further facilitated by improvements in communications, such as the invention of the electric telegraph. The extensive British – and other European – FDI in primary and service activities was related to imperialism, as a considerable portion of FDI went to colonial territories in the developing world.

The determinants of FDI in supply-oriented or resource-seeking activities have to be distinguished from those in market-oriented activities. Industrialization in Europe and the United States produced large markets for primary products, which were either found or grown in the developing world. Britain's position as the largest industrial economy before being overtaken by the United States meant that its entrepreneurs were well placed to perceive profitable opportunities in the extractive and commodity sectors. The high level of entrepreneurial activity was demonstrated by the level of firm creation (and destruction). Some 8,400 British companies are known to have been formed between 1880 and 1913 for mining and mine exploration abroad. The great majority of these firms generated little or no serious activity, but a tiny minority did. They became the predecessors of the large British extractive multinationals of the twentieth century (Harvey and Press 1990: 99).

British entrepreneurs were able to exploit worldwide opportunities in the extractive industries because of the availability of capital on the London Stock Exchange and because of Britain's position as the leading capital-exporting economy. The London Stock Exchange emerged as the world's largest source of mining finance in the late nineteenth century – and an enormous conglomeration of information about opportunities worldwide. The question arises why FDI rather than portfolio investment was frequently chosen to exploit such opportunities. Transactions cost theory provides important insights into the answer. Free-standing firms, it has been argued, provided an institutional alternative to capital markets with high transactions costs. High transactions costs arose in capital transfers in the nineteenth century because of the risks that debtors might not repay their obligations. Information asymmetries and opportunistic behaviour made the effective monitoring and screening of borrowers very costly. A strategy of taking collateral as security for a loan was possible, but not very effective for investments in mining and agriculture in which capital sunk into unsuccessful projects could not yield saleable assets. Free-standing firms enabled British lenders to monitor the use of their funds and exercise some managerial control over their investments (Hennart 1987, 1991). In many instances in the nineteenth century, however, British entrepreneurs were engaged in exploiting new opportunities at the frontiers of the expanding world economy. In such circumstances, FDI cannot be ascribed to the internalization process as there were no markets to internalize.

The determinants of British market-oriented FDI in manufacturing need to be treated differently. British manufacturing companies sought to exploit various ownership or competitive advantages in foreign markets through FDI. Probably the most important ownership advantage at this period was entrepreneurial ability. Thus William

Lever turned his attention to foreign markets soon after his firm started in 1885, and undertook a personal search for markets and, later, production sites (Wilson 1954: I, 89). Sometimes British firms possessed new technologies which they could exploit abroad. Courtaulds and its patented rayon technology provides one example. However, already at this stage, British manufacturing multinationals were much less active in new and technologically advanced industries, such as electricals, where competitive advantages were derived from extensive investment in research and development as well as the creation of managerial hierarchies. American and German firms emerged as the prominent multinational investors in such industries. British firms appeared more active in industries where advantages were derived from branding and product differentiation (Wilkins 1988a: 15).

The role of structural market failure in explaining the growth of the modern manufacturing multinational is well established. Using a sample of 119 British manufacturing firms which made a direct investment between 1870 and 1939, Nicholas has shown that 94 per cent of the firms for whom information is available exported their product before undertaking FDI (Nicholas 1982: 620). Tariffs and non-tariff barriers to trade often prompted the switch from export to overseas manufacture. The rise of trade protectionism in the United States and Continental Europe in the late nineteenth century was the single most important influence on the growth of manufacturing multinationals. Manufacturers of branded consumer or high-technology products which required markets with high per capita incomes and industrial sectors were under strong pressure to 'jump' tariff barriers to establish local manufacture (Jones 1986a: 9). Tariffs are less relevant, however, to explaining free-standing firms in manufacturing, such as the extensive British investment in beer-making in the United States in the late nineteenth and early twentieth century (Wilkins 1989: 324–30). A number of other non-tariff barriers to trade also stimulated FDI. Patent legislation in foreign countries occasionally encouraged British firms to manufacture locally rather than export in order to protect their technology. Armaments companies experienced pressure to manufacture locally from governments anxious to build defence capacity (Davenport-Hines 1986a: 44).

Market-oriented FDI was often an aggressive rather than a defensive reaction to market failures. British – and other foreign – enterprises were attracted to the enormous opportunities of the fastest growing and largest market in the world, that of the United States. British firms discovered that producing in a market gave them greater sensitivity to local tastes, and a better ability to respond quickly to market needs. The Gramophone Company, for example, built a record factory in Calcutta in 1907 which enabled it to shorten dramatically the six-month delay which had previously occurred when making a recording of popular music in India and getting a record on sale in that country (Jones 1985: 86).

British multinational manufacturing also grew as a response to transactional market failure. British firms grew across borders by internalizing markets for proprietary assets, such as technology and brands, because such markets were subject to high transactions costs. British manufacturing companies typically had agency agreements with foreign companies before investing abroad. These often involved high transactions costs in terms of enforcement by the principals, as many agents sought large discounts or were otherwise inefficient. Such problems led firms to replace agents with their own, wholly-owned selling companies (Nicholas 1982: 621−4).

The extensive British service sector FDI before 1914 had a number of determinants, although the UK's unique importance in world trade and in the world financial system was the critical factor. A distinction can be made between trade-supporting, location-bound and foreign-tradeable services. The first category included the British trading companies which operated throughout in Asia and Latin America. The business cultures and institutions of those regions were very different from Britain, and the trading companies reduced the risks of international trade in unfamiliar areas by collecting information and providing scarce managerial talent. British FDI in public utilities was also partly trade-supporting, arising from the absence of adequate infrastructure to support accelerating trade flows in Latin America and elsewhere. However, it was also in part location-bound, arising from entrepreneurial perceptions of profitable opportunities in supplying services where consumption could not be separated from production. British multinational banking had elements of all three types of service sector FDI. The banks specialized in international trade finance but they also provided domestic banking services, which was a location-bound service as FDI in the host economy was the only means to provide such retail banking (Jones 1993a: 30−40).

The size and spread of British FDI before 1914 was a reflection of the unique position of Britain in the world economy. FDI formed part of the torrent of British capital exports. The service sector investment came from an economy that still accounted for almost one-third of world trade before the First World War, and whose currency was used to finance most of world trade. The investment in the extractive and agricultural sectors came from the world's largest industrial economy in the nineteenth century. British entrepreneurs turned naturally to exploit overseas opportunities when much of the world was under British formal or informal political control, or else spoke English, as in the case of the United States.

THE INTER-WAR YEARS AND DEBATES ABOUT PERFORMANCE

Characteristics of British foreign direct investment in the inter-war years

The available statistical estimates suggest that the British share of world FDI stock declined marginally between 1914 and 1938, but the absolute stock is estimated to have risen from US$6.5 billion (£1,377 million) to US$10.5 billion (£2,160 million). It is probable that most of this increase occurred in the 1920s, given the disturbed political and economic conditions of the following decade. It would appear also that, while the majority of UK FDI remained in the primary and service sectors, there was an increase in multinational manufacturing; that, coincident with this development, new British FDI went to the developed world and especially the British settler countries; and that the free-standing firms declined sharply. These characteristics of British FDI will be explored below.

The evidence for the further expansion of British manufacturing multinational investment is strong. The number of British multinational manufacturers counted by Nicholas grew from over 200 in 1914 to 448 in 1939 (Nicholas 1991: 132). Case study evidence has established that many pre-1914 British manufacturing multinationals expanded the number of their overseas production plants. Dunlop, for example, undertook new FDI in production facilities in Canada, Australia, South Africa, Ireland and India in the inter-war years. Courtaulds undertook new investments in France, Germany and Italy in the 1920s. A new generation of British manufacturing firms developed. Before 1914 the British chocolate manufacturers had almost entirely relied on exports to penetrate overseas markets. This was a considerable contrast with the German chocolate manufacturer Gebrüder Stollwerck, which manufactured in various European locations and owned the second largest chocolate factory in the United States before 1914 (Chandler 1990: 399–400). In the inter-war years, however, Cadbury and Rowntree built factories in Australia, Canada, New Zealand, Ireland, South Africa and Germany. Other 'new'

British multinational investors included Glaxo (pharmaceuticals), GKN (engineering), Distillers (gin) and Metal Box (tin boxes) (Jones 1986a: 5, 9; Houston and Dunning 1976: 42–3). The extensive multi-national manufacturing operations of British American Tobacco, which began life in 1901 as a UK registered but American-dominated corporation with a one-third British shareholding, had also passed under full British ownership and control by the beginning of the inter-war years (Cox 1989: 60–1). It is noteworthy that FDI did not always come from the fast-growing sectors of the British economy. In the motor car industry, Austin and Morris made no effort to emulate the multinational strategies pursued by the leading American car companies. In contrast, the textile firms Bradford Dyers Association and Calico Printers Association invested in multinational manufacturing in Egypt and elsewhere in the 1930s (Tignor 1987: 53).

The further spread of protectionism was a major factor in the continued growth of British multinational manufacturing. The growth of tariffs in the settler Dominions, and even in British India and the dependent colonies, obliged British manufacturing exporters to those markets to consider local manufacture. Tariffs threatened the markets of companies such as Cadbury and Rowntree which depended on Empire markets for their products, and so stimulated local manufacturing. Few FDI strategies, however, were mono-causal. The influence of protectionism coexisted with the aggressive pursuit of market opportunities; with dissatisfaction with the costs of alternative means of servicing markets such as licensing; and with the need to emulate or threaten competitors (Jones 1986a: 8–10).

The extensive pre-1914 British FDI in the primary and service sectors stayed in place in the inter-war years, and expanded in some sectors, especially those – like petroleum and gold extraction – where world demand was strong. In the primary sector, there was a wide-spread trend towards merger and the creation of large firms, a process greatly stimulated by the growing capital intensity of many mining operations. These large firms frequently pursued horizontal integration strategies as they sought to utilize their skills and expertise developed in one country to others, and to diversify sources of supply, while vertical integration occurred when markets for raw materials and intermediate inputs were characterized by high transactions costs (Schmitz 1986; Hennart 1987).

The oil industry illustrated these processes. By the 1930s Anglo-Iranian and the part-British Shell Group were established as two of the 'seven sisters' which dominated the world oil industry, the other five companies being American. During the 1920s Anglo-Iranian developed rapidly as a modern managerial enterprise, making the Chandler-approved threefold investments in production, distribution and management. It built refining capacity in Britain, invested in oil tankers, and established distribution outlets in Continental Europe and other parts of the world (Chandler 1990: 298–303). The Shell Group's growth and degree of horizontal and vertical integration was even greater. In the inter-war years Shell had oilfields in the United States, Mexico, Venezuela and the Dutch East Indies, worldwide distribution facilities, and had also diversified into chemicals, establishing – for example – the Shell Chemical Company in the United States in 1929 (Beaton 1957: 502–31).

In contrast, many smaller free-standing oil companies disappeared, or shrank in importance. The small British oil companies active in Russia were wiped out by the Bolshevik Revolution in 1917, while the important Mexican production and oil distribution interests of the Pearson family were purchased by Shell in 1919 (Jones 1981: 217). Another free-standing venture, the Burmah Oil Company, declined in relative importance in the world oil industry as it was effectively confined to the oilfields and markets of British India (Corley 1983, 1988). Curiously, however, Burmah's 25 per cent shareholding in Anglo-Iranian and 4 per cent in Shell (acquired 1928) gave it such a high market value of shares that the firm was Britain's largest industrial enterprise by this measure in 1919, and tenth largest in 1930 (Chandler 1990: 666–79).

Large British-owned multinationals developed in other extractive industries in the inter-war years. Among the most important was the Rio Tinto Company, which diversified extensively from its Spanish mining interests by making large and successful investments in Zambian copper after 1929. It also diversified – less successfully – into chemicals in Europe and the United States. British-owned tin companies underwent considerable consolidation after the formation of the London Tin Corporation. By 1930 it had secured control over twenty British companies active in Malaya, and as a result accounted for one-third of the tin production of that country. It also secured control of many British tin companies in Thailand, Burma and Nigeria, where it controlled half of that country's tin production (Van Helten and Jones 1989: 168–9).

The performance of British multinational enterprise

There are two separate debates about the performance of British multinational business activities before the Second World War. Both raise important issues, but in the absence of aggregate rate of return statistics, or even reliable profitability data at firm level, solid conclusions remained elusive.

Discussion about the performance of British manufacturing multinationals before 1939 arose from archival research on a small number of large British companies, Dunlop, Cadbury and Courtaulds. It emerged that many of their investments in foreign manufacturing had yielded poor or negative financial results over long periods, although some investments – such as that of Courtaulds in the United States – had been highly successful. These British companies appeared to suffer from managerial weaknesses of the kind that could be predicted from the Chandlerian critique of personal capitalism. They had *ad hoc* management structures and control systems, and a preference for the negotiated business environment rather than fierce competition in the marketplace (Jones 1986a: 18–19; 1986b: 96–110).

Unfortunately, the interpretation of such case study evidence is difficult. Far too few companies have been researched in depth. There is little evidence on whether British companies performed any better or worse than multinationals of other countries, although Schröter's research on multinationals from smaller European countries before 1914, for example, confirms that FDI was a risky strategy which often resulted in unsatisfactory outcomes (Schröter 1991). Non-financial benefits from FDI – such as technological feedback from subsidiaries – are known to have existed, but their extent remains unresearched. The need to incorporate into discussions of success or failure an assumption about the effects of a firm's not undertaking FDI is widely acknowledged, but there is no systematic evidence as to the degree export markets would have been lost if FDI had not been undertaken (Jones 1986b: 102–4).

Perhaps the one aspect about the history of British multinational manufacturing companies before 1939 that can be quantified for a large population of firms is the location of foreign manufacturing subsidiaries. Nicholas's analysis of the regional distribution of production plants of 448 pre-1939 British manufacturing firms has confirmed earlier research indicating that British FDI was geographically widespread, although with a distinct shift to the Empire in the inter-war years (Nicholas 1991). However, this evidence has no clear relevance to debates about performance. Although the post-1945 preference of British firms for the Commonwealth has been interpreted as indicating a lack of competitiveness, there is a general recognition that the political and economic conditions of the inter-war years made the Empire an obvious and rational location compared with Continental

Europe or even the United States (Nicholas 1989: 129–30; Jones 1991: 112). The most that can be said is that the management burden faced by British multinational managers is likely to have been lessened by operations in culturally, linguistically and politically familiar markets.

There has been some systematic investigation of the financial performance of British FDI in the extractive and banking sectors. The absence of comparative data also renders the significance of the results difficult to interpret, and their main contribution has been to demonstrate the variety of outcomes between British enterprises active in the same environment. This emerges from a study of the rates of return of 123 British mining companies operating in Spain between 1851 and 1913. These firms generated internal rates of return varying from negative to 10 per cent or higher. Only one in five of these ventures was profitable, and ninety-eight of them eventually failed. As so often in mining ventures, pioneer companies tended to do much better than those that entered the business after the best prospects had been discovered (Harvey and Taylor 1987: 199–201). A calculation of the rates of return of a large sample of British overseas banks between 1890 and the Second World War likewise demonstrated considerable diversity in performance outcomes. The nature of business undertaken and the host region emerged as the most plausible explanatory variable, with the British banks active in Asia – the Eastern Exchange Banks – demonstrating a superior performance over the long term compared with those in Australia, Latin America and elsewhere (Jones 1993a: 388–9, 475–7, 486).

A second debate about the performance of British multinational enterprise has concerned the organizational capabilities of the British free-standing firms. The managerial structures of these firms were lean. Tiny head offices usually consisted of little more than a board of part-time directors, sometimes supported by a small secretariat, but more often with most financial, legal and technical functions contracted out. American-style managerial hierarchies were conspicuous by their absence. As a result, Wilkins suggests, they had no sustainable advantage in countries such as the United States and disappeared during the early twentieth century, although they persisted longer in countries which lacked strong indigenous management, such as Spain and Burma (Wilkins 1988b: 276).

The managerial inadequacy argument needs qualification. The fragile managerial hierarchies were inadequate before 1914 for high technology industries such as electricals or chemicals, but the British used the 'classic' multinational form when they invested abroad in such sectors (Wilkins 1988b: 277). However, in other sectors the absence of American-style managerial hierarchies did not necessarily translate into a lack of organizational capability. The nineteenth-century British overseas banks managed their large overseas branch networks by using socialization strategies of control, which were effective in minimizing potential agent–principal conflicts and reduced the need for large head offices to monitor staff (Jones 1993a: 47–53). Moreover, the existence of 'clusters' of free-standing firms suggests that the governance structures were not as weak as they appeared at first sight, and that markets for managerial skills and reputation were being internalized along with those for capital.

The decline in importance in the free-standing form of organization appears to have been the result of a number of factors. The corporate form was used for entrepreneurial ventures in the 'frontier' conditions of the late nineteenth century. As conditions matured, some free-standing enterprises such as Rio Tinto or Anglo–Iranian developed more extensive managerial hierarchies, and so evolved into fully fledged extractive multinationals. Others sold out to local investors. External shocks, such as the First World War – during which many British companies active in the United States were sold to American interests – and the Great Depression caused a high casualty rate. Further damage was inflicted by the introduction of exchange controls on capital exports in Britain after 1929.

However, in the service sector especially, British free-standing firms and trading companies remained strong and relatively vigorous through the inter-war years and beyond. They often derived substantial advantages from incumbency and experience. The British overseas banks, for example, had excellent franchises in many regions in which they operated. They had extensive physical assets in the form of networks of branches, as well as powerful intangible assets, especially in their reputations for honesty and stability (Jones 1993a: 200–1). Such advantages could only be quickly overcome by hostile host governments, but overt hostility was exceptional before 1939. One example was Iran, where the British overseas bank which had served as state bank found its activities restricted and a state-owned bank set up to compete with it (Jones 1986c: 184–241). However, this was a rare instance, and in other cases government restrictions could even strengthen British enterprises. In Brazil, for example, the St John d'el Rey Mining Company responded to restrictions on dividend remittances by reinvesting profits in Brazil, and underwent considerable growth as a result (Eakin 1989: 59–60).

BRITISH MULTINATIONALS AFTER 1945

Changes in distribution and corporate structure in the postwar world

British business lost none of its enthusiasm for FDI after the Second World War. The stock of British FDI grew rapidly, remaining much larger than that of either Germany or Japan, and possessing an importance relative to gross domestic product out of line with that of other similar Western European economies. Porter notes the 'ominous' loss of world export share by British industry between 1978 and 1985 (Porter 1990: 494). Yet that precise period saw a *fivefold* increase in British multinational investment. For the 1980−9 period the UK was the world's largest home economy for outflows of FDI, with average annual outflows representing 20 per cent of the world total. British multinational investment was also very 'dynamic' in the post-1945 period in the sense that it underwent a considerable transformation in geographical and industrial distribution, as well as in corporate structure.

The changing geographical location of British multinational investment was dramatic. In the first fifteen years after the end of the Second World War British firms became even more focused on the Commonwealth: one estimate is that 80 per cent of new British FDI in this period − equivalent to around £2.6 billion − went to Commonwealth countries, mostly Australasia, Canada and South Africa. British exchange controls after 1947 may have influenced this flow by their preference for investments in the sterling area. However, the Dominions were attractive for a range of other reasons. They had rising incomes and stable governments which pursued broadly import substitution policies. Competitive pressures were less than in the United States and Western Europe, while the still-extensive political links and the common English language continued to reduce the management burden. Sentiment and rational calculations about risks coexisted in corporate decision making. This can be seen in the case of Glaxo, which concentrated FDI in Commonwealth countries for two decades after 1945. The company's chief executive was said to be 'a poor linguist, with strong personal ties and sympathies with the Dominions . . . (who) concentrated in developing Glaxo's business in the Commonwealth for the good reason that the European mainland was too devastated and dislocated to offer stable or profitable business opportunities' (Davenport-Hines 1986b: 152). Whatever the exact reason, the upshot was that by 1962 around 55 per cent of the stock of

British FDI was in the Commonwealth: British companies had more assets in Malaysia and Nigeria than in France or Germany (Stopford and Turner 1985: 69–96).

However, by 1962 a change in the geographical location of British FDI had begun. It was a two-stage transformation as shown in Table 7.3. The first stage of the geographical redirection of British FDI was a sharp relative decline in the importance of investment in the developing world. Despite the continuing importance of certain developing economies through to the early 1960s, new FDI in the immediate post-war period went mainly to the developed Commonwealth. The British – and other foreign investors – faced restrictive and sometimes hostile policies of host governments in the Third World. The results were particularly dramatic in postwar Latin America. In Argentina the largely British-owned railway system was nationalized in 1948, and most of the rest of the once-extensive service sector investment disappeared. There were similar scenarios in other Latin American countries and in Asia and Africa as colonies became independent states. Investments in extractive industries such as oil became a particular target for host governments. BP's dominance over the Iranian oil industry was successfully challenged in the early 1950s, while Burmah Oil finally divested from Burma in the early 1960s after a decade of difficulties with the Burmese government (Bostock and Jones 1989: 48–9; Corley 1988: 254–71). The large British service sector and manufacturing direct investments in China had to be abandoned after the formation of the People's Republic in 1949. BAT, which had employed over 20,000 workers in a multiplant business in the 1930s, withdrew from China in 1952, followed soon afterwards by the trading companies Jardine Matheson & Company and Butterfield and Swire (Oster-hammel 1989: 210–14). The British may have lost 40 per cent of their total overseas business assets between 1938 and 1956 through sequestration, wartime destruction of property and obligatory sales (Houston and Dunning 1976: 45).

The second stage of the redirection of British multinational enterprise began in the 1960s as British firms invested on a large scale in the United States and Western Europe. The Western European share of British FDI rose from 13 to 23 per cent in less than two decades: the French veto on the British application to join the European Community in 1963 appears to have been the trigger. Subsequently the United States emerged as the single most important location for British FDI. In 1962 Canada had accounted for half as much investment again as the United States in the figure for FDI in North America given in Table 7.3. By 1981 the United States alone accounted for 28 per cent of

Table 7.3 Geographical destination of UK outward foreign direct investment by percentage of total book value of assets, 1929, 1962, 1981

	1929	1962	1981
Western Europe	7.4	13.4	23.2
North America	7.3	23.1	34.6
Other developed	10.9	27.1	20.4
Total developed	25.6	63.5	78.2
Rest of world	74.4	36.5	21.8
Total (world)	100.0	100.0	100.0

Source: Shepherd *et al.* 1985: 10

British outward FDI, with Canada providing the additional 6 per cent. The shifting geographical focus happened very rapidly. In the food industry 19 per cent of the output of leading UK firms was located in Europe and the United States in 1970, but only four years later the proportion had grown to 37 per cent (Houston and Dunning 1976: 117).

From the late 1970s the relative importance of the United States became even more striking. Around three-fifths of British FDI flows in the 1980s went to that country which came to account for half of the total stock of British FDI (Hamill 1988: 2). The result was a striking reversal of the investment relationship between the UK and the United States. Through the postwar period up to 1980 American FDI in Britain was in excess of British FDI in the United States. By the mid-1980s the value of British-owned assets in the United States considerably exceeded that of American companies in the UK (Dunning 1988: 235). Subsequently British acquisitions of American companies became even more frenetic. Between 1984 and 1990 British companies made 1,552 American acquisitions valued in excess of $111 billion (Hamill 1991: 29–30).

British acquisition activity was more modest in Continental Europe. The process of economic integration in Western Europe, and Britain's membership of the European Community since 1973, had a noticeable impact on the pattern of inward investment into the UK, but very little on British outward investment. This may have been because, as Ietto-Gillies has suggested, the long tradition of internationalization of British companies gave them a 'global' rather than a regional perspective (Ietto-Gillies 1993: 198). In Germany, British FDI increased over the 1970s and 1980s, especially in banking and finance but also in chemicals, but on nothing like the scale seen in the United States (Jones 1992: 98). Nevertheless, even in Continental Europe the number of British acquisitions was quite substantial. In the two years 1989 and 1990, British companies acquired 397 Continental firms valued at £12 billion (Hamill 1991: 30).

These changes in geographical location were matched by substantial shifts in industrial distribution. After 1945 British FDI ceased to be mainly in the primary and tertiary sectors, and manufacturing became predominant. By 1962 over half of the book value of British companies' FDI was in manufacturing industries, with a further 13 per cent in distribution. The relative importance of manufacturing subsequently grew further (Shepherd *et al*. 1985: 13–16). There are severe definitional problems in making international comparisons on sectoral distribution of FDI, but according to United Nations' estimates at the end of the 1980s the share of British FDI stock in the 'secondary sector' (38 per cent) was higher than that of Japan (27 per cent), exactly the same as that of France, but lower than that of Germany (49 per cent). The continuing international importance of the British oil and other extractive multinationals meant, however, that the proportion of British FDI in the primary sector (25 per cent) was much higher than that of France (13 per cent), Germany (2 per cent) and Japan (6 per cent), and only surpassed by the Netherlands (35 per cent) (United Nations 1992: 18).

The industrial composition of British manufacturing FDI also changed over time, as shown in Table 7.4. The industrial composition of British FDI has been analysed in terms of 'more technology intensive' and 'less technology intensive' sectors, based on expenditure on research and development. It is evident from the table that it fell heavily into the latter category in the immediate postwar period. In contrast, inward investment into Britain was heavily biased towards the 'more technology intensive' sectors. In 1964 around 70 per cent of the net foreign assets of British manufacturing multinationals can be regarded as falling into the 'less technology intensive' sectors, while almost 70 per cent of the net assets of foreign firms in Britain were in 'more technology intensive' sectors (Dunning 1985: 17). However, there were marked changes in the industrial composition of British manufacturing FDI over time. The chemicals sector grew in importance, as did to a lesser extent engineering, while food, drink and tobacco lost its overwhelming dominance of British manufacturing FDI. Conversely, from the 1970s the proportion of inward investment into Britain in the 'less technology intensive' sectors rose (Dunning 1988: 218). Nevertheless, an analysis of the world's 500 leading multinational enterprises in 1981 continued to show that the industrial composition of British FDI remained distinctive in its low technology content: 60 per cent of foreign production of all these companies was in industries that spent 2 per cent or more of sales on research and development. For the United States, the figure was 72 per cent, for Germany 84 per cent, for Sweden 89 per cent and for France 60 per cent. The British, on the other hand, had two-thirds of their foreign production in industries that spent less than 2 per cent of sales on research and development (Stopford and Dunning 1983: 65–75).

Table 7.4 Sectoral distribution of British overseas assets in manufacturing, 1954, 1964, 1981 (percentage of total net assets)

	1954	*1964*	*1981*
Food, drink and tobacco	47.3	39.0	27.1
Chemicals	11.9	14.2	28.0
Electrical engineering	5.4	4.9	10.0
Mechanical engineering	1.9	1.5	6.3
Vehicles	7.9	9.2	3.4
Textiles	8.1	6.9	4.3
Metal manufacture	7.3	9.7	2.0
Paper	5.4	8.7	5.5
Other manufacturing	4.7	5.6	13.4
Total	100.0	100.0	100.0

Source: Shepherd *et al.* 1985: 63

The distinction between 'high' and 'low' technology industry is misleading in some respects, and a more meaningful division may be between consumer branded and mechanized goods. British strength was visibly in the former category, and this has continued to be the case. During the 1980s food, drink and tobacco has accounted for over 30 per cent of Britain's stock of FDI in manufacturing – and contributed a remarkable 45 per cent of the total earnings of the manufacturing sector from FDI. It is worth noting, in this context, that the technology content of the food and drink industry rose markedly during the 1970s and 1980s, as a result of a growth in capital intensity of the production process and technical progress (Balasubramanyam 1993: 149).

The shifting geographical and industrial distribution of British

FDI in the post-1945 decades was matched by changes in its corporate structure. The further decline of the free-standing and other nineteenth-century forms of British FDI was closely associated with divestment from the developing world, where most of them had been based. The fates of individual firms were diverse, and by no means limited to sequestration. In Brazil, the St John d'el Rey Mining Company was gravely weakened by inflation and labour unrest by the 1950s, and was finally taken over by a group of New York investors in 1960 (Eakin 1989: 102–4). In Malaysia, the British agency houses, such as Sime Darby, Guthries and Harrison and Crosfield, had pursued flexible business strategies after the Second World War, diversifying successfully from plantation management and trading into manufacturing, as well as extending their business activities geographically, including in industrialized countries. However, during the late 1970s the Malaysian government orchestrated a series of share purchases on the London Stock Exchange and boardroom coups which resulted in the elimination of British control over these companies (van Helten and Jones 1989: 179–86). Similarly, in Hong Kong during the 1970s and 1980s many British-controlled trading and manufacturing enterprises (such as Hutchinson Whampoa and Wheelock Marden) were bought out by local entrepreneurs. Among the British overseas banks, the free-standing structure slowly disappeared between the 1960s and the 1990s. Some overseas banks were acquired by clearing banks. In one instance – that of the Hongkong Bank and Midland Bank in 1992 – the overseas bank took over the clearing bank. ANZ, one of the largest banks in Australia and New Zealand, 'emigrated' from Britain to Australia in 1976 (Jones 1993a: 321–71).

The large multinational corporation became the typical corporate form of British FDI. This reflected the transformation of the domestic economy into a US-style, big business economy during the 1950s and 1960s. As industrial concentration levels grew to be higher than those of the United States, the small and medium-sized enterprise sector shrank, and large corporations with M-form organizational structures became the typical British business enterprise (Channon 1973: 50–88; Jones 1993b: 10–18). Not surprisingly, British FDI became concentrated. In 1974 Britain's total net assets abroad (excluding banking, insurance and the oil industry) were held by 1,798 enterprises, but a mere fifteen enterprises accounted for 36 per cent of these assets, and for 1,130 out of the total of 12,303 overseas affiliates (Panic 1982: 144–5).

The competitiveness of British firms and the competitiveness of the British economy

It is this history of British multinationals after 1945 which raises the most acute problems for interpretations of overall British business performance. The paradox to be explained is the combination of the long-run deterioration in the international competitiveness of the British economy – as evidenced by the very sharp fall in the share of world exports of manufacturers after 1945 – and Britain's continued strength as a multinational investor. The evidence from Britain's multinational investment appears to contradict the familiar (and well-documented) catalogue of postwar British business failings, such as poorly educated managers, inadequately trained workers, 'short-termism' and much more (Lane 1989).

As in the case of the United States (Lipsey and Kravis 1987), a distinction has to be made between the international competitiveness of British firms and that of the British economy. It is apparent that the former has become progressively greater than the latter at least over the last three decades, and perhaps through the century. One result is that British firms shifted an increasing proportion of their total production to overseas countries. By 1971 Britain was one of three nations – the others being the United States and Switzerland – whose industrial output overseas was worth twice the value of goods exported. The British ratio of overseas output to goods exports was calculated at 214.6 per cent in that year, a considerable contrast with Germany (37.4 per cent), Japan (37.5 per cent) and France (93.5 per cent) (Houston and Dunning 1976: 10). Because British statistical data are less comprehensive than those of the United States, it is difficult to undertake a Lipsey and Kravis type of calculation for Britain of world market share by nationality of firm. Nevertheless, a series of studies by Dunning over the last twenty years has strongly suggested that the British-controlled share of sales has held up much better than that of exports from the UK. Thus, the UK share of world exports of manufactured goods fell from 16.3 per cent to 10 per cent between 1960 and 1972. Yet a calculation of the share of world sales by the largest British industrial firms showed only a slight decline from 8.3 per cent to 7.5 per cent between 1962 and 1972 (Dunning 1978: 10).

The most convincing explanation of the growing propensity of British firms to produce abroad is that they sought to escape from the deteriorating British economy by investing in more dynamic markets overseas (Hamill 1991: 31). As Panic has argued, among the most important determinants of FDI are the size and the growth of a market. The relative decline of the British market after 1945 increased the attractions of the markets of the United States and Continental Europe. The changing industrial distribution of British FDI, especially from the 1960s, suggested that British companies were seeking to produce a higher proportion of their more sophisticated or higher value added products in markets where income levels were higher (Panic 1982: 164–5).

The substantial British FDI in the United States since the late 1970s was part of a long-term strategy of diversification away from the slow growth British market towards the faster growth prospects offered by the United States (Hamill 1988: 12). The process can be demonstrated by case study evidence drawn from two industrial sectors in which British firms over the last twenty years have been widely regarded as internationally competitive – chemical and pharmaceuticals. In chemicals, during the 1980s ICI undertook large-scale FDI in the United States and Continental Europe. The company authorised £3.5 billion capital expenditure inside Britain between 1981 and 1991, and £7.6 billion outside Britain in the same period. According to the ICI Chairman, this was the result of decisions taken in 1984 when the firm 'concluded that the UK economy was unlikely to thrive and that the UK industrial base was declining. We came to . . . simple conclusions: that we had to increase our penetration of big overseas markets. . .' (*Financial Times*, 27 February 1993). A similar process occurred in the pharmaceutical industry, where British-based firms began manufacturing a growing proportion of their production overseas. By 1992 Glaxo manufactured 53 per cent of its product volume outside Britain (*Financial Times*, 1 March 1993). One outcome of these strategies was that in both chemicals and pharmaceuticals Britain's trade balance deteriorated sharply after 1980. The continued deterioration in world export share observed by Porter can be regarded as being due less to managerial inability to 'upgrade' than to British managers choosing to pursue growth opportunities outside the UK.

A striking feature of the strategy of British firms to escape from their home economy was the high level of internationalization of their research activities. By the 1980s British firms had become one of the most multinational in their organization of technological activity. Around 40 per cent of the patents that British companies were granted in the United States were attributable to research facilities located outside Britain. The figures for French, German and Italian firms were less than 15 per cent; for American firms around 7 per cent, and for Japanese firms 2 per cent. This extensive British international research and development was not in contradiction to the view that British FDI

was skewed towards 'low technology' industries. The British technological strengths, according to the patent statistics, lay in food, drink
and tobacco, construction equipment and textiles. The research in
these industries was often adaptive rather than fundamental, involving ways to match technology and production to quality of local
inputs and local consumer tastes. This extensive internationalization
also took place within the context of a decline in the technological
activities of British companies. The overall share of British-owned
firms in the US patenting of the world's largest companies fell from 7
per cent in 1969−72 to 5 per cent in 1978−86 (Casson 1991: 133−82).

There remains the problem of how British firms were able to sustain
their large foreign investment strategies given their alleged managerial
failings. It is likely that British multinationals over recent decades may
have possessed considerable advantages in capital-raising, derived
from their large size as well as the sophistication and size of the British
capital market (Clegg 1987: 102). This would help to explain why, in
contrast to Japanese multinationals, the British have primarily
expanded abroad through acquisition rather than greenfield investment. Thus a study of the 1,572 separate British direct investments
made in the United States between 1976 and 1986 revealed the predominant use of acquisition as the mode of entry (Hamill 1988). The
sums involved were considerable. Between 1985 and 1989 British food
and drink companies acquired thirty US-owned firms at a total cost of
£47 billion; another thirty-one firms were acquired in European Community countries at a total cost of £388 million (Balasubramanyam
1993: 157). The American acquisitions included some very large transactions, notably Grand Metropolitan's £3 billion purchase of Pills-
bury, the prominent American food company whose interests included
Burger King, as well as more modest ones, such as Tate & Lyle's acquisition of Staley, a leading corn sweetener in the United States, for £650
million.

Both the propensity of British companies to invest abroad and their
ability to do so can be related to the corporate governance of British
firms. Corporate dependence on capital markets for funds, together
with a business culture in which maintaining the share price is a vital
priority because of the need to thwart hostile takeovers, resulted in
pressure on British companies to maintain dividend growth. The slow
growth of the British economy meant that profitability could often be
best secured from operations in faster growing foreign markets. A
study of 304 large British manufacturing companies between 1972 and
1984 has indeed shown that increases in overseas production were
strongly associated with increases in sales and profitability (Grant

1987: 87). By the early 1990s almost 50 per cent of the earnings of the British corporate sector came from abroad. The method of corporate finance through the Stock Exchange, therefore, exercised a pressure on British firms to increase their foreign earnings. At the same time, the City was often willing to provide the large amounts of capital needed to fund expensive foreign acquisitions.

In so far as access to capital has been the main advantage possessed by British multinationals over the last decade, it raises serious questions about the likely performance of their investments. There is some evidence that the performance of British acquisitions in the United States in the 1980s has been unsatisfactory (Hamill 1988: 14–16). The greatest failure may have been in banking. From the late 1970s British banks sought to buy themselves into the US market. Between 1979 and 1981 four leading British banks paid between them $1,965 million for two American commercial banks and majority shares in two others. The banks in question were the eleventh, twelfth, twenty-fourth and thirty-seventh largest banks in the United States. Between 1985 and 1988 another $2,871 million was paid for four new banks, and for the minority shareholdings of the two banks partially acquired between 1979 and 1981. By 1992 these acquisitions, with two major exceptions, had all been sold again, often on poor terms. The worst case was the Midland Bank's acquisition of Crocker National of 1980, a disastrous investment which was eventually sold in 1986 only after Midland took over £2,500 million of Crocker's bad debts. Midland Bank was estimated to have lost around £1 billion on its American acquisition (Jones 1993a: 355–69).

The scale of the disaster which befell British banks in the United States does not seem to have been repeated in manufacturing. It seems likely, as Hamill has suggested, that British companies which made a large number of relatively low value acquisitions in the United States were more successful than those which attempted a small number of 'major shot' acquisitions (Hamill 1991: 42). There have certainly been many instances of successful American acquisitions: Glaxo's purchase of Meyer Laboratories Inc. in 1978 was a very significant step in that firm's development as a world-class pharmaceutical enterprise. At the end of the 1980s British non-bank affiliates in the United States yielded a considerable higher net income than their Japanese-owned counterparts (Wilkins 1990: 625). This raises again the question of the competitive advantages enjoyed by British multinationals in foreign markets. While British banks may have possessed no advantages at all except access to capital, it would appear that in the manufacturing sector firms had sufficient organizational and managerial skills to enable them to sustain extensive foreign investments. Otherwise, as Panic has observed, it is most unlikely that they could have continued to control a significant share of world industrial output (Panic 1982: 161–2). These skills were all the more important given the re-orientation from the Commonwealth to the more difficult and competitive markets of the United States and Europe.

Three points can be made about these British managerial skills. The first is that British managerial performance *was* improved, at least in manufacturing, by the growth of large companies and the professionalism of management seen from the 1950s. As a result, British companies were better equipped by the 1970s to manage operations in the United States and elsewhere in Europe than they had been a generation previously. This did not mean that all the defects of British business had been solved: the growing role of foreign-owned companies in many high technology and fast-growing sectors in Britain testified to continuing weaknesses there. Nevertheless, the improvement in the competitive performance of British multinationals over time is evident. In the first half of the 1960s US firms were considerably more profitable in their foreign operations than British firms (Dunning 1970: 258–9). Subsequently the profitability of British firms abroad has risen sharply relative to those of other nations, as well as compared with British firms operating only in the UK (Dunning 1988: 225).

Second, British management has had traditional skills in financial management and certain types of commercial activity which help to explain its extensive service sector FDI. It is possible to argue that these skills were of increasing use in certain manufacturing sectors in the 1980s. This may explain how British firms in the food and drink industry, with a low record of productive efficiency, were able to acquire more productive American firms in the 1980s. The leading British firms, such as Guinness and Grand Metropolitan, had evolved into conglomerates with diverse investments including hotels and real estate. The management of such enterprises required skills in marketing and financial management rather than production management. The reasons why British managers should have possessed such skills are debatable. Balasubramanyam points to continuities within the British inheritance of family firms and the managing agency system (Balasubramanyam 1993: 158–9). An explanation may also be found in the dimensions of national culture explored in the work of Hofstede (Hofstede 1984). It is a plausible hypothesis that the 'individualistic', 'masculine' and 'low uncertainty avoidance' dimensions of British culture identified by Hofstede inclined the British towards risky, entrepreneurial and trading activities, while they were less successful in industries and processes which involved complex production methods and long-time horizons (Jones 1993b: 9–10).

Third, using Michael Porter's concept of national 'diamonds' (Porter 1990), the improved performance of British multinationals over the last three decades may have been derived from their success in tapping into foreign diamonds. While uninational British firms were by definition trapped in the deteriorating British diamond, those firms that escaped overseas were stimulated into improved efficiency by the superior demand and factor conditions, more favourable clusters of individual activities and more competitive business environments.

This last argument raises the question of why the UK has been so attractive to foreign investors if its environment is so poor. During the 1980s Britain was the most successful of all European countries in attracting Japanese FDI, especially in the motor vehicle and consumer electronics sectors. Part of the answer is that Japanese companies were attracted to manufacture in Britain by low labour costs and the welcoming policy stance, but their market strategy was invariably focused on the European Community as a whole. A second element of the story is that the Japanese firms were able – by importing their own corporate cultures, investing in greenfield sites and employing young workers who were given training – to insulate themselves from some of the debilitating effects of the British 'diamond'.

CONCLUSION

The origins of the extensive British multinational investment in the twentieth century must be placed firmly in its historical context. The UK emerged as the world's largest multinational investor at a time when the British economy held a unique position in the world economy, in terms of its trading position, its role as the leading capital exporter and because of the existence of the British empire. These characteristics declined over the course of the twentieth century, but a strong 'outward-looking' tradition was established, reinforced no doubt by the use of English as an international language. As a result, when British market growth prospects deteriorated from the 1950s, many British firms had a propensity to sustain or improve corporate performance by establishing production facilities outside the UK.

Both the high level and the sustainability of British multinational investment were linked to the existence of extensive capital markets in the UK. This was obvious in the case of the huge sums of money raised by free-standing companies before 1914. Later, as Britain became a big business economy *par excellence*, large British multinational enterprises may have enjoyed advantages in capital-raising. In the post-1950 period the influence of the capital markets worked to reinforce the outward orientation of British business because of the importance of dividend growth to British companies. The pressure was rather less important where, as in Germany and Japan, companies were owned by interlocking domestic corporate interests, with less need to maximize short-term income and with strong commitment to their domestic economies. Moreover, their domestic economies offered far better growth prospects than the UK.

British multinational activity could not have been sustained without considerable organizational capability. The existence of this capability has been disguised because its nature was different from that possessed by American corporations. Especially before 1945 – but also afterwards – the British used socialization strategies and 'lean' types of organization to manage their overseas businesses. These often worked as effectively as US-style managerial hierarchies. The entrepreneurial and management skills of the British lay in activities involving commerce, risk and short-time horizons. These skills were of great value in their extensive extractive and service sector FDI before 1945, but after the Second World War the opportunities for multinational enterprise in these sectors was diminished by host government restrictions. However, British business remained prominent in certain extractive sectors, in financial sectors and in certain types of manufacturing activity, in which those financial and commercial skills were particularly appropriate. Improvements in British managerial and organizational practices in the post-1945 period showed through in improved efficiency, and over recent decades British multinationals were able to derive further advantages from the countries in which they operated.

The evidence from the history of British multinational enterprise has a number of implications for British business history more generally. British management and organization appear more effective than they would seem if judged against an American or German yardstick. British FDI was so extensive, especially after the Second World War, that the performance of British firms cannot be adequately captured by focusing on the trade performance of the UK economy. There is strong evidence that, over the last thirty years, the British-controlled share of world sales has declined much less sharply than British exports. This would imply that reasons other than management failure explain much of the relative economic decline of the UK. Public policy failures, especially after 1945, seem a more plausible candidate. The postwar macroeconomic failure to provide stable non-inflationary growth, and to invest in human resources, helped to create an uncongenial domestic environment from which flight was the only rational course.

NOTE

I would like to thank V.N. Balasubramanyam, Mark Casson and John H. Dunning and members of the Lancaster seminar held on 14–15 May 1993 for their comments on this chapter. Dunning provided the 1990 FDI stock figures given in Tables 7.1 and 7.2.

REFERENCES

Balasubramanyam, V.N. (1993) 'Entrepreneurship and the growth of the firm: the case of the British food and drink industries in the 1980s', in J. Brown and M.B. Rose (eds) *Entrepreneurship, Networks and Modern Business*, Manchester: Manchester University Press.
Beaton, K. (1957) *Enterprise in Oil. A History of Shell in the United States*, New York: Appleton-Century-Crofts.
Bostock, F. and Jones, G. (1989) 'British business in Iran, 1860s–1970s', in R.P.T. Davenport-Hines and G. Jones (eds) *British Business in Asia since 1860*, Cambridge: Cambridge University Press.
—— and —— (1994) 'Foreign multinationals in British manufacturing 1850–1962', *Business History* 36(1).
Casson, M. (ed.) (1991) *Global Research Strategy and International Competitiveness*, Oxford: Basil Blackwell.
Chandler, A.D. (1990) *Scale and Scope*, Cambridge, MA: Harvard University Press.
Channon, D.F. (1973) *The Strategy and Structure of British Enterprise*, London: Macmillan.
Chapman, S. (1992) *Merchant Enterprise in Britain*, Cambridge: Cambridge University Press.
Clegg, J. (1987) *Multinational Enterprise and World Competition*, London: Macmillan.
Coleman, D.C. (1969) *Courtaulds*, 2 vols, Oxford: Clarendon Press.
Corley, T.A.B. (1983) *A History of the Burmah Oil Company 1886–1924*, London: Heinemann.
—— (1988) *A History of the Burmah Oil Company 1924–1966*, London: Heinemann.
Cox, H. (1989) 'Growth and ownership in the international tobacco industry: BAT 1902–1927', *Business History* 31(1): 44–67.
Davenport-Hines, R.P.T. (1986a) 'Vickers as a multinational before 1945', in G. Jones (ed.) *British Multinationals: Origins, Management and Performance*, Aldershot: Gower.
—— (1986b) 'Glaxo as a multinational before 1963', in G. Jones (ed.) *British Multinationals: Origins, Management and Performance*, Aldershot: Gower.
Davenport-Hines, R.P.T. and Jones, G. (eds) (1989) *British Business in Asia since 1860*, Cambridge: Cambridge University Press.
Dunning, J.H. (1970) *Studies in International Investment*, London: George Allen & Unwin.
—— (1978) 'Ownership and country specific characteristics of Britain's international competitive position', University of Reading Discussion Papers in International Investment and Business Studies, no. 40.

—— (1985) 'The United Kingdom', in J.H. Dunning (ed.) *Multinational Enterprises, Economic Structure and International Competitiveness*, Chichester: Wiley.

—— (1986) *Japanese Participation in British Industry*, London: Croom Helm.

—— (1988) *Multinationals, Technology and Competitiveness*, London: Unwin Hyman.

—— (1993) *Multinational Enterprises and the Global Economy*, Wokingham: Addison-Wesley.

Eakin, M.C. (1989) *British Enterprise in Brazil*, Durham, NC: Duke University Press.

Feinstein, C. (1990) 'Britain's overseas investments in 1913', *Economic History Review* 43: 2.

Ferrier, R.W. (1982) *The History of the British Petroleum Company*, vol. 1, Cambridge: Cambridge University Press.

Fieldhouse, D.K. (1978) *Unilever Overseas*, London: Croom Helm.

Grant, R.M. (1987) 'Multinationality and performance among British manufacturing companies', *Journal of International Business Studies* 18(3): 79–89.

Hamill, J. (1988) 'British acquisitions in the United States', *National Westminster Bank Quarterly Review* August.

—— (1991) 'Strategic restructuring through international acquisitions and divestments', *Journal of General Management* 17(1): 27–44.

Harvey, C. and Press, J. (1990) 'The City and international mining, 1870–1914', *Business History* 32(3).

Harvey, C. and Taylor, P. (1987) 'Mineral wealth and economic development: foreign direct investment in Spain, 1851–1913', *Economic History Review* 40(2): 185–207.

Hennart, J.F. (1987) 'Transactions costs and the multinational enterprise: the case of tin', *Business and Economic History* 16: 147–59.

—— (1991) 'The transaction cost theory of the multinational enterprise', in C.N. Pitelis and R. Sugden (eds) *The Nature of the Transnational Firm*, London: Routledge.

Hertner, P. and Jones, G. (eds) (1986) *Multinationals: Theory and History*, Aldershot: Gower.

Hill, N.K. (1950) 'The history of the Imperial Continental Gas Association 1824–1900', unpublished PhD thesis, University of London.

Hofstede, G. (1984) *Culture's Consequences*, London: Sage.

Houston, T. and Dunning, J.H. (1976) *UK Industry Abroad*, London: Financial Times.

Ietto-Gillies, G. (1993) 'European Community integration and geographical spread of international production: the UK case', in H. Cox, J. Clegg and G. Ietto-Gillies (eds) *The Growth of Global Business*, London: Routledge.

Jones, G. (1981) *The State and the Emergence of the British Oil Industry*, London: Macmillan.

—— (1985) 'The Gramophone Company: an Anglo-American multinational, 1898–1931', *Business History Review* 59(1): 76–100.

—— (1986a) *British Multinationals: Origins, Management and Performance*, Aldershot: Gower.

—— (1986b) 'The performance of British multinational enterprise, 1890–1945', in P. Hertner and G. Jones (eds) *Multinationals: Theory and History*, Aldershot: Gower.

—— (1986c) *Banking and Empire in Iran*, Cambridge: Cambridge University Press.

—— (1988) 'Foreign multinationals and British Industry before 1945', *Economic History Review* 41(3): 429–53.

—— (1991) 'Locational choice, performance and the growth of British multinationals', *Business History* 33(1): 112–15.

—— (1992) 'British business in Germany since the nineteenth century', in H. Pohl (ed.) *Der Einfluss ausländischer Unternehmen auf die deutsche Wirtschaft vom Spätmittelalter bis zur Gegenwart*, Stuttgart: Franz Steiner Verlag.

—— (1993a) *British Multinational Banking 1830–1990*, Oxford: Clarendon Press.

—— (1993b) 'Big business, management and competitiveness in twentieth century Britain', University of Reading Discussion Papers in Economics, Series A, no. 268.

Kennedy, W.P. (1987) *Industrial Structure, Capital Markets and the Origins of British Economic Decline*, Cambridge: Cambridge University Press.

Lane, C. (1989) *Management and Labour in Europe*, Aldershot: Edward Elgar.

Lipsey, R.E. and Kravis, I.B. (1987) 'The competitiveness and comparative advantage of US multinationals 1957–1984', *Banca Nazionale Del Lavoro Quarterly Review* 155: 157–65.

Nicholas, S. (1982) 'British multinational investment before 1939', *Journal of European Economic History* 11(3): 605–30.

—— (1989) 'Locational choice, performance and the growth of British multinational firms', *Business History* 31(3): 116–20.

—— (1991) 'The expansion of British multinational companies: testing for managerial failure', in James Foreman-Peck (ed.) *New Perspectives on the Late Victorian Economy*, Cambridge: Cambridge University Press.

Osterhammel, J. (1989) 'British business in China, 1860s–1950s', in R.P.T. Davenport-Hines and G. Jones (eds) *British Business in Asia since 1860*, Cambridge: Cambridge University Press.

Panic, M. (1982) 'International direct investment in conditions of structural disequilibrium: UK experience since the 1960s', in J. Black and J.H. Dunning (eds) *International Capital Movements*, London: Macmillan.

Platt, D.C.M. (1986) *Britain's Investment Overseas on the Eve of the First World War*, London: Macmillan.

Porter, M.E. (1990) *The Competitive Advantage of Nations*, London: Macmillan.

Rippy, J.F. (1959) *British Investments in Latin America, 1822–1949*, Hamden, CT: Archon Books.

Schmitz, C. (1986) 'The rise of big business in the world copper industry, 1870–1930', *Economic History Review* 39(3): 392–410.

Schröter, H.G. (1991) 'Multinationale unternehmen aus kleinen Staaten 1870 bis 1930', Free University of Berlin.

Shepherd, D., Silbertson, A. and Strange, R. (1985) *British Manufacturing Investment Overseas*, London: Methuen.

Stone, I. (1977) 'British direct and portfolio investment in Latin America before 1914', *Journal of Economic History* 37(3): 690–722.

Stopford, J.M. (1974) 'The origins of British-based multinational manufacturing enterprises', *Business History Review* 48(3): 303–35.

Stopford, J.M. and Dunning, J.H. (1983) *Multinationals. Company Performance and Global Trends*, London: Macmillan.

Stopford, J.M. and Turner, J. (1985) *Britain and the Multinationals*, Chichester: Wiley.

Svedberg, P. (1978) 'The portfolio-direct composition of private foreign investment in 1914 revisited', *Economic Journal* 88 (December): 763–77.

Tignor, R. (1987) 'British textile companies and the Egyptian economy', *Business and Economic History* 16: 53–67.

United Nations (1992) *World Investment Report. Transnational Corporations as Engines of Growth*, New York: United Nations.

Van Helten, J.-J. and Jones, G. (1989) 'British business in Malaysia and Singapore since the 1870s', in R.P.T. Davenport-Hines and G. Jones (eds) *British Business in Asia since 1860*, Cambridge: Cambridge University Press.

Wilkins, M. (1977) 'Modern European economic history and the multi-nationals', *Journal of European Economic History* 6: 575–95.

——— (1988a) 'European and North American multinationals, 1870–1914: comparisons and contrasts', *Business History* 30(1): 8–45.

——— (1988b) 'The free-standing company, 1870–1914: an important type of British foreign direct investment', *Economic History Review* 61(2): 259–82.

——— (1989) *The History of Foreign Investment in the United States before 1914*, Cambridge, MA: Harvard University Press.

——— (1990) 'Japanese multinationals in the United States: continuity and change, 1879–1990', *Business History Review* 64 (Winter): 585–629.

Wilson, C. (1954) *The History of Unilever*, 2 vols, London: Cassell.

Young, S., Hood, N. and Hamill, J. (1988) *Foreign Multinationals and the British Economy*, London: Croom Helm.

8 The competitive environment of British business, 1850–1914

Oliver M. Westall

INTRODUCTION

Businesses cannot be seen in isolation. Their internal organization, strategy, growth and efficiency cannot be understood except in the context of the competitive environment in which they operate. This was transformed in nineteenth-century Britain by changes in the scale and structure of markets and industries. Some of these were the result of the evolution in the organization of business discussed in Chapters 3, 5, 6 and 9. Some were due to wider changes in the social and economic context of business. This chapter draws these developments together to show how firms adapted to this new competitive environment. It suggests that many of the changes in the scale, organization, conduct and efficiency of firms in the second half of the nineteenth century were in large part responses to the market, rather than the exercises in planned managerial discretion that have formed a recurrent theme in recent business historiography. The 'visible hand' usually required market dominance, a special competitive case, whose significance business history has tended to exaggerate because of its emphasis on the large and the long lived (Westall 1992: 5–9). British business has usually faced markets characterized by varying degrees of oligopolistic collusion and this, as Elbaum and Lazonick (1986) and Broadberry and Crafts (1992) would agree, has had important implications for its structure and performance.

Late nineteenth-century businessmen faced the three usual strategic options: competition, collusion or integration. Each option involved further choices. Competition could be by price, or by a variety of non-price means, including most significantly the differentiation of products to make them more attractive to consumers, and the innovation of entirely new products. Both of the latter helped avoid the full impact of price competition, which could reduce profit margins and increase uncertainty. Both gave a firm increased power over its market.

Collusion – co-operation between businesses designed to raise prices and profitability – was another way in which businessmen attempted to avoid the potentially painful consequences of price competition. Sometimes markets were structured in ways that made collusion so obviously in firms' interests that it took place effectively without any need for explicit consultation or co-operation. This was usually when the market was highly oligopolistic, being closely concentrated or containing a strongly dominant firm. In other, more diffused markets, it might only work if agreements were entered into with some formality, and were then monitored, strengthened and enforced by regular meetings, organizational arrangements and an increasing refinement of operation.

Integration – the process whereby firms increased in scale to comprehend larger shares of economic activity internally, rather than rely on market intermediation – could be directed along vertical lines, following the process of production and distribution; or it could be horizontal, concentrating activity in the same stage of production. This process is examined more closely in Chapter 6 and will be dealt with here only in so far as it cannot be separated from competition and collusion.

The stimulus to adopt particular strategies, and their subsequent success, was closely related to the structure and growth of the markets in which firms operated. Some aspects of strategy can be observed more easily by the historian than others. Competitive activity is sometimes highly visible from price data, the introduction of new products or advertising. However, other relevant factors, such as the significance of goodwill in long-standing business connections, or service and quality, are harder to identify.

Most types of collusion are difficult to study. Businessmen have never wanted customers to know about price fixing, and they have been even more careful when collusive activity has been illegal. But even here there are important distinctions to be made. The most obvious evidence of collusion comes from the creation of formal organizations, which leave evidence of their existence that can be traced by historians. By contrast, the informal collusion that does not require such a framework often leaves no clear indication of its existence. Yet in this case, as in the others suggested above, historians must be extremely careful to remember that the least evident activity is by no means likely to be the least important. Finally, apparent changes in the integration of economic activity can often be traced quite easily through company scale and activity, though the real impact of integration in terms of internal company organization and efficiency may be rather harder to assess.

COMPETITION DURING INDUSTRIALIZATION BEFORE 1850

It is sometimes easily assumed that, because most firms were small in the early nineteenth century, markets were always highly competitive. This was sometimes true. In the large markets that existed in bigger towns and cities, especially London, competition was no doubt vigorous. In some trades and industries special markets were created to generate greater efficiency in transactions. The cotton trade, with its sophisticated hierarchy of markets in Manchester, Liverpool, London and the cotton towns, is perhaps the most obvious of several possible examples (Edwards 1967: 172–81). Of course, there were important phases when price competition drove expansion and profitability in industries enjoying technological change or falling input costs. This was especially the case when rapid growth was found through opening up new markets with lower income consumers. Cotton is again an obvious case, but worsted saw a similar move to cheaper, lower quality products in the years from the late 1830s to 1860 (Sigsworth 1958: 50–2; Edwards 1967: 33–4). In these circumstances firms could indeed become price takers, with little opportunity to exercise control over their market environment. But these special cases must not be generalized too easily. Outside cities and larger towns, in many other products, markets were small because of transport costs, especially before the railways. Flows of information were inefficient, making it difficult for producers and consumers to recognize the possibilities for trade. Regional tastes and preferences remained strong, restricting entry. Limitations on the scale of firms made expansion into new markets difficult. Within individual trades, there were usually many specialized market segments that could not easily be entered by competing firms. Even in the cotton trade, for example, there were specialists in different counts or qualities of thread and cloth who would have had a clear idea of their principal competitors (Rose 1986: 42). In these circumstances, while price competition played an important role in marketing, its impact was substantially modified by differentiation and collusion.

Quality and reputation were certainly important elements in differentiation, creating importance for trade marks and in some cases branding. The dynamic activities of Wedgwood, for example, in creating a powerful position for his products by associating them with quality and social prestige have been well recognized (McKendrick 1960). The pin trade provides an interesting early example of the use of packaging for branding to allow consumers to re-purchase quality products regularly (Jones 1976: 51). But the most important forms of market power were derived from the inefficiency of the markets in finance and information. The provision of credit was undoubtedly a key element in building trading relations that were insulated to some extent against price competition. And the difficulty of transferring business to new connections with ease and confidence, when it was difficult to obtain authoritative information on their reliability, placed enormous importance on goodwill. The crucial role of the London warehousemen in the commercial structure of the country, with their privileged access to finance and their network of travellers linking them with consumers and suppliers, is perhaps the strongest example of these considerations. In differing degrees, credit and information flows were important in attracting and locking trading relationships throughout the economy.

The small scale of most markets outside London also encouraged collusion. For many products in most places there were only a small number of local firms, protected by transport and informational costs from competition. Pressures to avoid competition in such circumstances were probably so strong that there was little or no need to enter into formal agreements. It was obvious to all that, once competition began, all local firms would follow suit and drive down profitability across the market. The characteristic environment of British business activity before 1850 was almost certainly that of implicit collusion in local markets, which has left little or no evidence for the historian to detect, because its protagonists carried it out as a matter of common sense which required little or no discussion. The force of economic logic was often strengthened by ties created by family, religion or, more prosaically, the local country bank. Some flavour of these tight-knit local economies can be obtained from Taylor's study of Gillets' bank at Banbury (1964: ch. 3).

Even in industries dealing in national or international markets, collusion could still be relatively informal because of interdependence in particular market segments. In the cotton industry, for example, the leading firms in particular branches of the trade were often able to dominate pricing. In some cases price leadership was entirely implicit: in others there were loose agreements that were then secretly monitored (Rose 1986: 42). In larger markets, with more firms or little opportunity for differentiation, collusion required a more formal structure if it was to be successful. John Heathcoat used the licensing of his patented lace machine to other entrepreneurs as a means of establishing control over output (Dutton 1984: 194). In the northeast, the dominance of a few large coal owners allowed the Vend to control the price of the coal shipped out of the Tyne and Wear, but not without a complex process of output control regulated by a committee system and closely inspected. In the pin trade, collusion oscillated between implicit, explicit or non-existent forms, depending largely on the trade cycle (Jones 1973). As industrialization created a growing fire insurance market in the new industrial regions, new provincial insurers entered the market to challenge the three principal London insurance companies that had dominated eighteenth-century fire insurance. The latter had often been able to agree on premium rates without too much elaborate negotiation and organization. In the new and more competitive national market such informal collusion became impossible and the larger companies spent the years between 1820 and 1858 testing a series of more sophisticated methods of controlling competition that would force small and new concerns to co-operate with them (Dickson 1960: 149–56; Supple 1970: 121–9; Westall 1994).

The limits on the scale of the firm, discussed in Chapter 3, meant that integration was constrained. Between 1770 and 1825 some manufacturers ventured abroad to establish direct links with their markets, but financial disasters during the Napoleonic Wars and their aftermath discouraged all but the largest and bravest from continuing. Gradually a structure was established for the nineteenth century in which, in the traditional trades, independent merchants, financed by London acceptance houses, provided a specialized service for all but the largest of British manufacturers. These consequently had little direct contact with their foreign markets and were therefore subject to all the competitive pressures that operated in the domestic market (Chapman 1979). At home, for some specialist products such as Wedgwood's high class pottery and Carron's cast iron products, warehouses were established to display the products effectively in a range of provincial cities (McKendrick 1960; Campbell 1961: 202). In the cotton industry many of the larger firms maintained a merchant house in Manchester to represent their commercial interests (Rose 1986: 57, 81). But this forward integration was the exception reserved for larger and specialized firms, rather than the rule for the generality of concerns.

CHANGES IN MARKET STRUCTURES 1850-1914

Three trends lay behind the main changes in the organization and conduct of business between 1850 and 1914: the integration of markets; new possibilities for economies of scale and scope; and the changing balance of expansion between domestic and overseas markets.

Domestic market integration proceeded apace, largely as a consequence of railways. While their impact was never as dramatic as in the United States, because of Britain's already relatively compact market it was still substantial (Chandler 1990: 254-5). While the main shape of the system was clear by 1850, the creation of through routes and construction continued to intensify the impact of the network, and the economic implications of railways gradually became apparent. Barriers to entry evaporated in many previously protected local markets. Most product markets enjoyed a larger market size, creating the potential for a far greater exploitation of economies of scale, where production methods made these available. At the same time the speed of delivery made possible by railways also allowed stock holding to be reduced, creating important changes in the organization of distribution (Gourvish 1980: 30-1).

Beyond this, the impact of railways transformed the whole structure of social life, and in doing so it necessarily changed the environment of business. Perhaps the most obvious and important form this took was through urbanization. By 1851 a comparatively high proportion of 50 per cent of the population already lived in towns; by 1911 this has risen to 80 per cent – and within these totals the growth in the proportion living in large towns and cities was most striking (Thane 1981: 199). These towns and cities offered large, compact markets with ample scope for developing new forms of production and distribution. It became far more economical to create distributive networks of salesmen, branch offices and physical distribution systems of all kinds. And each one that was created could often be made more economical still by widening the range of products that it handled, offering opportunities for developing economies of scope. This, of course, was an important factor lying behind the striking changes in retail distribution in this period discussed in Chapter 9.

The final important form of market integration that took place was in the efficiency with which finance and information could be transmitted. At an accelerating pace, amalgamation and the development of a branch network created a far more integrated banking system, which allowed funds to be moved rapidly and with greater confidence

(Collins 1988: ch. 3). This allowed business to take a more relaxed view of long distance transactions. It also meant that the market in short-term finance through bank overdraft facilities was more accessible, freeing firms from a dependence on trade credit (Nishimura 1971: ch. 5). The transmission of information became easier for all through the increasingly efficient and economical postal service from the 1840s and, for more urgent requirements, the telegraph service, nationalized under the Post Office in 1870 (Daunton 1985). Cheaper paper, printing and the abolition of taxation on newspapers (1855) and advertisements (1853) facilitated an explosion in advertising and publicity of all types, allowing businessmen a quite new opportunity to acquaint consumers with the existence and merits of their products or services. The technical changes in printing and distribution of papers enabled the national newspaper to emerge, which created a national advertising market – with high barriers to entry, but large opportunities for those who could surmount them. Inexpensive printing and paper also allowed the proliferation of specialist magazines, especially for women, but for all interest groups, providing the possibility of targeted advertising (Nevett 1982: ch. 5).

Technical change in this period was sufficiently dramatic to lead some to dub it the 'second industrial revolution' (Chandler 1990: 62–3). It was characterized by a more rational application of scientific knowledge to production in such directions as chemicals and electricity, but its impact was not restricted to this. The key product across a far wider spread of industry was cheap steel (Landes 1970: 249–326). This had two implications for industrial organization. Steel enabled the construction of far larger vats and tubes which allowed raw materials and liquids to be processed and transported far more efficiently. The scale of processing could be larger and continuous so that heat was not lost. It became easier to integrate the handling of materials at one site. Brewing, milling, soap making, chemicals, food processing and chocolates are all good examples of industries which enjoyed new economies of scale as a result of this change.

Cheap steel also encouraged accurately machined tools and equipment which allowed mechanization to spread to a far wider range of production processes – and laid the basis for the manufacture of standardized components. Accurate machines allowed power to be applied to those many industries that had not benefited from that advantage in the pre-1850, largely textile centred revolution. Lathes, saws and sewing machines brought mechanization to many manufacturers such as the clothing trades, shoe manufacture, furniture, cutlery, cigarettes and calico printing that had all previously been handicraft in basis. Component assembly also became possible in the metal trades and in other directions such as furniture, laying the foundations for subsequent mass production, which saw an early example in bicycle production (Harrison 1969). Increased economies of scale became possible across a broad spectrum of British industry previously untouched by industrialization.

These trends in markets and production methods developed across three economic phases. Between 1850 and 1873 the macroeconomic environment was characterized by relatively buoyant home and foreign markets. Of course, there were cyclical trends, but the period was especially marked by innovational investment and rising prices. The pressure of demand meant that competition was not especially severe, except in a few declining sectors. It was a period of relative calm before the storm (Church 1975).

After 1873 the economic environment changed. With falling primary product prices the export markets on which many British industrialists depended grew less quickly. Over-capacity in export sectors reinforced the other sources of falling prices, making depressions longer and competition more intense. The emergence of foreign competition in manufactured goods, especially from the United States and Germany, began to impinge on British domestic markets and in third markets abroad. However, the same price fall, aided by reducing family size in middle-class groups and changes in the occupational structure, assisted important improvements in real incomes at home. While the export trade remained far more important to British industry than in any other country, the domestic market expanded more rapidly than before, reaching a climax in the boom of the 1890s. Because of the special importance of falling food prices to working-class groups, their capacity to purchase a widening range of consumer goods created opportunities for market expansion and the introduction of new products. Producers for these domestic markets therefore certainly enjoyed market growth, but this was offset by the implications of the market integration described above. Firms enjoying regional comparative advantages or technical competitiveness squeezed less efficient firms out of business. This occurred especially in those industries where economies of scale, based on the technical changes described above, were particularly potent. In these circumstances a process of creative destruction occurred, forcing many small-scale or country producers out of business. The concentration of business took place gradually. Scale economies emerged slowly, and the English preference for traditional trading connections and regional tastes and preferences remained strong. Attrition came first in districts most effectively penetrated by railways or which saw substantial urbanization. It was also particularly severe during slumps. However, the painful process of transition moved inexorably towards more concentrated national markets in many industries previously characterized by diffused production. The pain was shared by all because financially weak firms cut below cost, using reserves and other sources of finance, in a desperate attempt to remain in business. There were few knock-out blows in competitive markets; the process of attrition remained slow and bloody as producers adapted their competitive strategies in the search for success or survival.

Then in the Edwardian years after 1900, prices began to rise again, squeezing domestic incomes and once more shifting the emphasis from the domestic market to export markets fuelled by booming primary product prices. Some of the industries that had expanded on the basis of the growth in domestic demand in the previous two or three decades now suffered problems of declining growth in demand and over-capacity, creating a new and harsher competitive environment. By contrast, many of the export industries enjoyed easy markets which suggested – though it was an illusion – that their problems had been resolved.

COMPETITION

Price competition, or the potential price competition that costs might make possible, lay behind most of the competitive strategies deployed in the later nineteenth century. But its role often remained implicit. Businessmen sought to avoid it, for its action was more immediate and threatening than other forms of competition, and it could sap profitability more certainly. This became especially the case as the national concentration of business led to more powerfully oligopolistic markets. As the threat of self-destructive price warfare became more obvious, so they eschewed price competition and looked more energetically for other strategies. When they did so they discovered new possibilities for competitive activity, most obviously through advertising, branding and the creation of marketing and sales organizations.

Of course, there were plenty of directions in which price competition remained important. Many businesses were forced to accept its implications passively. In trades where they remained small in scale in relation to markets, and where products were relatively standardized, this was often the case. In the textile trades, the increasing scale, sophistication and efficiency of institutional markets in such centres as Manchester, Liverpool, Bradford, Leeds, Nottingham, and especially

London, created an environment in which many smaller firms were forced to take the market price. Even if they did establish special links with customers through goodwill or some other form of differentiation, the price on 'change' remained a powerful, if implicit, check on their opportunity to exploit this connection. This was especially the case in the cotton trade where increasing specialization by firms in its various processes fragmented production and opened up scope for competition at each of its stages. Farnie has described its competitive situation vividly:

> It remained severest in its incidence where firms were most numerous and where the product was simplest, undifferentiated, easily graded, sold in bulk, and therefore substitutable. Thus it proved keenest in the standard plain-goods trade, where prices were fixed in the slaughter-house of the Manchester Exchange.
>
> (Farnie 1979: 192)

In more general terms, this must have been the situation across most of the textile trades. While market institutions were never as prominent elsewhere, it seems reasonable to suppose that in the trade in clothing, boots and shoes, small metal wares, and in other trades where the market had become national but firms had remained small, there was only limited scope for escaping from the market price when the goods concerned were of standard design. This rigorous environment was reinforced by the importance of merchants and wholesalers. Their command of distribution to retailers and to export markets, along with their financial strength, gave them a powerful purchasing position which cut manufacturers off from their markets and forced them to remain competitive in the face of informed and shrewd purchasers (Payne 1974: 42–4; Chapman 1979; Hannah 1980: 64).

Price competition was also important in another more active context. In some cases it was used by firms Chandler has described as the 'first movers' – those who took the initial steps to achieve a dominant position in the national oligopolies that were emerging (Chandler 1990: 34–5). As firms took advantage of market integration, the new potential for economies of scale and scope and the potential of regional cost differences, those with the clearest competitive cost advantage could on occasion take advantage of this to move to a position of dominance in their industry, using price as their principal weapon. In practice this choice was usually made by firms operating in intermediate markets where trade customers were better informed and more hard-headed about their purchasing decisions because they were themselves subject to competitive pressures and were buying in bulk. This made them indifferent to peripheral forms of differentiation and almost entirely concerned with value, which, with standardized commodities, meant price. Although pricing agreements featured prominently in the chemical industry in some phases of its development, Brunner Mond exploited the substantial cost advantage of their Solvay process to establish a powerful market position in the soda business in price competition with the Leblanc producers (Richardson 1968: 282–3; Reader 1970: ch. 6). Pilkingtons were able to force steady price reductions in the glass industry from the 1870s on the basis of an economical cost base created by technological innovation and strict control of labour costs. This enabled them to establish themselves as the dominant British firm (Barker 1968: 318–19). In both cases the process was not one of dramatic price warfare but steady attrition, designed to expand market share without a significant fall in profitability.

However, whenever it was possible, firms tried to protect themselves from the need to compete on price. Even in the extreme case of the cotton industry its power was constrained. Farnie qualifies his earlier analysis of the directions in which it was most severe by pointing out that there were sectors where it was considerably limited. 'A wide and extending range of products dissolved the industry's superficial unity into a congeries of dissimilar and unconnected complexes of firms, producing different goods from different materials for different markets' (Farnie 1979: 193).

Many of the traditional forms of differentiation such as established trade connections and credit remained important, but their power was reduced. Widening markets opened up competition, and more efficient media provided more information on alternative trade connections, undermining the cosy relationships that had existed in local markets. The significance of trade credit in binding firms together was eroded by the increasing importance of the bank overdraft, which freed finance-hungry businessmen from the need to depend on suppliers or customers who would extract a price adjustment in return.

In other directions the late Victorian economy provided a framework for competition within which differentiation and specialization were deeply embedded. British goods retained many of the highly differentiated features of traditional production, including regional specialities and bespoke handicraft goods such as boots, tailored clothes or furniture. This was partly an aspect of Britain's cultural commitment, in a partially modernized society, to the trappings of an earlier age, with its hint of the rural and the non-industrial. Early British cars retained their polished carriage-like quality far longer than those in America. It also reflected a more skewed income distribution than in the United States with a narrow elite that determined design and manufacture for many less easily available goods. Britain's export emphasis also reinforced the tendency towards speciality production, for it served a multitude of overseas markets, each with its own distinct pattern of tastes and preferences. These patterns of demand fed back into the organization of production, emphasizing skilled labour intensity and the flexibility of small-scale firms. It was the ability of the British cotton trade, based on its flexibility and small-scale production runs, to produce for each and every one of these markets that provided part of its international competitiveness. This traditional emphasis in British business helped protect firms who could establish profitable niches.

This was in sharp contrast with the United States, where the market was increasingly dominated by inexpensive, mass-produced, standardized goods well suited to its homogeneous market with a narrow spread of incomes and less regional variation in tastes. The new possibilities of technology, economies of scale and distribution reinforced these tendencies. Yet there were changes in the British market in the closing decades of the nineteenth century that reflected the American mode. Rising working-class incomes and the important new economies in processing consumer goods from raw materials eroded the commitment to traditional, local and bespoke products. Market integration, new technology and economies of scale allowed new standardized versions of traditional products and some entirely new products to emerge and capture a national market. Sometimes the route to success lay through competitive pricing, as with the mass-produced clothing and boots imported from the United States in the 1890s. But in consumer markets differentiation was often equally successful, as this proved a route whereby an individual manufacturer could achieve national sales most successfully – and without squeezing margins too severely. One of the earliest products to take advantage of the railway to build a national market was the distinctive and superior Burton beer. 'Bass's home trade quadrupled within four years of the railway coming to Burton (1839).' By the 1870s Bass was the largest railway customer in the world with an agency system throughout the country (Gourvish and Wilson 1994: 150–6).

In some trades quality and design became increasingly important. William Morris's fabrics and wallpapers were perhaps an extreme case, designed for a wealthy and sophisticated market – though their influence increased the importance of simpler and lighter designs across the interior design market as a whole (Harvey and Press 1991:

ch. 3). With rising incomes the requirements of fashion involved an increasing proportion of the population. This was most obvious in the clothing trades, with the implications of fashion for design and finish permeating way back into the home trade in cotton and woollen cloths (Farnie 1979: 193; Fraser 1981: 61–4). The period also saw new products such as oil cloth and linoleum emerge, for which design and the range of colours was a key element in competition (Fraser 1981: 197).

But new possibilities for differentiation were far more obvious than these versions of traditional forms. The most strident was the efflorescence of advertising encouraged by the end of its taxation and that of the newspapers, and the cheap paper and printing which created the mass circulation newspaper and magazine. Initially newspaper advertising was conservative, set entirely in words in single columns. There was even strong resistance to display type. Improvements in printing technology allowed rapid changes to take place in the 1890s with newspapers accepting block illustrations. The placing of advertisements became far more professional, with the emergence of professional advertising agents and the publication of circulation figures. More efficient printing allowed the creation of papers with a national circulation, providing advertisers with a far more cost effective medium, including magazines that gave access to particular consumer segments.

Alongside newspaper advertising, other forms of advertising which benefited from cheaper printing and paper flourished. Posters were the most evident. Through the period they moved from an emphasis on words to visual messages. Lithography enabled more subtle designs including the effective use of colour printing. Some firms even purchased celebrated paintings – of which the most notable was Millais's *Bubbles*, bought to advertise Pears soap. Cheap postal rates for printed material encouraged some firms to begin circular mailings, with agencies offering address registers indicating special interests.

Alongside printed material, entrepreneurial imaginations dreamt up many other special advertising media. Victorian railway stations were richly decorated with enamelled advertisements. Liptons attracted publicity by parading thin men 'going to Liptons' and fat men 'coming from Liptons'. Beecham provided boatmen with free sails advertising his pills (Nevett 1982: ch. 5).

Local advertising for specific shops or manufacturers who could easily be identified by potential customers was a straightforward matter. But new problems arose when businesses were trying to expand their sales to capture regional or national markets. When so many products were by their nature relatively homogeneous, how could customers distinguish the product advertised by one supplier from any other? Traditionally this problem had been resolved by the use of trade marks, which in principle provided a clear indication and guarantee of the origin of a good (though it had always been subject to fraudulent misuse). In the late nineteenth century manufacturers exploited the idea of the brand in far greater degree to provide a clear indication to the consumer of the provenance of goods. They were appropriately packaged (often using the new possibilities of colour printing) in ways that reinforced the image that the business wished to create in the mind of the consumer and then advertised. In the period it became the characteristic mode of marketing for the repeat purchase consumer good. Many of the consumer goods that had previously been sold as homogeneous and indistinguishable 'commodities' were now converted into differentiated brands. This allowed the producer to reach consumers directly with a distinct product, putting pressure on distributors of all sorts to purchase it and then lock consumers into repeat purchases. For the consumer (and retailer) it reduced the cost of searching for consistent quality, which producers maintained because a reputable brand became a valuable asset (Wilkins 1992; R.G. Wilson 1994). The increasing importance of such devices was reflected in legislation designed to protect trade marks in 1875 (Alford 1973: 127; Fraser 1981: 146).

For firms operating in consumer goods markets, where customers were less well informed than in intermediate goods markets, brands provided an important route to a national market. Once they had established a production base that offered scope for economies of scale, they then established a marketing strategy based on branding that would expand their sales to take advantage of these new facilities. In contrast with the 'first movers' in the intermediate goods markets discussed above, they used their cost advantage to spend heavily on advertising brands that could penetrate markets more effectively (Chandler 1990: 263; Wilkins 1992). By adopting a strategy based on branding rather than price competition, they strengthened their position in two ways. Competition based on differentiation of this kind did not lead so quickly to a price response from squeezed competitors that would force market prices and profitability down. Furthermore, the time and cost involved in establishing a brand successfully created a barrier to competitive entry by a new contender.

The rapid growth in working-class demand created a market ideally suited to the expansion in sales of new products presented in a novel and lively way. One of the earlier mass markets created in this way was in sales of high quality beer, with Bass, Allsopps and Guinness creating strong and distinctive brands from the 1850s. This process was accelerated across the trade by the availability of cheap bottles and bottling from the 1890s (R.G. Wilson 1994). In biscuits, brand names became a crucial element in competition (Corley 1972). The most successful subsequent 'branders' included Lever Brothers, who developed such products as Sunlight, Lifebuoy and Lux soaps, and W.D. and H.O. Wills, with their Woodbine cigarette, which appealed to lower income groups (C.H. Wilson 1954: 27–8, 40–4, 55–8; Alford 1973: 97–8, 105–6, 125–7). But branding was certainly not restricted to this direction. The striking importance of branding in the marketing of the various new blended whiskeys, or of superior soaps such as that produced by Pears, indicates its equal appeal to middle income groups (Morgan and Moss 1993: 122–8). In some cases products such as Bovril and Oxo were created by the packaging of previously unusable raw materials. In others, branding created very specific products such as Crosse and Blackwell's ketchup. At the extreme, entrepreneurs devised brands whose chief merit probably lay in their advertising and packaging, whose promises offered far more utility than any content. Beechams pills, for example, were at the successful and enduring end of a spectrum which tailed off into the most fraudulent and dangerous of packaged patent medicines (Fraser 1981: ch. 10; Corley 1984; 1993: 109–11).

The final innovative form of differentiation was the creation of national marketing organizations. This was facilitated by increasing urbanization, which created larger markets that could be served by one office, shop or salesman, and the railway system, which allowed salesmen to travel more widely because of the reduced cost and time associated with travel. These were the same circumstances that allowed the dramatic changes in distribution described in Chapter 9.

Most British firms did not integrate forward into selling in the same decisive and structured way as many American firms did in this period. Their market was compact and distribution sufficiently well organized through specialist merchants to inhibit such a development (Hannah 1980: 61–5; Chandler 1990: 250). This encouraged the survival of smaller firms and placed most in the hands of wholesalers who could squeeze margins and insulate manufacturers from the contact with the market that might allow them to develop competitive edge. However, as markets became more competitive, some larger firms, especially those producing branded goods, developed sales forces to cultivate the market directly. In the 'free trade' in brewing, the Burton brewers and Guinness constructed complex commission agency networks. In the larger towns breweries used travellers (Gourvish and Wilson 1994). The late nineteenth century was the golden age of the commercial traveller, the humble hero of marketing who has scarcely received adequate attention from economic historians. In textiles, firms with distinctive products such as Horrocks, Tootals and Hollins began to attack the retail market directly (Chapman 1979: 230). Before 1900 Cadburys, Levers, Peek Frean in biscuits, Schweppes in soft drinks, Reckitts in starch and Pilkingtons in glass established branch offices and warehouses supporting sales forces (Chandler 1990: 263). Some firms moved to develop closer links with overseas markets as well, employing local salaried managers, at first in the newly settled Empire and then, after 1900, in Europe and the United States. Direct sales organizations sometimes laid the foundation for overseas production facilities. By 1914 Levers had plants in eleven other countries. Manufacturers were gradually clawing back market power from merchants.

Forward integration into the market on the American scale was more comprehensive in finance. The banks developed a national network of branches to capture customers (Collins 1988: ch. 3). This was matched by insurance companies who, from the 1860s, began to create their own branch office network. This provided a base for the growing army of inspectors who were sent out to attract, motivate and control the agents who could provide the most profitable business (Westall 1994). In both cases the forward integration was in part an attempt to compete by other means when cartels prevented direct price competition. Another striking case of forward integration was again in the brewing industry. For special reasons associated with the apparent restriction of licences for public houses, the 1890s saw a race between breweries to capture as many licensed premises as possible to protect or extend their market share (Gourvish and Wilson 1994: ch. 7).

Thus, in a variety of traditional and novel ways, businessmen were able to avoid the fiercest pressures of price competition. Beyond this some, such as Levers and Wills, were able to use marketing to build some of the largest companies in Britain at the start of the twentieth century. Between 1880 and 1914 were the heroic years of British marketing. The key problem was to develop sales on a scale that would allow British firms to enjoy some of the benefits of scale that were available to American companies. The successful establishment of some brands, backed by investment in new technology, created some businesses on an unprecedented scale. But in other markets these methods were either impracticable or insufficiently powerful alone to give businessmen the stability and profitability they sought. In consequence many complemented these methods of marketing by attempting to co-operate with other firms in collusive arrangements.

COLLUSION

From the 1880s the earlier widespread implicit collusion described above became increasingly formal and explicit, supported by written agreements and distinct organizations (Macrosty 1907: 23; Court 1965: 240). Though businessmen remained coy about these activities, and they remain difficult to trace in detail, their new form makes them more evident to the historian. Organizations linking businessmen developed in a variety of ways. Chambers of Commerce represented the interests of particular towns and local industries to government and the railways. Associations were also formed to negotiate collectively with trade unions. This wider co-operation facilitated the emergence of agreements to regulate competition.

But it should not be assumed that the new formality automatically implied increasing monopolistic power. The new guise assumed by collusion reflected its greater fragility in a harsher competitive environment. In earlier periods, local markets with few competitors had required little explicit organization to restrict competition (see pp. 210–11). Integrated national markets, new technologies and economies of scale, and the intervention of foreign competition changed the situation. This became especially clear with sustained deflation and over-capacity in the 1880s and was sustained to 1914 by the slow growth in the domestic market after 1914. It was a period of difficult transition for many British industries. Inefficient firms could no longer rely on high transport costs to protect them. Some were too slow to adopt new technology or grow to enjoy new economies of scale. As a result they faced competitive difficulties for which collusive arrangements seemed a solution. These sometimes also attracted the efficient, for they had little interest in a competitive scramble with firms facing extinction that would create sustained price warfare, reducing profitability for all. In any case, with their lower costs, higher prices offered an opportunity for superior profits that could be invested in expanding capacity or establishing brands that would consolidate their long-run competitive positions.

The number of firms involved and their disparate interests and competitive strengths made such arrangements unstable, and this promoted more organizational sophistication, making collusion more evident. In practice, however, it often proved an exercise in first aid, a temporary amelioration of a problem that required radical surgery. Over-capacity and inefficiency could not be permanently accommodated in this way. Eventually many of these attempts at formal collusion collapsed or led to more permanent amalgamations and reductions in capacity. By the early twentieth century this created an increasingly concentrated national market, with a more robust oligopolistic character, which was able to sustain collusion more successfully, sometimes without the need for the formality and complexity of the late nineteenth-century associations.

Collusion was unstable fundamentally because of the new competitive structure of markets, but the position was exacerbated by the usual complications inherent in its economic logic and by special features of the British business environment. In practice it ranged from the wholly implicit acceptance that one's prices should relate in some stable way to those of competitors, through occasional informal meetings, to the regularly organized trade association, or even highly disciplined sales agency, producing a far tighter control over the market that approached permanent merger. The degree of formality depended on the difficulties of achieving successful collusion, determined by the economic and technical possibilities of the market.

Many associations had an ephemeral life. Much collusion was cyclical in nature. A high proportion of all associations was found in the capital goods sector, often in industries with high capital costs, thus especially subject to the impact of trade fluctuations. By the First World War nearly one-fifth of the associations known to the Board of Trade were operating in iron and steel. The industries supplying the building trade – cables, baths, stoves, glass and so on – contained another concentration of agreements (Clapham 1963: 306–8, 316). In this context collusion tended to be sporadic, emerging after a phase of price warfare at the bottom of a cycle, to attempt to moderate the cost consequences of low capacity working by agreements to produce specified quotas. It might also be found at the peak of cycles, when capacity limitations meant that price advances could be carried successfully. Between these episodes formal collusion evaporated, though in many local markets we may imagine that informal contacts at Metal Exchanges and in other similar trade meetings moderated the course of competition (Macrosty 1907: 57). The steel rail and plate markets were prominent examples of this type of occasional cyclical organization. The imposing sounding National Consultative Council of the Iron Trade of Great Britain was formed in 1900 to integrate the activities of the various associations controlling iron bar prices, but when slump ensued, it collapsed (Macrosty 1907: 62). Similar associations came and went in the Birmingham finished goods trade (Macrosty 1907: 78–9).

More sophisticated forms of collusion emerged as firms demonstrated a dynamic tendency to move across the organizational spectrum from less to more formality, as they discovered the inherent problems of market control and sought to solve them. The market imposed an inexorable logic on those who tried to collude. Prices could only be fixed if output was controlled. This required adherence to the agreement by most firms in the market and barriers to prevent new entry. The more successful an agreement in raising prices, the greater the temptation for firms to exploit market control by cheating on the agreement, operating outside it, or entering the market, all of which would undermine the success of collusion. Price control could also shift the burden of competitive effort to non-price competition, by service, product differentiation, innovation or quality. This often proved beyond the scope of market control and could lead to an escalation in costs, as firms put increasing effort into winning business by these means.

When there were only a few members of a cartel it was not too difficult to control output by appointing independent accountants (for example) to inspect members' books and suggest some basis for output quotas. Compensatory penalties could be paid to other firms if a member exceeded the quota. Such an approach was characteristic of the capital goods industries such as steel (Clapham 1963: 305). It was how the Newcastle Vend, controlling coal sales by sea from the northeast, had operated (Church 1986: 66–8; Kirby 1993: 121–2). However, such forms of control became far more difficult to monitor as the number of firms increased, if there was significant market integration, or when the product involved was less tangible. Local associations in the iron and steel industry tried to cope with market integration by demarcation agreements between different geographical areas but these proved weak in practice (Macrosty 1907: ch. III). The Newcastle Vend collapsed in 1844 as a result of a substantial expansion in the number of collieries in the region and improvements in transport which opened up competition from new ports and by train, especially in the crucial trade to London. This fragmentation on the supply side meant that it subsequently proved difficult to resurrect price control (Kirby 1977: 9–10). For the rest of the nineteenth century coal became a 'fighting trade', with firms accepting market prices and concentrating on agreed wage costs as a second best alternative to controlling prices (Church 1986: 68–70). Intangibility of product meant that no attempt was ever made to control output by the Fire Offices Committee which controlled premium rates in fire insurance (Westall 1984).

If prices and output were successfully controlled, then it could be anticipated that firms would find other forms of differentiation by which to compete. Sometimes this led to agreements for the control of terms of delivery, discount scales, credit terms and transport charges (Macrosty 1907: 6). It usually proved difficult to control advertising or the scale and effectiveness of sales organizations. One of the most sophisticated of all pricing agreements – in the cotton thread trade – resolved this by the simple but effective means of insisting that all members sold their output through one shared marketing arm – the Central Thread Agency – which controlled all the terms and conditions of sale, but organized selling of this sort was otherwise practically unknown. It involved a usually unacceptable loss of goodwill with customers (Macrosty 1907: 136).

The more effective a pricing agreement became, the more tempting it was for an existing firm to break away from the agreement, or a new firm to enter the market, by shading its prices down. New products emerged to challenge those that were price controlled. Such considerations inhibited the formation of restrictive practices in many industries and their collapse in others. In some cases agreements were assisted by barriers to entry implicit in market structure. In the steel industry the scale of operation prevented rapid entry, which meant that the short-term cyclical basis of most associations was not threatened. In other industries, especially chemicals, absolute cost advantages such as patents provided an inherent strength for pricing agreements (Reader 1970: ch. 6). The energetic deployment of marketing to create distinct and attractive products in consumers' minds (described in the previous section) raised costly barriers to entry. In the soap trade, for example, successful brands made entry difficult.

Cartels could reinforce inherent barriers to entry. The principal cartel in fire insurance – the Fire Offices Committee – did not attempt to control the competitive creation of branch office organizations because they provided a costly barrier to entry for new companies. Similarly, successful cartels were rarely inert constructions. The same organization was capable of flexibly adjusting prices in threatened markets to discourage entry. Its members also purchased new entrants to remove the danger they created (Westall 1984). In the iron and steel trade the effectiveness of agreements could be strengthened by an acceptance of regional markets that would not be invaded from outside (Macrosty 1907: ch. 3).

Perhaps the most ambitious attempt to control entry was the series of Birmingham Alliances between businessmen and their employees' trade unions in the 1890s. Skilled workers were given a sliding wage scale related to prices, on the understanding that union members would only work for members of the relevant trade association. If a firm broke the price agreement, its union employees would strike to force it back into line. Through the decade this approach raised prices and wages dramatically though it eventually failed in one market because of entry from a different industry entirely – accounting for the change in fashion towards the wooden bedstead around 1900 (Macrosty 1907: 79–82; Clapham 1963: 304). Another approach was that of the Central Thread Agency, which used sole agency agreements with retailers to enforce a monopoly for their products in Britain. Any retailer selling the agency's products was not allowed to stock those of any competing concern, else it would no longer be served. Given the predominance of the agency in the trade, this was a powerful weapon which prevented entry.

This move forward into the retail sector was by no means unusual. Manufacturers increasingly tried to influence retailers by sole agency agreements and refusals to supply except to those who would sell at agreed retail prices – resale price maintenance. The main stimulus was closely akin to the pressure from low cost competition in manufacturing. The rise of multiple, department and co-operative stores placed traditional retailers under great pressure. Resale price maintenance was an attempt by traditional retailers to protect themselves against price competition. It spread most quickly when retailers were able to co-operate to force manufacturers to grant them guaranteed prices, but in some trades, such as books, there were also clear advantages for producers in encouraging the stocking of their goods (Yamey 1952).

The success of all these collusive arrangements was limited by two important aspects of the competitive structure of most British markets. The central role played by specialist wholesale merchants and their interest in retaining competitive purchase prices provided a powerful countervailing force to manufacturers. Such merchants were always prepared, with adequate financial resources, to support domestic or foreign entry in order to maintain alternative and competitive sources of supply (Clapham 1963: 308–9). And their position was reinforced by the growth of Co-operative Societies, who created the Co-operative Wholesale Society to offer alternative and competitive manufacturing and merchanting facilities. Both these sources could mount a powerful attack on attempts to collude in production or retailing. Furthermore, their position was reinforced by Britain's continued free trade policy, which provided the possibility of the relatively easy import of goods from the cheapest world sources. This was why the 1880s and 1890s saw the beginnings of significant manufactured imports from the United States and Germany, adding to the fashion and labour-intensive goods traditionally imported from France. Marshall and other British economists believed that the danger from restrictive practices was sufficiently limited by free trade and domestic entry (Freyer 1992: 56, 69).

There were potential strategies to control the threat of foreign entry. The Central Thread Agency relied on its largest member – J. & P. Coats – to establish branch factories in foreign markets to prevent the creation of potential overseas competition (Macrosty 1907: 127). In the chemical industry foreign entry was controlled by complex series of international agreements not to trespass on other national territories based on the shared possession of patent rights. Brunner Mond and Nobels were both able to benefit from this in their respective industries, ensuring the maintenance of their tight control over the British market (Reader 1970: ch. 4). Business abroad also saw one of the most successful and long lasting forms of collusion – the Shipping Conferences, through which ship-owners fixed rates and offered deferred rebates to merchants who agreed to use only their vessels. Starting with the Calcutta Conference in 1875, by 1908 virtually all outward trade from Britain, except in the North Atlantic, was controlled by such agreements. Rapid entry was difficult into such a business with such substantial capital at stake and loyalty agreements so effective (Clapham 1963: 314; Hyde 1967: chs 4, 5).

However, collusion was rarely able to rely on such opportunities. More commonly its practitioners moved from one potential threat to another. As one was fended off, the burden of competitive energy would be shifted elsewhere, requiring another organizational effort to obtain agreement on methods to control a new problem. Cartels only remained simple when they were short-term affairs intended to deal with problems of temporary over-capacity in capital goods industries. Other long-term attempts to cope with problems of over-capacity and falling prices or weakly oligopolistic markets were usually characterized by a steady attempt to control wider and wider aspects of competition – a process that was fraught with difficulty. A few pricing agreements were strikingly successful, many failed, and most were far less successful than sometimes imagined. It was only in the few situations where market structures were fundamentally conducive to cartelization that they were likely to be successful.

Collusive arrangements spread in a context in which their legality remained ambivalent. Early statute law had forbidden monopoly, but in such narrowly defined circumstances that it had become inoperative. Judge-made common law became most relevant. Civil actions against conspiracies in restraint of trade were successfully prosecuted by third parties as late as 1867. At the same time contracts in restraint of trade were in principle usually considered void, preventing their enforcement in the courts and adding to the fragility of agreements. However, judges swung with the wind in the closing decades of the century (Freyer 1992: 24). In the 1890s two important rulings weakened the impact of the traditional lines of argument. In the Mogul case (reported in 1892) it was ruled that businessmen must be free to enter into arrangements which were in their own interests and that this was not necessarily to be regarded as conspiracy against third parties unless a 'well defined tort' was committed. This was followed in 1894 by the Nordenfelt case which allowed the enforcement of a cartel agreement if 'reasonable both between the parties and in relation to the public interest'. The judgement reaffirmed that contracts in restraint of trade were contrary to public policy except in 'special circumstances' which were defined as when the contracts were in the interests of the contracting parties and the public. But the judges explicitly declined to rule on whether competition was fair or unfair, or to be tempted into creating economic policy. As a result, the law became increasingly permissive – albeit in a largely passive way – of collusive agreements. Essentially the attitude of British courts was dominated by an acceptance of *laissez-faire* and free trade – whatever the outcome (Freyer 1992: 77–9).

This was in striking contrast with the situation in America, where a combination of statute law (especially the Sherman Act 1890) and judge-made law was creating a legal environment that was hostile to collusion and monopoly (Freyer 1992: 79). France and Germany appear to have followed a similar path to Britain, changing law to encourage co-operation between businessmen, but at root there was a significant contrast. British law never actually encouraged collusion and monopoly, even if that was the apparent effect of the rulings made. Judges were constrained by their desire to avoid interference in the working of the market. It seems a paradox of liberal law that an unwillingness to interfere encouraged an increase in market power and monopoly. But there was an important context within which judges made these decisions and with which they would have been extremely familiar. The cohesiveness of the British business community allowed arbitration to play a central role in the settlement of disputes. Statute law encouraged this development and many collusive agreements were probably strengthened by the provision of cautionary deposits liable to loss by penalty clauses. Of course, the strength of the business community, based on shared values and the force of 'gentlemen's agreements' which allowed this form of control, similarly encouraged and supported collusive behaviour itself. And the passive role of the courts, including especially their unwillingness to enforce agreements, encouraged this process of negotiation and compromise (Freyer 1992: 3, 18). However, this merely reduced an important source of potential instability in the internal operation of collusive agreements. It did nothing to strengthen the underlying economic position of collusive agreements. None of the changes in English law provided much of a bastion against market forces.

INTEGRATION

Competitive and collusive strategies both contributed towards integration, which is investigated more exhaustively in the account of the emergence of the large-scale company provided in Chapter 6. British entrepreneurs were particularly successful in developing highly competitive branded, packaged goods. And one of the prizes of their marketing success was that they were able to develop large-scale, integrated production facilities. These concentrated manufacturing ability into far bigger businesses which enjoyed scale economies that reinforced competitiveness and generated profits that could be used to further develop the strength of brands. The firms involved are all familiar names: Lever Brothers, Imperial Tobacco, Distillers and Guinness were perhaps the largest. But behind them were such firms as Cadbury, Rowntree, Bovril, Colman, Huntley & Palmer and many more. As Chandler has shown, such firms became the single largest groups among the biggest industrial enterprises in Britain in the years before 1914. Sophisticated marketing was not merely imaginative froth on the surface of industrial life. It was the route to sustained growth and solid competitiveness, not least because the internal growth it allowed usually enabled such firms to retain strong central management (Chandler 1990: 262–8).

At the same time the fragility of pricing agreements and the continual difficulty of securing market control led some industries towards permanent amalgamation as the only way of achieving stability. Most of the horizontal amalgamations that were arranged around 1900 arose from the earlier difficulties of pricing agreements of various kinds. The names of many of the largest concerns betray their origins: United Alkali; Calico Printers Association; Fine Cotton Spinners and Doublers Association; Associated Portland Cement

Manufacturers; Bleachers Association; and Bradford Dyers Association (Payne 1967). In the alkali trade the firms using the Leblanc process tried through the 1880s to control soda prices by voluntary means. However, this proved quite unsuccessful in the face of competition from Brunner Mond using the lower cost Solvay method. As a result, the members of the Leblanc association formed the United Alkali Company in 1891, to take over all their capacity, convinced that its scale and opportunity for full control would offer a better chance of success (Reader 1970: ch. 6(i)). In the tobacco trade, a merger of previously colluding firms followed an attack on the British market by Americans in 1901 (Alford 1973: ch. 14). In the soap trade an attempt to convert unsuccessful collusion into permanent amalgamation was trumped in 1906 by a campaign run by the *Daily Mail* (presumably in order to protect its advertising revenue). Nonetheless, Lever took the industry in hand, and by 1914 he had brought most of its concerns under his ownership (C.H. Wilson 1954: ch. 8).

Pricing agreements often provided a route to amalgamation – and this proved important in shaping the organizational structure of the new companies, for they never lost their sense of being a voluntary association of independent concerns. Many operated as though they were no more than organizations designed to control competition. One of the chief activities of the Imperial Tobacco Company's central organization was to monitor and control the advertising expenditure undertaken by its constituent companies. The holding company that was to be such a feature of British industrial life was often the child of a failed attempt to control the market by other means. However, mergers were not the final staging post on the path to integration that began with attempts to control price. They usually focused on market control, rather than competitive production, ignoring the need for full integration of production facilities and centralization of management of the new amalgamation. For this reason, many were as unsuccessful as the terminable agreements they followed (Hannah 1979: 312–13).

CONCLUSION

Competition by price and differentiation, collusion and integration, the competitive strategies described in this chapter, were not alternatives. Many companies used them all with varying emphases through the late nineteenth century. Indeed they were related. Fierce price competition encouraged the quest for successful collusion. Collusion encouraged firms to compete by means other than price. Its problems drove them down the road to amalgamation – and if this achieved the market power they sought, it often pushed them back into collusion and differentiation within the context of a more robust oligopolistic market. These strategies were not the result of the whims of entrepreneurs. They were rational responses to the economic logic of their market environment. And it was this that laid the foundations of the distinctive and problematic large-scale company structure with which British business entered the twentieth century.

This chapter has tried to show how the large-scale firms discussed in Chapter 6 emerged from a specific competitive environment – that they were in part a consequence of the competitive strategies pursued by businessmen. The story comes full circle. We have seen that market integration and technological change in mid-century challenged the cosy oligopolies that had been so characteristic of the industrial organization of early nineteenth-century Britain. The late nineteenth century can be seen as a transitional phase in which the organization of business tried to come to terms with these new possibilities. With hindsight we can see that the potential for the large-scale company is writ large; the problem was to discover the route by which it could be realized. Two were found in the competitive strategies discussed here (there were other routes). Some large-scale firms emerged through the exploitation of brands to build an increasing share in already expanding markets. Others were founded on the wrecks of the attempts at collusion that many businesses found to be the most obvious way of coping with the difficulties of the transition. With the creation of the large-scale companies that were the outcome of these developments we can see the recreation of the possibility of stronger forms of collusion once more. Large firms moved to dominate national markets in ways that made them as sensitive to one another's competitive strategies as the small concerns had been in their local markets fifty and a hundred years before. And this provided the basis for a twentieth-century economy that was to become increasingly dominated by restrictive practices, sometimes encouraged, sometimes challenged, by governments.

BIBLIOGRAPHY

Alford, B.W.E. (1973) *W.D. & H.O. Wills and the Development of the U.K. Tobacco Industry, 1786–1965*, London: Methuen.

Barker, T.C. (1968) 'The glass industry', in D.H. Aldcroft (ed.) *Development of British Industry and Foreign Competition*, London: George Allen & Unwin.

Broadberry, S.N. and Crafts, N.F.R. (1992) 'Britain's productivity gap in the 1930s: some neglected factors', *Journal of Economic History* 52: 531–58.

Campbell, R.H. (1961) *Carron Company*, Edinburgh: Oliver & Boyd.

Chandler, A.D. (1990) *Scale and Scope: The Dynamics of Industrial Capitalism*, Cambridge, MA: Harvard University Press/Belknap.

Chapman, S.D. (1979) 'British marketing enterprise: the changing roles of merchants, manufacturers, and financiers, 1700–1860', *Business History Review* 53(2): 205–33.

Church, R. (1975) *The Great Victorian Boom, 1850–1873*, London: Macmillan.

—— (1986) *The History of the British Coal Industry*, vol. 3, *1830–1913*, Oxford: Clarendon Press.

Clapham, J.H. (1963) *An Economic History of Modern Britain: Machines and National Rivalries (1887–1914) with an Epilogue (1914–1929)*, Cambridge: Cambridge University Press.

Collins, M. (1988) *Money and Banking in the UK: A History*, London: Croom Helm.

Corley, T.A.B. (1972) *Quaker Enterprise in Biscuits*, London: Hutchinson.

—— (1984) 'Sir Joseph Beecham, 1846–1916', in D.J. Jeremy (ed.) *Dictionary of Business Biography*, vol. I, London: Butterworths.

—— (1993) 'Marketing and business history, in theory and practice', in R.S. Tedlow and G. Jones (eds) *The Rise and Fall of Mass Marketing*, London: Routledge.

Court, W.H.B. (1965) *British Economic History, 1870–1914: Commentary and Documents*, Cambridge: Cambridge University Press.

Daunton, M.J. (1985) *Royal Mail, The Post Office since 1840*, London: Athlone.

Dickson, P.G.M. (1960) *The Sun Insurance Office 1710–1960*, London: Oxford University Press.

Dutton, H.I. (1984) *The Patent System and Inventive Activity during the Industrial Revolution, 1750–1852*, Manchester: Manchester University Press.

Edwards, M.M. (1967) *The Growth of the British Cotton Trade, 1780–1815*, Manchester: Manchester University Press.

Elbaum, B. and Lazonick, W. (eds) (1986) *The Decline of the British Economy*, Oxford: Clarendon Press.

Farnie, D.A. (1979) *The English Cotton Industry and the World Market 1815–1896*, Oxford: Clarendon Press.

Fraser, W.H. (1981) *The Coming of the Mass Market 1850–1914*, London: Macmillan.

Freyer, T. (1992) *Regulating Big Business: Antitrust in Great Britain and America, 1880 to 1990*, Cambridge: Cambridge University Press.

Gourvish, T.R. (1980) *Railways and the British Economy, 1830–1914*, London: Macmillan.

Gourvish, T.R. and Wilson, R.G. (1994) *The British Brewing Industry, 1830–1980*, Cambridge: Cambridge University Press.

Hannah, L. (1979) 'Mergers, cartels and concentration: legal factors in the U.S. and European experience', in N. Horn and J. Kocka (eds) *Law and the Formation of the Big Enterprises in the 19th and Early 20th Centuries*, Göttingen: Vandenhoeck & Ruprecht.

—— (1980) 'Visible and invisible hands in Great Britain', in A.D. Chandler and H. Daems (eds) *Managerial Hierarchies: Comparative Perspectives on the Rise of the Modern Industrial Enterprise*, Cambridge, MA: Harvard University Press.

Harrison, A.E. (1969) 'The competitiveness of the British cycle industry, 1890–1914', *Economic History Review, 2nd series* 22(2): 287–303.

Harvey, C. and Press, J. (1991) *William Morris: Design and Enterprise in Victorian Britain*, Manchester: Manchester University Press.

Hyde, F.E. (1967) *Shipping Enterprise and Management 1830–1939 Harrisons of Liverpool*, Liverpool: Liverpool University Press.

Jones, S.R.H. (1973) 'Price associations and competition in the British pin industry, 1814–40', *Economic History Review, 2nd Series* 26 (2): 237–53.

—— (1976) 'Hall, English & Co., 1813–41: a study of entrepreneurial response in the Gloucester pin industry', *Business History* 18 (1): 35–65.

Kirby, M.W. (1977) *The British Coalmining Industry, 1870–1946: A Political and Economic History*, London: Macmillan.

—— (1993) *The Origins of Railway Enterprise: the Stockton and Darlington Railway, 1821–1863*, Cambridge: Cambridge University Press.

Landes, D.S. (1970) *The Unbound Prometheus: Technological Change and Industrial Development in Western Europe from 1750 to the Present*, Cambridge: Cambridge University Press.

Macrosty, H.W. (1907) *The Trust Movement in British Industry: A Study of Business Organisation*, London: Longmans, Green.

McKendrick, N. (1960) 'Josiah Wedgwood: an eighteenth-century entrepreneur in salesmanship and marketing techniques', *Economic History Review, 2nd Series* 12 (2): 408–33.

Morgan, N. and Moss, M. (1993) 'The marketing of Scotch whisky; an historical perspective', in R.S. Tedlow and G. Jones (eds) *The Rise and Fall of Mass Marketing*, London: Routledge.

Nevett, T.R. (1982) *Advertising in Britain: A History*, London: Heinemann.

Nishimura, S. (1971) *The Decline of Inland Bills of Exchange in the London Money Market 1855–1913*, Cambridge: Cambridge University Press.

Payne, P.L. (1967) 'The emergence of the large-scale company in Great Britain, 1870–1914', *Economic History Review, 2nd Series* 20 (3): 519–42.

—— (1974) *British Entrepreneurship in the Nineteenth Century*, London: Macmillan.

Reader, W. (1970) *Imperial Chemical Industries: A History*, vol. I, *The Forerunners 1870–1926*, London: Oxford University Press.

Richardson, H.W. (1968) 'Chemicals', in D.H. Aldcroft (ed.) *The Development of British Industry and Foreign Competition 1875–1914*, London: George Allen & Unwin.

Rose, M.B. (1986) *The Gregs of Quarry Bank Mill: The Rise and Decline of a Family Firm, 1750–1914*, Cambridge: Cambridge University Press.

Sigsworth, Eric M. (1958) *Black Dyke Mills: A History*, Liverpool: Liverpool University Press.

Supple, B. (1970) *Royal Exchange Assurance: A History of British Insurance 1720–1970*, Cambridge: Cambridge University Press.

Taylor, A.M. (1964) *Gillets: Bankers at Banbury and Oxford: A Study in Local Economic History*, Oxford: Clarendon Press.

Thane, P. (1981) 'Social history 1860–1914', in R. Floud and D. McClosky (eds) *The Economic History of Britain since 1700*, vol. II, *1860 to the 1870s*, Cambridge: Cambridge University Press.

Westall, O.M. (1984) 'David and Goliath: the Fire Offices Committee and non-tariff competition, 1898–1907', in O.M. Westall (ed.) *The Historian* and the Business of Insurance, Manchester: Manchester University Press.

—— (1992) *The Provincial Insurance Company 1903–38: Family, Markets and Competitive Growth*, Manchester: Manchester University Press.

—— (1994) 'Marketing strategy and the competitive structure of British general insurance, 1720–1980', *Business History* 36 (2): 20–46.

Wilkins, M. (1992) 'The neglected intangible asset: the influence of the trade mark on the rise of the modern corporation', *Business History* 34 (1): 66–99.

—— (1994) 'When and why: brand names in food and drink', in G. Jones and N. Morgan (eds) *Adding Value: Brands and Marketing in Food and Drink*, London: Routledge.

Wilson, C.H. (1954) *The History of Unilever: A Study in Economic Growth and Social Change*, vol. I, London: Cassell.

Wilson, R.G. (1994) 'Selling beer in Victorian Britain', in G. Jones and N. Morgan (eds) *Adding Value: Brands and Marketing in Food and Drink*, London: Routledge.

Yamey, B.S. (1952) 'The origins of resale price maintenance: a study of three branches of retail trade', *Economic Journal* 62: 522–45; reprinted in Bauer, P.T. and Yamey, B.S. (1968) *Markets, Market Control and Marketing Reform*, London: Weidenfeld & Nicholson, 273–301.

9 Concentration and competition in the retail sector *c.*1800–1990

Michael Winstanley

> There is not a man in the universe deserves the title of a complete
> tradesman like the English shopkeeper.
>
> (Daniel Defoe, *The Complete English Tradesman* (1726))

In recent years, at least from the 1960s, as Britain's industrial capacity
and international standing have declined, its retailing sector has
acquired an enviable reputation for efficiency and dynamic enterprise.
Despite the national, even multinational, nature of some businesses,
their success has often been portrayed in personal rather than
corporate terms, the product of specific individual's enterprise and
vision. This has been reflected in the output of business history over
the period which, in contrast to studies of manufacturing, has been
dominated by volumes dealing with successful companies; these have
dwelt on innovation, growth and personalities rather than stagnation
and relative decline (Briggs 1956; Mathias 1967; Rees 1969; Chapman
1973; Briggs 1985; Wilson 1985; Sigsworth 1990). If the British as a
nation have developed an aversion to manufacturing, the same, it
would seem, has not been true of retailing; from Defoe's day to the
present, shopkeepers, even in the unpromising decades of the late
nineteenth century, have epitomized the enduring triumph of British
enterprise (Wilson 1965: 189–94).

They have not always been viewed in such a favourable light.
Indeed, from the 1930s to the mid-1950s, the intense individualism of
many small shopkeepers was held to be responsible for the relatively
slow development of more efficient retailing by some economists, who
were both surprised and depressed about the apparently limited
market penetration achieved by the new forms of large-scale retailing
which had emerged in the late nineteenth century: surprised because
its cost advantages seemed indisputable and its inevitable supremacy
long forecast; depressed because numerous small retail units implied

high costs, low productivity, unjustifiably large margins and a waste of national human resources. Worse still, such inefficiency often seemed to have been deliberately engineered by collusive agreements and restrictive practices between manufacturers and trade associations, which operated against the consumer interest by maintaining artificially high prices or restricting choice. Rather than becoming more efficient in the inter-war years 'the retail market has been steadily becoming more imperfect, mainly because considerable expenditure has been devoted to the task of making it so' (Smith 1948: 130). During the 1930s in particular it exhibited 'a slowing down in the rate of development of new methods and new techniques of distribution . . . an element of rigidity that contrasted sharply with the fluidity of ideas, methods and structures in the decades before 1914' (Jefferys 1954: 96), with the result that 'the advantages of industrial progress were being dissipated on their way through distributive channels to the detriment of the consumer' (Fulop 1964: 8). This concern prompted a spate of academic and government enquiries designed to obtain precise information on distribution, and to suggest a range of measures to promote efficiency ranging from legislation to outlaw restrictive practices through to calls for wholesale commitment to co-operative trading (Levy 1948; Smith 1948; Jefferys 1950). Whether they were right to be concerned or whether British retailing has responded effectively to forces bearing on it forms the backbone of this chapter.

Any assessment of the structure and operation of retailing needs to recognize at the outset that it possesses characteristics which not only distinguish it from manufacturing, but make it difficult to measure, or even define, levels of business concentration, efficiency and competition, or to judge how far its operations serve the needs of consumers. Retailing is a barometer rather than an engine of change, its organization and marketing strategies *reflect* rather than *determine* levels of prosperity, class structure, social relations and settlement patterns. The nature of the market in which shopkeepers have operated has also been much more closely circumscribed by geographical location, a consequence of the fragmented nature of demand, consumers' imperfect knowledge and limited mobility. This has meant, with notable exceptions, that significant growth has been achieved by replication of outlets rather than expansion on a single site, a process which has demanded the establishment of complex management structures and knowledge of a wide range of local conditions. Unlike many manufacturers, retailers have also largely operated in a protected domestic market, and until the postwar era their overseas operations were generally concerned with securing sources of supply rather than expanding their distributive network.

The mixed nature of many shopkeepers' trade also means that it is rarely possible to relate the distribution of a product with a specific business organization, as is usual in histories of manufacturing or extractive industry, like cotton or coal. Tea, for example, in the nineteenth century was sold by itinerants, small neighbourhood shops, substantial grocers, high street traders like chemists and ironmongers, dedicated multiples, co-operative stores, tea and coffee taverns and even some department stores. Furthermore, there have been no clearcut functional divisions in many distributive sectors. The distinction between wholesaler and retailer in many trades is itself not only a comparatively recent one but one which is again now becoming less evident. Some firms, and indeed some individuals, have combined distribution with production or processing, making it difficult to assess the relative importance or efficiency of each activity. Most historical studies have sought to avoid these problems by concentrating on specific forms of business organization, but this, too, has its own conceptual difficulties, in terms of defining, for example, a 'multiple' or a 'department store', but also of determining their relationships with each other and the range of commodities they sold. 'General' stores have ranged from supermarkets to the corner shop.

Bearing in mind these considerations, this chapter reassesses three aspects which have dominated historical debate about retail development: the dating and speed of the transition from itinerant and market trading to fixed shop retailing; the comparative importance of large-scale retailers such as department stores, multiples and co-ops *vis-à-vis* independent family businesses; and the implications of changes in business structure for competitive strategies, operational efficiency and consumer interests. Central to its analysis is an attempt to explain why the retail sector, both in terms of number of outlets and market shares, has been dominated by the relatively 'small' family business. It concludes with a brief assessment of postwar trends which have significantly accelerated the dominance of large-scale retailing, in terms of both business structure and the size of outlets.

ITINERANTS, MARKETS AND THE GROWTH OF SHOPS

Jefferys' view (1954: 5–6) that it was only the years after 1850 which 'saw the triumph of the fixed shop as the dominant form of retailing' and that, prior to this period, open markets and itinerants played 'an important role', was reinforced by Davis (1966: 252–5). Both stressed the slow pace of change in the early nineteenth century and, although they acknowledged that shops were widespread before mid-century, they tended to see them as dominated by skilled producer/retailers or purveyors of luxuries to a relatively privileged, wealthy elite and contended that foodstuffs in particular continued to be bought at the market or in the street. The changes which had occurred by 1850 – the marginalization of fairs, the growth of intermediaries in the retail chain between producer and consumer and the gradual rise of fixed shop retailing – did not, on balance, deter Jefferys from insisting that 'the basic structure and character of the distributive trades . . . had not changed fundamentally', but 'still bore the marks of a pre-industrial economy'.

This position has been attacked on two very different fronts. On the one hand there are those who argue that older forms of non-shop outlets retained their importance beyond mid-century; on the other are those who maintain that developments in shop retailing were much more widespread far earlier.

Both Benson (1983: 98–114) and Alexander (1970: 61–86) have emphasized the continuing importance of itinerant trading. They point to a steady rise in numbers throughout the century at a rate in excess of population growth and the concentration of such traders in larger urban areas, suggesting that the importance of the cheap jacks, itinerant drapers and tea dealers, who feature so prominently in literary sources about rural life, has been overstated. Mayhew's vivid descriptions of London street traders in the early 1850s tends to support their view, as do analyses of census returns which suggest a continuing preponderance of itinerants of all descriptions in the most heavily urbanized counties until the early twentieth century (Shaw and Wild 1979: 280–2; Shaw 1986: 182; Phillips 1992: 54–6).

Others have stressed the continued vitality of market trading, especially for the working class. Davis asserted that 'markets were still of first rate importance to the housewife until nearly the end of the [nineteenth] century' (Davis 1966: 253). The number of specific market improvement acts continued to rise until the 1850s and their geographical distribution shifted away from the decaying, largely agricultural corporate towns of the south and west towards the industrialized towns of the North and Midlands (Shaw 1985: 290–1; Phillips 1992: 58–63). Further major redevelopments later in the century undoubtedly occurred, but frequency and scale are more difficult to chart since they were increasingly carried out under the aegis of general legislation or required no additional specific granting of parliamentary approval.

It is far less obvious, however, that all of this seriously challenges the view that retailing from fixed premises accounted for an increasing proportion of consumer spending in the nineteenth century. Street traders persisted primarily in commercial cities like London where they were symptomatic of the low level of demand and the relative lack of other employment opportunities in what were essentially casual labour markets, rather than a positive reflection of economic importance. Lancashire's continuing high level of itineracy throughout the century was largely due to the presence within its boundaries of two large commerical cities, Liverpool and Manchester, whose social characteristics reflected those of the capital with large immigrant populations and limited industrial employment. Here, as in London, street trading had become a 'marginal occupation' pushed to 'the periphery of the distribution system' as early as 1860 (Green 1982: 146; Scola 1992: 253). Its operators were invariably small scale, usually self-employed, and their involvement in the trade was often seasonal and restricted to selling perishable produce. Census figures clearly show that where there was well-paid, regular employment, as in the textile and heavy industrial towns, itineracy was even more marginalized.

Assessing the role of markets is also problematical since we still know virtually nothing about the scale of development on a national scale. Investment in new facilities in the early nineteenth century was undoubtedly much more widespread than the timing and distribution of market improvement acts suggests, since legislation reflected the regional geography of the growth of local authorities' powers rather than any obvious transformation in urban infrastructure, population growth or economic prosperity. Initial market improvements in unincorporated, urban settlements like Manchester were carried out under manorial control without the need to obtain specific powers from Parliament; elsewhere they relied on private, speculative capital to construct new premises, as in Leeds in the 1820s (Grady 1973–7: 165–95, esp. 170; Scola 1992: 150–61). Local authorities' activities in the industrial towns of the North and Midlands were restricted until after the Municipal Reform Act of 1835 established the principle and procedures for acquiring democratically accountable, borough administration. This provided the legitimacy to seek powers to purchase existing market rights and to erect purpose-built premises. These new facilities were ostensibly to house specialized food dealers, especially meat traders and greengrocers, but the motive for improvement was also partly ideological with Liberal-dominated councils seeking to use their new powers to dismantle private, often Tory-owned, market monopolies and to reap profits from municipal enterprise. Such initiatives also reflected the emergence of a civic consciousness, a desire to control public spaces, and a recognition of public health hazards like slaughterhouses. Not all of their grandiose schemes were successful (Alexander 1970: 42–58; Scola 1992: 161–74).

Market traders dealing in perishable foodstuffs tended to complement rather than compete with shops (Blackman 1963), and they continued to occupy an important retail role in smaller settlements or where consumer demand was insufficient to justify investment in permanent outlets for such produce, or even household goods and clothing. By the third quarter of the nineteenth century, however, their retail functions in larger conurbations were being devolved either to street traders or, increasingly, to fixed retail outlets. In Manchester, for example, the markets had by then become more specialized, physically distinct and effectively dominated by wholesalers who serviced the increasing number of fixed shops in the city who were the major retail beneficiaries of growing consumer demand (Scola 1992: 168). Markets survived, therefore, and they retained a key role in distribution, but their roles were transformed and their relative importance as retail outlets undoubtedly diminished over the century.

Recent research has also questioned Jefferys' late dating of the triumph of shop retailing. Relying primarily on trade directories, Alexander (1970: 89–109) argued that shop formations outpaced population growth from the 1820s and that it was the smaller retailer, especially the unclassified 'general shopkeeper', who was largely responsible for this expansion in numbers. It would now seem, however, that the directories he used grossly underestimated the numbers of such shopkeepers in the 1820s (Winstanley 1983: 12–15) and that Clapham's view that shop outlets were growing rapidly in number from at least the last quarter of the eighteenth century was largely correct (Clapham 1926: 219–28; Scola 1975; Mitchell 1981: 39–46; Mui and Mui 1989: 29–45, 135–47, 191–200). Their uneven spatial diffusion, however, reflected the regional diversity evident in other aspects of the economy (Langton 1984: 145–67). Provision was especially noticeable in the south, probably because nucleated settlements, agricultural prosperity, the decline of labourers' self-sufficiency and the growth of a wage economy were more evident than in the northern upland, pastoral areas which were both more self-sufficient and more easily served by travelling salesmen (Mui and Mui 1989: 37–45). By the end of the century shops were rapidly being established in northern industrial areas (Mui and Mui 1989: 195–6) but they do not initially seem to have posed a major challenge either to markets – since they sold essentially non-perishable produce like tea – or to the substantial skilled tradesman, since it was from him that they often purchased their supplies for resale to the poor.

Although accurate figures remain impossible to obtain, it is clear from trade directories and contemporary comment that shop numbers continued to rise dramatically in the nineteenth century, recurrent trade depression providing only a temporary hiatus. The expanding population was not only predominantly urban, but, possibly from the 1840s and definitely from the 1870s, it was increasingly affluent, generating sufficient concentrated demand to justify investment in fixed premises. Although each trade had its own distinct pattern of growth, and the pace of development varied regionally and between towns depending on size, social structure and the extent of suburbanization, it is clear that average rates of population per shop fell significantly over the century and that food retailing was everywhere the most dynamic sector (Shaw 1985: 291). Many would appear to have been small-scale operations, but it would be wrong to categorize all retail businesses in this way; they were ranged along a continuum from substantial concerns with workforces running into double figures whose proprietors were prominent figures in provincial society, through respectable family-run neighbourhood shops to marginal outlets established by the unfortunate or destitute with no other form of income. Although the more substantial among them often advertised themselves as specialists, divisions between trades would appear to have been blurred, especially outside the major cities where, as in the 'universal shop' in Mrs Gaskell's fictional *Cranford*, 'the profits of brown soap and moist sugar enabled the proprietor to go straight to . . . London' to purchase the latest fashions for his extensive upstairs showroom (Gaskell 1853: 60–1). Until well into the second half of the century, however, in every retail sector from grocery to jewellery, from drapery to confectionery, fixed shop retailing was the preserve of the individual or family business whose proprietor was personally involved in daily management, lacked the protection of limited liability or even the mixed benefits of partnership, and seldom operated more than one outlet.

THE EMERGENCE AND IMPACT OF LARGE-SCALE RETAILING

By the turn of the century, however, new forms of large-scale retailing – multiples, co-operatives and, to a lesser extent, department stores

– were being widely forecast to displace small family businessmen (Winstanley 1983: 39–40). These relied on exploiting the opportunities which arose out of a combination of transport improvements, an increasing urban population, enhanced consumer spending power and mobility, and new sources of supply, primarily of imported, non-perishable foodstuffs and mass-manufactured items of clothing and footwear.

Department stores reflected attempts, primarily by drapers, to increase turnover through diversification and expansion on a single site rather than by the opening of additional stores. There were distinct parallels between developments in Britain, Continental Europe and the United States, with the last increasingly recognized as the pace setter by the early twentieth century (Pasdermadjian 1954: *passim*; Ferry 1960: *passim*; Miller 1981: 19–47). Despite the publicity given to purpose-built stores like Selfridges West End store, whose theatrically staged opening in 1909 attracted much publicity (Pound 1960: 31–50), physical growth was usually achieved by piecemeal acquisition of adjacent properties, invariably on main thoroughfares in town centres, which were then adapted or totally redesigned to meet perceived changes in shopping fashions and to accommodate new lines of business or departments. Although they continued to rely heavily on their early reputation for women's and children's clothing, by the early twentieth century most of the stores also retailed gents' wear, footwear, furniture and furnishings, household appliances, foodstuffs, stationery, jewellery, glass and china and toys in an attempt to encourage customers to treat them as 'universal providers', a phrase initially promoted by William Whiteley whose premises, opened in 1863, are sometimes referred to as the first British department store (but see Alexander 1970: 107). To enhance their attractions to customers a variety of additional facilities were being provided by the 1900s: tea-rooms and restaurants, often with live entertainment; rest and club rooms; branch post offices; hairdressing salons; toilet and washing facilities. Selfridge's boast was that his store was 'a social centre, not a shop' (Pound 1960: 59–72). To cater for those unable to visit the stores themselves, comprehensive mail order catalogues were published (Jefferys 1954: 18–21; Adburgham 1964: 271–6; Shaw 1992: 135–53).

Multiples, or chain stores, represented a very different approach, seeking to expand their market share through geographical diffusion rather than single-site development. Apart from John Menzies and W.H. Smith's railway bookstalls they were virtually unknown before the 1870s. Concentrating initially on a narrow range of basic, largely non-perishable foodstuffs or manufactured products for which there was a guaranteed supply, they sought to tap the expanding working-class market of the period by keeping prices competitive, restricting lines, eschewing labour-intensive services and not offering credit. Bulk turnover enabled them to negotiate discounts from suppliers or to diversify vertically into production to reduce costs and to ensure regularity and consistency of supply. Liptons acquired tea plantations to supply its shops; Freeman Hardy and Willis relied on mass-manufactured shoes; Burton's opened tailoring factories to produce made-to-measure suits; Boots produced patent medicines. Less commonly the diversification was from manufacturing or importing into retailing: the River Plate Meat Company opened shops to retail its imported Argentinian beef; Singers to sell its sewing machines.

Between the mid-1870s and 1914 multiples appeared in virtually every sector of the retail trade although their impact was greatest in those sectors which dealt in mass-produced, standardized, non-perishable products (Jefferys 1954: *passim*). The majority remained relatively local but several rapidly acquired regional, even national reputations: Liptons, Home & Colonial, International Tea Company, Maypole (groceries and provisions); Jesse Boot (pharmacy); Hepworths, Foster Brothers and Burtons (men's outfitters); Dewhursts, Eastmans and James Nelson (frozen meat) and Marks and Spencer (Variety stores) (Jefferys 1954: 126–443; Mathias 1967: 96–194; Rees 1969: 1–38; Chapman 1973: 57–102; Shaw 1992: 153–9). The inter-war years witnessed further expansion, Burtons, for example, increasing its number of retail outlets from just forty in 1919 to 595 twenty years later (Sigsworth 1990: 43), but also, in line with the trend towards amalgamations evident in the rest of the economy and described elsewhere in this volume by Kirby, there were increasing numbers of mergers of large firms, especially in the grocery, footwear and pharmacy sectors (Jefferys 1954: 63–4; Mathias 1967: 237–97).

Despite marked differences in their organizational structure, patterns of ownership and market philosophy, co-operative stores shared many of the multiples' characteristics. They, too, concentrated initially on a narrow range of basic commodities, primarily non-perishable groceries such as tea, margarine and flour. They, too, expanded vertically, the Co-operative Wholesale Society, founded in 1863, co-ordinating buying for local retail societies, allowing them to enjoy the benefits of discounted bulk purchases, while manufacturing and processing a wide range of household and branded goods in its own factories (Redfern 1913: *passim*). Like the multiples, the co-operative movement expanded by opening new branches rather than diversifying on a single site and sought to remain competitive by restricting lines, economizing on services and dealing only in cash. Unlike the multiples, however, which were the brainchilds of individual entrepreneurs, co-operative societies had their roots in local community initiative. Both their origins and spectacular growth rates in the half century before 1914 lay in the industrial heartlands of the north where economic prosperity was accompanied by a sense of working-class identity and traditions of voluntary, collective organization which continued to underpin the movement's unique democratic nature (Cole 1944: 176–8, 212–41; Bonner 1961: 96–102; Purvis 1990: 325–9; 1992: 111–23). During the inter-war years, however, there was a conscious policy to move beyond these areas and to colonize 'co-op deserts' in the south, cities and rural areas. From a movement of just over half a million members in 1880, therefore, the co-op membership had grown to over 8.5 million by 1939 and was in a position to supply virtually every household need (Cole 1944: 371–2).

To many contemporaries writing before 1914 such developments presaged a rapid, comprehensive retail revolution with trade increasingly concentrated in fewer and larger hands. The precise impact of the newcomers' aggressive pricing, emphasis on cash sales and uninhibited advertising on independent shopkeepers' numbers, prosperity and marketing strategies, however, remains difficult to gauge, not least because each trade had its separate history. There is some evidence to suggest that shop numbers were falling in the first decade of the century, especially in food and clothing (Ford 1935), but by the 1930s it was clear that large retailers' share of leading sectors, although increasing, was doing so only slowly and that their overall market penetration remained relatively insignificant. There were even indications that the co-op and the department stores were struggling to maintain their market shares. Jefferys estimated that only in footwear, milk and furniture did independent retailers enjoy less than 50 per cent of the market just prior to the Second World War. They accounted for over 80 per cent of sales of new consumer durables such as motor vehicles and electrical goods, as well as fruit and vegetables, fish, newspapers, magazines, tobacco products, chocolates and sweets. Even in groceries and household goods, traditionally seen as the sectors where large-scale retailers had made greatest inroads, independents still enjoyed 54 per cent of trade. Collectively over two-thirds of total retail sales were accounted for by single-outlet retailers. Although co-ops enjoyed 25 per cent of milk sales, 20.5 per cent of groceries and 19.5 per cent of bread and flour, they had made negligible inroads in other areas: only in meat, coal and footwear did they account for 10 per cent or more of national sales. Overall their share of consumer spending was languishing around 10 per cent, their consumer loyalty apparently declining as they branched out beyond their early strongholds. Women's and children's wear and household furnishings continued to provide department stores with the bulk of their turnover, supplemented by high-class china and specialities, but overall they enjoyed only 5–6 per cent of the retail market. Multiples were rather more successful with over 20 per cent of turnover of a diverse array of products encompassing, in ascending order of market penetration, jewellery, poultry and game, groceries, milk, men's and boys' wear, stationery, pharmacy and furniture, but only in footwear, with 46 per cent, could they be considered to be dominant (Jefferys 1950: 125).

By the early 1930s, the pre-war forecasts of the imminent demise of the small shopkeeper seemed grossly misconceived. Instead, the possibility that Britain was 'over-shopped' was being discussed. Far from declining in the face of the combined onslaught of large-scale retailing, some argued that there had been 'a tremendously rapid multiplication of shops' (Smith 1948: 101). Amid mounting concern about business inefficiency, some economists called for the number of trading premises to be officially controlled by licences and, not surprisingly, received vociferous support from existing members of the trade, both the shop assistants' unions and the retailers' organizations which tended to represent the more substantial businessmen.

By the mid-1930s there was a growing realization that objective efforts to obtain accurate national statistics had to be undertaken. Ford's retrospective local studies, using evidence from trade directories, were designed to quell alarmist fears; he initially argued that shop numbers fell in most trades between 1901 and 1931, with grocers, butchers, bakers, pawnbrokers, and china and glass dealers experiencing the heaviest declines (Ford 1935). His subsequent work, however, showed that during the 1920s the downward trend was reversed in virtually every sector, regardless of region and size of settlement (Ford 1936; Ford and White 1937). More comprehensive national surveys suggested that in 1938 there were between 750,000 and 1,000,000 retail outlets depending on whether services such as hairdressing and cooked foods were included (Levy 1948: 32; Jefferys 1950: 123). When a government-sponsored Census of Distribution was finally introduced in 1950 it confirmed the findings of previous surveys: over 70 per cent of retail businesses still operated from a single site and further 11 per cent of outlets were owned by businesses which had four or less outlets (quoted in Jefferys 1954: 471).

Furthermore, practices did not seem to have been revolutionized. Many national grocery multiples had abandoned earlier price-cutting and diversified in attempts to raise gross profit margins, while smaller regional chains remained wedded to many labour-intensive, traditional practices such as delivery and personal service (Winstanley 1991: 23–31). As late as the mid-1950s the overwhelming majority of multiple businesses still fell into the latter category although the national organizations had overhauled them in terms of outlets and turnover (Jefferys 1950: 130; 1954: 471; *Stores and Shops Directory* 1955).

LIMITS TO GROWTH (1): SUPPLY-SIDE CONSIDERATIONS

To understand why large-scale retailing, defined both in relation to the scale of trading on a single site and to the number of outlets controlled by businesses, grew relatively slowly in the first half of the century, and to assess whether the preponderance of independent shops represented entrepreneurial failure, we need to appreciate not just the general forces which contrived to ensure the survival of the family firm in Britain, but the specific factors which operated within retailing itself.

Studies of family firms in manufacturing have largely concentrated on supply-side explanations of slow growth. These have emphasized possible entrepreneurial deficiencies, stressing particularly the reluctance of individual proprietors to lose overall control; a failure to delegate or to develop progressive managerial, promotional and accounting practices; unease about raising additional capital necessary for expansion, whether from partners, banks or through the adoption of limited liability; an inability to recognize either opportunities for growth or threats to their existence; and a decline in commitment by succeeding generations of the family. This business caution, combined with intense localism, seemed to amount to built-in barriers to growth which meant that firms which remained under family control were 'destined to be relegated or confined to the medium or even small size range' (Payne 1984: 179).

Unfortunately such theories have not been applied to the retail sector despite the fact that it was here that the predominance of small businesses was most evident. There are clues, however, even within studies of successful firms, to suggest that continued growth was often achieved despite, rather than because of, the roles of founding fathers, some of whom exhibited an almost obsessive desire to retain personal control. The 'critical phase', as Wilson observed in his history of W.H. Smith, was 'the conversion from individual, family or partner ownership to potentially fragmented public shareholding' (Wilson 1985: 392). Even those who recognized the need to raise additional capital, like Thomas Lipton, found it difficult to 'lay aside power, decentralise management (and) train up men as his successors' despite the fact that his business was 'outgrowing the limits of personal surveillance' (Mathias 1967: 114). Conflict over the control of Marks and Spencer characterized the 'interregnum' which followed their deaths, so completely had they dominated the shareholding and management (Rees 1969: 18, 36–8). Jesse Boot was equally reluctant to divest himself of close financial control and management, going so far as to buy up shares in the holding company which controlled his businesses and to withhold market and performance information from other shareholders (Chapman 1973: 128–30).

For many tradesmen, however, resort to share issue was used not to raise additional capital but to obtain the benefits of limited liability and to ensure that family members or close associates had guaranteed interests in the business. Such private companies had limited potential for growth and the structure may even have led to problems when family members sought to withdraw their holdings, forcing businesses either to scale down their operations or to seek additional funding for defensive reasons through borrowing or new partnerships (Ely 1976: 75).

As Rose has shown in Chapter 3, this reluctance to expand the capital base of a firm was usually indicative of a lack of desire among family businesses to expand operations beyond the level which individuals or family members could personally control. The development of a single site was consequently preferred to more unwieldy spatial expansion. In the case of department stores this usually entailed heavy investment in property development, both for the piecemeal acquisition of adjacent sites and for the partial or total rebuilding of premises. This, combined with the costs of diversification and the proliferation of labour-intensive services, obliged such stores to move up market to maintain high gross profit margins, while their central locations made them inconvenient for regular purchases of lower order commodities. Together these combined to limit further growth and to restrict their market penetration, despite attempts to promote mail order.

Such considerations also explain the reluctance of multiples to expand their branch network beyond a geographical area where each shop could be personally supervised on a regular basis by the proprietor or members of his family. Such decisions could also be justified on business criteria. There were considerable risks involved in expanding beyond the locality where a business had built up its turn-over and reputation. Massive advertising was needed to break down consumer loyalties to existing outlets and to build up a critical market share; a detailed knowledge of urban topography was indispensable to avoid investing in poor locations; any costs of expansion had to be offset by economies in bulk purchasing or wage bills; trained managers were not always easy to recruit and returns were uncertain.

Whether this amounted to entrepreneurial failure is less clear. For most retailers, trade was the means to a variety of ends, and the dedicated pursuit of growth was not necessarily viewed as the primary objective in life. Like their counterparts in manufacturing (see Chapter 3), it was safer and potentially more profitable to diversify into other aspects of the local economy, investing in housing or commercial premises for rent, local manufacturing concerns and land, or using profits to establish younger members of the family in different occupations or professions. To some extent, this reflected the essentially local nature of capitalism, but it was reinforced by a political and cultural provincialism which survived well into the twentieth century and which was increasingly socially dominated by the petite bourgeoisie (Crossick 1984: 81–7). By the end of the nineteenth century the personal involvement of manufacturers, merchants and professionals with their immediate locality, which, as Rose has demonstrated, was so strong in earlier decades, was waning since they increasingly operated in a mobile, national or international arena and developed general trade or vocational associations to champion their interests. Retailers' trade associations mirrored such developments, especially from the 1890s, but they remained essentially federal structures, their initiative and vitality emanating from local associations (Winstanley 1983: 75–92). The fixed location of retail capital, reliance on local trade and a continuing tendency to live within relatively easy reach of their place of work ensured that shopkeepers, along with builders, remained more committed to developing the prosperity and attractiveness of their urban environment than those engaged in manufacturing since, although many shopkeepers were no longer resident on their premises, they retained a significant interest in maintaining the appearance of, services to, and public order in the major thoroughfares where their premises were situated.

Not surprisingly, from the late nineteenth century until after the Second World War, such men dominated British local government and urban provincial society (Winstanley 1983: 101–2). Despite the gradual intrusion of central government, municipal authorities during this period retained substantial autonomy, controlling public utilities such as water, gas and electricity, operating public transport and promoting central redevelopment schemes, all of which had a direct bearing on retailing. The social status which political office brought continued to be bolstered by personal involvement in a wide range of associational activities ranging from churches and charities to sporting clubs and cultural societies. Such involvement in the local community and the benefits it brought in terms of status, power and the promotion of the local economy would have been jeopardized by spatial expansion. Not surprisingly, independent traders listed the destruction of local government as one of the inevitable consequences of the expansion of multiples from the turn of the century, extending this criticism even to co-ops which, despite their communal base, had loyalties to an ideal which transcended local concerns (Winstanley 1983: 90).

Co-ops faced rather different problems from those of the individual entrepreneur. Despite the movement's expansionist policies, capital resources, national conventions, ventures into advertising and sophisticated supply networks it was constrained by structural, cultural and ideological obstacles to growth. Unlike nationally controlled multiples the movement was federal, with power vested in individual societies whose leaders were democratically accountable to local shareholders. This posed considerable problems as far as co-ordinating activities was concerned. Not all societies were affiliated to the national Co-operative Union or felt obliged to purchase supplies from the Co-operative Wholesale Society. Despite attempts to effect mergers, the number of small societies remained stubbornly high especially in the old heartlands of southeast Lancashire. Debilitating competition between societies for customers and territory further weakened the movement. Even more seriously, there were tensions between the utopian ideals of mostly lay activists committed to establishing a co-operative commonwealth, the pragmatic concerns of business management and the materialism of many customers whose loyalty was largely dependent on the maintenance of the dividend. Policies which favoured the recruitment of committed co-operators restricted the pool from which managerial talent was drawn, while the commitment to become a 'universal provider' of wholesome foodstuffs and durable consumer goods under the umbrella of the Co-operative Wholesale Society often resulted in unco-ordinated diversification and wasteful vertical integration into production and processing at local level, the cross-subsidizing of unprofitable lines or stores, and the shunning of what was regarded as ephemeral, wasteful trends in fashion or design. Consequently the co-op tended to dissipate its efforts and its image remained a functional, utilitarian one, out of touch with increasingly materialistic, fashion-conscious consumers. Paradoxically, therefore, although collectively the movement seemed to possess both the capital and the will to expand, it lacked the entrepreneurial talent and single-minded pursuit of profit necessary to put this into effect.

In marked contrast to difficulties which businesses faced in expanding their operations, there were few barriers to entry into small-scale retailing. This continued to exert a powerful attraction for a wide range of people. In a society in which there were minimal welfare provisions until after the Second World War, general shopkeeping offered one of the few openings for widows, invalids, the unemployed and aged to maintain themselves independently. As household production retreated throughout the nineteenth century, the importance of retailing as one of the few sectors of the economy in which married women could combine family duties with profitable employment grew. In marked contrast to most areas of child employment, there were no legislative controls on families' exploitation of their own children as unpaid assistants. Above all, however, shopkeeping was seen by many entrants as a way of re-establishing personal control over their lives, of asserting their independence and staking a claim to enhanced social status within the local community (Lawson 1991: 312–26). For the small shopkeeper

> the possession of a business is not merely a matter of calculating profits. Sociological problems are involved which are quite alien to the department store or the big multiple shop or chain. The possession of a small shop means an independent livelihood though such independence may mean any amount of worry, drudgery, vexation and insecurity. . . . There is a feeling of pride in the possession which may obscure financial considerations.
>
> (Levy 1948: 10)

The apparently high failure rate among small shopkeepers was no deterrent to such entrants. They associated running a shop with independence and tended to believe that they had the personal qualities to survive where others had failed (Bechhofer *et al.* 1974: 478–9). Increasing opportunities to save, lump-sum payments from insurance companies, family legacies or, ironically, co-operative dividend enabled many to enter the trade. Until stricter planning controls were introduced in the inter-war years, especially on new housing estates, there were no legislative obstacles to converting residences into shops so that extra income could effectively be generated with minimal outlay. Small shops also benefited from national advertising campaigns by manufacturers keen to maximize outlets for their branded products, weaken the hold which general wholesalers had over many sections of trade and check possible dependence on oligopsonist multiples.

LIMITS TO GROWTH (2): MARKET IMPERFECTIONS

Such considerations, however, important though they are, are insufficient to explain the slow development of concentration in the retail sector, the presence of imperfect competition for goods and services was a major factor.

To some extent this was part of the trend towards explicit collusion at national level which, as Westall explains in Chapter 8, characterized business activity in the late nineteenth and early twentieth centuries. Shopkeepers' organizations and manufacturers were jointly responsible for enforcing agreements, either voluntarily or through legislative means, which restricted the ability of large retail organizations to capitalize on cost advantages which they may have had by lowering prices to the consumer to increase their market share. Resale price maintenance, whereby suppliers stipulated the prices at which their products were to be sold and withheld supplies from retailers who refused to recognize them, was the most important of these collusive arrangements. Originating in the 1890s (Yamey 1952: 522–45), it spread rapidly to cover a wide range of manufactured products by the inter-war years, including clothing, pharmaceuticals, photographic equipment, tobacco, soaps and toiletries, branded confectionery and groceries, books, newspapers and magazines, milk, motor vehicles, petrol and new electrical goods such as radios, gramophones and records (Levy 1942: 85–161; Jefferys 1954: 53–5; Winstanley 1983: 81–3). Such agreements adversely affected co-ops who suffered boycotts by some manufacturers since their policy of giving dividend to shareholding customers was interpreted as price cutting. Although multiples were usually able to negotiate discounts from manufacturers for bulk purchases they were unable to expand their market share by lowering prices, forcing them into competing on the smaller retailer's preferred ground of service and convenience. Rationing and price controls during and after the Second World War, although designed to prevent profiteering rather than price cutting, had similar effects, since prices were fixed to maintain existing outlets and to prevent large concerns from cornering the market.

Resale price maintenance reflected, and was bolstered by, manufacturers' continuing preference for strategies which encouraged competition based on product differentiation rather than price, a strategy also discussed by Westall in Chapter 8. Producers' vigorous advertising in the press, on billboards and through freely distributed shop signs proclaiming the qualitative superiority of their brands were designed to reinforce this, encouraging the consumer to demand their products by name even if they were more expensive than those of their competitors. Such policies had the desired effect not just of reducing the potential powers of wholesalers and large retailers over suppliers, but of sustaining a large number of outlets for the products concerned by guaranteeing a minimum rate of return (see, for example, Pasold 1977: 634, 644).

In other cases, product differentiation occurred more naturally. Variations in the quality and regularity of supply, a high degree of perishability, the necessary retention of a degree of processing on the premises, and after sales maintenance and repairs, all provided opportunities for the independent retailer to survive. Products as diverse as greengrocery, fish, meat, fresh provisions such as eggs, cheese and cold meats, bakery, confectionery, electrical goods, motor vehicles, some clothing and pharmaceuticals, and catering, including the ubiquitous fish and chip shop (Walton 1992: 88–100), all fell into these categories. A variety of personal 'services' were also emphasized depending on the nature of trade and clientele. Shopkeepers within working-class communities were 'dynamically involved in the culture of the community' (Hosgood 1989: 440) whether as 'bankers of the poor' providing credit lifelines during times of individual or collective distress, as the suppliers of congenial meeting places for the operation of women's informal domestic culture, or as the medium through which news and gossip were exchanged. Many such shops would appear to have remained open much longer than legally permitted shop hours, catering effectively as the 'poor man's larder' from which their customers purchased small quantities of basic commodities as and when they needed them. The extension of credit, whether through personal accounts or hire purchase, also featured prominently in the high street trader's competitive arsenal as did extensive, labour-intensive delivery networks, a feature which was greatly enhanced before the First World War by the bicycle and in the inter-war years by the commercial vehicle.

Some of these features were indicative of what was probably the most important constraint on the growth of large-scale retailing – the limited, fragmented, fluctuating and geographically dispersed nature of much consumer demand. Although inter-war surveys suggested that levels of primary poverty had declined, many members of the working class had little surplus income to devote to conspicuous consumption and may well have chosen to spend it on leisure rather than consumer goods. The rapid rise in real wages which had characterized the last quarter of the nineteenth century slackened off considerably in the first half of the twentieth while for many people between the wars, especially in the North and Midlands, unemployment and short time working, or fear of them, had a direct impact on the ability or propensity to spend. Credit remained important, not just for occasional purchases of durable consumer goods, but for weekly purchases, checking the growth of cash trading (Tebbutt 1983: 169–204).

As the tertiary sector of the economy continued to expand there was a marked redistribution of income in favour of the white collar professional and commercial classes. The areas to benefit most from this were London and the Home Counties, J.B. Priestley's 'newest England' which 'could almost accept Woolworths as its symbol', democratic because its cheapness made it accessible, 'a large-scale, mass production job' whose real birthplace, he concluded with regret, was America (Priestley 1934: 401–2). These new suburbanites provided the basis for the growth in consumer spending on durable household goods and clothing between the wars, products whose prices manufacturers and retailers alike were quick to control and which were marketed on brand names or fashion rather than 'value for money'.

Suburbanization, by dispersing purchasing power, also tended to check the concentration of food retailing and to encourage the proliferation of services. Although food storage facilities were more hygienic and public transport networks were dramatically expanded, the perishable or bulky nature of many products still dictated shopping patterns for most foodstuffs, obliging customers to make regular purchases of small quantities in the immediate vicinity of their homes or to rely on deliveries, rather than availing themselves personally of centrally situated outlets. Although private car ownership increased between the wars, it was insignificant in comparison with the United States and the predominantly male owners tended to use the vehicles for work or for family leisure pursuits at weekends. Newly affluent female customers may have visited town centres for higher order goods, but their continuing restricted mobility encouraged traders dealing in groceries, provisions and perishable produce to invest in commercial motor vehicles to expand their delivery networks, trading on service and convenience rather than price. This eroded the cost advantages which multiples had acquired through bulk purchasing and centralized handling procedures, while playing to the strengths of the local family tradesman who emphasized personal service, convenience and product differentiation.

Recognition of the demand constraints on large-scale retailers qualifies to some extent the views of those critics who claimed that the small-scale, labour-intensive nature of much distribution was inefficient and damaging to the public interest. Innovation was only possible when market conditions allowed. In view of the emphasis on brand loyalty and resale price maintenance promoted by manufacturers, the relative inelasticity of demand for basic foodstuffs and the geographical dispersal of demand, it is not surprising that food multiples, which had been at the forefront of change in the late nineteenth century, were obliged to diversify and trade on service to maintain market share, while businesses dealing in manufactured, non-perishable, higher order goods such as women's fashions and household furnishings were able to continue to rely on centrally located shops. Small-scale retailing in such circumstances was not an anachronism but reflected the imperfect nature of the market. Artificially imposed restraints on trade like resale price maintenance may have diluted competition, but they were not the major obstacle to the development of large-scale or price-competitive retailing; independent shops survived because market conditions allowed them to.

POSTWAR DEVELOPMENTS

While rationing and the array of legislative controls on the retail trade during and after the Second World War stifled any wholesale transformation until well into the 1950s, they also had the effect of significantly reducing the level of personal service offered and of raising labour productivity, thus providing a break with pre-war practices. Since then the pace of retail change has quickened dramatically with increases in both unit size and levels of business concentration and a consequent marked deterioration in the attractiveness and viability of smaller-scale retailing (*Retail Business* Annual Review of Trade; Dawson and Kirby 1979: 20–32; Bamfield 1980: 33–4). Some studies in the early 1970s suggested that much of the initial rapid decline was due to the once-for-all effect of the abolition of resale price maintenance and the widespread introduction of self-service, especially into grocery, and that the continuing imperfect nature of the market would ensure that 'the decline of the small firm sector of retailers will soon begin to slow down' with small shops continuing to perform a substantial role (Hall 1971: 46; Smith 1971: 2, 17–29). Others argued that there were market and managerial constraints to the growth of larger units (*Retail Business*, March 1970). But the numbers of shop outlets and businesses have declined remorselessly and with them has fallen the small retailers' market share. Although the gross value of their sales has risen as a result of increasing consumer spending, the annual rate of increase in turnover has been consistently lower than that of their larger competitors. By the mid-1980s they enjoyed little more than 30 per cent of the total market; significantly less in sectors such as grocery (about 13 per cent), clothing and consumer durables.[1]

Not all large organizations have benefited at their expense, however. The co-operative movement's market share also declined significantly to around 5 per cent by 1985, while many independent department stores either closed or became branches of one of the big five multiples (Debenhams, House of Fraser, John Lewis Partnership, Lewis's/ Selfridges and Allders) which together accounted for nearly 80 per cent of this sector's sales by the mid-1980s. Multiples have been the chief beneficiaries of retail changes in consumer durables, clothing and, to a lesser extent, alcohol, the sectors which have witnessed the most substantial rises in consumer spending. Food trades, however, have experienced even more dramatic changes. Early developments in the 1960s involved the aggressive expansion of outlets by a relatively large number of chains. Since then, however, there has been both a marked decline in the number of grocery multiples and a marked expansion of the range of goods which each outlet sells, offering to the consumer the possibility of 'one-stop' shopping. Although initial growth was at the expense of the independent trader, more recently such superstores have grown by taking trade from other large retailers, including the co-op and specialist multiples such as butchers, greengrocers, dairies and bakers. By the end of the 1980s the four leading chains accounted for nearly 80 per cent of total grocery sales.

The reasons for this dramatic transformation are not hard to find and were correctly forecast by economists in the immediate postwar years. Many independent shopkeepers agreed with commentators like Smith (1971: 17) that legislation outlawing collusive agreements between manufacturers to enforce resale price maintenance in 1956 and, more especially, the abolition of most individual suppliers' right to do so in 1964, sounded their death knell. Such legislation, however, reflected rather than caused the decline of the practice; it was already increasingly being abandoned by both large retailers and manufacturers who viewed it as a check to their expansion plans. There were more fundamental pressures which were at work. On the one hand, the relative attractiveness of owning a retail business was declining.

The consolidation of the welfare state removed the need for the elderly, disabled or widowed to take up retailing. In an era of relatively full employment, greater job security and choice, rising real wages, longer holidays and shorter working weeks, there were also easier avenues to social status and material benefits than running a shop in which long unsocial hours prevented the proprietors from participating in the new leisure pursuits which emerged with the increased free time, affluence and mobility. Improvements in housing also meant that fewer people were willing to tolerate the cramped living conditions which were invariably attached to small neighbourhood shops. The more substantial tradesman's status and political power in the local community was undermined by the erosion of local authority powers and the challenge of new professional classes.

The development of what Jefferys in 1950 described as a 'fully fledged distributive machinery' has worked to the advantage of the larger retailers. Refrigeration has expanded the scope for selling what were previously viewed as perishable products; bulk purchase, often of imported goods, has reduced handling costs and attracted considerable discounts; a more flexible national delivery network, based on road rather than rail, has lowered transport costs; computers have overcome problems of stock control and accounting associated with large-scale operations; national advertising by retail chains has broken down consumer loyalties to local shops or manufacturers' branded products. Above all, self-service and pre-packaging have reduced labour costs, raising staff productivity while effectively de-skilling the workforce, allowing the employment of cheaper female and casual labour.

All of this, however, was only implemented because the changing pattern of demand made it profitable to do so. Rising real incomes from the mid-1950s and, until the 1980s, relatively full employment and a reduction in income inequalities were clearly major elements in this. Changing settlement patterns were also significant, with slum clearance and new high-rise apartments and sprawling estates of the late 1950s and 1960s destroying many of the communal networks which had supported the neighbourhood shopkeeper. Of crucial importance, however, was the rapid extension of private car ownership which broke down the protected isolation of retail markets and reduced the need for new housing estates to contain their own shops. Customer mobility on this scale eliminated the need for expensive delivery services and opened up local shops to competition from more distant, cost-effective outlets by enabling consumers to travel more regularly and, even more significantly, to provide the means to carry their purchases home. Town centres were the initial beneficiaries of multiples' investment in new and enlarged premises, but rising property values, planning controls on the nature of development, urban congestion and insufficient parking have encouraged the development of out-of-town superstores, either individually or as part of new retail 'parks'. Where the small businessman has survived he or she has often done so by sacrificing a degree of independence, joining one of the voluntary grocery chains to obtain the benefit of discounts on bulk purchase or becoming a franchisee, contractually obliged to restrict his or her sales to products or services provided by a national or international company.

Retail developments on such a scale were not foreseen by critics of the small-scale retailing which they replaced. Even those writing in the late 1960s remained convinced that the possible disadvantages of greater concentration would be outweighed by the benefits of improved efficiency, and that ease of entry into a trade would check attempts to increase profit margins excessively (McClelland 1966: 291). The view that large-scale retailers are efficient and competitive is still widely held, but increasing concern is being expressed that rising levels of concentration do in fact jeopardize competition with a small number of big retailers able to dictate terms to suppliers and to determine the level of consumer choice available. Criticisms levelled at major retail chains by consumer organizations and the popular press echo those which were previously made of their small-scale predecessors. They have been accused of being reluctant to pass on cost savings to customers, preferring to maintain high gross margins to raise capital to acquire and develop sites convenient for 'one-stop' shopping, and of promoting product differentiation, emphasizing the superior quality and distinctiveness of their own brands instead of reducing prices. In some instances it has been argued that large retailers are now effective oligopsonists possessing power to dictate the nature, quality and price of products they buy from suppliers, and that there are agreements with manufacturers, especially of white electrical goods, not to stock brands or models sold by other local retailers, a practice which mirrors the restrictive practices of the inter-war years.

Barriers to entry, however, particularly in the form of high costs of property development and advertising, would now seem sufficiently high to rule out any substantial challenge from a rejuvenated small-scale business sector. The challenge is likely to emerge – is already emerging – from the incursion of new foreign-owned competitors like IKEA, Benetton and TOYSRUS into what had previously been viewed, despite the long-standing presence of a few overseas firms like Woolworths, Safeway and C & A, as a naturally protected market. Retailing organizations in the future, in short, are unlikely to be local, regional or even national, but international, reflecting the emergence of a more culturally-homogeneous mass market, at least in the developed Western world. How well British firms respond to this, in terms both of protecting their domestic market and of expanding their operations overseas, remains to be seen.

The real test of British retailing entrepreneurship may be yet to come.

NOTE

1 Figures from *Retail Business* drawing on Department of Industry data. Precise figures remain problematical because definitions of 'small' do not remain constant and annual estimates of retail shares are retrospectively revised.

BIBLIOGRAPHY

Adburgham, A. (1964) *Shops and Shopping, 1800–1914*, London: Allen & Unwin.

Alexander, D. (1970) *Retailing in England during the Industrial Revolution*, London: Athlone Press.

Bamfield, J.A.N. (1980) 'The changing face of British retailing', *National Westminster Bank Quarterly Review* May: 33–45.

Bechhofer, F., Elliott, B., Rushforth, M. and Bland, R. (1974) 'Small shop-keepers: matters of money and meaning', *Sociological Review* 22: 465–82.

Benson, J. (1983) *The Penny Capitalists: a Study of Nineteenth-century Working Class Entrepreneurs*, Dublin: Gill & Macmillan.

Benson, J. and Shaw, G. (eds) (1992) *The Evolution of Retail Systems, 1800–1914*, Leicester: Leicester University Press.

Blackman, J. (1963) 'The food supply of an industrial town', *Business History* 5(2): 83–97.

Bonner, A. (1961) *British Co-operation*, Manchester: Co-operative Union.

Briggs, A. (1956) *Friends of the People: the Centenary History of Lewis's*, London: Batsford.

——— (1985) *Wine for Sale: Victoria Wine and the Liquor Trade, 1860–1984*, London: Batsford.

Chapman, S. (1973) *Jesse Boot of Boots the Chemists*, London: Hodder & Stoughton.

Clapham, J.H. (1926) *An Economic History of Modern Britain*, vol. I, *The Early Railway Age 1820–50*, Cambridge: Cambridge University Press.

Cole, G.D.H. (1944) *A Century of Co-operation*, London: Allen & Unwin.

Crossick, G. (1984) 'The petite bourgeoisie in nineteenth-century Britain', in G. Crossick and H.-G. Haupt (eds) *Shopkeepers and Master Artisans in Nineteenth Century Europe*, London: Methuen, 62–94.

Davis, D. (1966) *A History of Shopping*, London: Routledge & Kegan Paul.

Dawson, J.A. and Kirby, D.A. (1979) *Small Scale Retailing in the U.K.*, Farnborough: Saxon House.

Defoe, D. (1726) *The Complete English Tradesman*, London; reprinted Gloucester: Alan Sutton, 1987.

Ely, V.N. (1976) *Fifty Years-Hard: Elys of Wimbledon*, London: Linen and Woollen Drapers' and Cottage Homes.

Ferry, F.W. (1960) *A History of the Department Store*, New York: Macmillan.

Ford, P. (1935) 'Excessive competition in the retail trades: changes in the number of shops, 1901–1931', *Economic Journal* 45: 501–8.

—— (1936) 'Decentralisation and changes in the number of shops, 1901–31', *Economic Journal* 46: 359–63.

Ford, P. and White, G.V. (1937) 'Trends in retail distribution in Yorkshire (West Riding), 1901–27', *The Manchester School* 119–25.

Fulop, C. (1964) *Competition for Consumers*, London: I.E.A./Deutsch.

Gaskell, E. (1853) *Cranford*, Oxford: Oxford University Press; reprinted 1980.

Grady, K. (1973–7) 'Profit, property, interest and public spirit: the provision of markets and commercial amenities in Leeds, 1822–9', *Thoresby Society* 54: 165–95.

Green, D.R. (1982) 'Street trading in London: a case study of casual labour', in J.H. Johnson and C.G. Pooley (eds) *The Structure of Nineteenth Century Cities*, London: Croom Helm, 129–52.

Hall, M. (1971) *The Small Unit in the Distributive Trades*, London: HMSO.

Hosgood, C.P. (1989) 'The "Pigmies of Commerce" and the working-class community: small shopkeepers in England, 1870–1914', *Journal of Social History* 22(3): 439–59.

Jefferys, J.B. (1950) *The Distribution of Consumer Goods*, Cambridge: Cambridge University Press.

—— (1954) *Retail Trading in Britain, 1850–1950*, Cambridge: Cambridge University Press.

Langton, J. (1984) 'The industrial revolution and the regional geography of England', *Transactions of the Institute of British Geographers, New Series* 9: 145–67.

Lawson, Z. (1991) 'Shops, shopkeepers and the working-class community: Preston, 1860–1890', *Transactions of the Historic Society of Lancashire and Cheshire* 141: 309–28.

Levy, H. (1942) *Retail Trade Associations*, London: Kegan Paul/Fabian Society.

—— (1948) *The Shops of Britain*, London: Routledge & Kegan Paul.

Mathias, P. (1967) *Retailing Revolution*, London: Longman.

McClelland, W.G. (1966) *Costs and Competition in Retailing*, London: Macmillan.

Miller, M.B. (1981) *The Bon Marché: Bourgeois Culture and the Department Store 1869–1920*, London: George Allen & Unwin.

Mitchell, I. (1981) 'Retailing in eighteenth and early nineteenth century Cheshire', *Transactions of the Historic Society of Lancashire and Cheshire* 130: 37–60.

Mui, H. and Mui, L.H. (1989) *Shops and Shopkeeping in Eighteenth Century England*, London: Routledge.

Pasdermadjian, H. (1954) *The Department Store: its Origins, Evolution and Economics*, London: Newman.

Pasold, E. (1977) *Ladybird, Ladybird: a Story of Private Enterprise*, Manchester: Manchester University Press.

Payne, P.L. (1984) 'Family business in Britain: an historical and analytical survey', in A. Okochi and S. Yasiwka (eds) *Family Business in the Era of Industrial Growth: its Ownership and Management*, Tokyo: Tokyo University Press, 171–206.

Phillips, M. (1992) 'The evolution of markets and shops in Britain', in J. Benson and G. Shaw (eds) *The Evolution of Retail Systems, 1800–1914*, Leicester: Leicester University Press, 53–75.

Pound, R. (1960) *Selfridge: a Biography*, London: Heinemann.

Priestley, J.B. (1934) *English Journey*, London: Heinemann/Gollancz.

Purvis, M. (1990) 'The development of co-operative retailing in England and Wales, 1851–1901: a geographical study', *Journal of Historical Geography* 16: 314–31.

—— (1992) 'Co-operative retailing in Britain', in J. Benson and G. Shaw (eds) *The Evolution of Retail Systems, 1800–1914*, Leicester: Leicester University Press, 107–34.

Redfern, P. (1913) *The Story of the CWS, 1863–1913*, Manchester: Co-operative Wholesale Society.

Rees, G. (1969) *A History of Marks and Spencer*, London: Weidenfeld & Nicholson.

Retail Business (Journal of the *Economist* Intelligence Unit).

Scola, R. (1975) 'Food markets and shops in Manchester, 1770–1870', *Journal of Historical Geography* 1: 153–68.

—— (1982) 'Retailing in the nineteenth century town: some problems and possibilities', in J. Johnson and C. Pooley (eds) *The Structure of Nineteenth Century Cities*, London: Croom Helm, 153–69.

—— (1992) *Feeding the Victorian City: the Food Supply of Manchester, 1770–1870*, Manchester: Manchester University Press.

Shaw, G. (1985) 'Changes in consumer demand and food supply in nineteenth-century British cities', *Journal of Historical Geography* 11: 280–96.

—— (1986) 'Retail patterns', in J. Langton and R.J. Morris (eds) *Atlas of Industrialising Britain, 1780–1914*, London: Methuen, 180–3.

—— (1992) 'The evolution and impact of large-scale retailing in Britain', in J. Benson and G. Shaw (eds) *The Evolution of Retail Systems, 1800–1914*, Leicester: Leicester University Press, 135–65.

Shaw, G. and Wild, M. (1979) 'Retail patterns in the Victorian city', *Transactions of the Institute of British Geographers, New Series* 4: 278–91.

Sigsworth, E.M. (1990) *Montague Burton: the Tailor of Taste*, Manchester: Manchester University Press.

Smith, A.D. (1971) *Small Retailers: Prospects and Policies*, London: HMSO.

Smith, H. (1948) *Retail Distribution*, Oxford: Oxford University Press (1st edn 1937).

Stores and Shops Directory (1955) London: Newman.

Tebbutt, M. (1983) *Making Ends Meet: Pawnbroking and Working-class Credit*, Leicester: Leicester University Press.

Walton, J.K. (1992) *Fish and Chips and the British Working Class*, Leicester: Leicester University Press.

Wilson, C. (1965) 'Economy and society in late Victorian Britain', *Economic History Review, 2nd series* 18: 183–98.

—— (1985) *First with the News: the History of W.H. Smith, 1792–1972*, London: Jonathan Cape.

Winstanley, M.J. (1983) *The Shopkeeper's World, 1830–1914*, Manchester: Manchester University Press.

—— (ed.) (1991) *A Traditional Grocer: T.D. Smith's of Lancaster, 1858–1981*, Lancaster: Centre for North West Regional Studies, Lancaster University.

Yamey, B. (1952) 'The origins of resale price maintenance: a study of three branches of the retail trade', *Economic Journal* 62: 522–45.

10 The growth of the firm in the domestic banking sector

Michael Collins

INTRODUCTION

Financial services are critical to the course of general economic development within a modern economy. The type of banking institutions that evolve in a country, and the functions they perform, will be of central importance to the form and pace at which modern business enterprises develop in a particular economy. In general terms, banks are intermediate between saver and borrower, mobilizing a country's savings (in the form of deposits) and making these available for productive investment (in the form of loans to customers etc.). For business firms, banks are essential to the conduct of modern commercial practices. Banks not only provide a sophisticated money transmission mechanism (allowing, for instance, for the transfer of payments and the settling of debts, say by the use of cheques or bills of exchange) but they also form an important source of loans for business enterprises. In Britain's case sophisticated financial markets and institutions emerged at a relatively early period and this made an important contribution to the nation's economic development in the eighteenth and early nineteenth centuries. Despite this, doubts have been expressed over the extent to which British banks were supportive of the needs of the productive sectors of the economy, especially manufacturing. In particular, doubts remain as to the degree and appropriateness of bankers' support for industry from the late nineteenth century when British industrialists were facing increasing competition from other developing industrial nations (Collins 1991; Capie and Collins 1992).

Part of the debate concerns the role of City of London financial institutions which were largely concerned with servicing overseas financial needs. By the end of the nineteenth century the business of many important City institutions such as the merchant banks, discount houses and Stock Exchange was dominated by the provision of loans from overseas borrowers and by the servicing of international trade and finance. It is acknowledged that there were major benefits accruing to the UK from this position of the City as the world's international financial centre. Nevertheless, some critics suggest that over the long term the consequences for British industry were detrimental because – it is alleged – the overall effect of the City's international function was to divert British savings into overseas investments rather than towards British industry (Kennedy 1987). According to this line of argument, if the business of British financial institutions had been more oriented to the needs of British firms than to overseas markets, then funds would have been cheaper and more readily available for British industrialists to undertake greater investment and thus retain their international competitiveness to a much greater extent than actually happened. One consequence of this hypothetical scenario may have been the more rapid growth of British firms and the earlier emergence of the large corporate enterprise in the UK.

However, these claims are hotly disputed. On the face of it, British financial markets were largely competitive and if it were true that a profitable opportunity existed to lend to British industry – an opportunity that remained available for a number of decades according to the critics – then surely, logic would suggest, profit-seeking banks would have taken steps to meet the demand and to participate in the profits. A more likely explanation for the City's relative 'neglect' of British firms is that British businesses in general were not demanding finance and funding from outside institutions. In fact, at this time most businesses were relatively small concerns which for the most part could finance investment from the firm's internal funds. Most businesses were also family concerns and this may have deterred them from seeking outside funding as it could have diluted family control over the business (e.g. through the issue of equity to a wider range of shareholders than family members). Indeed, the evidence suggests that when small and medium-sized firms sought to raise outside funding they could usually do so with little difficulty by drawing on local sources of funds (Michie 1990). Moreover, in those sectors where large corporate structures did emerge (e.g. brewing) and funds had to be raised on the capital market, London institutions responded positively. It seems not so much to have been that City institutions were biased against British industry but that British industry was not normally seeking investment capital from the financial markets.

In fact, for the most part the banking needs of British businesses would have been met not by the international institutions of the City of London but by retail banks such as Barclays, Lloyds and the Midland. There is another set of criticisms concerning the relationship between this type of bank and British business firms. It is sometimes alleged that the sort of bank−industry relationship that developed in Britain was not as conducive to international competitiveness and the emergence of large business enterprises as it was in some continental countries, particularly Germany. British banks were not investment banks, they did not buy shares of industrial companies. Instead, they favoured relatively liquid assets and, as regards loans, they preferred to lend for short periods. Thus, critics suggest, the support banks gave to Britain's business sector was restricted. The claim is that the banks did not seek to make good the deficiency of long-term funding from the capital market by offering long-term loans themselves and there was great reluctance to involve themselves in the business of their customers in a supportive manner. However, even if this allegation were true the explanation is unlikely to be one solely of inadequate supply of appropriate funding from the banks. The demand from businesses for bank involvement would be limited for some of the same reasons for their failure to use the capital markets for funding − the small size of most British firms meant that internal sources of funds were adequate for most purposes, and family owners would have been reluctant to relinquish some managerial control to a bank to whom they would have been in debt. Anyway, there is growing evidence that retail banks were, in fact, very supportive of most industrial clients and that they maintained long-term business relations with them. For example, whereas it was normal to lend over a relatively short period in the first instance there were frequent cases of continuous renewal which extended the full period of a loan over many years. There is yet another factor which should be taken into consideration and that is that, compared with overseas, British banks were remarkably stable institutions, with very few bank failures. This stability was partly derived from policy on liquidity and on avoiding too great a risk on lending. To the extent to which British business benefited from being serviced by a stable banking system, bank practice on asset distribution (including loans to business) made a positive contribution here.

An important part of the growing stability of British banking firms was the growth in scale of operations. It is with the changing nature and growth of the firm in this domestic banking sector that this chapter is concerned. More particularly, it examines developments in the organizational form favoured by British banking firms over the period 1826−1914. During the period the competitive structure of the market for retail banking services was transformed from one consisting of hundreds of small-scale suppliers (small 'private banks') to one dominated by a small group of giant corporate banks (known as 'joint-stock banks'). The result was the creation of a small number of banks which established offices throughout the country. The extensive branch networks so established gave access to massive sources of funds raised from depositors, and the large scale and geographical spread of business added to the stability of individual firms, a critical factor in a business so heavily dependent on public confidence. On the face of it, therefore, the large British retail banking firms that emerged during the nineteenth century were well placed to meet the financial requirements of Britain's growing economy. They were large, stable and conveniently sited. It is with this process of institutional change – with the emergence of the large firm in retail banking – that the chapter is concerned.

In particular, the chapter provides an examination of the reasons for, and pace of, the widespread adoption of the corporate structure within retail banking. One central argument of the chapter is that the nature of the business of retail banking itself meant that there were important commercial advantages accruing to those firms that could grow large enough to maintain extensive branch networks, spread risks and induce public confidence in their size and stability. Moreover, in contrast to other countries such as the United States, legislation in Britain was permissive enough to enable banks to adopt the corporate structure at a relatively early date compared with many other sectors of the economy. Within this permissive legislative framework aggressive branch formation and bank amalgamation formed the means for the marked growth in size of the typical retail bank in the period before the First World War, and the chapter presents data on this dramatic change in scale. The main consequence for financial market structure was the creation of an oligopoly dominated by a small number of firms. The chapter also considers this process and provides some measures of market concentration.

THEORETICAL PARAMETERS TO GROWTH

Two broad theoretical approaches are directly relevant to the overall growth achieved within the domestic financial sector over the nineteenth and early twentieth centuries, and to the structure of the firm within the sector.

The first of these concerns the pattern of long-term monetary growth and financial sophistication that occurs within such a developing economy as existed in pre-1914 Britain. It was this pattern of development that determined the growth of the market for different financial services and thus set important overall limits to the potential for growth of the firm. Over a very long period of economic progress and development – as real incomes rise, technology changes, and economic processes and transactions became more complex – there are bound to be profound effects on both the demand for the services of financial institutions and the ability of those institutions to deliver such services. Michael D. Bordo and Lars Jonung provide a formal statement of the general course of such development, and this can be usefully employed here (Bordo and Jonung 1987).

Bordo and Jonung identify two main phases of financial development associated with long-term growth within an economy and the chief characteristics of these two phases are termed 'monetization' and 'financial sophistication'. In the former, earlier phase, the most rapid development occurs in the provision of money balances. Here, it is assumed that the economy is at a relatively early level of development (say, such as Britain in the Industrial Revolution period, or even earlier) and the provision of banking and other financial services is similarly underdeveloped. In such circumstances, only a very small proportion of the population will hold a bank account. As the economy develops, however, there is increasing pressure for a monetary system effective enough to support the increasingly complex exchange mechanism inherent in the development of a market economy. In effect, economic development at this early stage calls for a disproportionate expansion of 'money'. Thus the banks – as providers of 'money' in the form of notes and cheques – are directly affected. The banking habit spreads beyond the initial narrow group of account holders, the number of banks increases, and rapid expansion takes place in the provision of those bank liabilities (deposits and notes) that generally function as money. Such rapid expansion at this stage of monetary experience obviously has direct implications for the potential growth and development of the firm.

Over time and as the economy continues to develop, financial requirements increase in complexity and there is an increased need for a much wider and more sophisticated range of financial services and instruments than was initially provided by the early banking institutions. It is at this point that Bordo and Jonung characterize the sector as undergoing a process of 'financial sophistication'. One feature is a relatively faster expansion of non-bank financial intermediaries (NBFIs) as they grow to meet the maturing economy's demands for a variety of financial assets (e.g. annuities) beyond those normally provided by the early banks. Some of these new financial instruments become effective money substitutes (e.g. building society shares which have some of the attributes of retail bank deposits) and, in consequence, there is a relative slowdown in the growth of bank money (compared with the assets held by NBFIs).

On the basis of this suggested process of development, therefore, we might expect to find a period of rapid growth for banking firms followed by one of greater acceleration for NBFIs. In other words, if the theoretical pathway is a fair representation of what actually happened, such a developmental path would have imposed a major general constraint on the possibilities for the growth of the firm in different parts of the financial sector – limiting non-bank financial intermediary growth in the early phase, and increasingly constraining retail bank growth in the later phase.

The second theoretical consideration which is of relevance to the study of the growth of the retail banking firm is that derived from Alfred D. Chandler's views on the emergence of the modern business enterprise within Britain (Chandler 1990). As in many of the other sectors covered in this volume, Chandler's analysis provides a useful starting point for the examination of changes in the organizational structure of the British market for financial services. In his general comparison of the evolution of industrial enterprises in the United States, Germany and Britain, Chandler emphasizes the continuing British commitment to 'personal capitalism', even into the twentieth century. This had a number of features but the most significant was the continuing personal involvement of owners in the management of firms. One consequence, he suggests, was the relatively slow development of professional managerial teams to run such enterprises.

Chandler's analysis concentrates on experience within the industrial sector, and it is important to test whether the general hypothesis is applicable to firms within the service (non-industrial) sector. In fact – as will become clear – development of the firm within the highly successful British retail banking sector conforms more closely to Chandler's model of the emergence of large, corporate firms than to a model of continuing British commitment to 'personal capitalism'. Thus, to the extent to which Chandler is correct in his assertion of the persistence of non-corporate business structures elsewhere in the British economy, the emergence of the firm in retail banking was an exception to this general developmental path. In retail banking the type of firm most closely resembling Chandler's 'personal capitalism' – the banking partnership or 'private bank' – lost pre-eminence at an early stage to the larger, corporate bank.

MONETIZATION AND FINANCIAL SOPHISTICATION

In this section data are presented for the overall growth of selective financial institutions and assets, giving some indication of the overall scale and direction of change in the three-quarters of a century or so before the First World War. Reliable estimates for bank liabilities are not available before the mid-nineteenth century but the figures presented for 1848–1913 in Tables 10.1 and 10.2 on the composition and growth of the British money stock lend credence to the general pattern of financial development suggested by Bordo and Jonung, at least as regards the commercial banks. As has been shown elsewhere (Collins 1988) they indicate that long-term monetary growth was slowing down in the period as a whole – from an average annual growth rate of 3 per cent in the third quarter of the nineteenth century to virtual stagnation in the early years of the twentieth century. Moreover, as Bordo and Jonung predicted, the ratio of the money stock to gross national product (the reciprocal of income velocity) first expanded – rising from 46 per cent in the middle of the nineteenth century to a peak of 55 per cent at the turn of the century – before falling away by the First World War.

Table 10.1 Relative growth of UK money stock and commercial bank liabilities, 1848–52 to 1910–13

Date (average of year-ends)	Ratio of money stock to GNP[a] (%)	Ratio of commercial bank deposits to GNP (%)	Ratio of commercial bank deposits and notes to the money stock (%)	Commercial bank deposits per head of population, constant prices (£)
1848–52	46	27	65	6.00
1873–7	51	38	78	13.30
1898–1902	55	45	84	20.50
1910–13	52	44	85	21.50

Source: Collins 1988: derived from Tables 2.1 and 2.2

Note: [a]Giving the following estimates for income velocity: 2.2, 2.0, 1.8, 1.9.

As is clear from Table 10.1 (fourth column) the bulk of the money stock in this period comprised commercial bank deposits and notes (which together accounted for some two-thirds of the total stock in mid century, rising to four-fifths by the start of the new century). It is also clear that the pattern of early rapid expansion followed by a marked slowdown was a major characteristic of the long-term growth of commercial bank liabilities. Deposit growth was strongest in the middle decades of the nineteenth century when the commercial banks were exploiting a relatively new market, opening up new offices and recruiting new customers. Thus in real terms the value of balances on deposit with the commercial banks per head of the population more than doubled between 1848–52 and 1873–7, and continued to rise sharply until 1898–1902. However, from the turn of the century when market opportunities were becoming more restricted, there was a noticeable levelling-off in the rate of expansion. Again, in general terms this is consistent with the Bordo and Jonung hypothesis of an eventual slowdown in the growth of money balances (including bank liabilities) as the early demands for a larger money stock were increasingly satisfied and relatively more sophisticated financial assets were being sought by the economic agents of the increasingly mature and complex economy.

Table 10.2 Compound rates of growth of UK bank deposits, 1848–52 to 1910–13 (per cent per annum)

Period	At current prices	At constant prices
1848–52 to 1873–7	4.7	4.0
1873–7 to 1898–1902	2.2	2.7
1898–1902 to 1910–13	1.6	1.1

Source: Collins 1988: derived from Table 2.3

Table 10.3 broadens the picture to include a bigger range of financial assets and institutions. The estimates are far from ideal. Information on this wider range is readily available (from David K. Sheppard) only from the 1880s, and for individual series exception may be taken to the coverage and detailed means of estimation (Capie and Webber 1985). They can nevertheless be used to indicate the broad direction of change. In general terms, they also reveal a long-term developmental pattern that is consistent with the Bordo and Jonung hypothesis (although there are, too, some detailed inconsistencies). What they do confirm is the relative slowdown in the expansion of bank assets in the early twentieth century, with their share of the total assets of the institutions listed falling from 63 to 60 per cent between 1898–1902 and 1910–14 and the share of bank loans and advances falling from 29 to 26 per cent. The share of the total assets of the NBFIs identified here (row 3) moved in the opposite direction, with a fall at the end of the nineteenth century and expansion in the early years of the new century. However, individual institutional experience was somewhat mixed. Savings banks underwent a very slow relative contraction throughout and the building societies' share contracted sharply. In contrast, insurance companies more or less held their relative position in the late nineteenth century before expanding very sharply in the years before the First World War (with their share of total assets rising from 20 to 25 per cent).

Table 10.3 Total assets of selected financial institutions (£million, percentage share of total given in parentheses)

	Date (five-year averages)		
	1880–4	*1898–1902*	*1910–14*
1 Commercial banks and discount houses – total	472 (58)	966 (63)	1233 (60)
2 Bank loans and advances	235 (30)	441 (29)	537 (26)
3 Non-bank financial intermediaries – total	317 (40)	564 (37)	827 (40)
of which			
Savings banks – total	89 (11)	192 (13)	250 (12)
Building societies – total	64 (8)	60 (4)	67 (3)
Insurance companies – total	165 (21)	312 (20)	510 (25)
4 Total assets of specified institutions (rows 1 + 3)	790	1530	2060

In conclusion to this introductory section, it can be said that the available data do lend support to the Bordo and Jonung financial development thesis. In particular, they suggest that the surmised developmental path is directly relevant in this period to the course of growth within financial markets. First, it appears that the rate of growth of the primary monetary institutions – the retail banks – reached its peak in the third quarter of the nineteenth century and slowed down noticeably in the early years of the twentieth century. Such general trends set the parameters to the growth and development of the firms operating within the market for banking services. Intuitively, for the retail banking market it could be anticipated that the era of most rapid growth in the middle decade of the nineteenth century would have been characterized by greater new firm creation and by freer entry to the market. Such characteristics would have been noticeably weaker in the later, slower growth period. In fact – as will be shown – this later period was marked by consolidation of the position of existing suppliers as large firms came to dominate and market concentration levels increased sharply.

ORGANIZATIONAL DEVELOPMENT: OVERVIEW OF BANKING SERVICES

Looking at the financial services sector as a whole, there was a great diversity of organizational responses to the opportunities created by the expanding markets of the nineteenth and early twentieth centuries. One important feature was the specialization of function adopted by most financial institutions. Particular types of institutions did not seek to offer a broad, generalized range of services but tended instead to concentrate on a relatively narrow provision. Thus, discount houses concentrated on the buying and selling of bills of exchange; merchant banks acted as underwriters and acceptance houses; building societies granted mortgages; and so on. In this way it is possible to view British financial markets as a series of parallel, discrete markets. There were important inter-linkages across these markets (as money and other assets could be transferred between them) but each traded in specialized services and financial instruments and each market was serviced by specialized institutions.

The reasons for this degree of financial specialization are not altogether clear. It has been suggested, for instance, that part of the explanation lay in the conservative attitude of British financiers who were risk averse and preferred to remain with familiar forms of business once these had become established (Kennedy 1987; Collins 1991). Indirect evidence for this comes from the actions of some commercial banks (which were amongst the country's largest financial institutions) and their attempts to suppress competition (Griffiths 1973). However, in this respect it is not possible to reach any firm conclusions regarding the degree and effects of banking conservatism and, undoubtedly, other reasons for specialization were important.

In some cases legislative stipulations were critical. This was true of savings banks and building societies, for instance. The former were directly regulated by the state's efforts to encourage and protect savings amongst low-income groups. Thus, a series of Acts fixed the maximum size of individual balances deposited with trustee savings banks (set, for instance, at £150 between 1828 and 1893), governed the rate of interest to be paid and the sort of investments to be undertaken, and imposed a general supervisory framework. More directly, in 1861 the state established its own Post Office Savings Banks (again with a clearly defined range of services) and by the early years of the twentieth century this was operating some 15,000 branches, compared with the 400 or so of the local trustee savings banks. Legislation also established a supervisory framework and prescribed the sort of business undertaken by the building societies (Boleat 1986: 1–3). Initially, building society regulations were incorporated within Friendly Society legislation although as early as 1836 the Regulation of Benefit Building Societies Act had afforded official recognition and established a register of societies' rules. But it was an Act of 1874 which established the basis of the specialized legal framework which has continued to the present. The supervisory stipulations were strengthened and the societies' activities closely prescribed, limiting their borrowing and investment powers – in effect, confining them to the provision of mortgages for home ownership.

In other instances – even in the absence of restrictive legislation – specialization of function provided some financial institutions with important economies of scale. This was the case, for instance, for the country's largest merchant banks based in the City of London. These banks developed specialized acceptance and issuing services. In the latter case, prestigious firms such as Barings confined their involvement to the top end of the market – to high quality, large-scale security issues made by the British and overseas governments, and by railways and other social overhead facilities. Such concentration of business made commercial sense as economies were derived from the cumulative knowledge and business contacts acquired over the years (Edelstein 1982). Specialization also meant that these firms became recognized experts in their chosen field and diversification (say, into small-scale industrial issues) may very well have damaged such a reputation, especially as the risks involved in any new, unfamiliar type of business were likely to be greater.

British merchant banks and a significant number of other financial institutions based in the City of London were involved in providing services to the international community. However, the rest of this chapter concentrates on the most important financial institution servicing the economy's domestic needs – the commercial retail bank.

ORGANIZATIONAL DEVELOPMENT: COMMERCIAL RETAIL BANKS

There is a difficulty with nomenclature for the institutions with which we are dealing, partly because the accepted usage of names has changed over time and partly because of problems in devising an exclusive definition. The concern here is with those domestic banks that offered normal high street commercial retail services – in particular taking deposits from the public, offering general lending and discount services, issuing cheques and/or bank notes and providing other financial remittance facilities. Thus, excluded are building societies, savings banks, merchant banks and overseas banks; included are that sort of institution that came to be known as a clearing bank, or a high street bank (such as Barclays or the Midland).

Some indication of the pace of growth in this sector has already been given in Tables 10.1 and 10.2. Table 10.4 provides some indication of the scale of business for which these institutions were responsible, with liabilities to the general public rising almost eightfold in England and Wales – to over £800 million – between 1848–52 and 1910–13, and fourfold in Scotland (where a separate banking system existed). In both cases deposit liabilities were much greater than notes, and became more so over time, although note-issuing continued to be of more importance in Scotland than in England.

Table 10.4 Commercial bank liabilities, 1848–52 to 1910–13 (£million)

Date (average of year-ends)	England and Wales		Scotland	
	Deposits	Notes	Deposits	Notes
1848–52	107	6	35	3
1873–7	366	5	80	6
1898–1902	664	1	105	8
1910–13	804	0.2	126	8

Source: Collins 1988: derived from Table 2.1

In the mid-nineteenth century much of this banking business was conducted on a personal basis and this was reflected in the institutional structure of banking, more especially in England and Wales where private banking was still the norm. Table 10.5 shows the total number of banks and banking offices operating in England and Wales and in Scotland at certain benchmark dates over the period 1825–1913. For England and Wales separate data are given for private and joint-stock banks. As can be seen, no joint-stock banks operated in 1825. This was because they were still prohibited by special legislation (operative since 1708) that had given the Bank of England a monopoly of joint-stock structure amongst all banks in England and Wales (but not in Scotland, nor Ireland), and had fixed the maximum number of

Table 10.5 Banks and banking offices, 1825–1913

Date (end of year)	England and Wales						Scotland		
	Private banks			Joint-stock banks					
	No. of banks	No. of offices	Offices per bank	No. of banks	No. of offices	Offices per bank	No. of banks	No. of offices	Offices per bank
1825	650	650	1	0	0	n.a.	36	173	4.8
1850	327	518	1.6	99	576	5.8	17	407	23.9
1875	236	595	2.5	122	1364	11.2	11	921	83.7
1900	81	358	4.4	83	4212	50.7	10	1085	108.5
1913	29	147	5.1	41	6426	156.7	8	1248	156.0

Source: Collins 1988: derived from Tables 2.4 and 2.5

partners in banks other than the Bank of England at just six. However, in two separate measures of 1826 and 1833 Parliament removed the Bank of England's monopoly and permitted the formation of banks with large numbers of partners, or shareholders. As the data in the table show, in the long run these new joint-stock banks came to dominate, with private banks dwindling throughout. From a peak of 650 in 1825, the number of private banks fell to 327 in 1850 and to 236 in 1875, even though this reduced number was still greater than the number of joint-stock banks at the time (and was not overtaken until the turn of the century). Thus, although there was a fairly rapid displacement of the private banks by the newcomers they managed to hold on for some considerable time. Contemporary supporters claimed that they could offer a more confidential service than the banking companies, and certainly the personal standing of partners could have been significant in maintaining customer loyalty, especially in small rural communities where most of the private banks survived.

However, although the number of private banking firms remained impressive for a good part of the nineteenth century, such private banks were typically much smaller than the joint-stock banks and therefore accounted for much less of the total retail banking business than their numbers alone imply. It was the joint-stock bank that came to dominate. Table 10.5 shows this clearly. In 1825 the market for commercial retail banking services was served by a large number of small, locally based firms – even in Scotland (where the ban on joint-stock banks did not exist) the average bank was operating fewer than five offices at that time. By 1913, however, the structure of the market had been transformed and had become dominated by a small number of large banking companies with London head offices and nationwide branch networks. With forty-one joint-stock banks in England and Wales and eight banks in Scotland, each company was then operating an average of about 156 offices. In other words, the form of ownership that most closely encapsulates Chandler's concept of personal capitalism was largely displaced in the retail banking market and the corporate form of ownership came to dominate at, what was for Britain, an early date.

LEGISLATION AND THE GROWTH OF THE JOINT-STOCK BANK

The particular form and timing of the adoption of the corporate structure by the retail banking sector was strongly influenced by legislative changes and general economic conditions.

As regards the legal position, a major distinction must be drawn between the banks in Scotland and those in England. The legal and banking systems of the two countries were separate and therefore the Scottish system had not been subject to the Bank of England's monopoly of joint-stock ownership. As a result commercial banks with large numbers of shareholders appeared much earlier in Scotland (Checkland 1975: chs 12, 17; Munn 1981). For this reason the effects of legislative changes on banking company structure during the nineteenth century were more important in England. In fact, it was the greater stability of the larger Scottish banks during the financial crisis of 1825–6 that led to Parliament removing the Bank of England's exclusive right to the joint-stock structure in England and Wales.

During that crisis at least ninety-three private banks in England and Wales ran out of cash reserves and/or went bankrupt. It was felt by many that one major reason had been the small size of these privately owned banks and the restricted access to resources that this imposed. The Banking Co-partnership Act of 1826 (known as the Joint-Stock Bank Act) sought to remove this institutional weakness. The Act permitted the formation of banks with an unlimited number of partners. However, the stipulations were applicable only outside a radius of sixty-five miles from London (where the Bank of England's privilege was retained). The Act was deficient in other respects, too. It did not attempt to establish a regulatory framework in which joint-stock banks could operate, but largely confined itself to removing the previous prohibition. In future non-London banks with more than six partners would be treated in much the same manner as the private partnership banks. For instance, all shareholders continued to carry unlimited liability for the debts of the bank, irrespective of the number of shareholders and irrespective of the size of their initial investment. The legal identity of the new companies was established by the permission granted under the legislation to sue and be sued in the name of company officials, but for the most part their duties and responsibilities were ill-defined and left to the vagaries of judgements under the Common Law.

One major advance came in 1833 when provision was made under the Bank Charter Act to permit joint-stock banks to operate in London. During the subsequent economic upswing of the mid-1830s there was a sharp increase in the number of these new banks, not only in London. In fact, expansion was especially marked in the industrial and commercial centres of the North and the Midlands. After the boom of the 1830s, though, there followed a marked lull in the creation of new joint-stock banks. This was partly a reaction to some of the more spectacular bank failures of that decade which must have deterred promoters and investors, but legislative constraints were also important. In this regard, a number of measures taken during the mid-1840s helped check further expansion. The first problem arose not from Parliament's attempts to reform company law, but from the imposition of monetary controls. In England the most important measure was the 1844 Joint-Stock Bank Act which imposed prohibitively severe regulations on the formation and operation of any new joint-stock banks (Crick and Wadsworth 1936: 26). As a result very few new banks were formed under this legislation and it was not until after its repeal (in 1857) that there was a noticeable change.

In fact, it was during the following decade of the 1860s that there occurred another joint-stock bank 'boom' reminiscent of the 1830s. As on the previous occasion expansion in the general economy was important to the timing of this boom, but enabling legislation created a favourable legal framework. In particular, changes in company law, 1858–62, allowed new banking companies to offer limited liability on their shares, and this was a feature of the 1860s banking expansion. However, many existing companies – in Scotland as well as England and Wales – retained unlimited liability because they believed it helped maintain depositors' confidence. This assumed advantage was strongly outweighed in 1878, however, when the City of Glasgow Bank failed with such large debts that many of its shareholders were financially ruined by having to meet creditors' claims that far exceeded the value of shareholders' original investments in the bank. Subsequent reform of company law in 1879 created a new category of limited shareholder liability for banks and most companies took advantage of its provisions.

Thus, from as early as the 1820s liberalization of company law had permitted the effective creation of joint-stock banks in England and Wales and, although not always assured a smooth path of development, subsequent reforms meant that by the end of the 1870s all major obstacles to joint-stock bank formation had been removed.

THE NATURE OF RETAIL BANKING AND THE EMERGENCE OF LARGE-SCALE BANKS

In fact, banks were amongst the most prominent of British business institutions to adopt the corporate structure in such a wholesale fashion during the nineteenth century. The reasons for this are closely tied to the nature of banking. Three requirements are critical to the successful conduct of retail banking: bank offices need to be sited in locations convenient for the general public; the banks need to establish an effective remittance system; and (in common with other financial institutions) high priority must be given to the maintenance of public confidence, especially in the light of the unusually short-term nature of retail banking liabilities.

The adoption of a corporate structure endowed major advantages on any retail bank trying to meet these requirements during the nineteenth century – providing the underlying rationale for the eventual dominance of the joint-stock structure that legislative liberalization made possible.

The bulk of a bank's liabilities are subject to repayment at little or very short notice. This meant that in the nineteenth century customers' deposits and notes were repayable in gold and silver coin or Bank of England notes (which were legal tender in England and Wales from 1833), more or less on demand. In normal conditions, of course, only a tiny proportion of liabilities would be converted to cash at any one time and a bank could comfortably conduct its business with a small cash reserve adequate to meet clients' everyday needs, with other assets lent and invested in order to earn interest. However, if there should be a general loss of confidence in a banker's ability to pay cash on demand, there could be a 'run' on a bank as customers sought to recover their deposits *en masse*. As such a bank's assets (loans, investments etc.) could not be converted to cash without some delay (and possibly on unfavourable terms), there could then exist a real danger of illiquidity, of the bank having to close through failure to meet customers' immediate demands for cash.

Such an occurrence was a real possibility in the nineteenth century, with a series of bank stoppages during the 'crises' of 1825–6, 1837, 1839, 1847, 1857, 1866 and 1878. It was thus essential for banks to maintain confidence. Careful management of assets so as to ensure adequate portfolio liquidity was crucial here. This was true for all banks, both big and small. However, to the extent that larger joint-stock banks had access to greater capital reserves than small private banks, company structure had an important effect on the ability of a bank to maintain public confidence (although, of course, it offered no guarantee against the effects of fraudulent or incompetent management which could still provoke bank failure). Indeed, it was the access to larger capital resources that enabled joint-stock banks, on the whole, to conduct larger businesses than the private banks, and 'bigness' itself may have been an important factor in boosting confidence amongst depositors.

Deposits from the general public were the main resource base on which the retail banking business could grow, and the opening up of new branches was a main means by which a bank could gain access to these deposits. And this is precisely what the system as a whole did. As the figures in Table 10.5 (third, sixth and ninth columns) show, the total number of banking offices in England, Scotland and Wales rose very sharply in the century to the First World War: from 823 in 1825 to 3,475 in 1875 and 7,821 in 1913. For individual banks, though, the creation of a large branch network necessitated the need for large capital resources and here, too, the joint-stock ownership of many shareholders provided obvious advantages over the smaller privately owned bank.

The establishment of a branch network was also important to another requirement of retail banking, the creation of effective remittance facilities. Retail banks are required routinely to remit cash, commercial information, securities and other documents throughout the country and beyond. Indeed, such services are a major part of the contribution to general economic development derived from the creation of an effective banking system. It is possible for these services to be provided through an agency network of small banks located in particular towns or regions – and this was the system that dominated early in the nineteenth century. However, there were direct economies to be gained for individual banks which, rather than depending on agents to handle their business, were able to establish their own offices in different parts of the country. In this way much of the routine remittance business could be carried out 'in-house'.

Nor was this the only motive for establishing branch networks. The bigger a bank's branch system the less pressing the need for it to resort to inter-bank markets. Imagine that a bank had no branch offices and operated in one town only. In such circumstances it was possible that, say, the demand for loans in the locality exceeded available deposits. In such a case, the bank would have to borrow from other banks (in the inter-bank market) in order to meet customers' needs for loans. In the opposite case, a bank confined to a locality with deposits in excess of the local demand for loans would need to lend in the inter-bank market in order to ensure fuller employment of its resources. In contrast, a bank with offices in a number of towns, in both net saving and net borrowing areas, could transfer the funds internally from branch to branch. In such a manner fees and payments to outside banks and agents would be reduced and customers' needs (either as depositors or borrowers) more readily accommodated.

Finally, the establishment of a branch network also helped spread and reduce risk. The larger the branch network being operated, the more geographically dispersed would be a bank's business. Business would thus be less concentrated on particular economic sectors, and the chance of stability was greater. In a bank with branches throughout the country, profits would depend on a great diversity of accounts, and losses on certain types of customers' accounts in particular parts of the country (say, following a downturn in grain prices in East Anglia, or a collapse in the market for West Riding textiles) could be more easily absorbed through the buoyancy of business elsewhere. In contrast, the business of a bank whose offices were unfortunately confined to an economically depressed region could be seriously undermined.

All such gains from establishing an extensive branch system created and sustained a powerful impetus towards big banks. Large branch networks required firms with large capital resources and the necessary managerial and organizational structure to control a large number of geographically dispersed offices. The drive to large-scale operations, in turn, augmented and consolidated the adoption of the corporate structure amongst retail banks. Size of firm and relative market share became critical performance indicators of success within the retail banking sector.

TREND TOWARDS GREATER MARKET CONCENTRATION

It is clear from the evidence already presented that the widespread adoption of the corporate structure transformed the institutional framework of British retail banking. In the case of commercial retail banking, banks with more than a few branches were invariably joint-stock banks. It can be seen from the data in Table 10.5 that the average private bank operated very few offices – even in 1913 there were only five per bank. In contrast, by 1913 forty-one joint-stock banks in England and Wales were operating a total of 6,426 offices, or some 157 per bank (a similar average pertained in Scotland).

In turn, the emergence and growth of the large-scale banking firm had a major impact on the competitive nature of the market, leading to a highly concentrated market dominated by a small number of large institutions. Part of the reason lies in the advantages (already discussed) that the corporate structure endowed on large banks. As we have seen, extension of a branching network was an important source of growth for individual banks. So, too, were mergers and takeovers, and it was by these means that in the period as a whole commercial retail banking was transformed from a highly atomized, competitive market with hundreds of institutions to an oligopoly dominated by just a few giant banks. Amalgamations occurred throughout the century but they tended to come in 'waves'. In Scotland a major phase of amalgamations occurred in the 1830s and 1840s (Checkland 1975: 465). In England, the merger movement proper began in the 1860s and there were further spates of activity in the 1880s and 1890s, and even then the largest joint-stock banks continued to engage in mergers until 1918 when government disapproval put a stop to it (Capie and Rodrik-Bali 1982).

The tables in the Appendices provide data on the changing size of each of the largest retail banks in the UK at three dates: 1875, 1900 and 1913. The ten largest banks are ranked according to the value of public liabilities (mainly deposits) and of capital funds. Appendix 1 summarizes some of these figures. These show that the degree of concentration in the retail banking market was already quite high in 1875, with the top ten banks accounting for 28.4 per cent of total deposits. However, while individually large, it can be seen from the figures that no one bank was dominant. Even the largest at that time (the London & Westminster) accounted for just 5.5 per cent of total deposits, though the largest five banks as a group were responsible for 22 per cent of the total. By the end of the nineteenth century there had been even greater consolidation and movement towards oligopoly – with the ten largest banks accounting for 41 (27.7) per cent of total deposits in 1900, and for a massive 60.7 (40.7) per cent in 1913. By that time individual banks were very large organizations indeed. In terms of value, the size of liabilities of the largest of the banks rose almost fourfold from £28.8 million, or 5.5 per cent of total deposits, in 1875 (London & Westminster), to £53.5 million, or 6.7 per cent of the total, in 1900 (Lloyds), to £100 million, some 9.7 per cent of total deposits, in 1913 (London, City & Midland) – with a smaller relative rise in capital funds from £2.7 million (London & Westminster), to £5.3 million (National Provincial), to £8 million (London, City & Midland) respectively. By the end of the First World War the 'Big Five' – Barclays, Lloyds, the Midland, the National Provincial and the Westminster – were amongst the largest banks in the world and accounted for some 80 per cent of domestic deposits in England.

CONCLUSION

British financial development over this period was characterized by functional specialization. In this regard retail banks were no exception. Therefore, the potential for growth through diversification to areas outside retail banking was limited. Within the retail banking sector, however, the scope for growth for individual firms was immense. Indeed, the history of the firm in the retail banking sector before 1914 is, in many senses, the history of the emergence of the giant firm. As a consequence, retail banking was unusual in British experience, with a sharp decline in the non-corporate firm at an early stage. The development of the firm in the retail banking sector is thus in contrast to Chandler's portrayal of the persistence of personal capitalism within the industrial sector. The process by which large banking firms could emerge was made possible by legislative changes which permitted banks to adopt incorporation. This the most successful firms did. However, legislation also made possible the widespread adoption of a corporate structure within the industrial sector. So legislation alone does not hold the key to the growth of the large corporation in retail banking. Permissive legislation was a necessary but not sufficient condition. It was the nature of the business of retail banking itself that made it such a suitable area for the extension and development of the corporate form of structure – because of the economies of scale associated with the maintenance of confidence, the operation of intermediary and remittance services, and reduction of risk. The banking firms' chosen means of expansion lay in mergers and the build-up of extensive branch networks. The consequence in the period was the transformation of a highly competitive market served by numerous small suppliers to an oligopoly market dominated by a small group of giant banks. In the period before 1914 no one bank could itself dominate the market and competition amongst the large firms seems to have been keen. However, following the First World War, official compliance and a more widespread collusive market environment meant that the early emergence of oligopoly market conditions left a legacy of co-operation and suppression of competition in British retail banking which was to last until the early 1970s.

REFERENCES

Boleat, M. (1986) *The Building Society Industry*, 2nd edn, London: Allen & Unwin.

Bordo, M.D. and Jonung, L. (1987) *The Long-run Behaviour of the Velocity of Circulation*, Cambridge: Cambridge University Press.

Capie, F. and Collins, M. (1992) *Did the Banks Fail British Industry?*, London: Institute of Economic Affairs.

Capie, F. and Rodrik-Bali, G. (1982) 'Concentration in British banking, 1870–1920', *Business History* 24: 280–92.

Capie, F. and Webber, A. (1985) *A Monetary History of the United Kingdom, 1870–1982*, vol. I, London: Allen & Unwin.

Chandler, A.D. (1990) *Scale and Scope. The Dynamics of Industrial Capitalism*, Cambridge, MA: Harvard University Press.

Checkland, S.G. (1975) *Scottish Banking. A History, 1695–1913*, Glasgow and London: Collins.

Collins, M. (1988) *Money and Banking in the UK. A History*, London: Croom Helm.

—— (1991) *Banks and Industrial Finance, 1800–1939*, London: Macmillan.

Crick, W.F. and Wadsworth, W.E. (1936) *A Hundred Years of Joint-Stock Banking*, London: Hodder & Stoughton.

Edelstein, M. (1982) *Overseas Investment in the Age of High Imperialism, United Kingdom, 1850–1914*, London: Methuen.

Griffiths, B. (1973) 'The development of restrictive practices in the UK monetary system', *The Manchester School* 41: 3–18.

Kennedy, W.P. (1987) *Industrial Structure, Capital Markets and the Origins of British Economic Decline*, Cambridge: Cambridge University Press.

Michie, R.C. (1990) 'The Stock Exchange and the British economy, 1870–1939', in J.J. van Helten and Y. Cassis (eds) *Capitalism in a Mature Economy*, Aldershot: Edward Elgar.

Munn, C.W. (1981) *The Scottish Provincial Banking Companies, 1747–1864*, Edinburgh: John Donald.

Sheppard, D.K. (1971) *The Growth and Role of UK Financial Institutions, 1880–1962*, London: Methuen.

APPENDIX I

Ten largest retail banks in the UK, ranked according to the size of deposit liabilities (gross): 1875, 1900 and 1913 (end of year)

	Bank	Value of public liabilities (£million)	Share of total bank deposits in the UK (%)
1875			
1	London & Westminster	28.8	5.5
2	National Provincial	25.6	4.9
3	London & County	23.6	4.5
4	London Joint Stock	19.4	3.7
5	Union Bank of London	18.3	3.5
6	Manchester & Liverpool District	12.6	2.4
7	City Bank, London	6.5	1.2
8	Manchester & County	5.6	1.1
9	Lloyds	5.1	1.0
10	North & South Wales	4.7	0.9
		150.2	*28.4*

Total bank deposits (gross) in UK £528 million

Appendix I – continued

Ten largest retail banks in the UK, ranked according to the size of deposit liabilities (gross): 1875, 1900 and 1913 (end of year)

	Bank	Value of public liabilities (£million)	Share of total bank deposits in the UK (%)
1900			
1	Lloyds	53.5	6.7
2	National Provincial	51.6	6.3
3	London & County	47.0	5.7
4	London, City & Midland	39.8	4.8
5	Barclays	34.6	4.2
6	Parr's	27.3	3.3
7	London & Westminster	27.0	3.3
8	Union Bank of London	20.5	2.5
9	Manchester & Liverpool District	18.6	2.3
10	London Joint Stock	18.3	2.2
		338.2	*41.0*

Total bank deposits (gross) in UK £824.6 million

	Bank	Value of public liabilities (£million)	Share of total bank deposits in the UK (%)
1913			
1	London City & Midland	100.0	9.7
2	Lloyds	99.0	9.6
3	London County & Westminster	96.0	9.3
4	National Provincial	68.7	6.7
5	Barclays[a]	55.8	5.4
6	Parr's	49.1	4.8
7	Union of London & Smiths	47.1	4.6
8	Capital & Counties[a]	41.0	4.0
9	London Joint Stock	40.8	4.0
10	Manchester & Liverpool District	28.6	2.8
		626.1	*60.7*

Total bank deposits (gross) in UK $1032.2 million

Source: *Bankers Magazine*; Capie and Webber 1985: Table II(1) for total deposits

Note: [a] June figures.

APPENDIX II

Ten largest retail banks in the UK, ranked according to the value of capital funds: 1875, 1900 and 1913 (end of year)

	Bank	Value of capital and reserve funds (£million)
1875		
1	London & Westminster	2.7
2	National Provincial	2.4
3	London & County	2.2
4	Union Bank of London	1.8
5	London Joint Stock	1.7
6	Manchester & Liverpool District	1.5
7	Manchester & County	1.0
8	Alliance	1.0
9	Consolidated	0.9
10	Liverpool Union	0.8
1900		
1	National Provincial	5.3
2	London City & Midland	5.0
3	Lloyds	4.7
4	London & Westminster	4.4
5	London & County	3.5
6	Barclays	3.4
7	London Joint Stock	3.0
8	Parr's	2.9
9	Manchester & Liverpool District	2.7
10	Union Bank of London	2.6
1913		
1	London City & Midland	8.0
2	London County & Westminster	7.5
3	Lloyds	7.2
4	Barclays[a]	5.2
5	National Provincial	5.0
6	Union of London & Smiths	4.7
7	Parr's	4.2
8	London Joint Stock	4.1
9	Manchester & Liverpool District	3.5
10	London & Provincial	3.0

Source: *Bankers Magazine*

Note: [a] June figure.

11 The state and British business since 1945

Helen Mercer

INTRODUCTION

The evolution of large-scale concerns in Britain is a main theme of this volume. This chapter addresses the role of governments in this process. The dominant tendency in existing literature is to deny or downplay any active role for British governments as 'trustpromotor'. For the inter-war period it is argued that governments' attitude towards the rise of the corporate economy was 'noncommittal' (Hannah 1983: 53); for the postwar period the words 'permissive' and 'liberal' are commonly used to describe governments' policies to mergers, the operations of large-scale firms and multinational corporations (MNCs) (Cosh *et al*. 1980: 232; George 1990; Jones 1990). Alternative interpretations, however, see governments 'actively fostering' the process of concentration, or extending a 'warm welcome' to foreign MNCs (Aaronovitch and Sawyer 1975: 306; Sugden 1990).

In this chapter we argue that the use of the word 'permissive' to describe government policies towards big business in Britain is misleading: successive governments have intervened in the competitive struggle between large and small firms on the side of the former, while attempts to control the monopolistic effects of the process or secure greater efficiency have failed. The bias is to be gleaned not only from industrial policies but also from policies towards British MNCs, foreign MNCs in Britain and the effect of the 'peculiarities' of Britain's financial sector on industrial development. Moreover, following Grove, we set the strength of business in relation to government against that of labour (Grove 1962: 77) and argue that uneven treatment of trade unions, compared with business, has reinforced the effect of policies aiding large and multinational firms.

Much recent work on government—industry relations has sought to identify the characteristics of state intervention affecting Britain's relative economic decline. For instance, on the one hand 'too much' government is accused of crowding out private entrepreneurship, reducing the size of the 'marketable' economy and handing decision-making on economic and industrial matters to politicians and bureaucrats (Broadway 1969: 180; Bacon and Eltis 1978). On the other hand a broad spectrum of opinion argues that Britain is peculiarly lacking in modernizing forces, including a modernizing state, and unflattering comparisons are made with 'the business of the state' in Germany or Japan (Fine and Harris 1985; Chick 1990; Wilks 1990). Most recently, the highly influential 'institutional rigidities' school blames the state for policies which harboured atomistic industrial organization until well into the twentieth century (Hall 1986). Otherwise the literature has traced the continued interweaving of government and business interests and debated the nature, extent and demise of a 'corporate bias' in British political economy (Blank 1973: Abraham 1974; Middlemas 1979; Vickerstaff and Sheldrake 1989). This chapter touches on these themes, but has a different focus, seeking to demonstrate that British governments have been successful: they have played an active part in helping to shape today's general business environment.

THE BRITISH BUSINESS ENVIRONMENT

The British business environment is markedly oligopolistic. In manufacturing Britain has come to boast one of the most highly concentrated industrial structures in the world. From the 1930s to the 1950s this industrial concentration was buttressed by cartel arrangements, from local to international levels, allowing the quasi-integration of retailing and processing of raw materials by dominant firms in the cartels (Aaronovitch and Sawyer 1975; Hannah 1983; Mercer forthcoming; Chapter 6 of this volume). Chapter 10 has shown that retail banking was by 1914 already dominated by five giant banks. Their position was buttressed by co-operation with the Bank of England and various collusive arrangements, especially regarding interest rates. In 1968 they became the 'Big Four', accounting for approximately 91.7 per cent of total deposits in the 1970s (Aaronovitch and Sawyer 1975: 111; Capie 1990). In distribution and construction a mass of small independent units have coexisted with a few large, dominating firms, and both sectors have been riddled with restrictive practices, sustained through trade associations and large manufacturing concerns in the various markets (Aaronovitch and Sawyer 1975: 104–13; Channon 1978: 56; Mercer 1989; Chapter 9 of this volume).

The dominance of large-scale firms is a feature not confined to the British business scene, but Britain exhibits it in a strong form and has a notable paucity of small firms: in 1975 only 25 per cent of manufacturing output in Britain was from small firms, in a league table where Britain was bottom and Japan was top with 66 per cent. This has prompted some authors to argue, in contrast to the institutional rigidities school, that at least some of Britain's economic problems stem from the weakness of the small-firm sector: Alfred Marshall, of course, saw them as the ultimate harbingers of entrepreneurship (Bannock 1980: 9; Burns and Dewhurst 1986: 60; Storey and Johnson 1987; Bannock and Albach 1991). A recent variant of this is the 'flexible specialization' school which argues that the future lies not with 'Fordist' methods of production with their emphasis on large-scale, long-term mass market orientation, but on a return to 'mechanized craft production' responding to ceaseless change with a strategy of 'permanent innovation' (Piore and Sabel 1984).

Alternatively, evidence that concentration of ownership has not been accompanied by commensurate concentration of plants has supported the argument that the economic success, for instance of West Germany, was related to its more numerous and larger scale plants in such key areas as engineering, electrical goods, chemicals and metal manufacture (Hughes 1976; Prais 1976). Furthermore, since the 1960s British companies have increasingly adopted the managerial hierarchies and the multidivisional form of organization advocated by the Chandlerian school. However, as this has been accompanied by long-standing financial short-termism and neglect of human capital the process has not reversed Britain's industrial decline (Chapter 6 of this volume). Increasingly it is shown that there is little evidence of efficiency gains from merger, or that innovation and technical progress are promoted by the process of concentration (Stoneman 1983; Cowling and Sawyer 1990).

Since 1945 Britain has been markedly affected by the globalization of capital. As Chapter 7 demonstrates, British-based MNCs are strongly represented among the world leaders, whilst the stock of British outward foreign direct investment as a proportion of gross domestic product is the highest in the OECD. The British economy has become increasingly attractive to foreign MNCs, especially those based in the United States and Japan with their presence concentrated in technically advanced sectors such as mechanical engineering and cars. Thus the contribution of foreign and domestic MNCs to Britain's gross national product, capital expenditure, employment, exports and profits is far greater than in any other industrialized

economy (Dunning 1985: 13, 18). This strong international orientation of British manufacturing, and increasingly also of British
retailing, is further seen in the banking sector. According to many
authors the latter has led to a 'divide' in British capitalism. The City's
relative autonomy from the demands of manufacturing and its ability
to dominate Treasury and government policies, especially regarding
the level of interest rates and the value of the pound on foreign
exchanges, has, this argument goes, adversely affected the environment for British manufacturing (Longstreth 1979; Ingham 1984;
Pollard 1984; Newton and Porter 1988). For Longstreth it has been
the alliance of 'the City' and MNCs, united by their common interest
in the free and flexible movement of capital around the world, which
has dictated government actions for much of the postwar period
(Longstreth 1979: 188).

Finally, Britain now boasts a weakened trade union movement, and
levels of pay are among the lowest, hours of work and unemployment
among the highest, and rights such as maternity leave among the
weakest in the European Community (Low Pay Unit 1993). Currently,
this situation is openly used abroad to encourage foreign direct investment in Britain. The weakness of trade unions, relative to large-scale
business, and the favour the latter finds with governments, means that
over a long period, and with vigour in the last thirteen years, this key
centre of 'countervailing power' has been weakened.

These then are the characteristics of the British business scene
today. It is policies towards all of these *taken together* which
demonstrate the very positive approach of British governments
towards large-scale firms and begin to explain the lack of a trade-off
in efficiency.

GOVERNMENTS AND LARGE FIRMS BETWEEN THE WARS

Relative to her rivals the British state, since the early to mid nineteenth
century, had maintained a *laissez-faire* stance. What little intervention
governments made in industrial structure up to 1914 mainly took the
form of control of monopoly, either through regulation – for instance
of the railways – or through ownership of 'natural' monopolies,
usually by local governments (Hannah 1980). In addition, continued
commitment to free trade was seen by liberal economists of the day as
fundamental to preserving Britain's relatively untrustified industrial
structure (MacGregor 1906).

Between 1914 and 1945 government encroachment into the sphere
of the businessman, and businessmen's encroachment into the affairs

of the state, became marked. Thus the inter-war period saw some detailed and general interventionist policies in the belief that the solution to Britain's failing international competitiveness in manufactured goods lay in promoting technical innovation accompanied by reaping the benefits of economies of scale. It was widely accepted that to leave the process of rationalization and the destruction of the inefficient firm to market forces could be painfully slow: the winds of 'creative destruction' needed some bellows (BPP 1929: 179). In the 1920s governments encouraged the formation of large firms in key sectors such as chemicals, and in the 1930s the government attempted to achieve amalgamations in cotton, coal and iron and steel. Sir Horace Wilson, appointed as Chief Industrial Adviser in 1930, was to initiate discussions with industries to encourage merger and rationalization (Hannah 1983: 50). However, the governments' ardour for large-scale firms as the route to international competitiveness was cooled and thwarted by divisions among industrialists. Together with the banks' failure to provide long-term finance this meant that government schemes intended to promote amalgamations became instead state-sponsored cartels (Aldcroft 1986: 128–9; Hall 1986: 275; Tolliday 1986; Kirby 1987). This situation prevailed into the Reconstruction discussions during the Second World War, civil servants being appalled at the extent to which industrialists, like the cotton spinners, spurned suggestions for reorganization and amalgamation, preferring stronger cartels (Mercer 1989; Johnman 1991).

Similarly, government policies on cartels reflected divisions among industrialists. Governments created hot-house conditions for cartelization in the 1930s. In particular, the emphasis on preserving British markets at home and abroad prompted a highly discriminatory system of tariffs and imperial preferences from 1931. This became a vehicle for increased cartelization, encouraged at the international level as the alternative to tariffs. Most international agreements were formulated by large firms with multinational interests. In turn they needed to control domestic markets through domestic cartels. Hence the mania for cartelization was mainly a large-firm strategy to keep smaller, independent competitors from undercutting prices (Hannah 1980: 51; Kirby 1987: 137). But the extensive and compulsory cartelization of the sort advocated by organizations representative of large firms in 1934 (by the Industrial Reorganisation League) and again in 1942 (by the National Policy for Industry) was vetoed by the National and Coalition governments respectively. This was partly for fear of the implications for democratic government and labour relations, but also because 'Conservative leaders were not prepared to go beyond the limits of contemporary industrial opinion' (Mercer 1989; Ritschel 1991: 61–2). The peak representative association of business then, the Federation of British Industries (FBI), articulating the interests of the smaller and medium-sized firms among its members, argued against any hint of compulsory amalgamation or adherence to trade association rules unless a majority of firms in the industry wanted it. Thus cartelization, viewed by governments as a means to maintain prices and profits (Booth 1987), was conducted in a way which accorded well with the views of the FBI. Hence contemporaries, both Marxists and mainstream economists, saw something amounting to businessmen's government in the industrial policies pursued (Allen 1935: 132F; *Britain without Capitalists* 1936; Hannah 1983: 52). More thorough-going policies, either for amalgamation or cartelization, were constrained primarily by divisions among industrialists reflecting the existing level of industrial organization.

The general belief in the merits of business organization, either amalgamations or trade associations, as defences against recession is perhaps illustrated by the fact that no anti-trust initiatives were made. The half-hearted attempts at the end of the First World War – the Committee on Trusts and the consequent Profiteering Acts – were used deliberately to quieten public feeling and 'educate' the working man in the view that large concerns and cartels were not against the public interest (Hannah 1983: 44; Mercer forthcoming).

Also in the inter-war period the key elements of policy towards inward investment had been laid down. Most important was the view that nothing should be done which might adversely affect the freedom of British MNCs abroad. In 1929 and again in 1945 proposals to limit the extent of foreign shareholdings were vetoed because of the ' "possibility of retribution by foreign countries and of its serious effect for the United Kingdom as a large investor in foreign undertakings" ' (Jones 1990: 197). It was accepted that certain 'strategic' areas be protected from foreign encroachment but, apart from armaments, these were mainly in the service sector – banking and shipping. For manufacturing a policy of promoting 'national champions' served instead: government involvement in the creation of the Anglo-Persian Oil Company and ICI may be seen as a part of this strategy (Jones 1990: 196–8). Again, government policies supported the tendency for British firms, notably those with multinational activities, to become heavily involved in the international cartel system, as the pace of overseas investment slackened in the depressed market conditions of the 1930s (Jones 1986: 5).

The Bank of England played a crucial role in formulating a generally positive policy towards multinational activity and in reinforcing the government's approach to rationalization. It responded speedily to American pressure for greater British openness to American investors (Jones 1990). The nature of the government's cartelization policy accorded well with the attitude of the Bank of England which sought to extricate itself from the overcommitment to the staple industries incurred after 1918. Rather than be an 'outside agency' proposed in 1931 by the Macmillan Committee on Finance and Industry to effect rationalization, it too preferred to leave detailed reform of industrial structure to industrial interests concerned through the trade associations and 'industrial self-government'. Its involvement in the rationalization of the staple industries was limited to spreading financial risks (Best and Humphries 1986). Thus the banking sector's involvement in industrial policy perpetuated failure to achieve major restructuring of British industry, as distinct from simply reducing capacity and banking risk.

While the tendency of British business was towards greater cohesion for both economic and political strategies through the trade associations, the British trade unions suffered a major loss of membership. Real wages rose in the 1930s, but unemployment never fell below 1 million and affected a much greater section of the labour force than this bald figure implies. Discussion of labour policies in the inter-war period has focused on business strategies to 'control' labour in the wake of the First World War which had brought widespread gains for trade unions. These changed from the adversarial tactics up to 1926 to attempts at conciliation and 'class harmony' initiated by representatives of large-scale industries in the aftermath of the General Strike. While the government adopted an arm's length approach to these experiments it was ready to intervene at times of serious conflict, for instance during the General Strike (Burgess 1980: 225).

In summary, governments in the inter-war years were willing to make detailed interventions in private industry, geared to promoting amalgamations or tighter business organization of other types, so long as those businesses concerned approved. As Chapter 6 has shown, concern with restructuring many utilities and staple industries increasingly eroded faith in either the market or industrial self-government as the mechanism to achieve it. Public ownership, as a means of overcoming divisions among industrialists and hostility among the workforce, had growing support. For the Labour party, nationalization of coal, iron and steel and the railways was the means to secure efficiency without enthroning private monopoly. After the war, therefore, many of the industries subject to interventionist policies before it were nationalized. Hence, in relation to privately owned industry governments appeared to have abandoned after the war some of the interventionist policies emerging before it (Grant 1991). Nationalization achieved substantial rationalization, but governments continued to pursue the quest for restructuring elsewhere in British industry. The quest took them down the road supportive of concentration of private ownership.

GOVERNMENT AND LARGE FIRMS SINCE 1945

Since 1945 industrial policies have been subservient to macro-policy objectives. The major discontinuities between Labour and Conservative administrations have been in the emphasis given by the former to microeconomic interventionism, although Labour's lack of success has prompted many writers to cast doubt on the extent of discontinuity. Nevertheless, in general terms enthusiasm has been greater under Labour governments through such initiatives as the National Plan of 1965, the Industrial Reorganisation Corporation established in 1966 and the National Enterprise Board and Planning Agreements of the 1970s, as well as nationalizations. Although Conservative governments have made some significant initiatives, such as the establishment of the National Economic Development Council (NEDC) in 1962, the general trend has been to favour 'disengagement' by the state and the free play of market forces. Hence industrial controls inherited from the 1940s were dismantled speedily from 1952 and steel was de-nationalized in 1953. In the early 1970s initial attempts at 'disengagement' were overtaken by other concerns, and state intervention actually increased in such noteworthy areas as aerospace and shipbuilding (Young and Lowe 1974). However, since 1979 Conservative governments have embraced the retreat of the state wholeheartedly, dismantling bodies like the NEDC set up by its predecessors, reining back on financial subsidies to business and engaging in substantive privatizations of public sector assets.

We look first at the interventionist strategies of Labour governments and their attempts to create efficient large-scale manufacturing concerns. While Labour did indeed foster the large firm, attempts to regulate the process to improve industrial efficiency failed.

One type of policy much favoured by Labour when in government was tri-partite discussions of the future and desired industrial structure and organization within each trade and industry. The policy had its roots in the consensual approach to restructuring embodied in the policies of 'industrial self-government' and 'industrial diplomacy' in the inter-war period (Roberts 1984). During the war, and drawing on inter-war experience, the Board of Trade evolved plans to secure business and financial co-operation in schemes of amalgamation. The resulting ideas were developed under the Labour government's Industrial Organisation and Development Act of 1947, with the added ingredient of trade union representation. The Act allowed for voluntary, tri-partite Development Councils in specific industries to be set up to review questions of technical development and industrial structure. The initiative tacitly accepted that the government could not enforce rationalization and instead hoped to provide, on an industry-wide basis, services 'essential to modern industrial development' but which were 'sometimes available to large organisations but not to smaller organisations' (Mercer 1991b: 79). However, the FBI organized to kill the measure. It saw such moves as back-door nationalization, opposed interference with existing trade associations, and heartily rebelled against bringing trade unions into managerial issues (Brady 1950; Rogow and Shore 1955; Mercer 1991b).

Nevertheless, Labour persisted with this form. The 1964–70 Labour governments developed the work of the NEDC, established by the Conservatives in 1962. The remit of the individual Neddies, the numbers of which were greatly expanded in Labour's first year of government, had many points of overlap with those of the Development Councils and working parties, including the application of research and development (R&D), standardization and consideration of industrial structure (Middlemas 1983: 203–6). One role of the Ministry of Technology (MinTech) (see below) was to provide services, namely R&D, which smaller firms could not themselves finance. It maintained large R&D centres whose resources could be drawn on by smaller-scale firms (Coopey 1993: 119). The system of Sector Working Parties under the 1974–9 Labour government continued a search for tri-partite solutions to Britain's industrial problems, although again with limited success (Sawyer 1991).

In 1950, reflecting on his experience as President of the Board of Trade, Harold Wilson argued that Development Councils had failed, in part because of the lack of coercion at company level (Mercer 1991b). Thus the second type of strategy was one of 'purposive' intervention to secure direct leverage on the individual firm. Such policies were devised in the 1960s in response to the realization that the gains of merger were 'disappointing', too motivated by financial and defensive considerations (Graham 1972: 191; Meeks 1977: 35; Hague and Wilkinson 1983: 5–11). The Labour government hence sought to promote mergers in key technical fields, and to direct the effects of merger. The two agencies established were MinTech in 1964 and the Industrial Reorganisation Corporation (IRC) in 1966. The main declared aim of the latter was to inject into the 'merger mania' of the time an awareness that concentration of ownership would not bring industrial regeneration unless used to increase economies of scale after merger. In its preamble, the White Paper announcing the IRC was an update of the conclusions of the Balfour Committee of 1929. It spoke of

> the need for more concentration and rationalisation to promote the greater efficiency and international competitiveness of British industry . . . many of the production units in this country are small by comparison with the most successful companies in international trade. . . . There is no evidence that we can rely on market forces alone to produce the necessary structural changes at the pace required.
>
> (cited in Hague and Wilkinson 1983: 17)

However, the IRC was constrained when it tried to direct the affairs of the firms it became involved in: while cash and influence were provided to bring forward some major mergers, perhaps more quickly than would otherwise have been the case, it found it a much harder task to ensure that reorganization brought with it 'the benefits of reorganization' (Young and Lowe 1974: 78). Indeed sceptics have criticized the absence of a staff of economists to work out sectoral strategies and the neglect of problems of rationalization such as job losses (Jones and Keating 1985: 89). The case of the GEC–AEI merger is illustrative. It had an immediate and beneficial impact on profits and dividends, but the new GEC proceeded to close many AEI research laboratories and scrapped certain innovations developed by AEI in telecommunications in favour of GEC's system. This may have been cheaper to develop, but it did not sell well abroad, although it had a captive market in the British Post Office. In addition there were 12,000 job losses in existing factories, while GEC received £1.7 million from the government for creating jobs by moving to Development Areas (Hills 1981).

Thus the initiative appears simply as pro-merger. Although only 2 per cent of total mergers in the period from 1967 to 1970 were promoted or financed by the IRC, these included some of the most significant mergers of the period, such as GEC and British Leyland. Although supposedly balanced by the Monopolies and Mergers Commission, established in 1965, it in fact provided a refuge for some firms from that body and promoted a merger which the Commission had previously rejected. The IRC persuaded the Board of Trade not to refer eight industries to the Monopolies Commission (Smith 1974: 95; Mottershead 1978; Cowling and Sawyer 1990: 79). Thus, although originally accused of 'back-door nationalization' by the CBI, the IRC, composed almost entirely of industrialists, became a forum for businessmen to discuss mergers ' "without talking to government but knowing that public money would be forthcoming" ' (Jones and Keating 1985: 88).

MinTech also embodied a commitment to reaping economies of scale, for, being concerned to promote science and technology R&D in civil industry, its staff believed it was possible to achieve an optimum size of firm to be determined by the scale of R&D and of production (Coopey 1993: 111). MinTech came to have very wide responsibilities covering computers, electronics, telecommunications, engineering, shipbuilding, atomic energy and the National Research Development Council. It supervised the Shipbuilding Industry Act of 1967 under which Upper Clyde Shipbuilders was formed, merging four previous shipyards, and, using funds provided under the Industrial Expansion Act, it supervised the merger which formed ICL (Smith 1974). But the level of intervention aroused business hostility. In 1968, when it acquired powers under the Industrial Expansion Act to acquire stakes in private companies, government–industry relations, according to *The Times* of that year, reached 'an unusually low point' (Coopey 1993: 118).

Still Labour governments persisted in trying to wed concentrations of ownership with economies of scale and scientific progress. By the time of the 1974 election, a more sophisticated theory served to validate the quest to assert leverage at company level. Stuart Holland argued that by concentrating economic policy on the 'meso-economic' or large-firm sector the government could link macroeconomic and microeconomic policies and give the state more leverage at the level of the firm (Holland 1976). The National Enterprise Board was to acquire substantial holdings in private firms to control large companies, to rescue 'lame ducks' and to promote planning for growth. Planning agreements to this effect would be made by the Board with the largest private manufacturing firms and public enterprise. Public ownership was also to be used to promote large-scale enterprise. Successful rationalization followed in the case of the aerospace industry, through the formation of British Aerospace, but the nationalization of shipbuilding and the formation of British Shipbuilders failed to produce integration of the constituent shipyards and research facilities (Sawyer 1991; 1992: 15–17). The system of planning agreements failed in the face of CBI opposition. Planning agreements had been a policy of the left of the Labour Party and carried little conviction in the Parliamentary Labour Party. Hence, in the course of its development the scheme, conceived to give governments control over large corporations, became, in the words of the Department of Industry discussion document, an opportunity for government ' "to attune its policies to the needs and plans of industry" ' (Wilks 1981: 405). The one planning agreement with a private firm, Chrysler, involved substantial government financial support for new projects: three years later Chrysler sold its UK operations to Citroen-Peugeot. Although the planning agreement gave the government a veto over such a sale, it, and the unions, were given no prior information (Sawyer 1991).

Labour governments also pursued more general policies to secure increased spending and application of R&D, standardization and the application of 'scientific management'. Such initiatives under the 1945–51 Labour governments, for instance, included the establishment of the British Institute of Management in 1946, the Anglo-American Council on Productivity and the National Research Development Corporation (Tiratsoo and Tomlinson 1993). Finally the nationalizations carried out under Labour governments were geared to securing rationalization of production, and in a number of key industries were successful. Thus we can see a general trend to support the process of concentration of ownership, with the attempt to follow that up with rationalization of production and the application of technology, to secure the perceived advantages of large-scale firms. However, except in publicly owned industries, the latter policies involved an interventionism in private industry which aroused intense opposition. The circumvention of opposition created policies which, as Hall has pointed out, 'reinforced the power of private sector actors' (Hall 1986: 277). The IRC and planning agreements were intended to allow the state leverage over large-scale firms. But, in so far as they operated, they had an opposite effect.

We now turn to Conservative policies. These included some similar plans: the initial establishment of NEDC, and some discriminatory intervention under the Heath government in the early 1970s in the form of the Industrial Development Executive. However, the more important contribution of Conservative administrations has been the emphasis on market forces and the winds of competition to bring about industrial restructuring. Many initiatives in this area were made under Labour governments – the 1948 Monopolies and Restrictive Practices Act and the 1965 Monopolies and Mergers Act – policies which had emerged with bi-party support under the wartime Coalition and the previous Conservative administration respectively. But since the 1950s the Conservatives have championed the cause of competition. They have introduced four major pieces of legislation – the 1956 Restrictive Trade Practices Act, the 1964 Resale Prices Act, the 1973 Fair Trading Act and the 1980 Competition Act. In the 1980s the encouragement of competition was declared to be the main concern of the Department of Trade and Industry (DTI 1988).

The promotion of competition policies is usually cited as the government's desire to control or regulate large-scale business. Thus for many writers a conflict in policy appears to arise when governments devise measures to encourage large-scale firms and then by introducing competition laws imply they can operate against the public interest (Smith 1974; Mottershead 1978; Freyer 1992). For instance, the mid-1960s saw the simultaneous creation of the IRC and the strengthening of the Monopolies Commission to enquire into mergers. A look at the actual effects of competition policies indicates that they conform to the pattern of promoting the large and, frequently, the multinational firm (see also Aaronovitch and Sawyer 1975: 307).

The first Monopolies and Restrictive Practices Commission (MRPC) of 1949 to 1956 was geared to the investigation, not of single-firm monopolies but of restrictive practices. On the whole the large firm was shielded from enquiry, either because it was held to be efficient or because competition existed with another large firm. In addition, civil servants cautioned Ministers not to take action against firms possessing strategically important positions in the industrial economy as a whole (Mercer 1991a). Where a large firm did come under scrutiny, as in the case of Dunlop, the effect of the MRPC's report was not to help smaller British firms but to open up the British market to foreign multinationals (McMillan 1989: 95–106).

The 'strong' legislation of 1956, which outlawed a wide range of cartels, did not touch arrangements which could be operated by the large firm acting alone, such as international cartels and certain distribution agreements like 'tied houses' or solus site arrangements in petrol distribution. While it abolished collective resale price maintenance it strengthened the right of the individual manufacturer to enforce his resale prices. As one assessment of monopolies legislation on small firms up to 1971 pointed out: 'The fact that the RTP Act is directed exclusively against collective and not against discriminatory and restrictive practices as such, discriminates automatically against the small firm' (Moos 1971: 15). In addition, the evidence indicates that the 1956 Act contributed to the developing wave of mergers, which reached its height in the early 1960s. One study shows that industries with high levels of cartelization before 1956 had a higher level of concentration afterwards (Aaronovitch and Sawyer 1975; Elliott and Gribbin 1977; Hannah 1983: 149; Fairburn 1989: 194; cf. O'Brien *et al.* 1979).

Interestingly, evidence from the public records indicates that Ministers and civil servants involved in policy formulation *expected* the 1956 legislation to affect adversely the smaller manufacturer who needed collective schemes to enforce his prices. Again in 1964 the complete abolition of resale price maintenance was *expected* by the Conservative cabinet to strengthen the competitive power of the large retailer, who could exist on smaller margins than the independent shopkeeper. Thus both the 1956 and 1964 measures aroused the keenest opposition from within the ranks of the Conservative Party, where many members were concerned lest the Party lose its basis among small businessmen. The Labour Party in 1956 opposed the Restrictive Practices Act as a charter for 'Big Business', prophesying that the abolition of cartels would lead to further 'trustification' (Mercer forthcoming).

The creation of the Monopolies and Mergers Commission (MMC) in 1965 had little impact on the current merger boom. In spite of growing concern with the levels of concentration of ownership and growing evidence that there were few efficiency gains from merger, policy was weak. Between 1965 and 1970 only 3 per cent of mergers qualifying for referral were in fact referred to the MMC. This represented fourteen mergers in the same period when the IRC *sponsored* about fifty. A 3 per cent referral rate has remained about the average (Fairburn 1989: 209). The procedure had some bite and, anticipating adverse decisions by the MMC, 31 per cent of the mergers referred between 1965 and 1983 were abandoned before judgement was passed and a further 31 per cent were found against the public interest. But the reports of the MMC did not try to be consistent, and the way the enquiries emphasized particular details of each case allowed 'participants to dictate the agenda of investigation and downgrades cross-referencing between reports' (Fairburn 1989: 227). Hence the last formal review of merger policy, in 1978, described merger policy as tending 'to operate in favour of mergers' (BPP 1977–8: 35). It concluded that mergers had yielded few efficiency gains and proposed that the government adopt a 'neutral' approach.

However, the 1980s saw substantial revision of these points (Littlechild 1989). In 1982 Norman Tebbit directed that competition be the sole consideration of the Commission in coming to a decision. This has led to a still more 'permissive' interpretation of legislation. Of twenty-three referrals between 1984 and 1986, only three were found against the public interest, while ten were abandoned (Fairburn 1989). Indeed, Stephen Littlechild has argued that mergers should be left and only instances of undesirable monopoly power tackled. However, such an approach could only be sustained if British policy had a history of willingness to tackle large concentrations of economic power (George 1990: 87).

If this large and daunting body of competition legislation has neither dealt with merger nor managed more purposive intervention in the 'public interest', what has been its function? Analysis of the curious referral procedures common to Britain's competition statutes indicates that the system functions as a sort of 'businessman's court', allowing businesses affected by another's monopolistic or controlling position some form of redress. For the period of the MRPC from 1949 to 1956 we can generalize from the Byzantine referrals screening procedure operated by the Board of Trade that the final reason for referring a large firm seems to have been the presence of 'countervailing' business interests. In the case of electrical engineering these were American interests, in the case of ICI/Fisons monopoly of chemical fertilizers, the National Farmers' Union (Mercer 1991a). The referral procedure under the monopolies and mergers legislation allowed the Mergers Panel (an internal government body consisting of representatives of the Board of Trade and interested government departments) effectively to make 'public interest' judgements ahead of the MMC. It may be, when the archives become available, that a similar situation prevailed in the Mergers Panel as in the Board of Trade's screening procedure of the 1950s. Competition legislation also served to diffuse popular hostility to 'big business', as studies of earlier anti-trust initiatives have shown.

Nevertheless, the use of regulatory bodies to maintain competition has been used to assuage fears concerning the recent Conservative governments' privatization programme. As Chapter 12 shows, that regulatory process is highly questionable. The overall effect of privatization conforms to the pattern already noted: fostering of concentration of ownership, this time exclusively in private hands. Indeed, as Chapter 12 shows, privatization has proceeded with the emphasis more on reasserting private ownership than on securing greater competition, a feature already apparent in the denationalization of steel in the 1950s.

Thus government policies towards the evolution of large-scale firms have been of two main types. Intervention has deliberately and overtly aimed to foster large-scale firms while also trying to secure efficiency gains from them. Competition policies have also fostered the tendency to concentration: being permissive of mergers and tender of the feelings of large firms in referrals policy. These two elements together add up to something stronger than 'permissiveness'.

Furthermore, policies towards small firms and towards multinationals underline the point that government policy has been weighted in favour of size.

Britain is notoriously weak in specific industrial policies for small firms, especially compared with Germany which provides financial support for R&D, start-up loans as well as 'soft' loans and guarantees (Bannock and Albach 1991). Following the Bolton report of 1971, governments have attempted to introduce some support for small firms. One role of the National Enterprise Board in the 1970s was to encourage them with grants especially in areas of high technology, Inmos being the best-known example (Sawyer 1991: 164). A report by the DTI in 1985 entitled 'Burdens in Business' proposed several reforms, ostensibly to aid small firms. Most referred to the removal of various forms of labour protection – conditions on health and safety, and the abolition of the Wages Councils, some of which have since been implemented (Burns and Dewhurst 1986: 89–90). However, such policies would actually benefit larger companies as well and conform more with the policy of allowing free enterprise full rein. Indeed, the paucity of policy for small firms contrasts markedly with the range of policies, direct and indirect, specifically to the advantage of multinational firms.

Policy towards MNCs has also been termed 'permissive' or 'passive', but compared with other countries, Britain gives a greater range of incentives to MNCs investing in Britain and makes fewer performance requirements (Young *et al.* 1988: 200). Restraints on MNCs wishing to invest in Britain have been weak, and this is well accepted in the literature. Screening of investment proposals through the Foreign Exchange Control Committee between 1945 and 1979 sometimes secured improvements 'of benefit to the United Kingdom' but these were usually 'marginal' especially as the government retreated if faced with the loss of a project, and approvals were usually swift (Young *et al.* 1988: 219; Jones 1990: 201). Monopolies legislation has been little used. A small number of cases of foreign acquisition have been referred to the MMC, but generally foreign companies face no greater threat from that source than domestic ones. Where a stronger stand has been taken under this legislation, it has generally been to protect the financial sector against foreign takeover

(Young *et al.* 1988; Jones 1990; Sugden 1990). This continues the pattern of policy established in the inter-war period, as has the continued promotion of national champions, for instance of British Leyland and ICL. There are other isolated cases of resistance to foreign acquisition: the IRC helped to ward off a bid by the Swedish ball-bearing firm, Skefco, for a greater share of the UK industry; in an isolated case transfer-pricing by foreign drug companies was investigated by the Monopolies Commission in 1973. But, the 'assurances' policy, used for a period in the 1960s, proved 'completely ineffective' (Jones 1990), nor, unlike countries like France and Italy, has Britain made an attempt to control MNCs through state-holdings.

On the other hand British governments have sought to provide incentives to attract foreign MNCs. Up to the 1970s this mainly took the form of speedy response to complaints, especially from the United States, of restrictions and continuing search to ease the path of MNCs. Since the 1970s the consensus is that governments have pursued a very positive policy (Young *et al.* 1988; Sugden 1990). This has taken two main forms. First, governments have set up various bodies to promote foreign investment, such as the Invest in Britain Bureau (in 1977), while various regional development agencies have competed to sell themselves to potential overseas investors. Part of this drive has been the frequent assertion that governments wish to encourage foreign investment. A 1982 statement of the government's policies gives a flavour of remarks typical since the 1950s:

> The Government is committed to maintaining and strengthening the operation of market forces in order to improve the country's economic performance. A free flow of inward direct investment contributes to this central policy objective by introducing additional productive capacity to compete with established sources in the UK and with imports, as well as to raise exports. . . . At the international level, freedom for companies to invest wherever they can exploit their strengths, like the flow of free trade, contributes to the efficient allocation and use of resources between countries. Further, the UK, with its heavy dependence on overseas trade, has a particular interest in preserving the open international trading system. . . . British exporters, for example often need to invest abroad in order to preserve and enlarge their markets. Treatment of British investors abroad is obviously influenced by the treatment accorded to inward investors at home. . . . For these reasons the Government, like its predecessors, welcomes inward direct investment into the UK. . . .

It is improvements in the country's overall economic performance
– lower inflation, higher productivity and a more positive and
realistic approach to industrial relations – allied to membership of
the EC . . . which, above all, will build up confidence of foreign
companies in Britain.

(NEDC 1982)

Apart from the theoretical free trade concerns outlined here, one
argument stands out as to why inward investment is encouraged – to
ease the path of British direct investment abroad. That is, foreign
MNCs are to be encouraged in the interests of British MNCs, when the
benefit of either to the British economy is at best in doubt.

The second way, as indicated in the quotation above, in which
Britain has been made attractive to overseas investors since 1979 has
been to change the image of the British workforce. Governments have
seen the labour practices of American and, more recently, Japanese
firms as beneficial to Britain (Fine and Harris 1985; Sugden 1990). In
turn, the current low labour costs are paraded abroad as an incentive
to invest in Britain.

These then are policies conducive to the dominance of large conglomerations of capital and their implementation goes some way to
explaining the accompanying weaknesses of Britain's industrial performance. We look now at two further factors reinforcing the character of government policies outlined so far – the banks and the trade
unions.

GOVERNMENT, INDUSTRY AND FINANCE

The financial sector has played its part in creating conditions supportive of merger and concentration while effectively undermining
attempts to secure the benefits of scale. First, the nature of Britain's
financial sector has given a fillip and particular flavour to the merger
movement. Unlike her European counterparts the sophistication of
the stock market in Britain means that stock market transactions have
played an important role in British mergers (Cosh *et al.* 1980: 227).
Prais has argued that financial factors have been the most important
determinant of mergers and concentration in Britain since the 1950s.
He notes how financial intermediaries (pension funds, life insurance
companies, unit trusts and investment companies) have seen a rise in
their control of the ordinary shares of UK quoted industrial companies from 18 to 41 per cent between 1957 and 1973. These have
channelled new capital funds towards larger concerns. Indeed, he sees

the rise in managerial control in British companies as promoting instability and encouraging takeover bids (Prais 1976: 135, 167).

Other elements of the financial sector serve to give an advantage to large firms. The increasing volatility of financial markets has prompted predominant concern with short-term performance by companies. Large companies, however, have been able to limit their vulnerability to these vagaries, mainly by directing more executive manpower into financial management. Thus large and multinational companies have had an advantage over their smaller competitors (Strange 1986: 119). The internationalization of British banking since the 1970s has meant that lending policies favour large firms. US banks in Britain, for instance, have mainly been involved in wholesale banking and have concentrated on lending to large corporations (Fine and Harris 1985: 140–2). The character of the banking sector's more detailed involvement in British manufacturing has meant that the investment programmes of large and small firms alike have been distorted. British banks have not 'failed' industry in the sense of failing to supply adequate amounts of finance, but they have adopted strategies to protect themselves against loss if the industrial borrower has difficulties. We have already seen how the policies of the Bank of England in the 1930s were motivated by this outlook. In the postwar era one analysis suggests that the use of the overdraft as the main form of bank loan to industry, and the form of collateral required have 'reinforced firms' lack of strategic planning of investment, production and finance' (Fine and Harris 1985: 131–42). British banks have proved a poor source of finance for the R&D programmes of small firms (Oakey 1984: 139).

Finally, government's willingness to give priority to international financial commitments has, at key conjunctures, overridden plans for industrial retrenchment which might have succoured indigenous manufacturing and sustained long-term investment programmes. The eclipse of free trade and emphasis on industrial development which began in the 1930s and was reinforced during the war gave industrial sponsoring departments in Whitehall a priority over policy. But despite all the attempts to lay down the basis for an active industrial policy after the war, the nettle was not seized and it is generally recognized that the abandonment of microeconomic planning and controls, together with the international settlement for a return to a new Gold Standard based on the dollar, returned the Treasury to dominance in economic policy-making (Leruez 1975; Coates 1984). Equally well-documented is the resurgence of liberal economic thought in the Conservative Party and in the actions of Conservative governments in the

1950s. Chief among these was 'a re-emphasis of monetary policy as the master control of economic activity, combined with a growing reliance upon the external strength of the pound as the regulator for internal policy (Harris 1972; Blank 1973: 123). Henceforth, the predominance of macroeconomic policies and the underdevelopment of microeconomic policies was to become a distinguishing feature of British management of the economy compared with our European rivals (Williams *et al.* 1983: 99).

By the 1950s the emerging lines of policy had provoked a reaction from the leaders of industry: the FBI had commented that the underdevelopment of microeconomic policy was a response to the increased influence of the City which sought to make London into an international financial entrepôt. By 1960 the FBI openly favoured a partnership of state and industry for long-term planning and growth (Ingham 1984: 209). One outcome, the establishment of the NEDC, was viewed at the time as an institution to ' "provide a rival source of expertise and policy-making on economic matters to the Treasury" ' and which ' "would promote the claims of growth as against those of sterling" ' (Leruez 1975: 104, citing contemporaries). These aims coincided with the 1964 Labour government's commitment to modernization. The attempt to downgrade the role of the Treasury can be seen in the creation of the Department of Economic Affairs in 1965 as an agency for long-term planning.

However, the key obstacle to implementation of many of the initiatives we have already described was the Labour government's immediate moves to deal with sterling crises and its assurances not to devalue. These were commitments which could only be met by traditional deflationary measures, including cuts and restrictions in public and private investment announced in the middle of 1965. Again the Bank of England's and the Treasury's concern to maintain the international standing of the City was buttressed by the government's concern to maintain the 'special relationship' with the United States, and it was seen that devaluation would put the dollar in the front line (Leruez 1975: 178–81).

Similar problems beset the industrial policies of the 1974–9 Labour government, although the speedy abandonment of nationalization and other proposals throws doubt on how wedded the leadership was to the plans. Nevertheless, sterling crises provided the background for the jettisoning of industrial policies (Artis and Cobham 1991).

Thus where governments (especially Labour) in the postwar period have set out to prioritize domestic manufacturing, investment and growth and have established institutions to achieve this, they have had to back down in the face of sterling crises.

GOVERNMENT AND LABOUR

Finally we may contrast British governments' 'permissive' attitude to business power with that towards trade union power. We may identify two ways in which governments have not been even-handed in regard to labour and business. These have produced policies conducive to the general tendencies outlined in the chapter so far.

First, labour was not incorporated into the sphere of government as private business was in the postwar period. The consensus around Keynesian full employment policies was always more apparent than real: labour had a subordinate role from the beginning (Middlemas 1986: 148; Coates 1991: 162; Tomlinson 1989). Although trade unions were represented on a large number of government committees, for instance the various tri-partite bodies established, their effectiveness was limited. The Trades Union Congress failed to take an active interest in their work, and trade unionists lacked relevant expertise for such work compared with representatives of business and government (Allen 1960: 34–41). In addition, governments have not flinched from direct and serious conflict with sections of their workers in the way that they have studiously avoided overt conflict with sectors of business. Until the 1960s attempts to restrain wages and raise productivity were essentially based on voluntary agreements, but since then more direct controls have been used. These have ranged from such policies as pay norms, linking pay rises with improvements in productivity, to attacks on the legal rights of trade unions, starting with the 1968 'In Place of Strife' and the 1972 Industrial Relations Act to the rash of such statutes in the 1980s. There have been direct confrontations with public sector unions.

Second, governments have been more ready to curtail 'restrictionism' by labour than by business. Low labour productivity was identified after the Second World War as 'Britain's essential problem' and tackling this has been a constant theme of postwar industrial policy. From the late 1940s, and aided by the nature of American involvement in the issues, such policies have centred on 'restrictive labour practices' (RLPs) and increasingly on trade unionism itself (Carew 1991; Tiratsoo and Tomlinson 1993). It might appear that dealing with RLPs is tackling the equivalent restrictionism in the world of labour to that of cartels in the world of business. In fact, at times, a hidden agenda of competition policies directed against restrictive business practices (RBPs) was to get at RLPs. When considering stronger legislation against cartels in 1955 leading Treasury officials and some members of Cabinet felt that RLPs were more objectionable. Such a train of argument had wide implications, for, as Walter Monckton, Minister of Labour, remarked when reporting back to his colleagues, 'from the purely economic viewpoint most of the negotiated terms and conditions of employment are restrictive practices' (PRO 1955; 1956). The equation of RBPs and RLPs is a false one. Trade unions and labour practices are the main form of collusions among workers regulating the price of labour. Their equivalent in the business world are not cartels but employers' federations. Hence, in policies against restrictionism governments have been biased in the treatment accorded to trade unions and businessmen.

Although the trade union movement has proved remarkably resilient both to labour policies over the last thirteen years and to the effects of recession on membership (Coates 1989: 136), it is undoubtedly weakened. The result is twofold. First, Britain is now indeed a low wage economy, a feature now aimed at attracting foreign investment in Britain. Second, the relative weakness of trade unions has implications for the future regulation of large-scale business. Research on the development of competition policies has shown that 'popular' feeling, mobilized through labour organizations, has been a powerful factor urging governments to do something about cartels, mergers, large firms and monopoly. The weakening of organizations of labour spells slimmer hopes of regulation of large-scale business.

CONCLUSION

This chapter is an attempt to make the emerging debate about the role of the state in the evolution of Britain's highly concentrated industrial structure more explicit, and to outline the wide area that the debate must encompass. It is necessary to survey a variety of policies, whose common thread was to foster the large firm and assist the free movement of capital. Attempts to regulate the process merely contributed to it. Governments have undermined, or failed to recognize, the possibilities of sustained 'countervailing power' in the form of the labour movement.

The chapter emphasizes the need to look at the general thrust of policies. Of course, when the details are examined more minutely disagreements and uncertainties within governments and parties appear. We have already mentioned the conflict within the Conservative Party over competition policies seen to harm small businesses. Nigel Harris has documented the continuing debate in the Party over the role of the state and the swings between étatist and competitive models of state action (Harris 1972). On labour policies it has been argued that sectors of business – usually large-scale firms – have favoured concordats with trade unions since the 1920s and into the 1960s (Longstreth 1979: 180). Even recently, larger firms did not rush to use the new powers provided in legislation (Coates 1989: 136). Nevertheless, the overall tendency of policies and the final outcome of disagreements has been consistent, and we can expect that, without some drastic change, close government support for the interests of large and multinational firms will remain.

We have only touched on the issues involved, but it is necessary to say something about the reasons for such policies. Keynes argued that 'the power of vested interests is vastly exaggerated compared with the gradual encroachment of ideas' (Keynes 1936: 383). There has certainly been a strong ideological component to government actions, often influenced by economists: the Labour Party by Fabians, the Conservatives by neo-liberals. But few 'academic scribblers' would endorse British governments' attitude to merger, concentration and MNCs, and the weaknesses of regulation. We are left with the unsurprising conclusion that conglomerations of economic power have had the political leverage to shape the character of government intervention.

NOTE

I am grateful to Maurice Kirby and Mary Rose for comments on an earlier draft of this chapter.

BIBLIOGRAPHY

Aaronovitch, S. and Sawyer, M. (1975) *Big Business*, London: Macmillan.
Abraham, N. (1974) *Big Business and Government. The New Disorder*, London: Macmillan.
Aldcroft, D.H. (1986) *The British Economy*, vol. 1, *The Years of Turmoil 1920–1951*, Brighton: Wheatsheaf.
Allen, G.C. (1935) *British Industries*, London: Longman.
Allen, V.L. (1960) *Trade Unions and Government*, London: Longman.
Artis, M.J. and Cobham, D. (eds) (1991) *Labour's Economic Policies 1974–1979*, Manchester: Manchester University Press.
Bacon, R. and Eltis, W. (1978) *Britain's Economic Problem: Too Few Producers*, 2nd edn, London: Macmillan.
Bannock, G. (1980) 'The economic role of the small firm in contemporary industrial society', in J. Curran, J. Stanworth and D. Watkins (eds) *The Survival of the Small Firm*, vol. 1, Aldershot: Gower.
Bannock, G. and Albach, H. (1991) *Small Business Policy in Europe*, London: Anglo-German Foundation for the Study of Industrial Society.

Bannock, G. and Peacock, A. (1989) *Governments and Small Business*, London: Paul Chapman.

Best, M.H. and Humphries, J. (1986) 'The City and industrial decline', in B. Elbaum and W. Lazonick (eds) *The Decline of the British Economy*, Oxford: Clarendon Press.

Blank, S. (1973) *Industry and Government in Britain. The Federation of British Industries in Politics, 1945–65*, Farnborough: Saxon House.

Booth, A. (1987) 'Britain in the 1930s: a managed economy?', *Economic History Review* 11: 499–522.

BPP (British Parliamentary Papers) (1929) *Final Report of the Balfour Committee on Industry and Trade*, Cmnd 3282.

—— (1977–8) *A Review of Monopolies and Mergers Policy*, Cmnd 7198.

Brady, R. (1950) *Crisis in Britain*, Berkeley, CA: University of California Press.

Britain without Capitalists (1936) London: Lawrence & Wishart.

Broadway, F. (1969) *State Intervention in British Industry 1964–68*, London: Kaye & Wood.

Burgess, K. (1980) *The Challenge of Labour. Shaping British Society 1850–1930*, London: Croom Helm.

Burns, P. and Dewhurst, J. (1986) 'Great Britain and Northern Ireland', in P. Burns and J. Dewhurst (eds) *Small Business in Europe*, London: Macmillan Education.

Capie, F. (1990) 'The evolving regulatory framework in British banking', in M. Chick (ed.) *Governments, Industries and Markets*, Aldershot: Edward Elgar.

Carew, A. (1991) 'The Anglo-American Council on Productivity (1948–52): the ideological roots of the post-war debate on productivity in Britain', *Journal of Contemporary History* 26(1).

Channon. D. (1978) *The Service Industries. Strategy, Structure and Financial Performance*, London: Macmillan.

Chick, M. (1990) *Governments, Industries and Markets. Aspects of Government–Industry Relations in the UK, Japan, West Germany and the USA since 1945*, Aldershot: Edward Elgar.

Clay, H. (1930) *The Post-war Unemployment Problem*, London: Macmillan.

Coates, D. (1984) *The Context of British Politics*, London: Hutchinson.

—— (1989) *The Crisis of Labour. Industrial Relations and the State in Contemporary Britain*, Oxford: Philip Allan.

Coates, K. (1991) 'The vagaries of participation 1945–1960', in B. Pimlott and C. Cook (eds) *Trade Unions in British Politics: the First 250 Years*, London: Longman.

Coopey, R. (ed.) (1993) *The Wilson Governments, 1964–70*, London: Pinter.

Cosh, A., Hughes, A. and Singh, A. (1980) 'The causes and effects of take-overs in the UK', in D.C. Mueller (ed.) *The Determinants and Effects of Mergers*, Cambridge, MA: Oelgeschlager, Gunn and Haines.

Cowling, K. and Sawyer, M. (1990) 'Merger and monopoly policy', in K. Cowling and R. Sugden (eds) *A New Economic Policy for Britain. Essays on the Development of Industry*, Manchester: Manchester University Press.

DTI (Department of Trade and Industry) (1988) *DTI – the Department for Enterprise*, Cmd 278, London: HMSO.

Dunning, J.H. (1985) 'The United Kingdom', in J.H. Dunning (ed.) *Multinational Enterprises, Economic Structure and International Competitiveness*, Chichester: Wiley.

Elliott, D.C. and Gribbin, J.D. (1977) 'The abolition of cartels and structural change in the United Kingdom', in A.P. Jacquemin and H.W. de Jong (eds) *Welfare Aspects of Industrial Markets*, Leiden: Leiden University Press.

Fairburn, J. (1989) 'The evolution of merger policy in Britain', in J. Fairburn and J. Kay (eds) *Mergers and Merger Policy*, Oxford: Oxford University Press.

Federation of British Industries (1935) *The Organisation of Industry*, London.

Fine, B. and Harris, L. (1985) *The Peculiarities of the British Economy*, London: Lawrence & Wishart.

Freyer, T. (1992) *Regulating Big Business. Antitrust in Great Britain and America 1880–1990*, Cambridge: Cambridge University Press.

George, K.D. (1990) 'Lessons from UK merger policy', in P.H. Admiraal (ed.) *Merger and Competition Policy in the European Community*, Oxford: Blackwell.

Graham, A. (1972) 'Industrial policy', in W. Beckerman (ed.) *The Labour Government's Economic Record 1964–1970*, London: Gerald Duckworth.

Grant, W. (1991) 'Government and manufacturing industry since 1900', in G. Jones and M. Kirby (eds) *Competitiveness and the State. Government and Business in Twentieth Century Britain*, Manchester: Manchester University Press.

Grove, J.W. (1962) *Government and Industry in Britain*, London: Longmans.

Hague, D. and Wilkinson, G. (1983) *The IRC – An Experiment in Industrial Intervention*, London: Allen & Unwin.

Hall, P.A. (1986) 'The state and economic decline', in B. Elbaum and W. Lazonick (eds) *The Decline of the British Economy*, Oxford: Clarendon Press.

Hannah, L. (1980) 'Government and business in Britain: the evolution of the modern relationship', in K. Nakagawa (ed.) *Government and Business: Proceedings of the Fifth Fuji Conference*, Tokyo: Tokyo University Press.

—— (1983) *The Rise of the Corporate Economy*, London: Methuen.

Harris, N. (1972) *Competition and the Corporate Society: British Conservatives, the State and Industry 1945–64*, London: Methuen.

Hills, J. (1981) 'The Industrial Reorganisation Corporation: the case of the AEI/GEC and English Electric/GEC mergers', *Public Administration* 59: 63–84.

Holland, S. (1976) 'The National Enterprise Board and planning agreements', in D. Lethbridge (ed.) *Government and Industry Relationships*, Oxford: Pergamon.

Hughes, A. (1976) 'Company concentration, size of plant and merger activity', in M. Panic (ed.) *The UK and West German Manufacturing Industry 1954–72: A Comparison of Structure and Performance*, HMSO: NEDO.

Ingham, G. (1984) *Capitalism Divided? The City and Industry in Social Development*, London: Macmillan.

Johnman, L. (1991) 'The Labour party and industrial policy, 1940–45', in N. Tiratsoo (ed.) *The Attlee Years*, London: Pinter.

Jones, B. and Keating, M. (1985) *Labour and the British State*, Oxford: Clarendon Press.

Jones, G. (1986) 'Origins, management and performance', in G. Jones (ed.) *British Multinationals: Origins, Management and Performance*, Aldershot: Gower.

—— (1990) 'The British government and foreign multinationals before 1970', in M. Chick (ed.) *Governments, Industries and Markets*, Aldershot: Edward Elgar.

Jones, R. (1987) *Wages and Employment Policy 1936–1985*, London: Allen & Unwin.

Keynes, J.M. (1936) *The General Theory of Employment Interest and Money*, London: Macmillan.

Kirby, M.W. (1987) 'Industrial policy', in S. Glynn and A. Booth (eds) *The Road to Full Employment*, London: Allen & Unwin.

Leruez, J. (1975) *Economic Planning and Politics in Britain*, London: Martin Robertson.

Littlechild, S. (1989) 'Myths and merger policy', in J. Fairburn and J. Kay (eds) *Mergers and Merger Policy*, Oxford: Oxford University Press.

Longstreth, F. (1979) 'The City, industry and the state', in C. Crouch (ed.) *State and Economy in Contemporary Capitalism*, London: Croom Helm.

Low Pay Unit (1993), figures cited in *The Observer*, 23 May 1993.

McMillan, J. (1989) *The Dunlop Story. The Life, Death and Rebirth of a Multinational*, London: Weidenfeld & Nicholson.

MacGregor, D. (1906) *Industrial Combination*, London: Bell.

Macrosty, M.W. (1901) *Trusts and the State*, London: Longman.

Meeks, (1977) *Disappointing Marriage: a Study of the Gains from Merger*, Cambridge: Cambridge University Press.

Mercer, H. (1989) 'The evolution of British government policy towards competition in private industry 1940–1956'. Unpublished Ph.D. thesis, University of London.

—— (1991a) 'The Monopolies and Restrictive Practices Commission 1949–1956: a study in regulatory failure', in G. Jones and M. Kirby (eds) *Competitiveness and the State: Government and Business in Twentieth Century Britain*, Manchester: Manchester University Press.

—— (1991b) 'The Labour Governments of 1945–51 and private industry', in N. Tiratsoo (ed.) *The Attlee Years*, London: Pinter.

—— (forthcoming) *Constructing and Competitive Order: the Hidden History of British Anti-trust Policy*, Cambridge: Cambridge University Press.

Middlemas, K. (1979) *Politics in Industrial Society: The Experience of the British System since 1911*, London: Deutsch.

—— (1983) *Industry, Unions and Government. Twenty-one Years of N.E.D.C.*, London: Macmillan.

—— (1986) *Power, Competition and the State*, vol. 1, *Britain in Search of Balance, 1940–61*, London: Macmillan.

—— (1990) *Power, Competition and the State*, vol. 2, *Threats to the Postwar Settlement Britain 1961–74*, London: Macmillan.

Moos, S. (1971) 'Aspects of monopoly and restrictive practices legislation in relation to small firms', *Committee of Enquiry on Small Firms* 13, London: HMSO.

Mottershead, P. (1978) 'Industrial policy', in F.T. Blackaby (ed.) *British Economic Policy 1960–74*, Cambridge: Cambridge University Press.

NEDC (1982) 'Direct inward investment. Memorandum by the Secretary of State for Industry', NEDC(82)7.

Newton, S. and Porter, D. (1988) *Modernisation Frustrated: the Politics of Industrial Decline in Britain since 1900*, London: Unwin Hyman.

O'Brien, D.P., Howe, W.S., Wright, D.M. and O'Brien, R.J. (1979) *Competition Policy, Profitability and Growth*, London: Macmillan.

Oakey, R.P. (1984) *High Technology Small Firms: Regional Development in Britain and the United States*, London: Pinter.

Piore, M.J. and Sabel, C.F. (1984) *The Second Industrial Divide*, New York: Basic Books.

Pollard, S. (1984) *The Wasting of the British Economy*, London: Croom Helm.

Prais, S.J. (1976) *The Evolution of Giant Firms in Britain*, Cambridge: Cambridge University Press.

PRO (1955) CAB 128/29 CM(55)47th meeting, 20/12/1955.

—— (1956) CAB134/1230 EP(56)18 'Restrictive Labour Practices', memorandum by the Minister of Labour 10/2/1956.

Ritschel, D. (1991) 'A corporatist economy in Britain? Capitalist planning for industrial self-government in the 1930's', *English Historical Review* 106: 41–65.

Roberts, R. (1984) 'The administrative origins of industrial diplomacy: an aspect of government–industry relations, 1929–1935', in J. Turner (ed.) *Businessmen and Politics. Studies of Business Activity in British Politics, 1900–1945*, London: Heinemann.

Rogow, A.A. and Shore, P. (1955) *The Labour Government and British Industry, 1945–1951*, Oxford: Blackwell.

Sawyer, M. (1991) 'Industrial policy', in M. Artis and D. Cobham (eds) *Labour's Economic Policies 1974–1979*, Manchester: Manchester University Press.

—— (1992) 'Labour's industrial policies in the 1970's: debates and deeds', Paper prepared for conference on 'Labour: the Party of Industrial Modernisation?', London School of Economics.

Smith, T. (1974) 'The United Kingdom', in R. Vernon (ed.) *Big Business and the State: Changing Relations in Western Europe*, London: Macmillan.

Stoneman, P. (1983) *The Economic Analysis of Technological Change*, Oxford: Oxford University Press.

Storey, D. and Johnson, S. (1987) *Are Small Firms the Answer to Unemployment?*, The Employment Institute.

Strange, S. (1986) *Casino Capitalism*, Oxford: Blackwell.

Sugden, R. (1990) 'The warm welcome for foreign-owned transnationals from recent British governments', in M. Chick (ed.) *Government, Industries and Markets*, Aldershot: Edward Elgar.

Taylor, R. (1991) 'The trade union "problem" in the age of consensus', in B. Pimlott and C. Cook (eds) *Trade Unions and British Politics: the First 250 Years*, London: Longman.

Tiratsoo, N. and Tomlinson, J. (1993) *Industrial Efficiency and State Intervention*, London: Routledge.

Tolliday, S. (1986) 'Steel and rationalisation policies 1918–50', in B. Elbaum and W. Lazonick (eds) *The Decline of the British Economy*, Oxford: Clarendon Press.

Tomlinson, J. (1989) 'Labour's management of the national economy 1945–51', *Economy and Society* 18(1): 1–24.

Vickerstaff, S. and Sheldrake, J. (1989) *The Limits of Corporatism*, Aldershot: Avebury.

Wilks, S. (1981) 'Planning agreements: the making of a paper tiger', *Public Administration* 59: 399–419.

——— (1990) 'Institutional insularity: government and the British motor industry since 1945', in M. Chick (ed.) *Governments, Industries and Markets. Aspects of Government–Industry Relations in the UK, Japan, West Germany and the USA since 1945*, Aldershot: Edward Elgar.

Williams, K., Williams, J. and Thomas, D. (1983) *Why are the British Bad at Manufacturing?*, London: Routledge & Kegan Paul.

Young, S. and Lowe, A.V. (1974) *Intervention in the Mixed Economy. The Evolution of British Industrial Policy 1964–72*, London: Croom Helm.

Young, S., Hood, N. and Hamill, J. (1988) *Foreign Multinationals and the British Economy. Impact and Policy*, London: Croom Helm.

12 Nationalization, privatization and regulation

Martin Chick

During the twentieth century, the relationship between British governments and some of the major utility industries has been somewhat circular in character. Some utilities such as railways, gas and electricity have passed from late nineteenth-century regulation, through early and mid-twentieth century public ownership and, more recently by virtue of privatization, back to the fact or prospect of regulation under private ownership. In contrast to this variously virtuous and vicious circle of state responses to these industries, the industries themselves have possessed a set of common and constant characteristics that have forced them upon the state's attention. These characteristics include public concern with the safety of output; externalities and spillover effects often resulting in the social value of output exceeding its private value; and, in general, elements within each industry in which the minimum efficient scale is large relative to the size of the market, and subject to decreasing costs. The purpose of this chapter is to trace the varying and developing responses of British governments towards these industries and to consider the extent to which the more recent developments in regulatory practice mark a continuous or new development on past responses.

MUNICIPALITIES, REGULATION AND EXTERNALITIES

Almost from their earliest days, utility industries sought contact with government. Given their large capital requirements, the utilities often required limited liability status, which could only be obtained from Parliament. This contact with central government was often reinforced at municipal level by the need for electricity, gas, telecommunications and water enterprises to gain local authority permission to dig up streets in order to lay mains and local networks. For its part, government became drawn into contact with utilities through its concern with safety. Beginning with the death of William Huskisson, sometime

President of the Board of Trade and keen deregulator, at the opening day ceremony of the Liverpool and Manchester Railway, Parliament had taken an interest in railway safety, although initially refraining from imposing safety restrictions on existing railways (Foster 1992: 20). By 1893, after a succession of railway accidents, public opinion shifted and legislation in that year provided the Railway Inspectorate with powers to improve safety requirements on the railways (Foster 1992: 53). Similar concerns prompted regulatory activity in the water, gas and electricity industries (Millward 1989: 200–4).

The immediate specific concern with safety of output developed to accommodate consideration of externalities and spillovers. Most utilities gave rise to a mix of beneficial and harmful externalities. Leaking gas was both noxious and dangerous, while gas lighting offered improvements in public safety. In turn, this concern with externalities coincided and blended with an emerging public concern to extend availability of output (Falkus 1977: 134–61). Improving the quality of often polluted drinking water offered improvements in public health, as too did extending the supply of mains drinking water to poorer areas (Millward 1989: 201). The development of a comprehensive integrated piped system under continuous pressure also offered to improve the effectiveness of fire-fighters, a point of most relevance to those propertied and commercial classes capable of influencing municipal policy (Hassan 1985: 531–47). Yet, although by the middle of the nineteenth century there was a growing demand that both the quality and quantity of the output of utilities like water and gas should be increased (Matthews 1986: 244–63), there was an apparent reluctance among suppliers to expand into ostensibly profitable areas.

CONTESTABLE MARKETS AND NATURAL MONOPOLIES

That this reluctance should exist in utilities is initially surprising, given that many of the network distribution utilities (gas, water, electricity, telecommunications) are standard economics textbook examples of industries which enjoy substantial economies of scale relative to market size with falling long-run average and marginal costs. These cost characteristics are often cited as providing the basis for these industries constituting 'natural' monopolies, in that competition in the field would simply result in replication of plant and networks at a cost to consumers in higher prices, lower quality or similar welfare losses (Millward 1991: 100). However, extension of supply did carry associated costs. In the water industry, there appears to have been uncertainty about the level of take-up of supply in poorer areas, economies of customer contiguity being important to the running and capital costs of networks (Millward 1991: 107). Extending the network also raised costs, as associated problems of leakage involved additional costs of inspection, as well as loss of output without income being earned (Matthews 1986: 244–63). There may also have been some concern at the possibility of other suppliers also attempting to enter a market which some economists regard as still having been potentially contestable (Demsetz 1968: 55–65; Baumol *et al.* 1977: 350–6; Bailey and Panzar 1981: 125–46; Millward 1991).

The emerging issue was the extent to which the state should intervene to provide guarantees of barriers to entry, enabling the incumbent to extend supply to the full quantity required. This issue was to recur in the contestable market literature, when particular attention centred on what precisely constituted a natural monopoly. Put in its simplest textbook form, a natural monopoly is held to exist when a single firm can produce the total market demand at a lower cost than two or more firms can. This cost advantage usually exists in conditions of long-run decreasing cost, which in turn often arise from the existence of fixed costs, which bulk large in total costs. Fixed costs are insensitive to variations in output and arise from indivisibilities in the productive process. It is the fixed costs which would be wastefully duplicated if two firms attempted to serve the same market. However, the existence of large fixed costs does not necessarily make for a natural monopoly; they are often a characteristic, but not an essential feature. It is possible, in the absence of internal economies of scale over a sufficient range of supply, for it to be equally efficient to have a number of producing firms (Kahn 1971: 119). More germane to natural monopoly than fixed costs are sunk costs. While closely related to fixed costs, sunk costs involve specialized forms of capital which are not easily converted into other productive uses (Sharkey 1982: 37). It is sunk costs which provide a fundamental obstacle to contestable markets. Contestable markets, with actual or threatened competition, assume that the means of production are quickly and fully available to all, that cost functions are identical, and that entry involves no sunk costs, therefore providing no barriers to exit. Sunk costs may also deter entry, as firms may benefit from building larger capacity than would be required in the absence of entry. That excess capacity then signals to potential entrants that the incumbent firm is willing to maintain or increase output if entry should occur (Spence 1977: 1–19). The potential entrant may also be deterred if it fears that its incremental output contribution will be absorbed by the market only if the price is reduced. Therefore, even though an entrant's costs may be as low as those of an incumbent, entry will be deterred. There may then be a case for franchise bidding schemes: for competition *for*, rather than *in*, the field (Williamson 1976: 73–104).

The issues involving government, market structures and natural monopoly gradually resolved themselves during the mid–late nineteenth century. By the middle of the nineteenth century, competition in the field had virtually ceased in the provinces, and Parliament was reluctant to sanction new companies if this created competition (Millward 1991: 101). While exclusive franchises were never given in the water industry, the issuing of franchises was initially the preferred method of defining the requirements and parameters of utility industries. The problem of high fixed and sunk costs requiring adequate pay-back periods was one of the main reasons behind the provision of franchises in these utilities. Legislation providing franchises for twenty-one years was quite common. However, in lumpy capital projects, franchises were often extended or open ended. In railways, the brevity of a twenty-one-year franchise allied to the expectation that competition along common routes would restrain prices resulted in railway franchises being free of a limited-term clause (Foster 1992: 18). In electricity, the initial twenty-one-year franchises were extended to forty-two years to provide an extended pay-back period (Hannah 1979: 5). Regulation of dividends and prices was deployed in an effort to provide a reasonable relationship between costs and prices, as well as offering efficiency incentives. However, effective arm's-length regulation proved difficult to achieve. Regulatory requirements were often under-specified, thereby facilitating evasion, enforcement proved difficult and monitoring was virtually absent. Price ceilings on gas became irrelevant as gas costs fell, and dividend regulation proved vulnerable to watering of the capital base.

PUBLIC OWNERSHIP AND NETWORKS

The difficulties experienced in attempting to regulate utilities placed local and central government in a position similar to that facing many enterprises towards the end of the nineteenth century. The difficulties and transaction costs of attempting to influence the activities of agents were becoming sufficiently high, and concern with the quality and quantity of output sufficiently politically important, to prompt authorities to move from regulation to ownership. The costs of using the market, which Coase identifies as persuading firms to replace transactions across markets by transactions within firms, were becoming equally relevant to governments (Coase 1937: 386–405). Such costs of using the market and its price system included those of discovering relevant prices, of bargaining, of negotiating contracts for each different transaction and of uncertainty if long-term contracts were required. Internalizing former market transactions within the firm seemed to offer the chance to improve the information asymmetry problems (Spence 1974). The main difference between the theory of the growth of the firm and that of government was that government came to be studied as part of the theory of public goods, a public good being held to have collectivity in consumption, i.e. one person's consumption does not reduce the availability of a good to another person. The concern with information was similar though, and prompted a move towards public ownership that pre-dated Labour governments. However, information asymmetries continued to beset regulatory arrangements. When arguing for the establishment of the London Passenger Transport Board, which would enable the Minister to take over many regulatory duties from the Tribunal, Herbert Morrison, as Minister of Transport, pointed to the consequent improvement in the information available to a minister supported by civil servants as a leading reason for such a change (Morrison 1933: 105).

As a result of such considerations, enterprises steadily shifted into public ownership. In water, the number of publicly owned water undertakings trebled from 250 to 786 in the period 1871–1915, and by 1912–15 approximately 80 per cent of authorized water undertakings were municipal (Millward 1989: 205–6). On the eve of the First World War there were 300 publicly owned gas enterprises accounting for nearly 40 per cent of the total of authorized undertakings (Millward 1991: 117). By 1944, 36.8 per cent of gas sales were made by local authorities, while in the electricity supply industry the publicly owned sector accounted for some 60 per cent of the industry measured in terms of employment (Chester 1975: 16–17).

A variation on the natural monopoly theme was where, as in electricity, the state promoted the establishment of a natural monopoly network (grid) so as to help break local monopolies in generation. Highly capital-intensive technological industries like electricity did appear to have scope to exploit economies of scale which improvements in transmission and steam-turbine technology had made available by the 1920s. However, the organization of electricity generation in a series of separate local monopolies, lacking both the stick of potential competition or the carrot of larger markets, appeared to many economists, engineers and industrialists to be preventing the full exploitation of the benefits of large-scale generation. In London, for example, seventy undertakings, each with separate power stations, inefficiently supplied electricity that could, in theory, have come from only four stations of optimum scale and technological characteristics (Hannah 1977: 208). Responding to industrial lobbying and increasing evidence of inefficiency, in 1926 the Baldwin government agreed to adopt the recommendations of the Weir Committee (1926) that a national grid should be constructed under the supervision of a Central Electricity Board (CEB). The grid offered generators the bait of access to a larger market, while also introducing the threat of competition to supply the grid. The CEB also had the power to close inefficient stations. Crucially, it left the ownership of the undertakings untouched. The strategy proved successful, the 1920s gap between British and American power station thermal efficiency virtually being closed by the late 1930s, and the price paid by the CEB to generating stations effectively falling by 69 per cent between 1923 and 1936 (Hannah 1977: 223).

The scope for deploying networks to stimulate competition among producers so as to achieve economies of scale was limited, however, not only by the extent of such networks but also by the characteristics of the output flowing across the network (Foreman-Peck 1987: 699–718). As on railways, forced amalgamations were often necessary, the scope for effective competition on the railways being limited by the presence of fixed and sunk costs (Starkie 1984: 16–19). By the early twentieth century, the view was growing that amalgamations between rail companies should be encouraged. Churchill's view in 1909 that 'there is no real economic future for British railways apart from amalgamation of one kind or another' reflected a growing opinion among independent, informed observers (Foster 1992: 56). With deteriorating finances and inefficiencies exposed by the First World War, and also facing increasing competition from road transport, the railways narrowly avoided being nationalized, being subject instead to an enforced amalgamation into four main-line railways in 1921 (Foster 1992: 59). The competition from road transport steadily eroded the monopoly status of the railway industry and ate into its previously captive freight business. Technological change, whether in the form of motor vehicles at the start of the century or microwave telecommunication towards the end, had the ability to cut across previously long-standing network monopolies in a fairly short time. However, the pace of technological change and shifts in market conditions were often not matched by a similar pace of change in the regulatory arrangements for the affected industries, this being the fate of the inter-war railway industry.

The enforced amalgamation of the railway companies anticipated an increasingly advocated approach towards industries in which market forces were held unlikely to achieve desired industrial restructuring. Industrial restructuring was driven in part by the growing faith in economies of scale, even in industries where the scope for and availability of economies of scale was not as common as was supposed (Buxton and Aldcroft 1979; Hannah 1979: 162). In the coal industry, which was not a natural monopoly but was an industry in which reorganization was sought, pursuit of rationalization in the 1930s was based on the two partly mythical beliefs that considerable economies of scale were available and that these economies of scale were most available in large pits (Greasley 1995).

The experience of the Coal Mines Reorganisation Commission in attempting to restructure the industry strengthened the later support for nationalization (Supple 1986: 236). While the interest in the issue of efficiency had only arisen as a secondary consideration behind government's prime concern with unemployment within the industry, the experience of the Commission's attempts to achieve some restructuring was influential in strengthening the Labour Party's espousal of nationalization. The Commission failed to overcome the resistance of a range of vested interests both inside and outside Parliament. This obscurantist resistance to restructuring was also experienced in such other industries as iron and steel and electricity distribution. By the late 1930s, and certainly during the war, opinion swung strongly against these vested interests, and exasperation at the inability of a range of industries to restructure themselves became increasingly apparent (Burn 1961; Supple 1987; Tolliday 1987; Chick 1995). By the end of the war, faith in the ability of markets and industries left to themselves to resolve structural deficiencies was at an all-time low, and it seemed clear that the compulsory restructuring of many utility and basic sector industries would be achieved. However, the compulsory reorganization of industrial structure did not necessarily require the transfer of ownership that was effected by the nationalization of industries. While the restructuring of the coal industry had long been advocated, and while nationalization had been favoured narrowly as the means by the Sankey Commission in 1919, the 1945 Reid Report which urged that a national authority be established to supervise the reorganization of the industry did not advocate public ownership as the means of achieving this (Reid Committee 1945: 137–8). The election of the Attlee Labour government in 1945 effectively settled the issue of ownership versus regulation. Most obviously, the Labour government was committed to implementing Clause IV of the Labour Party Constitution. The unsatisfactory experience with regulation had prompted a long-term drift into public ownership, while the obscurantist opposition of private owners in the coal industry in particular during the 1930s suggested to many that only nationalization was likely to break the power of such vested interests.

MONOPOLIES AND PRICING

With nationalization also came a further move towards monopoly. Just as public ownership had not been the only response available to the industries' problems, so too was there considerably more scope for preserving and promoting competition within what became monopoly industries in which cost and price information was suppressed. Alternative options might have been for sections of each industry, even sections of regions, to raise capital on their own account, with prices reflecting separate production costs of each unit. Certainly, the Treasury was prepared to consider a less strongly centralized nationalized electricity industry than the one which emerged (Chester 1975: 48). However, this ran counter to Morrison's wider aims. Monopoly was not only considered to be inevitable in many capital-intensive industries, but also to offer possibilities of improving the quality of the plant choices made by reducing supply-side uncertainties (Richardson 1960). Moreover, Morrison appeared to have a fundamental distaste for market mechanisms. His response to the suggestion that more use might be made of pricing mechanisms in securing co-ordination between industries within sectors was that such ideas were 'competition, not socialization'.

As nationalized monopolies, an immediate issue to concern economists was the basis of the pricing of output. During the Attlee government, this issue was much discussed within the advisory Economic Section, discussion being led in particular by James Meade. The general support given to marginal cost pricing built on earlier theoretical work, and was later augmented by contributions designed to secure the most efficient pricing arrangements while subject to budgetary constraints. In general, the theory of pricing in public enterprises subject to budgetary constraints is a synthesis of the views of both Hotelling and Coase, with a later take-up of the earlier ideas of Ramsey. In his work involving marginal cost pricing in 1938, Harold Hotelling drew upon an idea initially developed in 1844 by Jules Dupuit (Hotelling 1938: 242–69; Dupuit 1969: 255–83; Sharkey 1982: 14). While arguing that consumer welfare will be highest when prices are set equal to the marginal costs of production, it was anticipated that the revenue shortfall, which reflected fixed costs, would be paid for by a system of fixed charges or by subsidies from general taxation. However, taxation, or subsidy, involves a welfare cost exactly analogous to the cost of having the original price greater than the marginal cost (Little 1951: 577–84). Moreover, as noted by Coase, the existence of a subsidy introduces a distortion of its own, as non-users of a product are required to pay part of the cost for the users (Coase 1970: 113–28).

It was in an effort to resolve the problem of financial loss-making by increasing returns industries that the earlier ideas of Ramsey were developed (Ramsey 1927: 47–61). In short, Ramsey prices are raised above marginal cost in inverse proportion to the elasticity of demand. The appeal of Ramsey pricing was that it was posited on the assumption that a public enterprise must operate with its budget in balance. In firms with multiple outputs, the relative prices are decision variables of the firm, and therefore other prices are required. The Ramsey prices are the 'second best' prices that succeed in raising enough revenue to cover total cost with the smallest possible sacrifice in consumer welfare (Lindahl 1958: 168–76; Vickrey 1961: 8–37; Groves and Ledyard 1977: 783–809). More recently, various incentives have been developed to encourage a multiproduct monopolist to choose Ramsey pricing (Vogelsang and Finsinger 1979: 157–71; Loeb and Magat 1979: 399–404).

For all the theorizing, there was a great gulf between what economists might have wanted and what politicians understood and considered politically acceptable. Even some very straightforward arguments put forward in favour of marginal cost pricing by James Meade in the 1940s made little progress. Gradually, growing concern with allocative inefficiency as well as Treasury disquiet over the financial losses being incurred by some nationalized industries led to attempts to force stricter pricing and investment criteria on the nationalized industries. The 1961 White Paper began to address the problem and the White Paper of 1967 emphasized the virtues of (long-run) marginal cost pricing, discounted cash flow and the use of a test discount rate as set by the Treasury. However, while such developments were welcome, their impact was limited. Politicians often did not understand the issues and/or considered them mere academic concerns, industry largely ignored the pricing guidelines and the government's anti-inflation policies of the 1970s so distorted the input and price structures of the nationalized industries as to make any attempt to implement clear pricing policies largely irrelevant (Crossman 1976: 524; HMSO 1976).

DEFICITS AND PRODUCTIVITY

The Treasury's mounting concern with such issues as pricing practices in the nationalized industries arose from concern with the financial losses being made by some nationalized industries and the increasing capital demands of large projects, notably the nuclear power programme. Among the lossmakers, the two troubled industries of the inter-war period, coal and railways, continued on a trend decline and faced increasing competition. A number of responses to the problem were possible. Apart from tightening-up pricing practices and imposing apparently tougher criteria for investment, the industries could be encouraged to close loss-making activities. In railways, the Beeching Report of 1963 recommended a programme of cuts, many of which were implemented. However, while labour productivity rose as labour employed fell by one-third between 1925 and 1965, the industry continued to make financial losses (Dunkerley and Hare 1991: 391). Moreover, a programme of closures could only bring one-off gains in productivity, and such a strategy could not be continued indefinitely. Moreover, closure on financial criteria was complicated by the acceptance of social cost–benefit arguments, which justified the paying of subsidies to some loss-making lines. It is likely that these subsidies in turn reduced managerial incentives to keep marginal lines in profit, thereby increasing the subsidy bill. To this was added the complication of government interference with prices, particularly during periods of rising rates of inflation, when the prices of nationalized industries' output were held down. One consequence of this was to raise the demand for what was now a relatively cheaper product (compared with substitutes), thereby accelerating depreciation of the stock of equipment while reducing the flow of funds available for replacement capital investment formation. The trading difficulties of the coal, iron and steel, and railway industries increased the need for subsidies, while the rise in inflation increased the compensation payments made to nationalized industries in lieu of the price increases forgone as part of the anti-inflation programme. Both contributed to a public sector borrowing requirement which grew from being 2.3 per cent of gross domestic product (in market prices) in 1971 to a peak of 9.6 per cent in 1975 (Pratten 1990: 170).

While governments became increasingly concerned at the financial performance of the nationalized industries, economists were as much concerned with the productivity performance of these industries. On this, the evidence is not entirely clear. Direct comparisons between public and privately-owned enterprises are difficult to make because there are not many markets in which they were in direct competition. Where such coexistence was present in such activities as cross-channel ferries and the sale of gas and electric appliances, research based on limited data did find private operators to have a better record (Pryke 1982: 66−81). Other studies of railways and airlines in Canada and Australia, and water supplies in the United States, struggled to find any advantage to either form of ownership (Millward 1989: 189), while in the generation and supply of electricity, publicly owned utilities in the United States appeared to enjoy lower costs than privately owned firms during the 1960s and 1970s (Millward and Parker 1983). Research on the inter-war electricity industry showed a cost advantage to private firms, and earlier the CEB had increased the proportion of electricity it had bought from the more efficient private sector and forced the municipal authorities to take more of their electricity, something which the private enterprises had previously been unable to do (Foreman-Peck and Waterston 1985). In gas, no difference was found in the cost functions of public and private undertakings in late nineteenth-century Britain (Millward and Ward 1987: 719−37). More recently, comparisons of private and public water supply undertakings found no advantage in terms of cost-effectiveness (Feigenbaum and Teeples 1983: 672−8).

AGENCY PROBLEMS

In addition to concern with loss-making by some nationalized industries, and the increasing political importance attached to the level of the public sector borrowing requirement, there may also have been a more subtle cause of dissatisfaction with public ownership. While public ownership made governments wholly responsible for the performance of the nationalized industries, the monopoly structure of the industries allied to the public corporation form of control limited the ability of governments to influence their performance. The original intention had been for the board of each nationalized industry to be accountable ultimately to Parliament, but without Parliament or ministers becoming involved in the day-to-day management of the industry. Although the adoption of the public corporation form of organization was intended to allow nationalized industry managers to work at arm's length from government, ministers appear to have found it difficult to keep their distance from public industries. Parliament was supposed to set down the general principles for the operation of each industry concerning such issues as pricing and investment rules, but then refrain from interfering in managerial decisions. In fact, ministers failed to approve clear guidelines for the operation of the industry, but persisted in interfering in a range of matters of political interest, including decisions on the closure of works and railway lines, the siting of steel works (Ravenscraig), the pricing of output and the settling of wage disputes, and the national origin of particular types of plant purchases (SCNI 1968: 115, 226). However, there were also occasions when the monopoly nationalized industries were able to resist the will of ministers by exploiting their superior resources of information and expertise, and their knowledge that the government would not wish to push through politically unpopular decisions, such as increasing output prices or closing capacity, especially close to election time (Chick 1990b).

As problems of control became apparent, opinion within Whitehall moved in favour of the operation of external funding limits and the introduction of test discount rates and required rates of return. By the 1980s, the Thatcher government was relying almost exclusively on external financing limits, which did at least make the broad rules of play clear and did mean that government was only relying on manipulating those instruments over which it had better and fuller information than the industries. However, this did not solve the problem of vetting the veracity and quality of the managerial selection of projects which managers claimed met the required test discount rates.

The recurring problems characterizing relations between government and industry fall into the category of relations referred to by economists as principal–agent relations. In a principal–agent relationship, the principal (owner) and the agent (manager) do not share the same objectives. The principal wants to induce the agent to act in the principal's interest, but he lacks full information about the circumstances and behaviour of the agent, thereby presenting a monitoring problem (Vickers and Yarrow 1988: 9). The principal's main task therefore is to acquire this information, so that he may devise an incentive structure which will elicit from the agent a pattern of behaviour which approximates as closely as possible to that sought by the principal. In devising such an incentive structure, the principal will require information, not only to be able to monitor the agent's behaviour, but also to know what incentives are likely to be most effective on and attractive to the agent. In a relationship where the agent is a monopoly, acquiring this information could prove very difficult for the principal, particularly if the agent does not wish to release information and expertise under its control. In this situation, information is distributed asymmetrically between principal and agent, and these asymmetries of information are commonly seen as making the task of control or regulation considerably more difficult for the principal.

FROM DENATIONALIZATION TO PRIVATIZATION

The privatization of nationalized industries was not immediately seen as an answer to these problems. Indeed, even after the election of the first Thatcher government in 1979, there was little intimation of the importance which the privatization programme of the 1980s was to assume. It was one thing to dislike nationalization; quite another to know what to put in its place. While some sections of the Conservative Party, notably Enoch Powell and Rhodes Boyson, had long called for an end to nationalization, even such ideas of de-nationalization did not figure large in the 1979 election manifesto (Boyson 1971; Tivey 1973). Moreover, while ideas for somehow decoupling nationalized industries from the state were advanced in some quarters, they were different in emphasis from the later enthusiasm for actively promoting private ownership. It was only with time that the vocabulary of de-nationalization gave way to that of privatization. It was as part of the change in mood and toughening of approach provided by Geoffrey Howe in 1981, when amongst other things a very tight budget was announced and the Medium Term Financial Strategy was introduced, that the idea of privatization began to gain momentum. Howe also restated the theme of government dissatisfaction with its powers for improving the efficiency of nationalized industries:

> The Morrisonian constitution grants our nationalised corporations a degree of autonomy which is probably unique in the Western World. In the strict sense of the word they are constitutionally 'irresponsible'. . . . The Government's only real weapon is the threat to reduce or cut off external funds. This is far too drastic to be effective. It is like equipping traffic wardens with anti-tank guns but depriving them of the right to leave parking tickets.
>
> (Howe 1981)

When such admissions were being articulated, the government had only sold part of an inherited ragbag of equity holdings. In this ragbag with the utilities and natural monopolies were the likes of British Aerospace, British Leyland, British Steel and British Shipbuilders. The iron and steel industry, after a brief flirtation with public ownership during the tail-end of the Attlee government, was renationalized in 1967. Despite all attempts at the planned rationalization of the industry under private ownership, by 1967 nationalization was seen as almost the only remaining means of achieving the desired restructuring (Burk 1988). Others of the more recent state acquisitions had fallen into state hands as a last gasp attempt to fend off official liquidation. The rhetoric of rationalization accompanied these acquisitions but, as with British Leyland, while large companies were created, the plant often remained scattered and comparatively small. Elsewhere, government had acquired stakes in defence-related companies, some of which were to the fore in the early, tentative days of de-nationalization (Kramer 1988). In the spirit of de-nationalization, shareholdings were sold in ICL, Ferranti and British Petroleum in 1979, and in Fairey, Sinclair and Alfred Herbert in 1980 and 1981 (Foster 1992: 112). As part of a growing interest in liberalization, express coaching services were deregulated in 1980. The appearance of new entrants like British Coachways with fares set at roughly half those previously charged by the incumbent National Express gave rise to improvements in efficiency through competition which suggested the wider possibilities of shedding the nationalized industries into competitive environments. The sale of National Freight in 1982 to a consortium of managers, employees and company pensioners and the ninefold rise in pre-tax profits between 1981 and 1986 suggested that, given proper incentive structures, employees would respond with enthusiasm as well as accumulating considerable personal wealth. This emphasis on wealth accumulation through private ownership was increasingly a theme of the programme for the sale of council housing. Nearly 600,000 housing units were sold by local authorities between 1979 and 1983, more than in the entire postwar period at that time (Vickers and Yarrow 1988: 156). The programme was popular, and realized almost £2 billion in 1982.

It was in this environment that the ideas for privatizing nationalized industry gathered wider political and public support. While many of the early sales of shares had involved companies already operating in competitive markets, the privatization of British Telecom in 1984 marked the first large-scale sale of a monopoly, network-containing utility. The exhortations of a scruffy cartoon bird named Buzby to buy Telecom shares were followed in 1986 by an advertising campaign featuring the elusive 'Sid' to promote the sale of shares in the British Gas Corporation. More muted advertising campaigns accompanied the privatization of the British Airports Authority (1986), the National Bus Company, the water authorities (1989) and the electricity supply industry (1990–1).

PRIVATIZATION AND COMPETITION

Apart from its importance within a general government programme aimed at increasing private ownership and reducing the public sector borrowing requirement, it was hoped that the privatization of nationalized industries would lead to productivity improvements. To some commentators, the shift to private ownership itself was thought likely to result in improved efficiency (Beesley and Littlechild 1986: 35–57). Of more importance to most economists were the improvements in efficiency likely to result from introducing competition into these former monopoly industries. Initially, government ministers emphasized the incentives to efficiency likely to arise from increasing competition in the industries, but as the programme progressed such references to competition diminished (Moore 1986: 96). The initial privatization of the gas and telecommunication industries were widely criticized as failing to provide or encourage a higher level of competition within each industry. Greater scope for competition was provided for in the later privatization of the electricity industry, but even here this was less than some economists sought. Part of the economists' advocacy of increasing competition derived from the dissatisfaction with the performance of the nationalized industries and disillusion with the inability of such government instruments as the Monopolies Commission to put together an effective anti-trust policy (Gribbin 1978). There has also been an increase in suggestions from economic historians that inadequate competition and the extent of rings and cartel operations may have been an impediment to faster rates of growth in the inter-war British economy (Broadberry and Crafts 1992; Chapter 6 of this volume). The apparent early failure of government to introduce greater competition into many privatized industries provoked some economists to question whether the privatization policy had any remaining rationale (Kay and Thompson 1986: 18–32), many economists seeing the introduction of competition into former nationalized industries as likely to provide the greatest incentives to improvements in efficiency (Kay and Silbertson 1984: 8–16; Shackleton 1984: 59–73).

One explanation of why very limited, if any, competition was introduced into the newly privatized industries was that the transfer of ownership came to assume increasing importance during the period of the Thatcher governments. Building on the success of the sale of council houses and the early and large-scale sale of equity in British Telecom and British Gas, the increase of private ownership became a political aim of wide application. The possibility emerged of a rolling programme of privatizations, which might go on to include less attractive industries like steel, coal and rail. Indeed, leading advocates of privatization anticipated that the greatest benefits were likely to arise from privatizing the National Coal Board, British Rail, the Post Office, British Telecom and the CEGB (Beesley and Littlechild 1986). The wish to maintain the programme's momentum and the increasing political importance of the issue of ownership inclined ministers to seek the co-operation of managers within those industries marked out for privatization. Given the asymmetries of information and technical expertise enjoyed by the nationalized monopolies, securing such co-operation was crucial if any rolling programme was to gather momentum. As managers were unwilling to co-operate in privatizing their industries into highly competitive markets, thereby increasing the uncertainty both to managers and unionized labour, both government and the industry had a natural interest to ignore the economists' emphasis on increasing competition within these industries (Chick 1987: 104–16; 1990a: 1–9). Managers remained reasonably happy, not least because associated with privatization was a significant increase in managerial salaries.

The momentum of the privatization programme was broken by the crash of the London stock market on 'Black Monday', 19 October 1987, and, carrying in its wake, the subsequent failure of the British Petroleum issue. This provided government with pause for thought and there is some evidence that Cecil Parkinson, as Secretary of State for Energy, did attempt to ensure that a greater degree of competition would exist within the eventual structure of the next industry in line for privatization, namely the electricity industry. The consequences were instructive. While the chairman of the Central Electricity Council argued against any privatization of the industry into a competitive structure, the area board chairmen, who had been encouraged to stand on their own feet since the restructuring of the industry in the mid-1950s, fell in with the arguments being made by the supporters of greater competition. The subsequent argument was often conducted in public, with persistent cost investigations being made by the City who were attempting to evaluate the worth of the proposed equity issues. In this process, previously hidden and falsely reported factors concerning the costs of nuclear power in particular came out into the public domain. Not only was the government forced to remove the nuclear stations from the proposed privatization, but the cost to taxpayers of nuclear power and the extent of the allocative inefficiency involved became apparent. If the public was the ultimate principal in any principal–agent relationship, then it seemed clear that the principal had long suffered from overbearing asymmetries of information. Any public interest was likely to be better served by laws preventing people lying to the Stock Exchange than by public ownership on behalf of the people.

REGULATION (AGAIN)

The privatization of utility industries was necessarily accompanied by the return of regulation. Regulation of safety and minimum quality of product continued to be necessary, while regulation was also required to prevent abuse of concentrated market power, whether by restricting output, charging excessive prices, or condoning and protecting inefficiency. A regulator was appointed to each industry. The initial round of appointments saw Bryan Carsberg as Director General of Telecommunications at Oftel, James McKinnon at Ofgas, and later Stephen Littlechild at Offer and Ian Byatt at Ofwat. The main regulatory system chosen was price regulation, based on the RPI $-X$ formula where RPI was the retail price index and X the number chosen by the regulator. The other main form of regulation, that of return on capital which was commonly used in the long-regulated United States, was rejected, partly because of fears of regulatory capture. Being less discretionary, this was less of a danger for RPI $-X$. There was also the theoretical argument that rate of return regulation encouraged over-inflation of the capital investment rate base and distorted a firm's choice of inputs (Averch and Johnson 1962: 1052–69; Baumol and Klevorick 1970: 162–90). Rate of return regulation tended to push pricing towards being based on average cost and thus could prevent the firm from using a multipart tariff that could bring the price (for the marginal unit sold) closer to marginal cost. However, practical experience cast some doubt on whether the Averch–Johnson effect was occurring in practice, not least because American legislation had stopped stock watering, although not necessarily 'gold plating' over-investment (Kahn 1971).

Notwithstanding arguments over inflated rate base, the application of rate of return regulation to the privatized industries in Britain was likely to have faced regulators with the difficulty of obtaining information from monopolistic and oligopolistic industries. Not only did the concentrated structure of the privatized industries continue the principal–agent problems and associated information asymmetries which characterized government–industry relations during nationalization, but the search for appropriate cost–price relationships gave renewed vigour to the rumbling persistent issue of pricing output in utility industries.

The opting for the $RPI - X$ formula ostensibly removed from regulators the task of obtaining the level of information on product cost structure as required by capital return regulation. However, the formula is subject to inefficient strategic manipulation of both prices and costs, particularly as the date of the next regulatory review draws near. The industry may feel reluctant to reduce prices any further once the regulator's main requirements have been met, and in some circumstances may even welcome higher costs. While ostensibly different from rate of return regulation, on closer inspection the differences narrow. The setting of X is presumably determined with a specific return on capital in mind, and if entry deterring cross-subsidizing behaviour is to be prevented, then in places considerable information on costs is required. The $RPI - X$ formula did not afford an immediate check on cross-subsidization, and therefore entry deterrent behaviour. However, while British Telecom's decision to bring prices into line with costs by altering the balance between the charges for long-distance and for local calls did involve an entry deterring reduction of prices in areas where competition from Mercury was present or expected, it did also represent a gain in economic efficiency. That it was unpopular with many domestic users does not detract from its being a gain in economic efficiency (Foster 1992: 206).

The aim of preventing cross-subsidization required more detailed product cost information, exposing regulators to risk of regulatory capture and confronting them with information asymmetry problems arising from the principal (regulator)–agent (industry) problem where the agent was a monopoly or close relation. This information impinged on the setting of X within the $RPI - X$ formula, as the regulator had to know what was a sufficiently high level of X to drive the regulated industry to greater efficiency, but without at the same time squeezing profits so tightly as to deter entrants (Littlechild 1983: 32–3). The setting of a value of X often seems to be a process of trial-and-error and there is also the suspicion that the regulators are attempting to mould the $RPI - X$ formula, which they find inadequate, into a hybrid form of rate of return regulation which allows a better sight of the target of efficiency (Oftel 1985).

COMPETITION AND EFFICIENCY

It was the virtual absence of effective competition in many of the privatized utilities which both made regulation necessary and made effective regulation difficult. One strategy adopted by the regulators in response to the difficulties of obtaining adequate information and devising efficiency incentives was to push for more competition in their industries. In back-handed reflections on privatization, the annual reports of regulators frequently stressed the high priority which they laid on promoting effective competition. As Bryan Carsberg emphasized in his annual report for 1985, he attached a high priority to promoting competition, which he had quickly come to believe was 'one of the most important and urgent tasks laid upon me by the Act' (Oftel 1985: 8). More recently, both regulators and government departments have openly declared their wish to see more competition introduced into the gas and telecommunications industries.

Another strategy adopted in the pursuit of greater information on each industry's cost structure was to make very public threats of legal action against the industry, the object being publicly either to shame or to force the industry to release the information. Such exchanges were a hallmark of relations between James McKinnon at Ofgas and the gas industry (Ofgas 1989: 23–4; 1990: 19–20; 1991: 48–9). Just one such instance was the clash between British Gas and McKinnon in 1987 when McKinnon asked for details of the terms of various supply contracts. Threatened with legal action, British Gas backed down and released the information.

The promotion of competition involved regulators in the issue of interconnection, a term borrowed from the economics of telecommunications. It is particularly relevant to telecommunications, given the existence of network externalities where the utility of each customer is dependent on how many other subscribers are available on the same network. Thus, any new entrant would be at a considerable disadvantage if it was denied access to the existing network of subscribers. However, access to the network is of limited value if the incumbent continues to price so as to deter entry. The regulator therefore has the ultimate power to set the price of access to the network, once negotiations between the parties have come to an impasse. In the 1985 dispute between British Telecom and Mercury, Carsberg intervened to set Mercury a much lower tariff than normal for inland trunk calls, the tariff roughly covering marginal cost with some allowance for profit for Mercury. This did not put an end to disputes between British Telecom and Mercury over the terms of interconnection, but it did represent an improvement over what had gone before (Foster 1992: 171).

It is perhaps too early to offer more than a few commonsense observations and speculative comments on the effects of privatization on the productivity of the industries concerned. One obvious and immediate effect has been the shedding of labour, with employment in public corporations falling from 2.046 million in 1978–9 to 1.161 million in 1986–7, a fall of 43 per cent (Treasury 1988: 83). Some of the most marked improvements in productivity have come in industries awaiting possible privatization (post, steel, rail), one common manifestation being changes in management (Kay and Thomson 1987; Bishop and Kay 1988: 37–46). Alongside these changes in productive efficiency, there is evidence of improvement in allocative efficiency. If privatization is accompanied by a reduction in government interference and an increase in competition, it is likely that prices and costs will come more into line, with domestic consumers losing and industrial consumers gaining from such a development. The cross-subsidizing of domestic consumers by industrial consumers is likely to diminish (Jaffer and Thompson 1986: 45–68). Unprofitable activities are less likely to be tolerated unless a specific social cost–benefit subsidy is paid. Suppliers are also likely to look for the cheapest possible sources of inputs, which will bear hard on industries like coal which have enjoyed long-term supply contracts with the nationalized industries.

This chapter has traced the development of state involvement with utilities from regulation, through nationalization and back to regulation. The argument has been that, while the structures of control may have shifted, the characteristics of the industries (spillovers, decreasing cost, safety of output) which invited state concern have not. At the moment, the pursuit of increased competition in these industries is the dominant cry. This is not surprising. The first generation of regulators were unusually aggressive, with the belief in competition as the least worst system that is the hallmark of neoclassical economists. Many of the regulators were drawn from academic backgrounds. Bryan Carsberg was a Professor of Accountancy at the London School of Economics; Stephen Littlechild was Professor of Commerce at the University of Birmingham; Ian Byatt holds a PhD on the economic history of electricity, and was a lecturer in economics at Durham and in economic history at the London School of Economics between 1958 and 1967, before moving to economic positions within government (Hannah 1990: 369). As economists aware of the difficulties of regulation in monopolistic/duopolistic industries with associated information aysmmetries, they seem likely to press for competition to the greatest possible extent in their industries. This in part appears to derive from a greater understanding and a more explicit discussion of the nature of principal–agent relations as they affect the sometime nationalized industries. Problems clearly remain, but they do appear to be being considered more than they were and in a more open atmosphere in which the limitations arising from asymmetries of information are more keenly appreciated.

NOTE

I am grateful to the editors, Steve Jones and other conference participants for their comments on this chapter. Particular thanks go to Leslie Hannah who produced detailed responses to the first draft. The usual disclaimers apply.

BIBLIOGRAPHY

Averch, H. and Johnson, L. (1962) 'Behaviour of the firm under regulatory constraint', *American Economic Review* 52: 1052–69.
Bailey, E.E. and Panzar, J.C. (1981) 'The contestability of airline markets during the transition to deregulation', *Law and Contemporary Problems* 44: 125–46.
Baumol, W.J. and Klevorick, A.K. (1970) 'Input choices and rate of return regulation: an overview of the discussion', *Bell Journal of Economics* 1: 162–90.
Baumol, W.J., Bailey, E.E. and Willig, R.D. (1977) 'Weak invisible hand theorems in the sustainability of prices in a multiproduct monopoly', *American Economic Review* 67: 350–65.
Beesley, M.E. and Littlechild, S. (1986) 'Privatisation: principles, problems and priorities', in J.A. Kay, C. Mayer and D. Thompson (eds) *Privatisation and Regulation: The UK Experience*, Oxford: Clarendon, 35–57.
Bishop, M. and Kay, J.A. (1988) *Does Privatisation Work?*, London: London Business School.
Boyson, R. (ed.) (1971) *Good-Bye to Nationalisation*, Enfield: Churchill Press for the Constitutional Book Club.
Broadberry, S. and Crafts, N.F.R. (1992) 'Britain's productivity gap in the 1930's: some neglected factors', *Journal of Economic History* 52(3): 531–58.
Burk, K. (1988) *The First Privatisation*, London: Historians Press.
Burn, D. (1961) *The Steel Industry, 1939–59*, Cambridge: Cambridge University Press.
Buxton, N.K. and Aldcroft, D.H. (1979) *British Industry Between the Wars*, London: Scholar Press.
Chester, D.N. (1975) *The Nationalisation of British Industry, 1945–51*, London: HMSO.
Chick, M. (1987) 'Privatisation: the triumph of past practice over current requirements', *Business History* 29: 104–16.
—— (1990a) 'Politics, information and the defence of market power', in M. Chick (ed.) *Governments, Industries and Markets*, Aldershot: Elgar.
—— (1990b) 'Marginal cost pricing and the peak-hour demand for electricity, 1945–51', in M. Chick (ed.) *Governments, Industries and Markets*, Aldershot: Elgar.
—— (1995) 'The political economy of nationalisation: the case of electricity distribution', in R. Millward and J. Singleton (eds) *The Political Economy of Nationalisation in Britain, 1920–50*, Cambridge: Cambridge University Press.

Coase, R.H. (1937) 'The nature of the firm', *Economica* 4: 386–405.
—— (1970) 'The theory of public utility pricing and its application', *Bell Journal of Economics* 1: 113–28.
Crossman, R. (1976) *The Diaries of a Cabinet Minister*, London: Hamish Hamilton, vol. II, p. 524.
Demsetz, H. (1968) 'Why regulate utilities?', *Journal of Law and Economics* 11: 55–65.
Dunkerley, J. and Hare, P.G. (1991) 'The nationalised industries', in N.F.R. Crafts and N. Woodward (eds) *The British Economy Since 1945*, Oxford: Clarendon Press.
Dupuit, J. (1969) 'De la mesure de l'utilité des travaux publics', *Annales des Ponts et Chaussés*; reprinted in Arrow, K. and Scitovsky, T. (eds) (1969) *Readings in Welfare Economics*, Homewood, IL: Irwin, 255–83.
Falkus, M.E. (1977) 'The development of municipal trading in the nineteenth century', *Business History* 19(2): 134–61.
Feigenbaum, S. and Teeples, R. (1983) 'Public versus private water delivery: a hedonic cost approach', *Review of Economics and Statistics* 65: 672–8.
Foreman-Peck, J. (1987) 'Natural monopoly and railway policy in the nineteenth century', *Oxford Economic Papers* 39(4): 699–718.
Foreman-Peck, J. and Waterston, M. (1985) 'The comparative efficiency of public and private enterprise in Britain; electricity generation between the World Wars', *Economic Journal* 95, Supplement.
Foster, C.D. (1992) *Privatisation, Public Ownership and the Regulation of Natural Monopoly*, Oxford: Clarendon Press.
Greasley, D. (1995) 'The coal industry: images and realities on the road to nationalisation', in R. Millward and J. Singleton (eds) *The Political Economy of Nationalisation in Britain, 1920–50*, Cambridge: Cambridge University Press.
Gribbin, J.D. (1978) 'The post-war revival of competition as industrial policy', Government Economic Service Working Paper 19.
Groves, T. and Ledyard, J. (1977) 'Optimal allocation of public goods: a solution to the free rider problem', *Econometrica* 45: 783–809.
Hannah, L. (1977) 'A pioneer of public enterprise: the Central Electricity Board and the National Grid, 1927–1940', in B. Supple (ed.) *Essays in British Business History*, Oxford: Clarendon Press.
—— (1979) *Electricity before Nationalisation*, London: Macmillan.
—— (1990) 'Economic ideas and government policy on industrial organisation in Britain', in M.O. Furner and B. Supple (eds) *The State and Economic Knowledge*, Cambridge: Cambridge University Press.
Hassan, J.A. (1985) 'The growth and impact of the British water industry in the nineteenth century', *Economic History Review* 38(4): 531–47.
HMSO (1976) *A Study of U.K. Nationalised Industries: A Report to the Government by the National Economic Development Office*.
HM Treasury (1988) *Public Expenditure Survey*, London: HMSO.
Hotelling, H. (1938) 'The general welfare in relation to problems of taxation and of railway and utility rates', *Econometrica* 6: 242–69.
Howe, G. (1981) *Privatisation: The Way Ahead*, Conservative Political Centre.
Jaffer, S.M. and Thompson, D.J. (1986) 'Deregulating express coaches: a reassessment', *Fiscal Studies* 7(4): 45–68.

Kahn, A.E. (1971) *The Economics of Regulation: Principles and Institutions*, vol. II, New York: Wiley.

Kahn, A. (1970) *The Economics of Regulation*, Boston, MA: MIT Press.

Kay, J.A. and Silbertson, Z.A. (1984) 'The new industrial policy – privatisation and competition', *Midland Bank Review* Spring: 8–16.

Kay, J. and Thompson, D. (1986) 'Privatisation: a policy in search of a rationale', *Economic Journal* 96: 18–32.

—— and —— (1987) 'Policy for industry', in R. Dornbusch and R. Layard (eds) *The Performance of the British Economy*, Oxford: Oxford University Press.

Kramer, D.C. (1988) *State Capital and Private Enterprise*, London: Routledge.

Lindahl, E. (1958) 'Just taxation – a positive solution', in R.A. Musgrave and A.T. Peacock (eds) *Classics in the Theory of Public Finance*, London: Macmillan, 168–76.

Little, I.M.D. (1951) 'Direct versus indirect taxes', *Economic Journal* 61: 577–84.

Littlechild, S. (1983) *Regulation of British Telecommunications Profitability*, Department of Industry, London: HMSO.

Loeb, M. and Magat, W.A. (1979) 'A decentralised method for utility regulation', *Journal of Law and Economics* 22, 399–404.

Matthews, D. (1986) 'Laissez-faire and the London gas industry in the nineteenth century; another look', *Economic History Review* 39(2): 244–63.

Matthews, R.C.O., Feinstein, C.H. and Oddling-Smee, J.C. (1982) *British Economic Growth, 1856–1973*, Oxford: Clarendon Press.

Millward, R. (1989) 'Privatisation in historical perspective: the U.K. water industry', in D. Cobham, R. Harrington and G. Zis (eds) *Money, Trade and Payments*, Manchester: Manchester University Press.

—— (1991) 'Emergence of gas and water monopolies in nineteenth century Britain: contested markets and public control', in J. Foreman-Peck (ed.) *New Perspectives on the Late Victorian Economy*, Cambridge: Cambridge University Press.

Millward, R. and Parker, D. (1983) 'Public and private enterprise: relative behaviour and efficiency', in R. Millward, L. Rosenthal, M.T. Sumner and N. Topham (eds) *Public Sector Economics*, London: Longman.

Millward, R. and Ward, R. (1987) 'The costs of public and private gas enterprise in late nineteenth century Britain', *Oxford Economic Papers* 39: 719–37.

Moore, J. (1986) 'The success of privatisation', in J.A. Kay, C. Mayer and D. Thompson (eds) *Privatisation and Regulation: The U.K. Experience*, Oxford: Clarendon Press.

Morrison, H. (1933) *Socialisation and Transport*, London: Constable.

Ofgas (1989) *Annual Report 1989*, 12 February 1990, London: HMSO.

—— (1990) *Annual Report 1990*, 12 February 1991, London: HMSO.

—— (1991) *Annual Report 1991*, 11 February 1992, London: HMSO.

Oftel (1984) *Annual Report 5th August to 31 December 1984*, 3 July 1985, London: HMSO.

—— (1985) *Annual Report 1985*, London: HMSO.

Pratten, C. (1990) *Applied Macroeconomics*, 2nd edn, Oxford: Clarendon Press.

Pryke, R. (1981) *The Nationalised Industries: Policies and Performance since 1968*, Oxford: Martin Robertson.

—— (1982) 'The comparative performance of public and private enterprise', *Fiscal Studies* 3(2): 66–81.

Ramsey, F. (1927) 'A contribution to the theory of taxation', *Economic Journal* 37: 47–61.

Reid Committee (1945) *Committee Report on the Coal Industry*, Cmnd 6610.

Richardson, G.B. (1960) *Information and Investment*, Oxford: Clarendon Press.

SCNI (1968) Select Committee on Nationalised Industries, vol. I, London: HMSO.

Shackleton, J.R. (1984) 'Privatisation: the case examined', *National Westminster Bank Review* 1984: 59–73.

Sharkey, W. (1982) *The Theory of Natural Monopoly*, Cambridge: Cambridge University Press.

Spence, A.M. (1974) *Market Signaling: Informational Transfer in Hiring and Related Screening Processes*, Cambridge, MA: Harvard University Press.

—— (1977) 'Entry, capacity, investment and oligopolistic pricing', *Bell Journal of Economics* 10: 1–19.

Starkie, D. (1984) 'B.R. privatisation without tears', *Economic Affairs* 18(4): 16–19.

Supple, B. (1986) 'Ideology or pragmatism? The nationalisation of coal, 1916–46', in N. McKendrick and R.B. Outhwaite (eds) *Business Life and Public Policy*, Cambridge: Cambridge University Press.

—— (1987) *The History of the British Coal Industry*, vol. 4, Oxford: Clarendon Press.

Tivey, L. (ed.) (1973) *The Nationalised Industries since 1960*, London: Allen & Unwin.

Tolliday, S. (1987) *Business, Banking and Politics*, Cambridge, MA: Harvard University Press.

Vickers, J. and Yarrow, G. (1988) *Privatisation: An Economic Analysis*, Cambridge, MA: MIT Press.

Vickrey, W. (1961) 'Counterspeculation, auctions and competitive sealed tenders', *Journal of Finance* 16: 8–37.

Vogelsang, I. and Finsinger, J. (1979) 'A regulatory adjustment process for optimal pricing by multiproduct monopoly firms', *Bell Journal of Economics* 10: 157–71.

Weir Committee (1926) *Report of the [Weir] Committee appointed to review the National Problem of the Supply of Electrical Energy*, HMSO.

White Paper (1961) *Financial and Economic Obligations of the Nationalised Industries*, Cmnd 1337.

—— (1967) *Nationalised Industries: A Review of Economic and Financial Objectives*, Cmnd 3437.

Williamson, O.E. (1976) 'Franchise bidding for natural monopolies – in general and with respect to CATV', *Bell Journal of Economics* 7: 73–104.

13 Investment in human capital and British manufacturing industry to 1990

Mary B. Rose

One of the most striking contrasts, in comparing British business development with the United States, Germany and Japan over the last century and a half, is the attitude displayed towards human capital investment by employers, workers and the state. Amongst Britain's principal competitors, employers have long viewed training of their workforce as an investment, the return on which would be enhanced business performance and competitiveness. In Britain, by contrast, training has more often been viewed as a cost. As a consequence, it has been neglected and only comparatively rarely and belatedly in the twentieth century viewed as a vital part of business strategy. Thus, whilst by the 1980s leading employers in Japan, West Germany and the United States were devoting 3 per cent of annual turnover to training, the comparative figure in Britain was 0.14 per cent (Gospel 1992: 158; Fitzgerald 1993: 97).

The failure of firms to value human resources during the nineteenth and early twentieth centuries was not only reflected in education. The patchiness of company welfare schemes and personnel management before 1914, for example, whilst partly a consequence of the slow development of large-scale companies in Britain, is also indicative of a neglect of human capital. This is because welfare, especially pension schemes, were initially associated with efforts to create an internal market of firm-specific labour, even if they subsequently were extended to manual labour (Hannah 1986: 67; Gospel 1992: 74–5). Although by no means the only supply-side explanation of the loss of competitive advantage by many of Britain's manufacturing firms in the twentieth century, the significance of this negligence with respect to human resources, whilst difficult to measure, should not be underrated.

At all levels, state educational policies also diverged. In the late nineteenth century, for example, the German government pursued centrally co-ordinated education policies. In the United States, too, both State and Federal governments gave priority to the development of education. In twentieth-century Japan, on the other hand, education came second only to national unity and defence (Lazonick 1986: 105–19; Lockwood 1965: 510). In Britain in the late nineteenth century, however, although governments showed some awareness of the importance of education, central co-ordination was avoided in favour of local control. At the same time, state funding of education remained distinctly limited until after the Second World War (Barnett 1986: 231–2).

Not only has human capital been perceived differently in Britain, but the levels of educational attainment of managers appear to have been markedly higher elsewhere. In Britain in the mid-1950s, therefore, less than half of directors and around 20 per cent of managers had degrees, a level of graduate participation in business which was surpassed in Germany, Japan and the United States in the 1920s (Keeble 1992: 51–2). Although the next twenty years saw a rise in the proportion of senior executives with degrees, by the early 1970s Britain was still lagging behind the rest of the industrialized world. Only half of top management in Britain's large manufacturing firms (and far less in smaller firms) were graduates, compared with between 80 and 90 per cent in Europe and the United States. In addition, few British executives, outside the leading companies, either received specialist management training or had achieved a high level of technical competence. Instead, as generalist administrators, either with degrees totally unrelated to their business career or with a training in accountancy, they often lacked any technical understanding of manufacturing (Aldcroft 1992: 103–9).

The postwar deficiencies in the education of managers and executives pale into insignificance in comparison with the formal education and levels of training of the workforce. In terms of mass education, the twentieth century has been littered with lost opportunities, especially with respect to continuation education. This was especially true in the period following the 1944 Education Act. Then, despite a general rise in educational opportunities, the provision of training and education, for the non-academic teenager, was woefully inadequate and compared unfavourably with Britain's main competitors (Sanderson 1988: 38–50). The absence of any defined educational route for the majority of school leavers, especially following the decline in apprenticeships from the 1970s, has led to a serious waste of human resources and has limited the impact of any training schemes devised by employers (Keep and Mayhew 1988: vii).

This chapter explores precisely why British attitudes towards human resources should have diverged so markedly from practice elsewhere. It balances the long-term influence of practices evolved during the Industrial Revolution against changes in human capital investment, by both employers and the state, in response to foreign competition, war and social change since 1870. The chapter is divided into four sections. The first focuses on the Industrial Revolution. It highlights the extent to which the peculiar configuration of demographic and labour market conditions, with pre-existing industrial patterns, meant that Britain's industrialists had little cause to devote much of their firm's resources to training. The second section, which covers the late nineteenth century and inter-war period, illustrates the way in which foreign competition led to changes in educational provision, if not to attitudes of employers. In the third section deficiencies in the provision of training and indeed in the educational system which have emerged since 1945 are explored. In the fourth conclusions concerning the impact of human capital deficiencies on the performance of British manufacturing industry are drawn.

1780–1830: THE INDUSTRIAL REVOLUTION

The decision of an employer to invest in the human capital of the workforce is informed by a number of considerations. These include the elasticity in the supply of labour, especially skilled labour, the nature of the product and of markets served, and hence the likely return on any investment. Where employers make substantial provision for training and where, by implication, their competitive advantage is dependent upon a highly trained labour force, employers tend to be keen that they, rather than their competitors, are the beneficiaries. Thus in firms where training has been internalized, welfare, especially pension schemes and other non-pecuniary benefits, may be used in an effort to create an internal labour market (Gospel 1992: 9–10). In Britain during the Industrial Revolution few factory and mine owners made extensive investments in human capital or made strenuous efforts to retain labour. Just why this was so can best be appreciated in the context of local labour markets.

It is generally accepted that the availability of an abundant supply of cheap labour was of fundamental importance during British industrialization (Pollard 1978: 102; Habakkuk 1962). Population growth, steady before 1780, accelerated afterwards to reach a rate of 0.91 per cent per annum over the next twenty years. By 1800 Britain's population had reached 10.5 million and over the next fifty years had doubled to stand at 20.9 million in 1851. It is now clear that the initial rise in Britain's population owed most to changes in the birth rate, although the precise causality remains the subject of debate (Lee and Schofield 1981: 17–35; Wrigley and Schofield 1981; Mokyr 1983; Anderson 1985). The result was an abundance of labour which influenced both industrial technology and the organization of work. Whether attention is directed towards those few industries which became factory based or to the numerous sectors organized on an outwork basis or in workshops, British industry between 1780 and 1850 was overwhelmingly labour intensive. The boundaries between the factory and the non-factory sector were often blurred. As Samuel has argued:

> Mechanization in one department of production was complemented by an increase in sweating in others; the growth of large firms by a proliferation of small producing units; the concentration of production in factories by the spread of outwork in the home.
>
> (Samuel 1977: 17)

That this occurred was partly a product of the relatively slow evolution of efficient technology, but was also a reflection of a cheap and plentiful supply of labour in industrial communities.

What is especially striking about British demography in this period is the relative youthfulness of the population. By the early nineteenth century it would seem that around 24 per cent of the population was aged between 5 and 14 (Wrigley and Schofield 1981: 528–9). Given such high dependency rates, it is not surprising that child and female labour was to play a significant role in Britain's early industrialization. In a world where children were an economic asset, the family rather than the individual wage earner represented the normal economic unit (Nardinelli 1980: 739–55).

Child and female labour was especially widely used in textiles in the late eighteenth and early nineteenth centuries in both the factory and non-factory sectors, and women were also extensively employed in the metal trades (Berg 1985: 12; 1987: 64–98; Berg and Hudson 1992: 35–8; Hudson 1992: 162–4). Coal mining, on the other hand, with a few regional exceptions such as eastern Scotland, was predominantly male. In this sector, however, juvenile labour was important. Indeed in a significant number of areas the use of child labour continued into the second half of the nineteenth century (Church 1986: 192–5).

The link between demographic and economic change during the eighteenth and early nineteenth centuries was undoubtedly a complex one and national trends mask significant regional variations. The specific social and economic characteristics of different protoindustrial areas undoubtedly influenced patterns of nuptuality and migration, and hence demographic trends (Medick 1976; Hudson 1992: 140). There was not a simple relationship between increasing economic opportunity and population growth, especially in areas of high in-migration or where there were declining sectors. As a result of disequilibria and lags between the existence of employment opportunities and rising birth rates, it can be argued that the British Industrial Revolution occurred against a background of pockets of surplus labour. In London, for example, in the second half of the eighteenth century, there was a crisis of poverty, the most intractable problem being child poverty (Rose 1989: 7–9). Similarly underemployment was not unusual in many agricultural areas in mainland Britain and Ireland in the eighteenth and nineteenth centuries (Berg 1985: 65–102).

Population growth, therefore, sometimes exceeded the ability of a local economy to absorb labour. Similarly, especially between 1780 and 1820 the quest for water power led manufacturers into ever more isolated locations whilst, especially in the northeast, the spread of coal mining activity was often to areas far from centres of population (Pollard 1965: 191–6; Chapman 1967: 156). Certainly, indigenous labour supplies were sometimes scanty and it was often necessary to import both skilled and unskilled labour. Yet for the factory sector employers' difficulties should not be exaggerated, for labour requirements were modest. In addition their quest for workers should be set against the policies and attitudes of the Poor Law authorities.

The idea that the owners of isolated mills and mines supplemented indigenous sources of labour by using the parish apprenticeship system is well rehearsed in the literature (Smelser 1959: 104–10; Pollard 1965: 194–6; Chapman 1967: 156–83). Recent research has shown, however, that it was only the larger employers, and those with especially notorious local reputations, who found it necessary to bring batches of children long distances (Rose 1989: 5–32). The rest were able to rely on the connivance of local parochial authorities in their quest for supplies of poor children (Lane 1977: 267), especially if other sources of employment were declining. Eager to reduce the burdens of supporting the poor, eighteenth-century Poor Law authorities sometimes welcomed factories as a source of employment, even if they were subsequently horrified by conditions of work (Rose 1989: 21–3). Conversely, it is probable that some eighteenth-century factory masters chose districts because good water power was accompanied by plentiful supplies of poor children (Chapman 1967: 167).

Against this background of a growing population where pockets of poverty could overburden parish authorities, it would be surprising if much factory labour, but especially child labour, was viewed by employers as anything more than a renewable resource. Although some children were doubtless employed for their manual dexterity, many child textile factory workers were engaged in little more than sweeping floors and cleaning machinery. In mines, on the other hand, children often spent their time opening trap doors to allow the passage of trucks (Church 1986: 194; Rose 1986: 109). As a result, the level of human capital investment by factory and mine owners in much of their substantial juvenile workforces was very limited, as inevitably were the efforts to retain their labour within the firm.

It should not be concluded, however, that skill was irrelevant to the success of individual firms in the late eighteenth and early nineteenth centuries. What is particularly striking is the extent to which factory owners used internal and external contracts, based upon the reservoir of skills in their community, rather than devoting their own resources to training. There were of course instances, especially amongst the patentees such as Arkwright, Wedgwood and Watt, where skills were firm specific. In such cases the firm's continued competitive advantage was dependent partly on their patent but also on the often difficult task of ensuring that skilled workers did not leave (Dutton 1984: 111). They were the exceptions, however, and in the majority of factories and mines in the Industrial Revolution training was external to the firm, though often internal to the community.

Isolated by their dependence on water power or by geological peculiarities, early factory or mine owners were especially reliant on skills originally gained outside the firm. They may have been able to rely upon pockets of poverty for their unskilled labour force, but they normally had to attract mechanics or hewers and encourage them to remain. In such circumstances, even though their own personal investment in the skill of their workforce was limited, their very isolation meant that they were keen to create a skilled labour market which was internal both to the firm and the community.

They did this especially by providing housing. In regions such as the Midlands, north Lancashire, northeast Cheshire, in Scotland and North Wales, reliance on water power by factory owners led to a proliferation of factory villages. In mining in northeastern England, on the other hand, free housing became part of the labour contract and was so entrenched by the late nineteenth century as to be part of the collective bargaining process (McKendrick 1961: 30–55; Pollard 1964; Chapman 1967: 158–9; Daunton 1980: 164–5; Church 1986: 277;

Rose 1986: 38–9, 111–21). Specific skilled groups were often the eighteenth-century targets of housing, a selectivity which anticipated attitudes detected in the second half of the nineteenth century (Lazonick 1979: 231–49; More 1980). In the late nineteenth century, for example, Clydeside shipbuilders used housing to counteract shortages of particular grades of labour rather than as a response to a general labour shortage (Melling 1981: 288).

In some instances, especially amongst the larger and more successful employers such as Arkright, Strutt, Owen and Greg, cottage building was a precursor to wider development. Through the adoption of paternalist strategies they created labour markets which were internal to the community and hence the firm (Pollard 1965: 231–42; Butt 1971: 84; Rose 1986: 13–35). These factory owners sought to improve work efficiency, which included reducing labour turnover, through the provision of reasonable working conditions, regularity of employment and community development. Schools, shops, chapels and recreational facilities gave form and values to isolated communities from which, by the 1820s and 1830s, employers might draw an increasing proportion of all types of labour (Pollard: 1963: 513–19; Rose 1986: 102–22; Fitton 1989: 187–9).

Contingency, tempered by religious principles and sometimes the influence of an entrepreneur's wife, therefore, encouraged the establishment of educational facilities within factory colonies (Child 1964: 293–311; Davidoff and Hall 1987: 99–100). It would be misleading, however, to interpret this, in the majority of cases, as an investment in the human capital of the workforce. Some employers undoubtedly viewed education as essential to the improvement of the individual. Yet the suspicion remains that the return which factory colonizers anticipated from providing schools was a rise in productivity from greater docility rather than from enhanced skill (Boyson 1970: 95). After all, for the majority of factory jobs at this time literacy was of limited importance except among such key workers as bookkeepers and mechanics.

Manufacturers during the British Industrial Revolution may have relied heavily upon water power, but by the early 1800s steam power was becoming increasingly popular. By the 1820s, technological improvements to steam engines contributed to a growing locational concentration in industry (Musson 1976: 420–5). Access to coal resources became crucial and factory-based industry became increasingly urban. Moreover, by the 1840s migration and population growth saw the merging of some industrial villages with existing towns (Marshall 1968: 216–20). As a predominantly rural industrial environment gave way to one which was increasingly urban, so it is possible to detect some adjustment to the attitude of employers to their community and inevitably to their workforce. In urban areas employers were able to rely on local concentrations of skill rather than relying on skills which had been imported and housed in communities of their own making. In this environment training was more often based in the community than in the firm and was provided via an array of internal and external contracts.

Systems of internal contracting, whereby factory and mine owners passed such managerial functions as recruitment and training to skilled, usually male, workers, were widespread and were to be found in textiles, ironmaking, shipbuilding, mining and pottery (Gospel 1992: 19). Factory mule spinners, for example, controlled virtually all aspects of their work from maintenance of their machinery to the choice of helpers. Out of piece-rate wages they recruited, trained and remunerated their piecers who, in turn, could look forward to the prospect of rising to become spinners. It was a hierarchical system, therefore, which almost exactly replicated the craft-based apprentice system (Chapman 1900: 468–9; Taylor 1960: 215–35). In a range of other skilled activities, including shipbuilding and engineering, sub-contracting underpinned formal rather than informal apprenticeship. Themselves the product of custom, craft apprenticeships can be traced back to the Elizabethan Statute of Artificers. Such apprenticeships, which were usually of fixed duration and provided transferable skills, formed the basis of shopfloor training during the Industrial Revolution (Elbaum 1991: 196–7).

Internal contracting of this sort is indicative of the attitude of many nineteenth-century employers and workers to human capital. The reservoirs of traditional skill in Britain's developing industrial communities meant that it was feasible to pass responsibility for the recruitment and training of future skilled labour to key members of the workforce. This substantially reduced the burdens of management, made it easier to control and train a juvenile workforce and allowed flexibility in the face of market fluctuations (Littler 1982: 66–7). Such relationships were inseparable from the paternalist strategies which Joyce has identified for much of urban Lancashire in the second half of the nineteenth century. There the 'minder piecer system' persisted in mule spinning, and overlookers, themselves often drawn from the ranks of skilled workers, combined key factory positions with prominence in the community. This role

as the master's agent and yet part of the workforce gave [the overlooker] a crucial and mediating role in the life of the factory.

(Joyce 1980: 101)

From the perspective of workers, on the other hand, personal skill was equated with bargaining power. It was the skill of hand mule spinners, for instance, which had given them the market power to perpetuate a traditional practice in the factory age (Lazonick 1990: 95). By restricting entry into skilled trades, internal contracting helped to preserve this labour market strength. Thus the introduction of the self-acting mule in the 1830s and 1840s did not undermine the traditional organization of work. Instead the craft orientation of mule spinning was reinforced by both unions and employers, with internal contracting surviving until after 1945. Similarly in skilled trades where apprenticeship was the norm, foremen, themselves usually skilled workers, retained considerable control over the training process (Lazonick 1990: 95; Elbaum 1991: 194–212; Singleton 1991: 53).

The existence in some communities of reservoirs of traditional skill did not just give rise to internal contracting in factories. It could mean that some skilled activities remained outside the factory well into the nineteenth century. Indeed a remarkably small proportion of Britain's skilled labour worked in factories during the Industrial Revolution. The 'other industrial revolution' included:

> industry and artisan workshops much more than it did the factory system. [It was an] industrial revolution which relied on tools, small machines and skilled labour much more than it did steam engines and automatic processes . . .
>
> (Berg 1985: 12)

Clusters of skilled outworkers and artisans employed in small workshops can sometimes be found serving the needs of the factory owner. In volatile markets, the ability to tap skill, which was external to the factory but internal to the community, allowed factory owners flexibility in the face of rapidly changing demand (Lyons 1985: 419–26; Berg 1993). This merely served to reinforce the view of employers that training need not be internalized within factories.

There was as a result little need to create internal labour markets in urban areas. Huberman has argued that, even in large urban centres like Manchester and Bolton before 1850, the bargaining power of skilled cotton workers in large firms ensured that they enjoyed a relatively high degree of job security and developed long attachments with particular firms (Huberman 1986: 987–98; 1987: 177–92). Just how far such practices extended beyond a few large firms is unclear

(Rose *et al.* 1989: 89–103). But generally, it is likely that labour markets remained external to individual firms, although often specific to a particular urban community, a phenomenon which was reflected in paternalist strategies.

In the 'model' colonies resources had been directed towards creating economic and social microcosms where labour was tied to one employer. Where skill and training derived from the community rather than being transplanted and where there was a range of employment possibilities, firm-specific paternalist investments were not an option. Instead, in this setting investments made by employers were rarely directed specifically towards their own workforce, but rather to the entire community in which, until the late nineteenth century, they were usually resident. By endowing churches, hospitals, schools, mechanics institutes, parks and public buildings, the owners of family firms were able to enhance their social and political prestige within the community (Howe 1984: 307). Yet just as schools in the rural factory colonies should not be confused with human capital investment, so it should not be assumed that by endowing mechanics institutes urban employers expected to improve the skill of their workforce. Such moves were very much a reflection of a belief in the importance of self-help and self-improvement for the individual rather than developments intended to enhance business performance.

FORMAL EDUCATION AND INDUSTRY, 1870–1939

The role of formal education in Britain's Industrial Revolution was distinctly limited. The modest technological requirements of the world's first industrializer meant that experience was more significant than scholarship. Indeed, amongst textile workers levels of literacy actually fell during the Industrial Revolution, though the obligation of textile mill owners to provide schooling for children they employed began to reverse this trend by the 1830s (Sanderson 1972a: 75–104; Schofield 1973: 450). The limited impact of formal education was not confined to the workforce. Only that minority of businessmen who had attended the Dissenting Academies and taken courses at the Scottish universities had received much formal education. Nevertheless the impact of the community-based scientific studies on the dissemination of knowledge should not be underestimated (Schofield 1972; Keeble 1992: 39). Practical skill rather than academic aptitude was thus deemed to be the basis of business success in many spheres. In engineering, for example, even in the mid-nineteenth century, the only technical training that many leading practitioners such as

Armstrong, Mather, Whitworth and Fairbairn had received was an apprenticeship. Equally Brunel was openly suspicious of theoretical training (Roderick and Stephens 1972: 117; Buchanan 1989: 163). On the other hand, as far as management was concerned, in the majority of family firms in textiles the most normal training was in-house experience (Keeble 1992: 39). It is true that from the mid-nineteenth century there was an increased tendency for the sons of industrialists to receive public school education, yet its classical bias had little relevance for business. In any event, it was a trend confined to a small elite of successful, long-established, industrial families. For the majority of owners of small family businesses, formal education remained limited throughout the nineteenth century.

Not surprisingly, given the Classical bias of Oxford and Cambridge, there were virtually no links between English universities and industry in the late eighteenth and early nineteenth centuries (Sanderson 1972b: 1–30). This is not to say that science was irrelevant to industry at this time. Rather it is to argue that, just as employers tapped the indigenous skill of their communities for practical expertise, local institutions proved invaluable conduits of scientific information (see Chapter 3 for further discussion of business communities). Informal links were reinforced between predominantly nonconformist scientists and businessmen through the provincial scientific societies such as the Birmingham Lunar Society (Schofield 1972: 136–47; Thackray 1974: 675–705).

In the late nineteenth century, the upsurge of foreign competition, the beginnings of a shift in the industrial base, technological changes and an increase in the size of firms all altered the economic environment. The First World War, on the other hand, exerted unprecedented pressure on British industry and highlighted the need for technical expertise, if productivity growth was to be achieved. These trends undoubtedly influenced both the supply of and demand for formal and especially technical education. There was, moreover, a proliferation of professional associations and qualifications after 1880, in spheres such as accountancy and engineering (Roderick and Stephens 1972: 121–2; Buchanan 1989: 96–103; Perkin 1989: 20). Yet if British experience in this period is compared with that of Germany or the United States, the response to challenges seems muted and patchy. These contrasts are perhaps best explained with reference to differing historical influences on economic and social development, as well as on government policy.

More than any other late-nineteenth-century trend, it was the chastening effect of foreign competition which focused attention on deficiencies in British education. Growing foreign prowess in science-based sectors was combined with the difficulties of the staple industries between the 1870s and 1890s. As steel replaced iron in the second half of the nineteenth century, Britain, from being a world leader, was overtaken first by the United States and then by Germany. In chemicals too British producers lost market share to German firms which, by 1913, controlled 85 per cent of the world dyestuffs market (Wrigley 1986: 170). There emerged by the late 1860s a vociferous applied science lobby, composed primarily of professional men, academics, politicians and, interestingly, comparatively few industrialists, who were convinced that Britain's ability to retain industrial leadership was dependent upon scientific and technical education (Hennock 1990: 300). This view was confirmed by the findings of several Select Committees and Royal Commissions, of which the most important were those on Scientific Instruction (1867–8), Technical Instruction (1882–4) and Depression in Trade and Industry (1886). These pointed especially to unfavourable contrasts with educational practice in Germany (Pollard 1989: 272–3; Sanderson 1988: 39). There is, indeed, ample evidence that where industrialists needed scientifically trained personnel in the late nineteenth century, as in the Merseyside chemical industries, they looked to Germany either for substitute education or for scientists (Roderick and Stephens 1972: 122–9).

Cultural and institutional explanations of British economic decline have highlighted the deficiencies in Britain's late nineteenth century education system, especially with regard to science and technology. Designed for the socialization of gentlemen and based on outmoded values, the British education system, it has been conventionally argued, failed to meet the needs of industry in the changing world of the late nineteenth century (Landes 1969: 347; Wiener 1981; Lazonick 1986: 101–46; 1991: 48; Wrigley 1986: 162–3). Yet even with respect to the public school system there is remarkably little evidence of a negative influence on economic growth (Berghoff 1990). Similarly, the idea that education generally failed British industry in the late nineteenth century cannot be sustained. This is because many of the deficiencies in the quality, if not the quantity, of scientific and technical education identified in the parliamentary inquiries were removed between 1890 and 1910 (Sanderson 1988: 38–40).

Much of the development was on a local rather than a national level, however, with individual business communities spawning technical schools, colleges and universities to meet their specific requirements. Between 1851 and 1902, therefore, a period which also saw the continued proliferation of provincial scientific societies, eleven new provincial civic universities and university colleges were founded. These were initially financed primarily by industrialists. The array of scientific departments in these institutions thus reflected local industrial profiles, with high quality departments of metallurgy at Sheffield and textile chemistry at Manchester and Leeds. This expansion stimulated a sixtyfive-fold growth in the numbers of science and technology graduates between 1870 and 1910 (Roderick and Stephens 1972: 124; Sanderson 1972b: 1–30; Floud 1984: 7; Pollard 1989: 162–204). Curricula innovation was not, however, confined to science and technology. At the London School of Economics and the civic universities, especially Birmingham and Manchester, late-nineteenth-century developments in scientific education were matched, in the early twentieth century and inter-war period, by the expansion of economics and business-related subjects (Keeble 1992: 97–124).

Shortcomings in sub-university technical education were also met at a local level. In London, where the apprenticeship had virtually disappeared, technical colleges and polytechnics were established under the auspices of the City and Guilds Institute (Sanderson 1988: 42–3). Similarly the Technical Instruction Act of 1889 empowered local authorities to levy a rate to establish municipal technical colleges. The Local Taxation (Customs and Excise) Act of the following year also made substantial additional revenue available for technical education (Pollard 1989: 162–204; Sanderson 1988: 38–43; Hennock 1990: 310–11).

The largest late-nineteenth-century gap in the education system, in comparison with Germany, was in school level and continuation technical education. Plans for junior technical schools were aired following the 1902 Education Act, though provision remained patchy and localized throughout the inter-war period, with only 230 junior technical schools established in England by 1937–8. In Leeds, for example, during the inter-war period only one in thirty boys proceeded from elementary school to a junior technical school (Barnett 1986: 232; Jenkins 1987: 116; Sanderson 1988: 43–4). It was the wartime skill shortage, however, which prompted government-controlled initiatives under the umbrella of the Ministry of Munitions. Yet neither the hundred technical schools and twelve instructional factories, established during the First World War, nor central government co-ordination of continuation education long survived the war (Fitzgerald 1993: 86). The 1918 Education Act did raise the school leaving age to 14 and required compulsory part-time continuation education. But along with other plans for postwar reconstruction, continuation education was a victim of the Geddes axe of 1922, and further significant expansion of technical education had to await rearmament in 1938 (Barnett 1986: 233; Sanderson 1988: 43; Kirby and Rose 1991: 32).

Despite government concern over the manifest shortcomings of British technical and scientific education there was therefore remarkably little central co-ordination of educational reform. In addition, whilst there was some growth in state funding of education after 1880, British government investment in human resources lagged behind Germany and the United States (Aldcroft 1992: 21). Rather than creating a centrally controlled education system, the reforms of the late nineteenth century confirmed the symbiotic relationship between the needs and resources of localities and all levels of educational provision. Where taxation (as opposed to private donation or rates) was used to finance education, as under the Local Taxation Act of 1890, 'county and borough authorities [enjoyed] all the discretion normally associated with local finance' (Hennock 1990: 311). Condemned by Barnett as the British 'instinct for localism' (Barnett 1986: 232) this tendency, which contrasts so sharply with experience in Germany, is the result of more than the legacy of a generation of limited government intervention.

The willingness of individual German states and later the German government to invest in education is well known. But even in the less interventionist United States government funding of the Land Grant institutions, which included the Massachusetts Institute of Technology, was of great importance to the spread of high level technological education (Lazonick 1986: 105–15). That successive British governments behaved so differently from those of their major competitors can partly be explained by the prevailing *laissez-faire* orthodoxy. This attitude, inseparable from a belief in balanced budgets, persisted throughout the late nineteenth and early twentieth centuries and certainly restricted government expenditure. In the inter-war period, on the other hand, as so often in the twentieth century, British macroeconomic policy was driven by external rather than domestic considerations. Thus in the 1920s the anti-inflationary measures necessary to restore the Gold Standard at pre-war parity meant the sacrifice of expanded government expenditure on technical education. Yet the apparent straitjacket of budgetary and fiscal orthodoxy was not the only explanation of limited central government involvement in technical and scientific education. Differences in the experience of industrialization were also important explanations of variations in government policy.

The relative backwardness of later industrializers in comparison with Britain, and the consequent shortage of skilled labour, created a need for a more co-ordinated, centralized approach to education (Pollard 1989: 146–7). In Germany the demand for technical personnel for state service contributed to a closely co-ordinated education policy (Hennock 1990: 300–1). Equally, the early superiority of British manufactures forced the conclusion that

> We are obliged to make up for our lack of money and limited experience by means of intellectual power and scientific insight.
> (Quoted by Hennock 1990: 301)

In Britain, on the other hand, state demand for technical personnel was more limited. In addition early industrial development had been dependent upon extensive supplies of pre-industrial skill, whilst heavily localized industrial development had created pockets of wealth and influence in provincial business communities (Garrard 1983; see Chapter 3 for a discussion of provincial business communities). This made the finance of localized educational development to meet the needs of industry feasible before the 1890s. The comparative autonomy of county and borough councils in educational policy also perpetuated local control of education.

A local rather than national solution to the late-nineteenth-century shortcomings of British scientific and technical education may have been the natural consequence of past development, but it had long-term implications. At all levels, scientific and technical education was patchy and this limited the overall scale of provision. In comparison with the United States and Germany, for example, the numbers of technological graduates in Britain remained paltry. Thus, whereas in Germany and the United States there were respectively 10,740 and 13,465 technology graduates in 1901–2, in Britain the figure stood at 3,370, a deficiency which influenced both industrial performance and industrial mix. Conversely, in the case of Germany it has been argued that the sheer volume of engineering graduates was of fundamental importance to superior industrial performance before 1939. During the inter-war years, commercial and related subjects proved even less popular in Britain, with only 647 people taking commerce degrees at Manchester, Birmingham and London in this period. Since many of these were civil servants and teachers, the impact on industry must have been slight indeed (Roderick and Stephens 1972: 114; Locke 1989: 98; Keeble 1992: 97–124; Guagnini 1993: 37; König 1993: 65). In the sub-university sector, on the other hand, the sharp variations in the provision of technical education in the inter-war period served to perpetuate nineteenth-century experience (Marsden 1987: 25–59).

Investment in education and training by British employers has been described as a missing dimension. Only a minority of large nineteenth-century firms, usually outside the staple industries, encouraged their employees to gain professional qualifications. Similarly, it was normally only those firms facing specific skill shortages in engineering, such as the textile machine makers Mather and Platt, which internalized training (Fitzgerald 1993: 78–84). Whereas in the United States and Germany the industrial demand for graduates and formal qualifications rose in the late nineteenth century and inter-war period, in Britain any increase was very modest (Chandler 1977: 466–7; Locke 1984: 80–1; Lazonick 1986: 105–19). Even with the limited numbers of science, technology and commercial graduates in Britain, there is no evidence of a supply deficiency. Rather employers and indeed trade unionists demonstrated an ambivalence bordering on hostility to formal qualifications in general and to graduates in particular. A degree was seen as a positive disadvantage for managerial employment in many industries and indeed also in insurance and banking. In the staple industries, for example, a science or engineering graduate was thought to have spent too long with theory at the expense of shopfloor experience. This suspicion of theory was also extended to graduates in economics or other business-related disciplines (Coleman 1973: 113; Pollard 1982: 198; Keeble 1992: 85).

Rarely highly educated themselves, few employers saw sub-university level technical education for shopfloor workers as bringing important benefits to their firms. In engineering and other skilled trades, therefore, despite an increasing professionalization, five- or seven-year apprenticeships remained the most popular form of training for work on the shopfloor and for aspirant managers (Gospel 1992: 23). Trade unionists, on the other hand, were suspicious of anything which might undermine the apprenticeship which had for so long reinforced their status and, more important, their bargaining power (Sanderson 1988: 42). Thus one supporter of on-the-job training suggested:

> technical education can surely only mean the teaching of an art. . . .
> I can conceive of no better school than the workshop. You have the experience and skill of the best artisans . . . you are in the very atmosphere of your craft . . . you are learning by doing.
>
> (quoted by Court 1965: 171–2)

The proliferation of professional qualifications from the late nineteenth century certainly increased the academic training of some engineers. Yet since subsequent apprenticeship brought transferable skills, few manufacturing employers were prepared to educate workers at the firm's expense. Partly a survival of Victorian notions of educational self-help, this meant that, throughout the inter-war period, where employers encouraged workers to gain qualifications it was to be at night-school in their own time. Similarly in 1920 the Federation of British Industry, whilst not dismissive of the advantages of technical education, was dubious of the benefits of compulsory continuation education, and feared disruption to production as a result of day release (Fitzgerald 1993: 86–7). The only exceptions to this attitude were among leading, large-scale firms such as those in the Coventry motor and cycle industry (Thoms 1990: 46–7).

In emphasizing the differences in the attitudes of employers towards human capital in Britain, the United States and Germany, however, it is all too easy to neglect the similarities. If British industrialists were often reluctant to employ graduates they were, like their American counterparts, eager to endow higher education (Guagnini 1991: 74–5). In Germany, on the other hand, shopfloor training, as in Britain, was prized, and indeed before 1914 there is evidence of resistance in some firms to graduates. Yet, in contrast to Britain, craft training tended to be firm specific and by the inter-war period was widely viewed as a supplement to rather than a substitute for formal education (Locke 1984: 80–1). Precisely why the attitudes of British employers, despite apparently beginning from a similar stance, diverged from those in its principal competitors is a complicated issue. There were, for example, sometimes contrasting historical influences in the three countries. These, combined with differences in the technological base of industries, in the structure of firms and in the nature of markets helped to explain why British employers were often apparently indifferent to education and training.

On the face of it, it seems strange that Britain's provincial universities were financed by Victorian businessmen who were then reluctant to employ their graduates. Yet the apparent contradiction was not as great as it appears. The endowment of education by industrialists in Britain and America, in the first half of the nineteenth century, has been interpreted as being a reflection of business success and a passport to social standing in predominantly business communities (Howe 1984: 307; Dalzell 1987: 88–98). This trend continued in the late nineteenth century. In Britain it was the relatively small proportion of successful, long-established families operating in the staple industries who, along with industrialists in science-oriented industries like chemicals, endowed the new civic universities. It was they who formed the vanguard of the applied science movement (Guagnini 1991: 72–80).

These families, who for the most part owned large profitable firms, were prepared to employ graduates. They were also more likely to have received a university education themselves, albeit at Oxford or Cambridge. The majority of nineteenth-century owners of short-lived, small-scale firms in the staples and in engineering were not in a position to endow higher education nor to have received much by way of formal education of any sort. Instead, they were likely to have been shopfloor trained. For these men, the employment of graduates was a luxury they could neither afford nor appreciate. The wave of defensive mergers in the late nineteenth century, combined with the privations of the inter-war period, did little to alter perceptions. Throughout the period in question, therefore, in Britain as elsewhere, graduates tended to be employed in larger firms, irrespective of sector, and in those firms with a strong scientific bias. It comes as no surprise to find that these were the very firms most likely to attempt to create internal labour markets for their professional staff through the introduction of pension schemes and other welfare provisions (Fitzgerald 1988).

In America late-nineteenth-century endowment of higher education by wealthy industrialists continued apace, yet differences in technology and the scale of firms meant that the growth in demand for graduates was more rapid than in Britain. Shortages of skilled labour in many areas of America had led, for example, to a substitution of technology for skill. As a result, whilst shopfloor labour was increasingly unskilled, there was a growing demand for highly educated personnel, especially for engineers, to deal with ever more complex technologies in large-scale firms. Such pressures affected a far larger proportion of industry than was the case in Britain (Gospel 1991: 1–12).

Differences in industrial structure and industrial base, combined with contrasting government policy, help to explain variations in the status of shopfloor training in Britain and Germany. In both Germany and Britain well-established craft traditions meant that there were conflicts between the graduate engineer and the shopfloor-trained skilled worker in the late nineteenth century. Yet, as Locke has argued, this similarity was superficial. In the first place the absence of school-based technical education in Britain meant that the average German shopfloor worker was likely to be better educated than his British contemporary. In the second, whilst there was some resistance to the employment of graduate engineers in German manufacturing before 1914, this was only to be found in small craft-oriented firms. It did not extend to the relatively substantial proportion of larger firms.

During the 1920s government action ensured that, in engineering, shopfloor training alone became rare (Locke 1984: 80–1).

British patterns of human capital investment before 1939, therefore, contrasted with those detected in the United States and Germany. International differences in the nineteenth-century experience of industrialization, combined with variations in industrial mix, the scale and organization of business and the attitude of the state all contributed to this divergent experience. The ramifications of the comparative neglect of formal training and education for the performance of British business before the Second World War are difficult to isolate and quantify. Nevertheless, the productivity gap between British and American manufacturing industry in the 1930s has been traced, in part, to skill deficiencies (Broadberry and Crafts 1992: 536). At the same time, the small numbers of scientifically and managerially trained graduates provided an extremely limited pool of specialist expertise, in comparison with Britain's major competitors. This must have retarded the potential for a shift away from the staple industries towards more skill-intensive sectors.

INVESTMENT IN HUMAN RESOURCES SINCE 1945

In many sectors after the Second World War, deeply entrenched work practices and the scepticism of managers concerning the value of training and education for their specific firms, the legacies of past experience, clearly helped shape postwar practice. The general apprenticeship was so firmly embedded in the minds of both unions and management as to be an accepted part of the collective bargaining process (Sanderson 1988: 42). Past practice is not, however, the only explanation for the relative neglect of human capital investment in British companies. A combination of deficiencies in the education system and a tendency towards short-termism in British business also influenced strategy concerning human resources.

The Second World War marked a watershed in government attitudes towards expenditure on education and in theory to scientific and technical education. The 1944 Education Act addressed the problem of compulsory education, so often shelved in the inter-war period, and left open the option of a three-tier system of grammar, technical and secondary modern schools to cater for the needs of both academic and non-academic pupils as recommended by the 1945 Ministry of Education's pamphlet, *The Nation's Schools*. Prompted by the fear that continued neglect of technical education would undermine industrial performance, the Technical Education White Paper of 1956 emphasized the importance of education for economic growth. It proclaimed that

> Unless we can get every intelligent youngster on to the further education ladder, our hopes of meeting industrial needs will not be fulfilled.
>
> (quoted by Davis 1990: 136)

Similarly the Robbins Report of 1963 signalled a dramatic expansion of the university sector, whilst calling for five 'Special Institutions for Scientific and Technological Education and Research' of the American and Continental type (Barnett 1986: 292). Public expenditure on education rose accordingly, from £284 million in 1948 to £6,626 million in 1975 and, as a percentage of gross national product compared favourably with leading postwar industrial powers such as Japan and West Germany (Landymore 1985: 691–2; Aldcroft 1992: 22–3).

Despite the priority accorded to education by successive postwar British governments before 1979, the benefits for manufacturing industry have been limited (Daly 1982: 48–56). Indeed, in terms of human capital investment in an industrial workforce, British education policy since 1945 has been marked more by lost opportunities than achievement (Sanderson 1988: 44). In devoting a disproportionately high level of resources to the academically able, the 1944 Act, and indeed the Robbins Report, did little to prepare the majority for the world of work. Some 75 to 80 per cent of school pupils in the 1950s and 1960s were consigned to secondary moderns and emerged at 15 or 16 with few qualifications and even fewer skills. Moreover, school attainment levels were generally poorer than in Continental Europe and Japan. The much heralded technical schools declined in number from 321 in 1947 to 225 in 1962, with only 1.2 per cent of the school population attending this type of school. They were the victims of the shift in attitudes in both Whitehall and at the local level in favour of the grammar school (Sanderson 1991: 162–9). The decline and ultimate demise of the technical school has created one of the most serious deficiencies of the British education system and one which has been recognized as a major cause of Britain's skill shortage (Sanderson 1991: 170). Thus, despite expanded government expenditure, the education system continued to produce a workforce suited to the labour-intensive but declining staple industries and the low skill sectors (Baxter and McCormick 1984: 42). It was a workforce, however, which was patently ill-fitted for the technologically advanced sectors which grew so rapidly in the rest of the industrialized world during the 1950s and 1960s. In other words the 'education gap' between the average British worker and those in other major industrial economies, identified even before the end of the nineteenth century, was not closed in the postwar era – if anything it became wider.

The expansion of the university sector in the 1960s has been condemned for a liberal arts/social science bias, which was at the expense of technology. A higher education sector which accorded low status to engineering has contributed, Wiener suggested, to 'Britain's psychological and intellectual deindustrialisation' (Wiener 1981: 134–5). Scholars have been justifiably sceptical of Wiener's seductive, but simplistic, cultural interpretation of British economic decline (see especially essays in Collins and Robbins 1990). Yet the limited supply of engineering graduates and their relatively modest position in the hierarchies of British companies, at the very least, distinguishes British practice from that in Germany, the United States and Japan (Lazonick 1986: 110; Locke 1993: 62; Yasamuro 1993: 76–101). The foundation of first the London and then the Manchester Business School during the 1960s marked, on the other hand, the beginning of graduate management education on the American model. Yet these comparatively modest developments were half a century behind those in the United States. Such tardiness in the development of academic managerial education meant that, as industrial concentration rose in the 1960s, British managers were less well equipped than their American counterparts to cope with the challenges of big business. Influenced no doubt by generations of industrial practice, managers for their part saw experience rather than managerial education as the key to business success (Locke 1993: 65). Where British managers had a formal qualification at all it was more likely to be in accountancy rather than an MBA as in the United States or in engineering as in Germany (Jones 1993: 23).

If universities neglected both technology and management training in the postwar period probably the greatest lost opportunity, at the tertiary level, lay in the development of the polytechnics in the 1960s and 1970s. Their original aims of providing high grade, tertiary, vocational education, at both degree and sub-degree level, were often subordinated as subject mix shifted in response to academic drift (Landymore 1985: 711). The transformation of old polytechnics into 'new' universities, with the removal of the binary funding line in 1992, has only served to confirm this move away from the continental notion of technical education in the tertiary sector.

Perhaps the greatest deficiency in British postwar education, and one which has had especially serious consequences for British industry, has been at the intermediate level for the non-academic school leaver (Prais and Wagner 1983: 46). Here neither the state nor firms have been prepared to close the education gap. Government expenditure on post-compulsory education throughout the postwar period has lagged behind that in much of Europe, the United States and Japan (Keep and Mayhew 1988: vii). In Germany, on the other hand, firms have given training a far higher priority than was the case in Britain (Aldcroft 1992: 62). As a result, whilst 60 per cent of the German workforce gained an intermediate qualification, the proportion was only 30 per cent in Britain (Prais and Wagner 1983: 46). Moreover in Britain, until 1970, although workers had the opportunity to gain additional qualifications through day release, the apprenticeship remained the favoured qualification. Many workers had completed it without passing any theoretical tests and employers were under no legal obligation to provide study time (Peters 1967: 109). With the decline of apprenticeship from its peak of 240,000 in 1964 to just 63,700 in 1986, the position with respect to industrial training has become far worse (Keep and Mayhew 1988: x). The Industrial Training Act of 1964, designed to promote firm-specific training, enjoyed only mixed success (Fitzgerald 1993: 93). Many initiatives fell foul of recession in the 1970s and the Industrial Training Schemes, starved of funding, withered on the vine under the Thatcher government during the 1980s. They were replaced by Youth Training Schemes which, whilst reducing unemployment, did little to close the skill gap with Britain's continental competitors (Lane 1989: 73; Jones 1993: 26–7). This attempt aside, it was only the larger firms and those with a long tradition of valuing human resources which offered much by way of systematic training. The culture of a corporation like ICI, for example, informed as it was by the technical and scientific requirements of its products, therefore emphasized expertise and skill far more than was the norm (Aldcroft 1992: 55).

The flaws in postwar educational development have constrained business strategy towards human resources in several ways. The limited training and technical expertise of managers in this period is likely to have restricted their interest in training their workforce. Low levels of scientific and technological graduate participation at board level doubtless reinforced prejudices (Keep and Mayhew 1988: vii). At the same time, in many British firms a short-termism in both financial and labour arrangements, not to be found in either Germany or Japan, has discouraged long-term investment in human capital (Keep and Mayhew 1988: vii). From the perspective of the workforce, in sharp contrast to experience in Germany, dwindling wage differentials between skilled and unskilled workers and more especially between the shopfloor and foremen has given little incentive to gain additional qualifications (Prais and Wagner 1988: 40). Yet it was primarily the inappropriateness and inadequacy of education received by the average worker which completed the vicious circle, limiting as it did the value of training a young shopfloor worker received (Keep and Mayhew 1988: ix).

The slow response of British industry and the inappropriateness of all levels of postwar education policy has had serious consequences for the international competitiveness of industry. As Pollard has observed, it was the failure to rejuvenate the supply side of the economy which has most hampered macroeconomic performance since 1945 (Pollard 1982: 124). His emphasis was primarily on the barriers to the development of effective investment strategies and the implications which this had for British industrial performance. Yet, physical investment is unlikely to reap maximum productivity rewards if set against an inadequate framework of human capital investment.

The growing productivity gap in British relative to American industry since the inter-war period, and relative to Europe and Japan especially between 1950 and 1980, has received growing attention (Rostas 1948; Broadberry and Crafts 1990: 375−402; Broadberry and Fremdling 1990: 403; Van Ark 1990: 343−73; Broadberry and Crafts 1992: 531−58). By the mid-1970s, for example, German output per employee in manufacturing was about 50 per cent higher than in Britain, and in the region of 80 per cent higher in mechanical engineering and vehicle production. Compared with Japan, the gap was even wider (Daly *et al.* 1985: 48; Carr 1992: 80). The precise impact of skill deficiency on productivity is difficult to quantify. Nevertheless, a series of comparative studies by the National Institute for Economic and Social Research since 1982 has explored the implications of the limited education and poor training for British productivity performance (Roy 1982: 30−47; Daly 1982: 48−56; Prais and Wagner 1983: 46−65; 1985: 53−73; 1988: 34−47; Daly *et al.* 1985: 48−61; Prais 1985: 48−61; Steedman and Wagner 1989: 55−78; Mason *et al.* 1992: 45−57). They have concluded that an important explanation of Britain's twentieth-century productivity gap was a lack of technical expertise and training for managers, supervisors and shopfloor workers which inhibited the understanding of production techniques. Such deficiencies may have slowed down the introduction of advanced technologies in some sectors. Yet it was the manifest failings in intermediate, rather than advanced, education which were the most damaging. These meant that machinery breakdowns were longer and more frequent than, for example, in Germany where operatives were better able to take care of their machinery than their British counterparts (Daly *et al.* 1985: 61).

The experience of foreign multinationals in Britain serves to confirm the suspicion that the key to the productivity gap must lie with human capital deficiencies. It is undoubtedly true that the subsidiaries of foreign-owned firms, operating in Britain, enjoyed higher rates of productivity than equivalent British firms (Dunning 1958: 179–83; 1976: 71–4, 92–5; Bostock and Jones 1994). Yet if the productivity of foreign subsidiaries in Britain is compared with that achieved in the home economy (using identical technology, plant size, product, production runs) the gaps are quite startling. One Japanese manufacturer reported that advanced automatic machines were produced at only 60 per cent of the rate achieved in Japan. Similarly a German multinational reported that productivity in their UK plant was between 30 and 50 per cent of the level in their German plants (Prais 1985: 41; Carr 1992: 80).

The damaging impact of skill deficiency on British business performance has not merely been confined to productivity. From the 1950s, and especially since 1970, the most rapidly growing sectors, internationally, have been those producing technologically sophisticated, skill-intensive goods for high income markets (Fitzgerald 1993: 96–7). These have been sectors where the flexibility of the workforce in the face of rapidly changing markets has held the key to competitive advantage. In Germany, for example, high levels of human capital investment have facilitated a shift in product range to 'high quality' goods (Prais and Wagner 1988: 42). In Japan, on the other hand, human resources have lain at the heart of competitive strategy. There, the skill and knowledge of an educated and skilled workforce, using computerized, lean production techniques, have generated a combination of productivity gain and product flexibility (Locke 1993: 53–75). Britain even today, by contrast, remains overspecialized in product areas of low skill intensity. In the British food and drink industries performance has been better than in manufacturing generally in the 1970s and 1980s (Balasubramanyam 1993: 144–60). Nevertheless, in biscuits, for example, there is evidence that, where the markets served dictated variety rather than standardization of production, British workers lacked the flexibility to achieve the same level of productivity as Continental competitors (Mason *et al.* 1992: 56).

Even though there has been some narrowing of Britain's productivity gap with Europe since 1980 (Carr 1992: 83), skill deficiencies are likely to continue to have a damaging impact on the British economy.

High levels of foreign direct investment represent the only really significant growth in manufacturing capacity since 1979. Britain has been an especially popular destination for Japanese firms, anxious to penetrate European markets. Yet criticism of the skill levels of UK job applicants by Japanese companies casts doubt on the extent to which this will continue when they start to produce more sophisticated goods abroad (Strange 1993: 411).

CONCLUSIONS

This chapter has shown that, by the inter-war period British governments, employers and trade unions in general took formal education far less seriously than their contemporaries in other industrialized economies. Governments, whilst aware by the late nineteenth century that there was a link between education and economic performance, were nonetheless disinclined to co-ordinate policy or to make substantial financial commitments to education. The majority of employers, on the other hand, believed that shopfloor training rather than formal education underpinned business success. Like the state, most did not devote a substantial proportion of their firm's resources to either formal education or training. Rather, following practice during the Industrial Revolution, they delegated reponsibility for training to foremen and were rarely prepared to finance (through time or resources) the acquisition of formal qualifications by employees. For the skilled worker, on the other hand, education appears to have been viewed as being quite distinct from the world of work, where anything that undermined the apprenticeship was suspect. This is not to discount the importance of such movements as the Workers Education Association, but these were the embodiment of working-class self-help, rather than being linked to the work process.

Even before 1939 these attitudes began to inhibit productivity growth. Yet it has been after 1945 and most especially since 1970 that the effect of Britain's human capital deficiencies have been most damaging. Perceptions of training that had their origins in the nineteenth century lingered on in many sectors and continued to shape human resource policies through the 1950s and 1960s. Only in those sectors such as chemicals and pharmaceuticals, where competitive advantage had long been dependent upon scientific knowledge rather than practical skill, was formal education, rather than shopfloor training, valued. Education did however, become a major priority of postwar governments. Yet despite a sharp rise in educational expenditure since 1945 the needs of industry, especially with respect to intermediate education, have not been met.

Britain continued to produce a labour force better suited to the industrial demands of a bygone age, where the majority of the workforce were unskilled or semi-skilled and where training was informal rather than dependent upon formal education. In modern economies, however, competitive advantage is based upon an ability to compete in high income and rapidly changing markets. In such a world a new balance has emerged between physical and human capital where constant learning is critical to the full enjoyment of returns on investment. As a consequence, as was observed in an OECD report in 1985,

> education and training are more than ever central to modern economies that are based on rapidly changing knowledge and skills, many of them highly complex.
>
> (quoted by Aldcroft 1992: 19)

Yet in evaluating the causes of Britain's loss of competitive advantage in many skill-intensive sectors Porter has concluded:

> The British workforce is well behind in education and skills compared with many other advanced nations. There is a shortage of managers trained in technology entering manufacturing industries, and a technological background has been uncommon in top management.
>
> (Porter 1990: 498)

The implications for Britain of human capital failings are manifestly clear. Hastened, it must be said, by the excesses of government monetary policy in the 1980s, there has been an absolute decline in manufacturing since the mid-1970s which has been accompanied by a sharp rise in unemployment. At the same time, as illustrated in Chapter 7, the more dynamic British firms have increasingly sited their activities overseas. Inward investment by foreign, especially Japanese, multinationals has been seen as an important source of new manufacturing employment. Yet, without wide-ranging improvement in the education of the workforce, Britain may be destined to lose even that panacea. There is a substantial education gap between shopfloor workers in Britain and those on the Continent. As a result, the UK could become an offshore producer of goods of low skill intensity, supplying technologically sophisticated Japanese-owned factories elsewhere in Europe.

NOTE

I am grateful to the participants at the 'Business Enterprise in Modern Britain' symposium held at Lancaster University 14–15 May 1993 and especially to Geoff Jones and Maurice Kirby who also submitted written comments. Thanks are also due to Michael Sanderson for his helpful observations on this chapter. All errors are of course mine.

REFERENCES

Aldcroft, D.H. (1992) *Education Training and Economic Performance, 1944 to 1990*, Manchester: Manchester University Press.

Anderson, M. (1985) 'Historical demography after *The Population History of England*', *Journal of Interdisciplinary History* 15: 595–608.

Balasubramanyam, V.N. (1933) 'Entrepreneurship and the growth of the firm: the case of the British food and drink industry', in Jonathan Brown and Mary B. Rose (eds) *Entrepreneurship, Networks and Modern Business*, Manchester: Manchester University Press.

Barnett, C. (1986) *The Audit of War*, London: Macmillan.

Baxter, J.L. and McCormick, J.B. (1984) 'Seventy per cent of our future: the education, training and employment of young people', *National Westminster Bank Quarterly Review* 1984: 36–44.

Bendix, R. (1956) *Work and Authority in Industry*, New York: Wiley.

Berg, M. (1985) *The Age of Manufactures*, London: Fontana.

—— (1987) 'Women's work, mechanisation and the early phases of industrialisation in England', in P. Joyce (ed.) *The Historical Meanings of Work*, Cambridge: Cambridge University Press.

—— (1993) 'Small producer capitalism in eighteenth century England', *Business History* 35: 17–39.

Berg, M. and Hudson, P. (1992) 'Rehabilitating the industrial revolution', *Economic History Review* 45: 24–50.

Berghoff, H. (1990) 'Public schools and the decline of the British economy, 1870–1914', *Past and Present* 129: 535–68.

Bostock, F. and Jones, G. (1994) 'Foreign multinationals in British manufacturing, 1850–1962', *Business History* 36 (forthcoming).

Boyson, R. (1970) *The Ashworth Cotton Enterprise*, Oxford: Clarendon Press.

Broadberry, S.N. and Crafts, N.F.R. (1990) 'Explaining Anglo-American productivity in the mid-twentieth century', *Oxford Bulletin of Economics and Statistics* 52, 375–421.

—— and —— (1992) 'Britain's Productivity gap in the 1930s: some neglected factors', *Journal of Economic History* 52: 531–58.

Broadberry, S.N. and Fremdling, R. (1990) 'Comparative productivity in British and German industry', *Oxford Bulletin of Economics and Statistics* 52: 403–21.

Buchanan, R.A. (1989) *The Engineers: A History of the Engineering Profession in Britain, 1750–1914*, London: Jessica Kingsley.

Butt, J. (ed.) (1971) *Robert Owen: Prince of Cotton Spinners*, Newton Abbott: David & Charles.

Carr, C. (1992) 'Productivity and skills in vehicle component manufacturers in Britain, Germany the US and Japan', *National Institute Economic Review* 79–87.

Chandler, A.D. (1977) *The Visible Hand. The Managerial Revolution in American Business*, Cambridge, MA: Belknap Press.

Chapman, S.D. (1967) *The Early Factory Masters*, Newton Abbott: David & Charles.

Chapman, S.J. (1900) 'Some policies of the cotton spinners' trade unions', *Economic Journal* 10–467–73.

Child, J. (1964) 'Quaker employers and industrial relations', *Sociological Review* 12: 293–311.

Church, R. (1986) *The History of the British Coal Industry*, vol. 3, *1830–1913*, Oxford: Clarendon Press.

Cohen, I. (1990) *American Management and British Labour: A Comparative Study of the Cotton Spinning Industries*, Westport, CT: Greenwood Press.

Coleman, D.C. (1973) 'Gentlemen and players', *Economic History Review* 26: 92–116.

Collins, B. and Robbins, K. (1990) *British Culture and Economic Decline*. London: Weidenfeld & Nicholson.

Court, W.H.B. (1965) *British Economic History, 1870–1914*, Cambridge: Cambridge University Press.

Daly, A. (1982) 'The contribution of education to economic growth in Britain: a note', *National Institute Economic Review* 101: 48–56.

Daly, A., Hitchens, N. and Wagner, K. (1985) 'Productivity, machinery and skills in a sample of British and German manufacturing plants: results of a pilot inquiry', *National Institute Economic Review* 48–61.

Dalzell, R.F. (1987) *Enterprising Elite: The Boston Associates and the World They Made*, Cambridge, MA: Harvard University Press.

Daunton, M.J. (1980) 'Miners' housing: South Wales and the Great Northern coalfield', *International Review of Social History* 25: 148–65.

Davidoff, L. and Hall, C. (1987) *Family Fortunes: Men and Women of the English Middle Class, 1780–1850*, London: Hutchinson.

Davis, M. (1990) 'Technology, institutions and status; technological education, debate and policy, 1944–56', in P. Summerfield and E.J. Evans (eds) *Technical Education and the State since 1850*, Manchester: Manchester University Press.

Dunning, John H. (1958) *American Investment in British Manufacturing Industry*, London: George Allen & Unwin.

—— (1976) *U.S. Industry in Britain*, London, Wilson House Publications.

Dutton, H.I. (1984) *The Patent System and Inventive Activity during the Industrial Revolution*, Manchester: Manchester University Press.

Dutton, H. and King, J.E. (1982) 'The limits of paternalism: the cotton tyrants of North Lancashire, 1836–54', *Social History* 7: 59–74.

Elbaum, B. (1991) 'The persistence of apprenticeship in Britain and the decline in the United States', in H.F. Gospel (ed.) *Industrial Training and Technological Innovation: A Comparative and Historical Study*, London: Routledge.

Fitton, R. (1989) *The Arkwrights: Spinners of Fortune*, Manchester: Manchester University Press.

Fitzgerald, R. (1988) *British Labour Management and Industrial Welfare, 1846–1939*, London: Croom Helm.

—— (1993) 'Industrial training and management education in Britain; a missing dimension', in N. Kawake and E. Daito (eds) *Education and Training in the Development of Modern Corporations*, Tokyo: Tokyo University Press.

Floud, R. (1984) *Technical Education, 1850–1914: Speculations on Human Capital Formation*, London: Centre for Economic Policy Research.

Garrard, J. (1983) *Leadership and Power in Victorian Industrial Towns, 1830–80*, Manchester: Manchester University Press.

Gospel, H.F. (1988) 'The management of labour: Great Britain, the United States and Japan', *Business History* 30: 104–15.

—— (1991) *Industrial Training and Technological Innovation: A Comparative and Historical Study*, London: Routledge.

—— (1992) *Markets, Firms and the Management of Labour in Modern Britain*, Cambridge: Cambridge University Press.

Guagnini, A. (1991) 'The fashioning of higher technical education in Britain: the case of Manchester', in H. Gospel (ed.) *Industrial Training and Technological Innovation: A Comparative and Historical Study*, London: Routledge.

—— (1993) 'Worlds apart: academic instruction and professional qualifications in the training of mechanical engineers in England, 1850–1914', in R. Fox and A. Guagnini (eds) *Education, Technology and Industrial Performance in Europe, 1850–1939*, Cambridge: Cambridge University Press.

Habakkuk, J.H. (1962) *American and British Technology in the Nineteenth Century: the Search for Labour Saving Inventions*, Cambridge: Cambridge University Press.

Hannah, L. (1986) *Inventing Retirement*, Cambridge: Cambridge University Press.

Hennock, E.P. (1990) 'Technological education in England, 1850–1926: the uses of the German model', *History of Education* 19: 299–331.

Howe, A. (1984) *The Cotton Masters, 1830–1860*, Oxford: Clarendon Press.

Huberman, M. (1986) 'Invisible handshakes in Lancashire: cotton spinning in the first half of the nineteenth century', *Journal of Economic History* 46: 987–98.

—— (1987) 'The economic origins of paternalism: Lancashire cotton spinning in the first half of the nineteenth century', *Social History* 12: 177–92.

Hudson, P. (1992) *The Industrial Revolution*, London: Edward Arnold.

Jenkins, E.W. (1987) 'Junior technical schools, 1905–1945: the case of Leeds', *History of Education* 16: 105–17.

Jones, G. (1993) 'Big business, management and competitiveness in twentieth century Britain', University of Reading Discussion Paper in Economics, no. 268.

Joyce, P. (1980) *Work, Society and Politics*, Brighton: Harvester Wheatsheaf.

—— (1984) 'Labour capital and compromise: a response to Richard Price', *Social History* 9: 67–76.

Keeble, S.P. (1992) *The Ability to Manage: A Study of British Management, 1890–1990*, Manchester: Manchester University Press.

Keep, E. and Mayhew, K. (1988) 'The assessment: education, training and economic performance', *Oxford Review of Economic Policy* 4: i–xv.

Kirby, M.W. and Rose, M.B. (1991) 'Productivity and competitive failure: British government policy and industry, 1914–19', in G. Jones and M.W. Kirby (eds) *Competitiveness and the State: Government and Business in Twentieth-Century Britain*, Manchester: Manchester University Press.

König, W. (1993) 'Technical education and industrial performance in Germany: a triumph of heterogeneity', in R. Fox and A. Guagnini (eds) *Education, Technology and Industrial Performance in Europe, 1850–1939*, Cambridge: Cambridge University Press.

Landes, D. (1969) *Unbound Prometheus*, Cambridge: Cambridge University Press.

Landymore, P.J.A. (1985) 'Education and industry since the war', in D. Morris (ed.) *The Economic System in the UK*, Oxford: Oxford University Press.

Lane, C. (1989) *Management and Labour in Europe*, London: Edward Elgar.

Lane, J. (1977) *Apprenticeship in Warwickshire, 1700–1834*, unpublished PhD thesis, University of Birmingham.

Lazonick, W. (1979) 'Industrial relations and technical change: the case of the self-acting mule', *Cambridge Journal of Economics* 3: 231–49.

—— (1986) 'Strategy, structure and management development in the United States and Britain', in K. Kobayashi and H. Morikawa (eds) *Development of Managerial Enterprise*, Tokyo: Tokyo University Press.

—— (1990) *Competitive Advantage on the Shop Floor*, Cambridge, MA: Harvard University Press.

—— (1991) *Business Organization and the Myth of the Market Economy*, Cambridge: Cambridge University Press.

Lee, R.D. and Schofield, R.S. (1981) 'British population in the eighteenth century', in R.C. Floud and D. McCloskey (eds) *The Economic History of Britain since 1700*, Cambridge: Cambridge University Press.

Littler, C. (1982) *The Development of the Labour Process*, London: Heinemann.

Locke, R. (1984) *The End of the Practical Man: Entrepreneurship and Higher Education in Germany, France and Great Britain*, Greenwich, CT: JAI Press.

—— (1989) *Management and Higher Education since 1940*, Cambridge: Cambridge University Press.

—— (1993) 'Education and entrepreneurship: an historian's view', in J. Brown and M.B. Rose (eds) *Entrepreneurship Networks and Modern Business*, Manchester: Manchester University Press.

Lockwood, W.W. (1965) *The State and Economic Enterprise in Japan*, Princeton, NJ: Princeton University Press.

Lyons, J.S. (1985) 'Vertical integration of the British cotton industry, 1825–1850', *Journal of Economic History* 45: 419–26.

Marsden, W.E. (1987) *Unequal Educational Provision in England and Wales: the Nineteenth Century Roots*, London: Woburn Press.

Marshall, J.D. (1968) 'Colonization as a factor in the planting of towns in North West England', in H.J. Dyos (ed.) *The Study of Urban History*, London: Edward Arnold.

Mason, G., Prais, S.J. and Van Ark, B. (1992) 'Vocational education and productivity in the Netherlands and Britain', *National Institute Economic Review* 45–57.

McKendrick, N. (1961) 'Josiah Wedgwood and factory discipline', *Historical Journal* 4: 30–55.

Medick, H. (1976) 'The proto-industrial family economy: the structural function of household and family during the transition from peasant to industrial capitalism', *Social History* 1: 291–316.

Melling, J. (1981) 'Employers, industrial housing and the evolution of company welfare policies in Britain's heavy industry: West Scotland, 1870–1920', *International Review of Social History* 26: 255–300.

Mokyr, J. (1983) 'Three centuries of population change', *Economic Development and Cultural Change* 32: 183–92.

More, C. (1980) *Skill and the English Working Class*, London: Longman.

Musson, A.E. (1976) 'Industrial motive power in the United Kingdom, 1800–70', *Economic History Review* 29: 415–39.

Nardinelli, C. (1980) 'Child labour and the factory acts', *Journal of Economic History* 40: 739–55.

Payne, P. (1967) 'The emergence of the large scale company in Great Britain, 1870–1914', *Economic History Review* 20: 519–42.

Perkin, H. (1989) *The Rise of Professional Society: England since 1880*, London: Routledge.

Peters, A.J. (1967) *British Further Education*, Oxford: Pergamon.

Pollard, S. (1963) 'Factory discipline in the Industrial Revolution', *Economic History Review* 16: 254–71.

—— (1964) 'The factory village in the Industrial Revolution', *English Historical Review* 79: 513–31.

—— (1965) *The Genesis of Modern Management*, Harmondsworth: Pelican.

—— (1978) 'Labour in Great Britain', in P. Mathias and M.M. Postan (eds) *The Cambridge Economic History of Europe*, vol. 7, part 1, Cambridge: Cambridge University Press.

—— (1982) *The Wasting of the British Economy*, Beckenham: Croom Helm.

—— (1989) *Britain's Prime and Britain's Decline: The British Economy, 1870–1914*, London: Edward Arnold.

Porter, M. (1990) *The Competitive Advantage of Nations*, London: Macmillan.

Prais, S.J. (1985) 'Educating for productivity: comparison of Japanes and English schooling and vocational preparation', *National Institute Economic Review* 48–61.

Prais, S.J. and Wagner, K. (1983) 'Some practical aspects of human capital investment: training standards in five occupations in Britain and Germany', *National Institute Economic Review* 46–65.

—— and —— (1985) 'Schooling standards in England and Germany: some summary comparisons bearing on economic performance', *National Institute Economic Review* 123: 34–47.

—— and —— (1988) 'Productivity and management: The training of foremen in Britain and Germany'.

Roderick, G.W. and Stephens, M.D. (1972) *Education and Industry in the Nineteenth Century*, Newton Abbot: David & Charles.

Rose, M.B. (1986) *The Gregs of Quarry Bank Mill: the Rise and Decline of a Family Firm, 1750–1914*, Cambridge: Cambridge University Press.

—— (1989) 'Social policy and business: parish apprenticeship and the early factory system, 1750–1834', *Business History* 31: 5–32.

Rose, M.B., Taylor, P. and Winstanley, M.J. (1989) 'The economic origins of paternalism: some objections', *Social History* 14: 89–98.

Rostas, L. (1948) *Comparative Productivity in British and American Industry*, Cambridge: Cambridge University Press.

Roy, A.D. (1982) 'Labour productivity in 1980: an international comparison', *National Institute of Economic Research* 101: 9–16.

Samuel, R. (1977) 'The workshops of the world: steam power and hand technology in mid Victorian Britain', *History Workshop* 3: 6–72.

Sanderson, M. (1972a) 'Literacy and social mobility in the Industrial Revolution' in England', *Past and Present* 56: 75–104.

—— (1972b) *The Universities and British Industry, 1850–1970*, London: Routledge & Kegan Paul.

—— (1988) 'Education and economic decline, the 1890s–1980s', *Oxford Review of Economic Policy* 4: 38–50.

—— (1991) 'Social equity and industrial need: a dilemma of English education since 1945', in T. Gourvish and A. O'Day (eds) *Britain since 1945*, London: Macmillan.

Schofield, R.E. (1972) 'The industrial orientation of science in the Lunar Society of Birmingham', in A.E. Musson (ed.) *Science, Technology and Economic Growth*, London: Methuen.

Schofield, R.S. (1973) 'Dimensions of illiteracy, 1750–1850', *Explorations in Economic History* 10: 437–54.

Singleton, J. (1991) *Lancashire on the Scrap Heap: The Cotton Industry, 1945–1970*, Oxford: Oxford University Press.

Smelser, N.J. (1959) *Social Change in the Industrial Revolution*, Chicago, IL: Chicago University Press.

Steedman, H. and Wagner, K. (1989) 'Productivity, machinery and skills: clothing manufacture in Britain and Germany', *National Institute Economic Review* 40–57.

Strange, R. (1993) *Japanese Manufacturing Investment in Europe: Its Effect on the UK Economy*, London: Routledge.

Taylor, A.J. (1960) 'The subcontracting system in the British coal industry', in L.S. Pressnell (ed.) *Studies in the Industrial Revolution*, London: Athlone.

Thackray, A. (1974) 'Natural knowledge in cultural context: the Manchester model', *American Historical Review* 675–705.

Thomas, D. (1990) 'Technical education and the transformation of Coventry's industrial economy', in P. Summerfield and E.J. Evans (eds) *Technical Education and the State since 1850*, Manchester: Manchester University Press.

Tolliday, S. (1986) 'Management and labour in Britain, 1896–1939', in S. Tolliday and J. Zeitlin (eds) *Between Fordism and Flexibility: The Automobile Industry and its Workers*, Oxford: Polity.

Tolliday, S. and Zeitlin, J. (eds) (1991) *The Power to Manage? Employers and Industrial Relations in Comparative Historical Perspective*, London: Routledge.

Van Ark, B. (1990) 'Comparative levels of manufacturing productivity in post war Europe: measurement and comparisons', *Oxford Bulletin of Economics and Statistics* 52: 343–74.

Wiener, M. (1981) *English Culture and the Decline of Industrial Spirit, 1850–1980*, Cambridge: Cambridge University Press.

Wrigley, E.A. and Schofield, R. (1981) *The Population History of England, 1541–1871: A Reconstruction*, London.

Wrigley, J. (1986) 'Technical education and industry in the nineteenth century', in B. Elbaum and W. Lazonick (eds) *The Decline of the British Economy*, Oxford: Oxford University Press.

Yasumuro, K. (1993) 'Engineers as functional alternatives to entrepreneurs in Japanese industrialisation', in J. Brown and M.B. Rose (eds) *Entrepreneurship Networks and Modern Business*, Manchester: Manchester University Press.

Index

acceptance houses 99, 107, 211, 272
accountancy 349
advertising 213, 219–20, 249
AEI 296
agency houses 195
agency problems 325–7
agriculture 97
aircraft industry 163–5
airlines 325
Alexander, D. 239
Anglicans 77
Anglo-American Council on
    Productivity 1951 298
Anglo-Iranian Oil Company 185,
    189, 292
Argentina 177, 191, 244
arsenals 117
Ashton, T.S. 41
Ashworth, Henry 65
attorneys 94, 107
Australia 177, 180, 184, 188, 190

Balfour Committee on Trade and
    Industry 1929 147, 296
Bank Charter Act 1833 277
bank–industry relations 265
banking 10, 21, 24, 63, 75, 95,
    101–5, 109, 133, 187, 192, 195,
    198, 263–86, 288, 305; see also
    commercial retail banks,
    corporate banking, joint stock
    banks, multinational banking,
    overseas banks, savings banks
Banking Co-partnership Act 1826
    277
Bank of England 100, 103, 113, 118,

148, 276, 277, 279, 288, 292, 293
bankruptcy 64, 69–70, 90–1, 265,
    278, 279
Barclays Bank 80, 265, 274, 282
Beeching Report 1965 324
Belgium 178
Benetton 258
Benson, J. 239
bill of exchange 66, 101, 104, 107,
    272
Birmingham 3, 32, 37, 39, 40, 79,
    81, 92, 95, 99
Birmingham Alliances 227
Bordo, Michael D. 267–8, 269
Bordo and Jonung hypothesis
    270–2
Boyson, Rhodes 327
Bradford 215
branch network 280–1
branding 182, 194, 210, 220, 221,
    222, 223
Brazil 177, 189, 195
brewing 96, 117, 221–2
Bristol Aeroplane 163
British Aerospace 297, 327
British Aircraft Corporation 163
British Airports Authority 328
British Gas 329
British Institute of Management 298
British Iron and Steel Federation 152
British Leyland 327, 328
British Petroleum 328
British Shipbuilders 297, 327
British Siddeley Engines 163
British Steel 327
British Telecom 329, 331